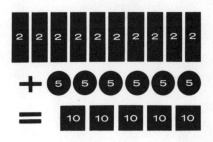

Basic Mathematical Concepts

F. LYNWOOD WREN
Professor of Mathematics
San Fernando Valley State College

basic
mathematical
concepts

McGRAW-HILL BOOK COMPANY
New York, St. Louis, San Francisco,
Toronto, London, Sydney

To Alleyne

PREFACE

This book has been written with the hope that it will provide for the person with slight background in mathematics an opportunity to acquire an understanding and appreciation of the basic structure of elementary mathematics. The nature of the number system we use is traced carefully from its beginnings in the natural number system to its full structure in the field of complex numbers. A very significant theme of this development is the important contribution which *place value* makes to the simplicity of our system of numeration and to the efficiency of our computational techniques. Other basic concepts and principles which contribute to the subject-matter content of the book are position, shape, and size; measurement, both direct and indirect; relation and function; and problem solving.

No discussion of the structure of number systems could have any semblance of completeness without some attention to the nature and importance of deduction. The limitations imposed here by the context of minimum prerequisites restrict this development to a brief consideration of the nature of implication. Some of the simpler theorems are proved, while others are left as exercises for the reader to develop. Both the formality of deduction and the informality of intuition play very important roles in shaping the content of this presentation.

A prefatory section, Guidelines for Careful Study, appears at the beginning of each chapter. These guidelines include questions designed to assist the reader in getting the most from the chapter. In the main, they point out key concepts and principles which the discussion of the chapter develops. Some of the questions serve as refresher ties with previous chapters. Each set of guideline questions thus can serve in a dual capacity for the reader: (1) as a partial review of previous chapters and (2) as a preview of the new chapter.

At the end of each chapter there is a section entitled Invitations to Extended Study. Here the reader will find questions and suggestions for pursuing the development of the preceding material in further detail and also, in some cases, to more advanced levels. It is hoped that at least some readers will be challenged to accept some, if not all, such invitations.

Finally, a fairly extensive bibliography of pertinent references follows the final chapter. In these references the reader will find more elaborate treatment of some subjects and, in general, effective support of all topics discussed.

It is the sincere hope of the author that this book will answer, both authentically and satisfactorily, the question of what is meant by the word "structure" when applied to mathematics. Also, it is hoped that at least some readers may be challenged to further study of the basic concepts and principles of elementary mathematics. The principal motivation which has inspired the author from the beginning, however, has been a desire to provide, in language not too highly technical in nature, a discussion which would present mathematics—even arithmetic—as something more than a mere composite of figures and formulas to be used as tools for more efficient puzzle solving, bookkeeping, scorekeeping, and tax computation.

The content of the book, in its present organization, has evolved out of lecture notes gathered over several years of attempting to provide a stronger mathematics background for those aspiring to become teachers in the elementary school. It has been checked carefully against the "Recommendations for Level I" of the Committee on the Undergraduate Program in Mathematics (CUPM). There is substantial treatment of the topics recommended in their preliminary report, *Course Guides for the Training of Teachers of Elementary School Mathematics.*

The author is deeply indebted and sincerely grateful to many individuals for their suggestions and criticisms in the preparation of the manuscript, namely, (1) his students, who have served both as a source of inspiration and as a leaven of guidance; (2) Professors J. Houston Banks, Irving H. Brune, John R. Hatcher, Johnathan W. Lindsay, John W. McGhee, Jr., Maria A. Steinberg, James C. Smith, Warren C. Willig, and Mr. Sidney Sharron, who gave him the benefit of their comments and criticisms after either reading the manuscript or using the preliminary edition as a text in their classes; and (3) certain unknown reviewers for their evaluation and criticism. Finally, the author owes no greater debt of appreciation and gratitude than that due his wife, Alleyne T. Wren, who not only typed the manuscript but also criticized, counseled, and encouraged through the months of writing and rewriting necessary to get it in its final form.

F. Lynwood Wren

CONTENTS

3 the natural number system 42

4 the domain of integers 78

5 the field of rational numbers 104

6 the number field of elementary mathematics

7 modular arithmetic

8 the concepts of position, shape, and size

190

9 the concept of measurement

248

10 the concepts of relation and function

the nature of number

GUIDELINES FOR CAREFUL STUDY

The simplicity and effectiveness of symbolism are not too generally realized or appreciated. For example, when the driver of an automobile looks at a traffic signal he sees a green light, an amber light, or a red light. These lights can be very simple and effective symbols for use in giving information about traffic control at the street crossing. They will have this effectiveness if and only if the traveler thinks into each symbol the meaning it carries. If he sees only a green, amber, or red light with no thought of traffic regulations, the significance of the signal is completely lost. An analogous situation exists in the study and use of mathematical concepts and symbols. If, in the attempt to use a concept or symbol, no effort is made to think of its full meaning, then one might as well be flipping disks in tiddlywinks.

In this chapter certain concepts and symbols are introduced and discussed. They are of basic significance for the intelligent comprehension not only of the content of this chapter but also of that of the entire book. For this reason, clear understanding, which results in accurate interpretation and ready use of each concept and symbol discussed, is very essential.

The following questions can serve you well as guidelines for careful study of the content of this chapter.

1   What is meant when one speaks of a set of elements?

2   What is the meaning of each of the symbols $\in$, $\subset$, and $\subseteq$? What is the distinction between them?

3   What is meant by and what is the symbol for each of these concepts: intersection and union of two sets, universal set, empty set, complement, relative complement, disjoint sets, equal sets?

4   What are the accepted symbols for indicating a set?

5   What is a set builder?

6   What is meant by one-to-one correspondence?

7   What is meant by the cardinal number of a set?

8   What is meant by $n(S)$ where S represents a set?

9   What is the distinction between the cardinal and ordinal concepts of number?

10   What is meant by place value, or positional value?

INTRODUCTION

What is number? It would be a rather difficult task to give an answer to this question that would be satisfactory from a logical point of view or even intelligible from a utilitarian point of view. As evidence of the truth of this statement one might consider this dictionary definition: Number is "the, or a, total, aggregate, or amount of units." Even if the key words of this definition carry no ambiguous or confusing implications to the reader, there is still difficulty in getting a clear comprehension of just what concept of number this definition attempts to convey. In spite of these logical and utilitarian difficulties, it is possible to use our quantitative experiences to shape an intuitive concept of number which will serve as a satisfactory foundation upon which to build for appropriate understanding of the number system of elementary mathematics. It is the purpose of this chapter to lay the first stones in the structure of this foundation.

In order to pursue this development in an intelligent manner, it is first desirable to introduce certain terms and symbols which can be used advantageously to induce clarifications and avoid ambiguities of discussion.

1–1   THE CONCEPT OF SET

In the contemplation of his environment man observes and studies objects, either as individuals or as members of some *collection* or *family* of objects.   The teacher has concern for his *class* as well as for each pupil.   The grocer buys canned goods by the *case* and, in general, sells them by the single can.   The hunter attempts to flush a *bevy* of quail in order to concentrate upon and bring down one for his game bag. The big-game hunter may seek a *herd* of elephants or a *pride* of lions so that he may be successful in bagging an individual animal as the trophy of his hunt.   The fisherman seeks the habitat of a *school* of fish before dropping his line.   A bridge *hand* of 13 cards is dealt from a *deck* of 52 cards.   The tennis player concentrates on winning the individual game in order that he may win enough games to claim first the *set* and then the *match*.

Names for collections of objects

The italicized words in the above paragraph are simply different names used to refer to an identifiable collection of objects.   There are many other such words: assemblage, assembly, congress, congregation, flock, troop, posse, ensemble, club, to list a few.   Whatever the terminology to specify a particular collection may be, all designated collections will have one characteristic in common, namely,

It will, at least in theory, be possible to identify any given object as either a member of the specified collection or not a member.

Common characteristic of all collections

Possibly the simplest, and certainly the most general, term used to designate such clearly delineated collections of objects is *set*.   The concept is indeed basic in our culture and has been referred to as the unifying and clarifying concept in the study of mathematics.†

Set

For any particular discussion there exists a "universe of discourse" which is the all-inclusive set of elements clearly identified by the specific orientation of the discussion.   This set will be known as the *universal set* and, in general, will be designated by the symbol *U*.   All other sets entering into the discussion will be *subsets* of *U*.   In fact, in general, they will be *proper subsets* of *U*.

Universe of discourse

Universal set

Definition 1–1   The set *P* is a *subset* of the set *Q* if and only if every element of *P* is also an element of *Q*.   The symbol $P \subseteq Q$ is to be read "*P* is a subset of *Q*." *P* is a *proper subset* of *Q* if and only if the ele-

Subset and proper subset

---

† The terms *collection* and *class* are used at times in mathematics as synonymous with set. Also, attention is called to the fact that the concept of set used here is that of a *well-defined set* in contrast with such sets as "the set of all interesting books" and "the set of all funny jokes," whose elements are not so clearly and distinctly recognizable.   We shall be interested only in those sets which are well defined.

Well-defined set

ments of P are also elements of Q and there is at least one element of Q which is not an element of P. The symbol $P \subset Q$ is to be read "P is a proper subset of Q."

Example In any discussion concerning the correct spelling of words of the English language the universal set U is the English alphabet. The 26 letters of the alphabet are the elements from which selections are made to form combinations which we recognize as correctly spelled words. The letters of each word are then elements of a proper subset of U.

Relation

The symbols $\subseteq$ and $\subset$ indicate what we shall call a *relation* between two sets. At this point it will be sufficient to state that the term relation simply implies the consideration of two elements or objects which are linked to each other in some specified manner. Later, it will be desirable to give a more precise definition of the concept of relation. In the symbol $P \subseteq Q$ the set on the left (P) is linked to the set on the right (Q) by the phrase "is a subset of." From Definition 1–1 it should be evident that any set is a subset of itself $(P \subseteq P)$. Since P is seen here both on the left and on the right of the symbol, the relation $\subseteq$ may be said to have the effect of reflecting the image of the object. Any relation

Reflexive

which has this property is said to be *reflexive*. Is the relation $\subset$ reflexive? Why?

Transitive

A property which is common to both relations $\subseteq$ and $\subset$ is that of being *transitive*. This means that each relation has the property of passing on successively from element to element. It should be clear from the definition that if $P \subseteq Q$ and $Q \subseteq R$, then $P \subseteq R$. In other words, the relation "is a subset of" passes on successively from P to Q to R. Likewise, if $P \subset Q$ and $Q \subset R$, then $P \subset R$.

Most frequently in discussions concerned with the relationships existing between two sets, we are not too greatly concerned with whether or not the proper-subset relation holds, but merely with which set, if either, is a subset of the other. In other words, are the elements of the set P also elements of the set Q? If the answer to this question is yes, then we say "P is a subset of Q," "P is contained in Q," or "P is included in Q" and write $P \subseteq Q$.

If we can establish for two given sets P and Q that $P \subseteq Q$ and also $Q \subseteq P$, then we say that set $P =$ set Q.

Equality of
two sets

Definition 1–2 Set $P =$ set Q if and only if $P \subseteq Q$ and $Q \subseteq P$.

The full implication of this definition is, of course, that two sets are identical if every element of each is an element of the other.

Element of
a set

Any object o of a particular discussion will be an element of the universal set U for that discussion. The symbol $o \in U$ will be used to indicate this fact, and is to be read "the object o is in the set U," "the object

o is a member of the set U," "the object o belongs to the set U," or "the object o is an element of the set U." If P is any given set and o is any object, then either $o \in P$ or $o \notin P$ (o is not an element of P).

The three most generally accepted forms for indicating a set are:

Methods of indicating sets

1   $S = \{s_1, s_2, s_3, \ldots\}$. This symbol is read "$S$ is the set whose elements are s_1, s_2, s_3, and so on." The three dots ($\ldots$) are used in any case to indicate an omission, whether the omission be of an unending number or of a fixed number of elements. For example, $N = \{1,2,3,4,\ldots\}$ is the symbol for the unending set of the counting numbers, otherwise called natural numbers; the set $D = \{1,2,3,\ldots,9\}$ could be used to indicate the set whose elements are the one-digit natural numbers 1, 2, 3, 4, 5, 6, 7, 8, 9.

2   $S = \{s|s$ has certain prescribed characteristics$\}$. This symbol is read "S is the set of all elements s such that s has certain prescribed characteristics." Of course, different prescriptions will distinguish different sets. For example, the two sets N and D can be represented by $N = \{n|n$ is a natural number$\}$ and $D = \{d|d$ is a one-digit natural number$\}$. Such a symbol is called a *set selector* or a *set builder*. It indicates the pattern or formula for selecting the elements of the set.

3   S = the set all of whose elements are s_i or even "S is the set all of whose elements are s_i." This is the least formal of the three and merely makes a statement which is sufficiently precise to identify the elements of the set. For example, N = the set of all natural numbers and D is the set of all one-digit natural numbers.

Example   There are both boys and girls enrolled in the sixth grade of Valley Elementary School.   Let

$V = \{$all pupils of Valley Elementary School$\}$
$C = \{c|c$ is a child enrolled in the sixth grade of Valley Elementary School$\}$ (this is read C is the set of all c such that c is a child enrolled in the sixth grade of Valley Elementary School)
$B = \{b|b$ is a boy in the sixth grade of Valley Elementary School$\}$
$G = \{g|g$ is a girl in the sixth grade of Valley Elementary School$\}$
$P = \{$all boys and girls attending school at Valley Elementary School$\}$
$T = \{t_1, t_2\}$ (where t_1 and t_2 represent one each of a set of twins, a brother and sister, enrolled in the sixth grade of Valley Elementary School)

1   $V = P$. Since any pupil of Valley Elementary School is either a boy or a girl attending the school, $V \subseteq P$. Also, since any boy or girl attending the school is a pupil of the school, $P \subseteq V$.

2   $C \subset V$. Each child of the sixth grade is a pupil in the school, but there are pupils in the school who are not enrolled in the sixth grade. Why is it also true that $C \subset P$?

3　$B \subset C$ and also $G \subset C$. Why?

4　$B \subset C$ and $C \subset V$; therefore $B \subset V$. This is merely the symbolic way to say that any boy enrolled in the sixth grade of the school is a child enrolled in the sixth grade of the school and is therefore one of the pupils enrolled in the school.

5　T is not a subset of B ($T \not\subset B$) since one of the elements of T is not an element of B. Similarly, $T \not\subset G$. Why is $T \subset C$?

The entire context of this example is portrayed in a vivid manner in the diagram of Fig. 1–1.

The rectangle represents the set V which is the universal set of the example, and, since $P = V$, it also represents the set P. The set C, which is a proper subset of V, is represented by a circle contained entirely within the rectangle. Thus the interior of the rectangle is represented as containing all elements of the set V (all pupils of Valley Elementary School), and the interior of the circle as containing all elements of the set C (all children enrolled in the sixth grade of Valley Elementary School). The sets B, G, and T, which are proper subsets of C, are represented by circles, each of which is contained within the circle C. Since B and G have no elements in common, the circles representing these two sets do not overlap (do not have any portion in common). The set T has one element in common with set B and one element in common with set G. For this reason the circle for T does overlap the circle for B and also the circle for G.

Venn diagrams　Diagrams such as that of Fig. 1–1 are called *Venn diagrams*. They can be used very effectively to give vivid portrayal of indicated relationships between sets. Frequently the picture can be made even clearer and more expressive by the proper use of shading or color. In Figs. 1–2 through 1–6, colored circles are used to symbolize sets of elements selected from the universal set U, which, in turn, is represented by the rectangle.

There are three basic operations used in working with sets. They are *complementation*, *union*, and *intersection*. Each of these operations will now be defined and also illustrated by an appropriate Venn diagram.

Complement　*Definition 1–3*　When the universal set U is clearly defined, the complement of P is the set of all those elements of U which are not elements

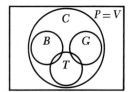

FIGURE 1–1　Venn diagram

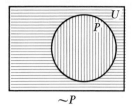

FIGURE 1–2   The rectangle represents U.   The vertical lines represent P.   The horizontal lines represent $\sim P$, that is, all those elements of U which are not elements of P.

$\sim P$

of P.   The symbol $\sim P$ is read "the complement of P," sometimes abbreviated to "not P."   (See Fig. 1–2.)

Example   If U is the set of all letters of the English alphabet and P is the set of all letters used to spell the word "mathematics," then $\sim P$ is the set of all letters of the English alphabet not used in spelling the word "mathematics."

$U = \{$all letters of the English alphabet$\}$
$P = \{a,c,e,h,i,m,s,t\}$
$\sim P = \{b,d,f,g,j,k,l,n,o,p,q,r,u,v,w,x,y,z\}$

At times one is concerned not so much with a clear-cut definition of the universal set as with those elements of one set P which are not elements of another set Q.

Definition 1-4   The *relative complement of set Q in set P* consists of all elements of set P which are not also elements of set Q.   The symbol $P - Q$ is to be read "the relative complement of Q in P" or, in abbreviated form, P minus Q."   (See Fig. 1–3.)

Relative complement

Notice that the diagram emphasizes the fact that the relative complement of Q in P has meaning even when $Q \not\subset P$ (Q *is not a proper subset of P*).   What is the diagram when $Q \subset P$?

Example   Given $T = \{1,2,3,4,5,6,7,8,9\}$, $S = \{3,5,7,9,10,12,13\}$, and $R = \{2,4,6,8\}$.

$T - S = \{1,2,4,6,8\}$ $S - T = \{10,12,13\}$
$S - R = \{3,5,7,9,10,12,13\} = S$ $R - S = \{2,4,6,8\} = R$
$T - R = \{1,3,5,7,9\}$ $R - T$ contains   no   elements
                since $R \subset T$

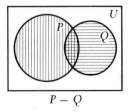

FIGURE 1–3   The rectangle represents U.   The vertical lines represent P and the horizontal lines represent Q.   The portion of P containing vertical lines *only* represents $P - Q$, that is, those elements of P which are not also elements of Q.

$P - Q$

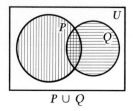

$P \cup Q$

FIGURE 1–4   The rectangle represents U. The vertical lines indicate elements of P. The horizontal lines indicate elements of Q. The set $P \cup Q$ is represented by lines in *either* direction.

These same sets T, S, and R will be used to illustrate the concepts of union and intersection of two sets, which are now defined.

Union of two sets

Definition 1–5   The *union* of two sets P and Q consists of all those elements which are either in P or in Q or in both P and Q, with no duplication of elements.   The symbol $P \cup Q$ is read "P union Q" or, more simply, "P cup Q."   (See Fig. 1–4.)

Intersection of two sets

Definition 1–6   The *intersection* of two sets P and Q consists of all those elements which are common to both P and Q.   The symbol $P \cap Q$ is to be read "P intersection Q" or more simply, "P cap Q." (See Fig. 1–5.)

Example   For the sets T, S, R, of the preceding example we have

$T \cup S = \{1,2,3,4,5,6,7,8,9,10,12,13\}$ $T \cap S = \{3,5,7,9\}$
$T \cup R = \{1,2,3,4,5,6,7,8,9\} = T$ $T \cap R = \{2,4,6,8\} = R$
$S \cup R = \{2,3,4,5,6,7,8,9,10,12,13\}$ $S \cap R$ contains no elements since S and R have no elements in common

In this example the intersection of sets T and S and the intersection of sets T and R are sets with easily identified elements.   The intersection of sets S and R, however, presents a problem.   The two sets have no elements in common, so there are no elements which we can identify as belonging to the set which is their intersection.   In order that there will be no exception to the concept of the intersection of two sets

Empty or null set

it thus becomes necessary to define the *empty set, or null set, as that set which has no elements.*   The symbol $\emptyset$ is read "the empty set" or "the null set"; the two expressions are used interchangeably.   We may now

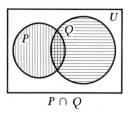

$P \cap Q$

FIGURE 1–5   The rectangle represents U. The vertical lines indicate elements of P. The horizontal lines indicate elements of Q. The set $P \cap Q$ is represented by crossing lines.

write $S \cap R = \emptyset$, which is read "the intersection of sets S and R is the empty set." Similarly, in the example following Definition 1–4, we have $R - T = \emptyset$, or the relative complement of T in R is the empty set.

The sets S and R are disjoint sets in accordance with the following definition.

Definition 1-7   Two sets P and Q are said to be disjoint sets if their intersection is the empty set, that is, if they have no elements in common.   (See Fig. 1–6.)   *Disjoint sets*

What sets of Fig. 1–1 are disjoint sets?

Attention is called to the fact that the set $\{0\}$ is not the null set.   This set is not empty since it contains one element, the element zero.   This new set $\emptyset$ allows the use of the complement of a set with no exceptions. For example, $\sim U$ is $\emptyset$.   Similarly, $\sim\emptyset$ is U.   Although we shall make no effort to prove the statement, it is possible to prove that the empty set is a subset of every set.   Symbolically, this statement may be written $\emptyset \subseteq P$ for every set P.

Example   Consider the following sets:

U (the universal set) $= \{$all letters of the English alphabet$\}$

$A = \{a,b,c,j,k,l,s,t,u\}$
$B = \{j,k,s,t\}$
$C = \{l,m,n,u,v,w\}$
$D = \{a,b,c,l,u\}$
$T = \{l|l$ is a letter in the word Tennessee$\}$
S is the set whose elements are the letters e, n, s, t
$\emptyset$

1   All sets, including U, are subsets of U, and $\emptyset$ is a subset of all sets, including $\emptyset$.

2   When any element from U is being considered, one can determine clearly and convincingly whether or not it is a member of any selected subset of U.   For example, a is a member of A ($a \in A$) but a is not a member of B ($a \notin B$).

3 B is a proper subset of A ($B \subset A$), since all elements of B are also elements of A and there is at least one element in A which is not in B.

FIGURE 1–6   The rectangle represents U.   The vertical lines indicate elements of P.   The horizontal lines indicate elements of Q.   The set $P \cap Q$ is $\emptyset$ since there is no portion of U which has crossing lines.   The sets P and Q have no elements in common.

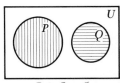

$P \cap Q = \emptyset$

4   *C* is not a subset of *A* ($C \nsubseteq A$). Although the elements *l* and *u* which are members of *C* are also members of *A*, there are other elements of *C* which are not elements of *A*, namely, *m*, *n*, *v*, *w*.

5    $C \cap A = \{l,u\}$, since *l* and *u* are the only elements which the two sets have in common.

6    $A \cup B = A$, since $B \subset A$.

7    $A - B = D$, since the elements of *D* are left in *A* after the elements of *B* have been removed.

8    $B \cap C = \emptyset$, since *B* and *C* have no elements in common. They are disjoint sets.

9    $S = T$ since $T = \{t,e,n,s\}$, because the set selector selects *only* the letters used in the word Tennessee and says nothing about how many times any one letter is used nor anything about the arrangement of the letters. It follows then that $S \subseteq T$ and $T \subseteq S$.

10    $S - T = \emptyset$.

Exercises

1   Use the form $S = \{s_1, s_2, s_3, s_4, \ldots\}$ to describe each set.
   (a) $I = \{i | i$ is a positive integer$\}$
   (b) $S = \{s | s$ is an integer greater than 5 but less than 20$\}$
   (c) $G = \{g | g$ is a state of the United States one of whose boundaries lies along the Gulf of Mexico$\}$
   (d) $L = \{l | l$ is the name of one of the Great Lakes of the United States$\}$
   (e) $E = \{e | e$ is a positive even integer$\}$
   (f) $M = \{m | m$ is a state of the United States bordering on Mexico$\}$

2   Write a symbol which will be the set selector for each of these sets:
   (a) $O =$ the set of all odd integers
   (b) $T = \{2,4,6,8,10,12\}$
   (c) $R = \{$Oregon, Hawaii, Alaska, California, Washington$\}$
   (d) $V = \{a,e,i,o,u\}$
   (e) $A = \{3, 1 + 2, 2 + 1, 1 + 1 + 1\}$
   (f) $B = \{5,7,9,11,13,15,17,19\}$
   (g) $P = \{1,3,5,7,9\}$
   (h) $Z =$ the set of all integers

3   Given the two sets

   $$M = \{0,2,4,6,8\} \quad \text{and} \quad N = \{0,1,3,5,7,9\}$$

   Is this a true statement: $\emptyset = M \cap N$? Give reasons to support your answer.

4   Is it true that $\emptyset$ is not equal to $\{\emptyset\}$? Give reasons to support your answer.

5   Are these true or false statements about the sets of Exercises 1 and 2?

(a) $I = Z$ (b) $O \subset I$ (c) $E \cap T = \emptyset$
(d) $E \cup T = E$ (e) $M \cap R = \emptyset$ (f) $P \cup O = O$

6   What is a symbol for each of these sets? The letters represent sets of Exercises 1 and 2.

(a) $B \cap P$ (b) $O \cup E$ (c) $G \cap M$
(d) $B - P$ (e) $B \cup S$ (f) $B \cap S$

7   Consider these sets:

$F = \{\text{apple, peach, pear, orange}\}$
$V = \{\text{onion, carrot, potato, bean}\}$
$C = \{\text{apple, pear, carrot}\}$
$D = \{\text{apple, peach, orange}\}$
$E = \{\text{onion, carrot}\}$

Which of the following statements are true and which are false?

(a) $F = V$ (b) $C \subseteq F$ (c) $E \subset V$ (d) $V \subset V$
(e) $D \cup C = F$ (f) $C \cap D = E$ (g) $F - D = \{\text{pear}\}$

8   If U is the universal set, what is the set $A \cup U$? What is the set $A \cap U$?

9   What is the set $A - \emptyset$? What is the set $A - A$?

10 What is the set $A \cup {\sim}A$? What is the set $A \cap {\sim}A$?

11 Draw Venn Diagrams to show each of the following sets:

(a) $(A \cup B) \cup C$ (b) $A \cap (B \cap C)$
(c) $A \cup (B \cap C)$ (d) $(A \cup B) \cap C$
(e) $(A \cup B) \cap (A \cup C)$ (f) $(A \cap B) \cup (A \cap C)$
(g) $A - B$ when $A \cap B = \emptyset$ (h) ${\sim}[A \cap B]$
(i) ${\sim}[A \cup B]$ (j) ${\sim}[(A \cap B) \cup C]$

12 Use Venn diagrams to illustrate the truth of the following statements:

(a) $A \cup B = B \cup A$
(b) $A \cap B = B \cap A$
(c) $(A \cup B) \cup C = A \cup (B \cup C)$
(d) $(A \cap B) \cap C = A \cap (B \cap C)$
(e) $A \cup (B \cap C) = (A \cup B) \cap (A \cup C)$
(f) $A \cap (B \cup C) = (A \cap B) \cup (A \cap C)$

13 Let $C = \{\text{all the different letters in the word Cincinnati}\}$ and $M = \{\text{all the different letters in the word cinema}\}$. Are these sentences true or false? Give reasons for each answer.

(a) $C - M = M - C$ (b) $C = M$
(c) $C \cup (C - M) = C$ (d) $M \cap (C - M) = M$

14   Give six examples of the empty set.

15   Is the following statement true or false?   The empty set has a subset but it has no proper subset.   Give reasons to support your
answer.

1–2   THE CARDINAL NUMBER OF A SET

From history we learn that the shepherds of ancient times used an
interesting technique for keeping records of their flocks of sheep.   As
the sheep filed into the pasture the shepherd would set aside one pebble
and only one pebble for each sheep that passed.   Furthermore, he was
careful that no pebble was placed in the pile unless it was placed there
to represent a sheep.   By using this technique he was assured of the
Object-to-
object
correspondence
fact that there was an object-to-object correspondence between the
pebbles in the pile and the sheep in the flock.   There were just as many
sheep as there were pebbles, and as many pebbles as sheep.

Tallying
One modern version of the shepherd's technique is the process of
tallying, which is frequently used in counting votes in a class or school
election.   One and only one tally mark is made for each vote cast, and
no mark is made which does not represent a vote.   In this way there is
an object-to-object correspondence between the register of tally marks
and the total number of votes cast.   When such a procedure is followed,
there will be just as many tally marks as there are votes cast, and, conversely, there will be just as many votes cast as there are tally marks
made.

If one enters a classroom and sees that each chair in the room is occupied by one and only one student and that there are no students for
whom there are no chairs, one knows immediately that there exists an
object-to-object correspondence between the chairs in the room and the
students in the class.   There will be just as many chairs as there are students, and, conversely, there will be just as many students as there are
chairs.

One-to-one
correspondence
The object-to-object correspondence of each of the above three illustrations is an example of what is known as a *one-to-one correspondence*
between the elements of one set and the elements of a second set.

Definition 1–8   Two sets *A* and *B* are said to be in *one-to-one corre-*
spondence with each other when the elements of the two sets are so
paired that to each element of set *A* there corresponds one and only
one element of set *B*, and to each element of set *B* there corresponds
one and only one element of set *A*.

The correspondence of the first illustration is a one-to-one correspondence between the set (pile) of pebbles and the set (flock) of sheep;

in the second illustration, the one-to-one correspondence is that between the set (register) of tally marks and the set (total number) of votes cast; and in the third illustration the one-to-one correspondence is that between the set (room) of chairs and the set (class) of students. In each case the two sets which are in one-to-one correspondence would be said to have the same *cardinal number,* or the same *cardinality.*

Counting is a familiar process in which the set of cardinal numbers $1, 2, 3, 4, 5, 6, \ldots$ is used. Just what is the cardinal number 1; what is the cardinal number 2; what is the cardinal number 3; ... ? For the purpose of this discussion it is not essential that we get too involved in the philosophical subtleties involved in these questions.† Suffice it to say here that all sets which can be placed into one-to-one correspondence with the set $\{a\}$ have the cardinal number *one,* that is, they each contain one and only one element. Similarly, all sets which can be placed into one-to-one correspondence with the set $\{a,b\}$ have the cardinal number *two,* that is, they each contain two and only two elements, and so on. Thus, through the simple technique of establishing one-to-one correspondence between sets, the numbers 1, 2, 3, 4, 5, ..., familiar to us as counting numbers, are seen to be cardinal numbers of sets.

The cardinal number of a set P is sometimes called the *count of the set P.* It tells how many elements are contained in the set. This is the context in which 0 is identified as the cardinal number of the empty set. There are 0 elements in the empty set. If any given set is such that its count exists and is one of the cardinal numbers 0, 1, 2, 3, 4, ..., the set is said to be *finite;* otherwise it is said to be *infinite.* It will be convenient to use the symbol $n(P)$ to indicate the cardinal number of P. For example, $n(\emptyset) = 0$ and $n(\{1,2,3,4,\})$ is 4. Thus, we may refer to the set $C = \{0,1,2,3,4, \ldots\}$ as the set of all cardinal numbers or the set of all counting numbers. They answer the question, How many elements in a given set?

A counting number gives a distinct quantitative characterization of a collection of objects. Just as "brother" gives a distinct relation characterization, so "four" gives a distinct quantitative characterization, namely, that which we recognize as possessing the property of one-to-one correspondence with that collection to which the English-speaking people of the world have given the name "four," whether it be the legs of a horse, the number of individuals necessary for a game of bridge, or the main points of the compass. A very effective illustration of the use of 0 to give such a quantitative characterization of a set may be found in a consideration of the box score of one of the games in a recent baseball World Series game (Fig. 1–7). Note that this game was played in Los Angeles, and that it is the custom in such box scores to place the record for the home team on the lower line of the box. The numbers across the

Cardinal number

Finite or infinite

† A more thorough treatment may be found in Norman T. Hamilton and Joseph Landin, "Set Theory: The Structure of Arithmetic, pp. 74–106, Allyn and Bacon, Inc., Boston, 1961.

FIGURE 1–7   A baseball scoreboard.   0 and 1 are cardinal numbers used to tell the number of runs scored during each team's effort to score.   The × has no significance other than that of a mere placeholder.

	1	2	3	4	5	6	7	8	9	R
New York Yankees	0	0	0	0	0	0	1	0	0	1
Los Angeles Dodgers	0	0	0	0	1	0	1	0	✕	2

top line enumerate the innings of play.   They serve either as cardinal numbers or as ordinal numbers (see Sec. 1–3), depending on the way in which they are used.   One example of a cardinal use is the following: For *four* innings neither team scored.   An ordinal example is: The Dodgers scored in the *fifth* inning, and each team scored in the *seventh* inning.

In each of the first four innings neither team was able to score any runs.   This information is shown by the 0's recorded in the boxes provided.   This same pattern was followed in the sixth and eighth innings. In the fifth inning the Yankees failed to score but the Dodgers were able to score 1 run.   In the seventh inning each team scored 1 run.   In the Yankee half of the ninth inning they again were unable to score.

Zero as a number

Throughout this box score each 0 means an effort was made to score and *zero* runs were scored, just as each 1 means *one* run was scored.   Thus, each symbol 0 has as much numerical significance as the symbol 1 has. Each colored symbol, 0 or 1, tells the number of runs scored during a period of effort to score runs.   What does the symbol × in the lower part of the ninth inning mean?   When it became Los Angeles' time to attempt to score in this inning they were already ahead in the total number of runs scored.   They had already won the game, so there was no reason for them to make any additional effort to score.   The × is

Placeholder

simply a *placeholder:* the frame might as well have been left empty except that it is the custom to write in a symbol.   It would be entirely incorrect to replace the × by a 0, just as it would be entirely incorrect to replace any of the 0's by the symbol ×.   In this illustration each zero is the cardinal number of a set of runs which has the same cardinal number as the set of "all icebergs found in the Mojave desert during the month of July."   In the frame labeled R, the 1 and 2 indicate the total number of runs scored by each team.

Suppose three different people were given the assignment to count the chairs in some given classroom.   While they might use three distinct techniques in making their individual counts, the number reported should be the same from all three.   This illustrates a very important property of sets, namely,

The cardinal number of a set is a property of the set only, and is independent of the count used to obtain it.

This is intuitively reasonable and we shall accept it without proof, although it is possible to derive it by rigorous argument. This property of a set, which is as real and significant as such properties as color, size, shape, sourness, sweetness, length, and width, might be called the *number property of the set.* We can thus say that number is that prop- erty of a set of objects which the set has in common with every other set with which it can be placed in a one-to-one correspondence. It should be noted that to say $n(A) = n(B)$ is not to imply that set $A =$ set B. For example, if $A = \{1,2,3,4,5\}$ and $B = \{a,b,c,d,e\}$, then $n(A) = n(B)$, but the elements of A and B are not identical, and $A \neq B$.

Number property of a set

1–3   THE CONCEPT OF ORDINAL NUMBER

We have seen that one important concept of number is that of the cardinal number of a set, which answers the question, How many? Another important notion is that of an *ordinal number,* which answers the question, What is the order of the elements in a set? When one states that there are seven contestants entered in a race, there is no particular concern over the order of their arrangement; only the cardinality of the set is of consequence. At the end of the race, how- ever, there is no particular concern about "how many" entrants there were; the major concern is the order in which they finished. Who was first, who was second, and even, at times, who was last?

Ordinal number

What basic principles control the determination of order? To answer this question let us consider, for example, the sets A, B, C, and D which are all subsets of the same universal set. Furthermore, let the sets be such that $A \subset B, B \subset C$, and $C \subset D$. By the transitive property of the relation "is a proper subset of," it follows that $A \subset B \subset C \subset D$. Thus a specified ordered arrangement is determined for the four sets. When such an ordering has numerical significance the names "first," "second," "third," and "fourth" are associated with sets A, B, C, and D, respec- tively. Other titles such as "earliest," and "tallest" may be given to a member of set A, depending on the criteria used in ordering the sets. In contrast, a member of set D may be labeled "latest," "slowest," or "shortest."

The same four sets could be ordered in another way. The fact that A is a subset of B can also be expressed by stating that the set B contains the set A, that is, $B \supseteq A$. It thus follows that if $A \subset B \subset C \subset D$, then $D \supset C \supset B \supset A$. The principle for ordering here would label an element of set D as first and of set A as fourth. Such a scheme is used in popularity contests, political elections, and other such contests.

Example   Suppose the seven contestants in a footrace are Bob, Tom, Joe, Jim, David, John, and Bill. The universal set for the race = {Bob, Tom, Joe, Jim, David, John, Bill}. If the sets of finishers, in their respective order of occurrence, are {David}, {David, Joe}, {David, Joe, Jim}, {David, Joe, Jim, Bob}, {David, Joe, Jim, Bob, John}, {David, Joe, Jim, Bob, John, Tom}, and {David, Joe, Jim, Bob, John, Tom, Bill}, then we say that David was *first;* Joe was *second;* Jim, *third;* Bob, *fourth;* John, *fifth;* Tom, *sixth;* and Bill, *seventh.* From another point of view we might say that David was the *fastest* runner, and Bill the *slowest* runner, in the race.

Man, through the ages, has possessed both a cardinal and an ordinal sense of number in varying degrees of refinement. In its ordered sense, number maintains a somewhat closer contact with concreteness than it does in its cardinal sense. However, there are many basic uses of the cardinal concept of number in which man may engage intelligently without having any clear concept of the cardinality of the set, or sets, with which he is dealing. He can tell when one set contains more elements than another; he can tell when "*all* the parade has passed" or when there are "more apples to be placed in the sack"; and so on. To attain higher levels of number recognition and number use, man has had to evolve more refined techniques for observation of symmetric patterns, mental recognition of equal sets, subdivision into significant subsets, and counting.

1-4   THE NEED FOR A SYMBOLIC LANGUAGE

Suppose that, for the moment, you remove from your thinking all number names and number symbols with which you are familiar. What are some of the major problems with which you are confronted if you have a need to count and record the results of your counting? For example, how would you answer the question, How many letters are there in the word "number"? You start with the letter n, but you have neither a name nor a symbol to record the result of your count. These must be invented or determined. If the set of elements to be counted is fairly large in content, it becomes desirable to use some pattern of grouping in order to simplify the system of symbols and names. The principle

Place value   of *place value,* or *positional value,* can be used as a most effective aid in building symbols for large numbers. By place value we mean the value which a digit symbol acquires by virtue of its position in any given numeral. Place value has no significance at all, however, until some

Base of a numeral system   agreement has been reached as to the cardinal number of the set to be used in grouping. This number is called the *base* of the system. In the number system that we use the base is ten because in forming the symbols for larger numbers we group in terms of the set whose cardinal number is ten. Hence this system is called a *decimal* system, from the Latin word *decem*, meaning ten. Thus, if the symbol ☐☐☐☐ represents a four-digit number, the square on the extreme right is the ones place, the next to the left is the tens place, the next is the place for ten × ten, and the next is for ten × ten × ten. In other words, in the number 2,345 the 2 is in the thousands place, the 3 is in the hundreds place, the 4 is in the tens place, and the 5 is in the ones place.

Decimal numeral system

It is the purpose of this discussion to outline the salient problems in building a system of numeration. We shall use place value and the principle of addition of these values to obtain the symbol for any expressed quantitative concept such as how many letters there are in the word "number." To illustrate, 2,345 means 2 thousands + 3 hundreds + 4 tens + 5 ones, or two thousand three hundred forty-five.

Building a system of numeration

The only thing left for us to determine before we can begin our experiment of building the system of number symbols is the cardinal number of the set we shall use as the base. Let us choose as the base of our system the number which is the cardinal number of all sets which can be placed in one-to-one correspondence with the set {a,b,c,d,e}. If we were counting in the familiar decimal number system this number would be five, represented by the symbol 5. In the number system we are constructing we have neither the number name "five" nor the number symbol 5. We shall use the number name *verto* and the number symbol I0 to indicate the base of our new number system. In Fig. 1–8 there are suggested number names and symbols to assist you in understanding just what takes place in the building of a number symbolism. Note that I0 is the symbol for verto, that is, it is the symbol for the base of the system. Similarly, I00 is the notation for base × base, or verto × verto, and I000 represents base × base × base, or verto × verto × verto.

Base **verto**

Now to count the letters in the word "number," starting with *n*, we have vert; *u* is perp; *m*, trang; *b*, sar; *e*, verto; and *r*, verto-vert (II). In

FIGURE 1–8   Number names and symbols in base verto.

I vert	I0 verto	I00 vertoo	I000 vertong
⊥ perp	⊥0 perpo	⊥00 perpoo	⊥000 perpong
△ trang	△0 trango	△00 trangoo	△000 trangong
☐ sar	☐0 saro	☐00 saroo	☐000 sarong

This system uses 0(zero) as it is used in the decimal system.
I0 (verto) represents the base.
I00 (vertoo) represents the base × the base.
I000 (vertong) represents the base × the base × the base.

the word "arithmetic" there are perpo ($\perp 0$) letters, and in the words "elementary mathematics" there are saro-vert ($\square$I) letters. Count the letters to check these statements. As a final check on your ability to count in this new system, count the words and then the letters in this entire sentence.† To interpret symbols such as $\square\square$, $\triangle\square\triangle$, and $\square\perp\triangle$I we use place value and the additive principle: $\square\square = \square 0 + \square$; $\triangle\square\triangle = \triangle 00 + \square 0 + \triangle$; $\square\perp\triangle$I $= \square 000 + \perp 00 + \triangle 0 + $I. This last symbol is read sarong perpoo trango-vert.

This experiment may be pursued as far as one likes. It has been designed merely for the purpose of giving the reader some opportunity to understand some of the basic principles which have fostered the evolution of our system of enumeration out of the confusion and awkwardness of more primitive systems.

Exercises

1 When are two sets of objects said to be in one-to-one correspondence with each other?

2 Without counting, use one-to-one correspondence to show that you have just as many fingers on your left hand as on your right hand.

3 Under what conditions can the empty chairs of a classroom be counted to determine the number of pupils absent from class?

4 Give four illustrations, other than those of the text, of one-to-one correspondence between sets.

5 What is meant by the "number property" of a set?

6 Can you cite evidence from the literature or from your experience of the existence of a number sense among animals, birds, or insects?

7 Give two illustrations, other than those in the text, of situations in which man might exhibit number sense without recourse to counting.

8 Team up with someone to try this experiment:

(*a*) Each present the other with groups of objects in disarray, and in varying numbers, for example,

```
XX X   X
XXX X   X
  X X X   X
   X X   X
```

the object being to determine the upper limit of immediate recognition.

† There are saro-sar ($\square\square$) words and trangoo-saro-trang ($\triangle\square\triangle$) letters in the entire sentence.

(b)   Each present the other with groups of objects in various forms of orderly array, for example,

```
X X   X X   X X
 X     X     X     X
X X   X X   X X
```

also to determine the upper limit of immediate recognition.

9   What are some illustrations of the use of tallying as an aid to counting?

10   Distinguish between the concepts of cardinal and ordinal numbers. Give illustrations.

11   What is the cardinal number of each of the following sets?

(a)   All circles which are square
(b)   All letters common to the words "bar," "call," and "saw"
(c)   All occurrences of the letter "e" in the word "cough"
(d)   The days in a week
(e)   The minutes in an hour

12   Classify each of the following numbers as a cardinal number or an ordinal number.

First day of the week	Baseball score 3–0
32 children	6 months
1309 18th Avenue S	7-day week
Dickens 5-1141	December 25
24 hours in a day	75 pages
Page 75	Mascot number 0

13   List the sets which would show the set of racers = {Linda, Carol, Cathy, Sharon, Marly, Diana} finishing in this order: Linda, first; Sharon, second; Diana, third; Marly, fourth; Cathy, fifth; and Carol, sixth.

14   List the sets which would show the girls of Exercise 13 finishing in this order: Diana and Marly tied for first place; Cathy, third; Carol and Sharon tied for fourth place; and Linda sixth.

15   Write the numeral in the verto system for each of these numbers:

(a)   Perpoo, verto-trang
(b)   Sarong, trangoo, vert
(c)   Perpong, perpo-perp

16   Write the number for each of these numerals:

(a) $| \perp \triangle$ (b) $\triangle 0 \square$
(c) $\square \triangle 0$ (d) $\square | \triangle \square$

17   Determine whether the statement

$$n(P \cup Q) = n(P) + n(Q) - n(P \cap Q)$$

is true or false under each of the given assumptions on P and Q:

(a) P and Q are disjoint sets.
(b) P and Q are not disjoint sets.

INVITATIONS TO EXTENDED STUDY

1   Investigate the significance of symbolism in such areas as high-way travel, home life, business, industry, and religious and organization ceremony.

2   When are two sets A and B said to be *equivalent?* What is the significant difference between the statement that two sets are equivalent and the statement that two sets are equal?

3   Use Venn diagrams to illustrate these relations between sets. They are known as De Morgan's laws.

$$\sim(A \cup B) = \sim A \cap \sim B \qquad \text{and} \qquad \sim(A \cap B) = \sim A \cup \sim B$$

4   Develop the argument needed to establish De Morgan's laws.

5   Develop the argument needed to establish the statements of Exercise 12 on page 11.

6   Invent number names and symbols for a number system using 卌 || as a base. Assume place value and the additive principle in constructing symbols for numbers larger than the base.

systems
of numeration

GUIDELINES FOR CAREFUL STUDY

One of the significant benefits to be derived from a study of the historical background of any cultural aspect of modern civilization is the
acquiring of a better orientation for the evaluation and appreciation of
the cultural characteristics of the present. As was pointed out in the
preceding chapter, two basic problems in the construction of any system of numeration are number symbols and number names. Furthermore, the concepts of a base and place value, and the additive principle
for combining values, are essential to an efficient structure of number
symbols. It is beneficial and of interest to review the struggles past
civilizations have had with these problems in the development of
numeration systems.

In this chapter brief analyses are made of some of the more significant
of the primitive systems of numeration. A careful study of these systems can help you to a clearer understanding and deeper appreciation
of the one which we use today. Also the study of number systems in

bases other than ten provides a context for significant comprehension of the advantages and limitations of the decimal system.

Guidelines for intelligent study of this chapter are:

1   Observe carefully the nature of the number symbolism characteristic of each culture discussed.   What base was used?   Did it make use of any form of place value?   Did it make use of the additive principle?

2   How readily did each of the numeration systems adapt to computation and other quantitative uses?

3   Did the absence of a concept of place value affect the efficiency of any of the systems?

4   Did the absence of simplicity of form affect the efficiency of any of the systems?

5   What are the essential characteristics of a decimal system of numeration?

6   What are the basic characteristics of our numeration system which contribute to its effectiveness?

7   What is the historical origin of our system of numeration?

8   Why did the writer Tobias Dantzig attribute such great significance to the discovery of "the symbol for an empty column"?

9   What is the contrast between the digit value and the place value of each digital symbol in the symbol for any number larger than the base of a numeration system?

10   Does each of the digital symbols 0, 1, 2, 3, 4, 5, 6, 7, 8, 9 have significance both as a number symbol and as a placeholder in symbols for large numbers in a decimal system?

11   Why do symbols such as 10 and 20,456 have no meaning until they are given orientation within the context of a specified base?

12   Under what conditions does 10 not mean ten?

INTRODUCTION

What is the one characteristic of the Hindu-Arabic numeration system in use today that has caused it to supersede other numeration systems? Any informed person would most likely answer "the use of place value in the structure of our number symbols." A study of the numeration systems of some of the more significant of ancient cultures clearly reveals the difficulty in operating with these systems due to the absence of the simplifying contribution of *place value* in the structure of the numerals† used.

Place value is
of great
significance

---

† The word "numeral" is the name given to the symbol for the cardinal number of a set.

2-1 PRIMITIVE SYSTEMS

The approximate date 3500 B.C. is accepted as the beginning of the use of numerals in a definite number system. The Sumerians, Egyptians, and Chinese all used methods which seemed to imply that their numerals developed from the natural process of tallying. Each Babylonian, Egyptian, and Chinese numeral up to nine is represented by means of a series of strokes, while numerals of higher denomination, such as tens and hundreds, are denoted by special strokes. Straight marks for the smaller numbers appeared quite early, while ten has always been indicated by some special symbol.

The Egyptian numeral system was basically decimal in nature, but without the concept of positional, or place, value. Distinct symbols represented the different powers of ten (10; 100; 1,000; 10,000; 100,000, and 1,000,000). Figure 2-1 exhibits the symbolism used for each of the basic denominations. Multiples of each specific power of ten were symbolized by repetition of the appropriate symbol. The symbol for 40, for example, was 4 of the symbols for ten, the symbol for 500 was 5 of the symbols for one hundred, the symbol for 9,000 was 9 of the symbols for one thousand, and so on.

Egyptian numerals

In composing large numerals the Egyptians used only the principles of repetition and addition. Thus $\begin{smallmatrix}9\\9\end{smallmatrix}\ \begin{smallmatrix}\cap\cap\cap\\\cap\cap\end{smallmatrix}\ \begin{smallmatrix}|\,|\,|\\|\,|\,|\end{smallmatrix}$ would be used to represent two hundreds plus five tens plus six ones;† we write this number as 256.

† The symbol has been written here to read from left to right, although it was the practice among the Egyptians to read from right to left.

FIGURE 2-1   The Egyptian numerals

OUR NUMBER	HIEROGLYPHIC SYMBOL	OBJECT REPRESENTED
1	|	vertical staff
10	∩	heel bone
100	9	scroll
1,000	𐦀	lotus flower
10,000	𓂭	pointing finger
100,000	∽	burbot fish
1,000,000	𓀠	man in astonishment

Babylonian
numerals

Writing in Babylonia was done on damp clay tablets with a stylus which produced a wedge-shaped symbol, known as cuneiform. In writing numbers only two elementary characters were used: the wedge $\vee$, a symbol for one; and the arrowhead $<$, a symbol for ten. These were combined in a simple manner and so constituted a satisfactory system of notation. Two systems were employed by the Babylonians: the decimal and the sexagesimal (base sixty.) Cantor states that the scale of sixty was adopted so that each god could be denoted by one of the whole numbers from one to sixty, which told of his rank in the heavenly hierarchy.†

Two principles, the additive and multiplicative, were employed in this system of notation. All numbers below 100 were expressed by symbols whose values had to be added. The special symbol for 100 was $\vee >$, and in writing hundreds the smaller symbol was placed to the left of the 100 and used as a multiplier; thus $<\vee >$ was the symbol for 1,000, that is, 10 times 100. This then became a new symbol and the multiplicative principle was applied to it to write thousands; thus $<<\vee >$ was read 10 times 1,000 and not 20 times 100. Biblical as well as secular history seems to indicate rather definitely that the use of large numbers was very rare. Some historians state that the principle of positional value was used in writing large numbers with sixty as the base, but that for numbers smaller than sixty a special pattern of grouping, using ten as a base, was used. Can you think of any illustration in our use of number that implies a scale of sixty?

Rhind papyrus

The Rhind, or Ahmes, papyrus,‡ a rather comprehensive Egyptian arithmetic written about 1650 B.C. and representing the highest arithmetical attainments of the Egyptians, gives Egypt the distinction of a decimal system as old as that of Babylonia. Although their knowledge was probably not so profound as we might expect, it shows marked proficiency in mathematics at the time when Abraham visited Egypt and brought the art of numbers from Chaldea to Egypt.

2-2 THE GREEK AND ROMAN SYSTEMS

The Greeks probably obtained their knowledge of mathematics from the Egyptians, since active trade had sprung up between Greece and Egypt about the seventh century B.C., giving opportunity for an exchange of ideas as well as merchandise.

† M. Cantor, *Vorlesungen über Geschichte der Mathematik*, vol. I, p. 43, B. G. Teubner Verlagsgesellschaft, mbH, Leipzig, 1922.
‡ A. B. Chace, L. S. Bull, H. P. Manning, and R. C. Archibald (eds.), "The Rhind Mathematical Papyrus," vols. I and II, Mathematical Association of America, Inc., Buffalo, N.Y., 1927 and 1929.

FIGURE 2-2   The Greek numerals

1	α	alpha	10	ι	iota	100	ρ	rho	1,000	α'
2	β	beta	20	κ	kappa	200	σ	sigma	2,000	β'
3	γ	gamma	30	λ	lambda	300	τ	tau	3,000	γ'
4	δ	delta	40	μ	mu	400	υ	upsilon	4,000	δ'
5	ϵ	epsilon	50	ν	nu	500	ϕ	phi	5,000	ϵ'
6	F	digamma*	60	ξ	xi	600	χ	chi	6,000	F'
7	ζ	zeta	70	o	omicron	700	ψ	psi	7,000	ζ'
8	η	eta	80	π	pi	800	ω	omega	8,000	η'
9	θ	theta	90	φ	koppa*	900	λ	sampi*	9,000	θ'

* Obsolete symbols

As early as the third century B.C. the Greeks represented numbers by the initial letter of the numeral names. Later in writing their numerals they used the 24 letters of their own alphabet and three special symbols.[†] Their method was to assign the numbers from one to nine to the first nine letters of the alphabet; then 10, 20, 30, . . . , 90, to nine more; and 100, 200, . . . , 900 to nine more. There being only 24 letters in the Greek alphabet, three more were necessary; so they made use of three obsolete letters. An examination of Fig. 2-2 reveals that the obsolete letters were used as symbols for 6, 90, and 900.

The additive principle only was used in numbers smaller than 10,000. For example, $\sigma\mu\beta$ was interpreted to mean $200 + 40 + 2$ or, as we should write it, 242. An accented letter was used to indicate multiplication by 1,000. For example, δ' became the symbol for 4,000, and $\delta'\rho\lambda\delta$ the symbol for 4,134. For numbers larger than 10,000 an additional symbol, M, was introduced to indicate multiplication by 10,000. There seems to be some ambiguity as to where the number to be multiplied would be written. It occurs in print sometimes above, sometimes before, and sometimes after the M. Thus, $\overset{\epsilon}{M}$, ϵM, and $M\epsilon$ might be found as the symbol for 50,000. We shall use ϵM. In writing numbers larger than 10,000 both the multiplicative principle and the additive principle were used. For example, $\theta M\gamma'\psi\pi\eta$ would be interpreted as

$$90,000 + 3,000 + 700 + 80 + 8$$

or, as we should write it, 93,788. It is said that, when numbers were used in a context, a line might be drawn above the numbers to distinguish them from words. For example, the Greek word $\tau\iota\eta$ means "why?"; as a numeral it means 318. In such cases the over-stroke could well be used to remove ambiguity of meaning. Thus $\tau\iota\eta$ would mean "why?" and $\overline{\tau\iota\eta}$ would mean 318.

Greek numerals

† Howard Eves, "An Introduction to the History of Mathematics," p. 14, Holt, Rinehart and Winston, Inc., New York, 1953.

FIGURE 2-3   Abacus showing 7,510,269

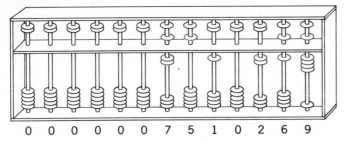

0 0 0 0 0 0 7 5 1 0 2 6 9

The numeral system used by the Greeks was so clumsy that they made very little progress in calculations. It seems from accounts of most historians that, when the fingers were not adequate, some kind of abacus was used. According to tradition, Pythagoras first introduced this instrument into Greece after his travels in Egypt.† As to the kind of abacus, we know very little. Herodotus is given credit for the statement that "the Egyptians calculate with pebbles moving the hand from right to left." We might infer from this statement that the abacus was some kind of board divided into vertical columns in which each column was used for the units of different denominations. This would indicate some conception of the notion of the principle of position which appeared at an earlier date in tables of squares constructed by the Babylonians. In Fig. 2-3 the colored discs show how the number 7,510,269 would be recorded on a modern abacus.

The system of notation used by the Romans was much better suited to computation than that of either the Greeks or the Egyptians. It made use not only of the addition principle but also of a principle of subtraction which was found occasionally among the cuneiform characters of the Babylonians. The use of these two principles is seen in the three numbers X (ten), IX ($10 - 1$, or nine), and XI ($10 + 1$, or eleven). This notational pattern was a decided improvement over that used by the Greeks, since it was less cumbersome and did not burden the memory with numerous symbols, only seven being necessary: I, V, X, L, C, D, M. For large numbers, the overscoring bar was used to indicate multiplication by 1,000; for example, $\overline{\text{X}} = 10 \times 1,000 = 10,000$. The number 2,070,849 would be written as the Roman numeral $\overline{\text{MMLXX}}\text{DCCCXLIX}$.

Roman numerals

For several centuries the Greek and Roman systems contended for popular favor among mathematicians, the Roman being finally adopted for reckoning in medieval Europe. It has been said that the Roman system of calculating on the reckoning board was one of the most important steps in the development of the decimal system.

† F. Cajori, "A History of Mathematics," p. 52, The Macmillan Company, New York, 1919.

2-3 THE MAYAN SYSTEM

To the Maya of Central America seems to belong the distinction of first having the principle of place value and the use of a zero symbol in a fully developed numeral system.   Research has revealed numerous records of their calendars and chronology which have been successfully deciphered, disclosing the fact that the Maya possessed this system five or six centuries before any Asiatic country.† Their system, as found in their calendars, rituals, and astronomical observations, was not decimal but vigesimal (base twenty) in nature, except for one position. "Twenty units of the lowest order (kins or days) make one unit of the next higher order (uinal or 20 days), 18 uinals make one unit of the third order (tun or 360 days), 20 tuns make one unit of the fourth order (katun or 7,200 days), 20 katuns make one cycle or 144,000 days, and finally 20 cycles

Mayan numerals

† F. Cajori, The Zero and Principle of Local Value Used by the Maya of Central America, *Science*, **44**:715 (1916).

FIGURE 2-4   The Maya numerals

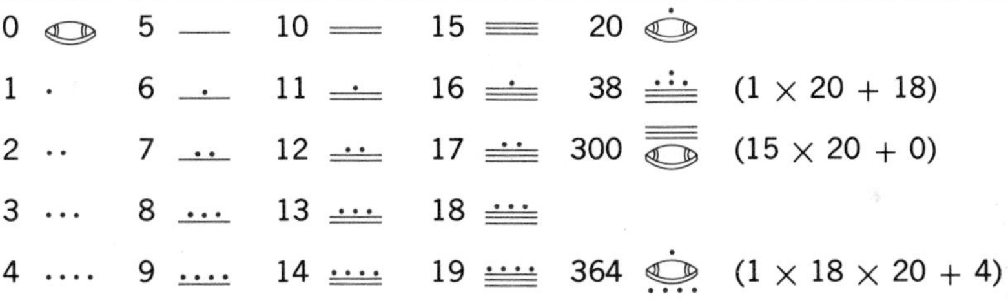

The *kin* of the Mayan system has the same value as the *one* of our decimal system.   Therefore, any numeral of the Mayan system may be converted into its equivalent numeral in our system by changing each position symbol into its equivalent number of kins.

⋯	3 great cycles =	3 × 2,880,000 kins =	8,640,000 kins
⬯	0 cycles	= 0 ×	144,000 kins =	0 kins
═	10 katuns	= 10 ×	7,200 kins =	72,000 kins
⩶	18 tuns	= 18 ×	360 kins =	6,480 kins
⠒	2 uinals	= 2 ×	20 kins =	40 kins
≐	11 kins	=	11 kins =	11 kins
				8,718,531 kins

The equivalent numeral in our decimal system is 8,718,531.

make one great cycle or 2,880,000 days."† The numbers from 1 to 19 are represented by bars and dots, each dot standing for one unit and each bar for five, the value of the bars and dots being added in each case. In writing twenty, the principle of local value enters for the first time as it is represented by the symbol for zero (⬭), with a dot placed over it. Figure 2–4 shows how place value is used in writing large numbers. For example, thirty-eight is expressed by the symbols for 18 (three bars, three dots) in the *kin* place and one dot representing 20 placed above 18 in the *uinal* place. Conant says: "In the Maya scale we have one of the best and most perfect examples of vigesimal numeration ever developed by any race."‡ There is no evidence of digital numeration in the first ten units; but, judging from the almost universal practice of the Indian tribes of both North and South America, this may have been the origin of the Maya counting. Can you think of any illustration in our use of number that implies a scale of twenty?

Exercises

1 Translate each of these symbols from the Egyptian numerals to our numerals:

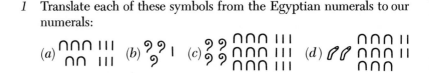

2 Translate each of these symbols from the Greek numerals to our numerals:

(*a*) ψπη   (*b*) ε′ε   (*c*) λ′μ   (*d*) δΜρα   (*e*) η′ΜχΜγ′ωλδ

3 Translate each of these symbols from the Roman numerals to our numerals:

(*a*) CCXLVII   (*b*) MI   (*c*) MCMLXII
(*d*) MCDXCII   (*e*) M̄M̄MIV   (*f*) M̄D̄C̄XCCX

4 Translate each of these symbols from the Mayan numerals to our numerals:

(*a*) ⬭   (*b*) ⋮   (*c*) ☰   (*d*) ⬭   (*e*) ⬭

5 Translate each of these symbols first to Egyptian numerals, then to Greek numerals, then to Roman numerals, then to Mayan numerals:

(*a*) 467   (*b*) 2,508   (*c*) 40,720   (*d*) 1,492
(*e*) 3,004   (*f*) 400,500   (*g*) 1,610,430   (*h*) 4,201,897

† *Ibid.*, p. 716.
‡ L. L. Conant, "Number Concept," p. 200, The Macmillan Company, New York, 1931.

6   What do you think is the reason the Egyptian, Greek, and Roman
    numeration systems had no symbol for zero?

2–4   THE DECIMAL SYSTEM

The numeral system we use is called a decimal system, since it uses ten
as its base, or radix.   Any such system, which also uses the principle of
positional value, must have ten primary digital symbols.   We use the
nine digit numerals 1, 2, 3, 4, 5, 6, 7, 8, and 9 to represent the presence
of value and the numeral 0 to represent the absence of value.   These
symbols, along with the use of the concept of positional value, or place
value, and the additive principle, enable us to write any number we
wish, no matter how large or how small.   Positional value simply means
the value of any one of the above symbols as determined by its relative
position in the numeral.   The additive principle tells us that the value of
any numeral is found by getting the sum of all the respective implied
products of digit and place values.   For a clearer comprehension of the
intrinsic part the ten digital symbols play in the structure of our system
of numeration, let us consider a symbol such as 1,203.   For this particular illustration let us think of this numeral in parallel with the word
"teeter" ($t_{ee}t_e{}^r$).   Because of the place the symbol 1 holds in 1,203, it
has a place value of "one thousand."   How many "thousands" are in
1,203?   We say "one," but what is "one"?   In *this* illustration, it is the
number that is associated with the concepts of "thousands in 1,203"
and "the number of times the letter 'r' is used in the word 'teeter'."   It
is the same as the cardinal number to be associated with the set of "all
Empire State Buildings in New York City," with the set of "all oceans
named Atlantic," or with all sets whose elements can be placed in one-
to-one correspondence with the elements of any one of these sets.   Thus,
in addition to its *place* value of thousand, the digit symbol 1 in the number 1,203 has a *digit* value we call "one."   Similarly, in this illustration,
the symbol 2 has a place value of "one hundred" and a digit value of the
number that is associated with the concepts of "hundreds in 1,203"
and "the number of times the letter 't' is used in the word 'teeter'."   In
like manner, the symbol 0 has a place value of "ten" in the number 1,203
and a digit value of the number to be associated with the concepts of
"tens in 1,203" and "the number of times the letter 'a' is used in the
word 'teeter'."   The symbol 3 has a place value of "one" and a digit
value associated with "ones in 1,203" and "the number of times the
letter 'e' is used in the word 'teeter'."   Thus, in the structure of any
numeral, the digital symbols 0, 1, 2, 3, 4, 5, 6, 7, 8, and 9 have, each in its
own right, both a place value and a digit value.   They are used *both* as
placeholders *and* to represent numbers.

Ten as the
base of a
numeral
system

Place
(positional)
value

Additive
principle

Digit value and
place value in
numerals

The additive principle then gives the numerical significance of the numeral 1,203 as being $1(1,000) + 2(100) + 0(10) + 3(1)$, or $1,000 + 200 + 3$. It is clearly understood that, in a decimal system of numeration, the value of each position in any given numeral is ten times the value of the next position to its right and one-tenth the value of the next position to its left. This fact is more explicitly displayed when 1,203 is written as $1(10^3) + 2(10^2) + 0(10^1) + 3(1)$. Natural numbers used as exponents simply tell how many times a given number is used as a factor. In other words, $10^3 = 10 \times 10 \times 10 = 1,000$; $10^2 = 10 \times 10 = 100$; and $10^1 = 10$. With this notation, increasing the size of the exponent of 10 is all that is needed to indicate positional values of greater value: $10^4 = 10 \times 10 \times 10 \times 10 = 10,000$; $10^6 = 10 \times 10 \times 10 \times 10 \times 10 \times 10 = 1,000,000$; and so on. Decreasing the size of the exponent of 10 indicates positional values of smaller value: $10^1 = 10$; $10^0 = 1$. Also, we have $10^{-1} = \dfrac{1}{10}$; $10^{-2} = \dfrac{1}{10^2} = \dfrac{1}{10 \times 10} = \dfrac{1}{100}$; and so on. This use of 0 and negative numbers as exponents is in accordance with the definition

For any nonzero number a, $a^0 = 1$ and $a^{-n} = \dfrac{1}{a^n}$ where n is any positive number.

Thus $10^0 = 1$ and $10^{-2} = \dfrac{1}{10^2}$.

The real significance of such a numeration system lies in its compactness and adaptability in form and in the great simplification it contributes to computation. The principle of place value is the most important single attribute of our system of numeration which has given to it the power and usefulness that has resulted in its almost universal acceptance by the nations of the world.

2–5   ORIGIN AND DEVELOPMENT OF OUR NUMERALS

It is not known just who was the originator of the numeral symbols which we use, nor just what process of reasoning affected their forms. Many theories have been advanced as to their origin, but the one which seems to be the most generally accepted is that they are of Hindu origin. The authorities who adhere to this hypothesis seem also to be agreed upon the fact of Arabic influence in transmittting these symbols to other civilized nations and ultimately to the civilizations of the present. For this reason our numeral system is usually called the Arabic, Hindu-Arabic, or Indo-Arabic numeral system, with Hindu-Arabic probably the most generally accepted.

Margin notes:

Relative place values in numerals

Use of exponents in numeral structure

Significance of place value

Hindu-Arabic numerals

The value of these numerals was not recognized at once, nor were they readily accepted. Even as late as the fifteenth and sixteenth centuries the use of these numerals was very rare, since merchants still made use of the Roman system for keeping their accounts. In fact, the transition from the Roman numerals was incomplete even up to the time of the first Queen Elizabeth of England (1558–1603).

The forms of the symbols 0, 1, 6, 8, and 9 have not changed much; those for 2, 3, and 7 have changed some; while the forms for 4 and 5 have been greatly altered. The changes which these forms underwent were brought about not so much from a desire for improvement as by the fact that all manuals and documents were written by hand. It was with the invention of printing that the numerals assumed some permanency of form. So it is that our symbols of today are practically the same in appearance as those of the fifteenth century.

The date of the invention of 0 as a symbol in our numeral system is not known. Maximus Planudes, a Byzantine writer, thought that the Hindu numeral system made use of such a symbol and gave A.D. 738 as the first known instance of it.† There is additional evidence for the theory that the earliest Hindu notation neither contained such a symbol nor used the principle of place value. The rules used by Aryabhatta (A.D. 476) for extracting roots involved the principle of position and the zero, making it appear that they were both introduced about the fifth century. In an Indian inscription of A.D. 876, the numbers fifty and two hundred seventy are both written with zero. Dantzig attributes the discovery of zero to an attempt to record a permanent counting-board operation, for without some symbol to represent the empty columns "such an entry as ≡ = might represent 32, 302, 320, 3002, or many other numbers." He further states:‡

0 as a symbol

Conceived in all probability as the symbol for an empty column on a counting board, the Indian sunya was destined to become the turning-point in a development without which the progress of modern science, industry, or commerce is inconceivable. And the influence of this great discovery was by no means confined to arithmetic. By paving the way to a generalized number concept, it played just as fundamental a rôle in practically every branch of mathematics. In the history of culture the discovery of zero will always stand out as one of the greatest single achievements of the human race.

The ancient Babylonians used in their documents, but not in their calculations, a symbol to indicate that the units of a certain class were missing, and as early as the second century B.C. the Greek astronomers made use of their letter *omicron* for the same purpose. Because of this

† M. Cantor, *op. cit.*, p. 603.
‡ Tobias Dantzig, "Number, the Language of Science," 3d ed., p. 35, The Macmillan Company, New York, 1945. Used by permission of the Macmillan Company.

historical and notational emphasis given to 0 as a symbol for the "empty column," or "absence of value," incorrect interpretations of the full significance of the symbol are sometimes made. Some writers have been inclined to argue that zero is not a symbol for a number but is merely a placeholder. This is an entirely false argument since the symbol 0, just as does each of the remaining nine digital symbols of our numeral system, has distinct stature both as a symbol for a number and as a placeholder.

2-6   THE NUMERATION OF LARGE NUMBERS

After printing had, to a certain degree, stabilized the shape of the numerals used in counting and computation, there still remained the question of notation and terminology to enable one to read and write the various combinations that might be made from these 10 digital symbols. Up to the seventeenth century many different methods were used in the numeration of large numbers.

Names for large numbers

A decided advance was made by the introduction of the word *millione*. It occurs first in the year 1484 in the "Arithmetic" of the Italian, Piero Borgi, and next in the "Suma" of Luca Pacioli. During the sixteenth century the use of *millione* to denote $(1,000)^2$ spread to other European countries and to England, where Tonstall in 1522 speaks of it as being commonly used but "rejects it as barbarous."

The words "billion," "trillion," etc., date back almost as far as "million," as they seem to have been used first by the Frenchman, Nicholas Chuquet, in 1520. He used the words *byllion, tryllion, quadrillion, quyllion, sixlion, septyllion, octyllion,* and *nonyllion* to denote the second, third, etc., powers of one million, or 10^{12}, 10^{18}, etc. Names with the same significance appeared in Germany in 1681 and in England in 1687, but did not become used generally until the eighteenth century. When the people of France began grouping digits in groups of three, "billion" was assigned the new meaning of a thousand millions or 10^9, "trillion" a thousand billions or 10^{12}, etc. This difference in notation and terminology still prevails today, for in England, Germany, and certain North European countries "billion," "trillion," etc., are used for 10^{12}, 10^{18}, etc., while in the United States, France, and certain South European countries they designate 10^9, 10^{12}, etc. In other words, in the United States one billion is one thousand million or 1,000,000,000, while in Britain it is one million million or 1,000,000,-000,000. Such ambiguity in interpretation loses its significance when contrasted with the effectiveness of a system of numeration which can express the estimated weight of one atom of hydrogen as 0.00000000000000000000000175 gram (175 hundred-septillionths

Ambiguity of the symbol for one billion

Flexibility of our numeral system

gram) and at the same time tell us that a handful of uranium will produce as much useful power as about 50 trillion (50,000,000,000,000) pounds of coal. If these numbers do not impress the reader, there is the estimated mass of an electron, 0.00000000000000000000000000000199 pound (199 hundred-nonillionths pound), the number of times a voice is amplified in a coast-to-coast telephone call† ($10^{3,000}$), Sir Arthur Eddington's estimate of the number (136×2^{256}) of protons in the universe, the googol (10^{100}), the number sometimes mentioned as the total possible number of moves in a chess game ($10^{10^{50}}$), the googolplex ‡ ($10^{10^{100}}$), or the really big number known as Skewes' number,

$$10^{10^{10^{34}}}$$

Googol and googolplex, and Skewes' number

These are all finite numbers which theoretically can be written out by using the concept of place value, the nine digits, and zero. The googol would be fairly simple to write, as it is 1 followed by 100 zeros; but do not try to write the googolplex, for it has been said that there would not be enough room to write it if you went to the farthest star, touring all the nebulae and putting down zeros every inch of the way.

Exercises

1 Why is our system of numerals referred to as the Hindu-Arabic system?
2 What is meant by the statement that our system of numeration is a decimal system?
3 Use the symbol 1,056.013 to illustrate what is meant by place value.
4 Contrast the Hindu-Arabic system of numerals with (a) the Mayan system; (b) the Babylonian system; (c) the Egyptian system; (d) the Roman system. Point out the major similarities and differences.
5 What are some of the more important reasons that the Hindu-Arabic system has prevailed over each of the other systems of numeration named in Exercise 4?
6 If one digit is annexed to the right of the numeral 342, how is the value of each digit in the symbol affected?
7 If one zero is removed from the right of 26,500, how is each digit of the symbol affected?
8 Answer the question of Exercise 7 if two zeros are removed from the right of 26,500.
9 How could one-dollar bills (or pieces), dimes, and pennies be used to illustrate the basic principles of place value?

† *Telephone News,* August, 1963, Pacific Telephone, Los Angeles, California.
‡ Edward Kasner and James Newman, "Mathematics and the Imagination," pp. 18–35, Simon and Schuster, Inc., New York, 1940.

2-7 BASES OTHER THAN TEN

We have noted how the Babylonians used sixty as a base of their numeral system, and the Maya Indians used twenty. In modern literature on the subject there is to be found argument in support of the use of numbers other than ten as the base in the structure of our numeral system. Also, it is a well-known fact that electronic computation uses a binary number scale (base two) and that significant modifications of the straight binary code are used in many types of computer coding. Except for the use of two and certain powers of two as bases in electronic computation, sixty in measures of time, twenty in expressions such as "three-score years and ten," and twelve in certain forms of measurement, our numeral system quite likely will retain ten as its base. Nevertheless, profit can be derived from a study of numeral systems constructed on bases other than ten. We shall pursue in some detail an examination of systems with bases twelve and five, respectively. In this analysis we shall assume place value and the use of the additive principle, as in our decimal system. Furthermore, while we recognize the possibility of inventing new number symbols and names, we shall yield to the simple pattern of using, where possible, those already established, and shall not invent unless it becomes necessary to do so.

2-8 BASE TWELVE

In the title to this section, why is the word "twelve" written in place of using the symbol 12? The answer is simple. It is merely because the symbol **12**† (call it "one-two") in a duodecimal (base twelve) system of numeration is no longer the symbol for the concept of that which can be put in one-to-one correspondence with the strokes in Fig. 2–5. When we say we are going to use "twelve" as a base, we mean that we plan to group in "groups of twelve" and in such a grouping there are **10** (read this "one-oh"; it is no longer "ten") strokes in Fig. 2–5. There is one group of "twelve strokes" and zero strokes left over. Thus the symbol **12** (one-two) in base **twelve** means 1 group of twelve and 2 more (1 of the base and 2 more). If **10** (one-oh) no longer means ten, how can we write the number ten in this base? Since ten is smaller than twelve, it must be represented by a digital symbol; so we are in need of a one-figure symbol which can occupy only one position in the structure of

10 (One-oh) represents the base

---

† In the remainder of this section and in subsequent sections boldface will be used to indicate numerals which are to be interpreted in bases other than ten.

FIGURE 2–5

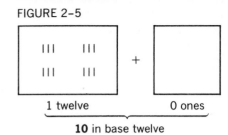

1 twelve   0 ones

10 in base twelve

numbers larger than the base. We shall use **t** and read it "tē" just as we read the letter. Similarly, we shall use the letter **e** to represent eleven, since eleven is also less than twelve and we need a one-figure symbol and a name by which to identify it. Thus, in a number system of base **twelve** our digit symbols will be **0, 1, 2, 3, 4, 5, 6, 7, 8, 9, t, e.** To be able to count and compute satisfactorily in this number system, now that we have satisfactory digital symbols, we still have to invent number names. For example, what is the number **ee?** We shall avoid this difficulty simply by calling each digit separately in order to read any number. For example, just as we read the symbol **12** as "one-two," we shall read the symbol **ee** as "e-e." For what does the symbol **3t4** stand? It means **300 + t0 + 4,** or **3 × 100 + t × 10 + 4 × 1.** This means **3 ×** (twelve × twelve) + **t** × (twelve) + (**4** × one). We read it "three-te-four." In terms of our definitions "one dozen" = twelve units and "one gross" = twelve dozen, the number **3t4** might also be read "**three gross te dozen four.**"

Digital symbols in base **twelve**

Reading numerals in base **twelve**

2–9   BASE FIVE

In order to operate efficiently in base **five** the only invention necessary, under our present agreement, will be that of number names. As digital symbols we can use **0, 1, 2, 3, 4.** In Fig. 2–6a the days of the month of July are shown enumerated in the familiar way using the decimal system. In Fig. 2–6b the corresponding numerals are shown as they would be written in a system using five as the base. Note that the symbols 0, 1, 2, 3, and 4 are used as digital symbols here as well as in base ten and base **twelve.** While they have the same cardinal significance in the languages of all three bases, they differ considerably in the meanings they carry, depending upon the base orientation of the numeral in which they occur. 23 as a symbol in base *ten* means 2 tens + 3 ones; as a symbol in base **twelve** it means **2** twelves + **3** ones; and as a symbol in base **five** it means **2** fives + **3** ones.

Digital symbols in base **five**

FIGURE 2-6   The days of the month of July enumerated in base ten and in base **five.**

July

S	M	T	W	T	F	S
1	2	3	4	5	6	7
8	9	10	11	12	13	14
15	16	17	18	19	20	21
22	23	24	25	26	27	28
29	30	31				

Base ten
(*a*)

July

S	M	T	W	T	F	S
1	2	3	4	10	11	12
13	14	20	21	22	23	24
30	31	32	33	34	40	41
42	43	44	100	101	102	103
104	110	111				

Base **five**
(*b*)

2-10   EQUIVALENT NUMERALS IN DIFFERENT BASES

How many letters in our alphabet?

How many letters are there in our alphabet?   As an aid in answering this question, we might follow some pattern of arranging the letters in readily countable groups, as shown in the colored blocks of Figs. 2-7, 2-8, and 2-9.   If we arrange them in groups of ten, there are 2 groups of ten each and 6 more.   We say there are 26 letters in the alphabet, because the symbol 26 in base ten means 2 tens and 6 ones (see Fig. 2-7). If the letters of the alphabet are grouped in groups of twelve, there are two groups of twelve and two more.   We shall write this **22—twelve**† and call it "two-two."   There are 26—ten or **22—twelve** letters in our alphabet (see Fig. 2-8).

What symbol should be used if the letters were grouped by fives?

† This symbolism will be followed throughout the book to call attention to the use of bases other than ten.   In all cases not printed in boldface the base is to be understood to be ten.

FIGURE 2-7   The number of letters in the English alphabet as enumerated in base ten.

a	*b*	*c*	*d*	*e*	ten	
f	*g*	*h*	*i*	*j*		2 × ten
k	*l*	*m*	*n*	*o*	ten	
p	*q*	*r*	*s*	*t*		+ = 26
u	*v*	*w*			six } 6 ones	
x	*y*	*z*				

FIGURE 2-8   The number of letters in the English alphabet as enumerated in base **twelve**.

a	*b*	*c*	*d*	*e*	*f*	twelve
g	*h*	*i*	*j*	*k*	*l*	
m	*n*	*o*	*p*	*q*	*r*	twelve
s	*t*	*u*	*v*	*w*	*x*	
y	*z*					two} 2 ones

2 × twelve
+
22—twelve

There is one group of five × five, no groups of five, and one more (see Fig. 2-9). The symbol in base **five** for the number of letters in our alphabet is **101.** The symbol to be used to represent a quantitative concept depends on the base that is used for the purpose of grouping:

26—ten = **22—twelve** = **101—five.**

What base is used if one says there are **35** (three-five) letters in our alphabet?

FIGURE 2-9   The number of letters in the English alphabet as enumerated in base **five**.

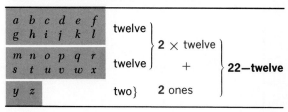

a	*b*	*c*	*d*	*e*	five
f	*g*	*h*	*i*	*j*	five
k	*l*	*m*	*n*	*o*	five
p	*q*	*r*	*s*	*t*	five
u	*v*	*w*	*x*	*y*	five
					five}
z					one} 1 one

1 × five × five
+
0 × five
+
1 one
= **101—five**

FIGURE 2-10 Interpretation of certain symbols in different bases

Symbol	Meaning			
	Any base	Base ten	Base twelve	Base five
10	1 (base) + 0 ones	1 (ten) + 0 ones	1 (twelve) + 0 ones	1 (five) + 0 ones
$100 = 10^2$	1 (base × base) + 0 (base) + 0 ones	1 (ten × ten) + 0 (ten) + 0 ones	1 (twelve × twelve) + 0 (twelve) + 0 ones	1 (five × five) + 0 (five) + 0 ones
$1{,}000 = 10^3$	1 (base × base × base) + 0 (base × base) + 0 (base) + 0 ones	1 (ten × ten × ten) + 0 (ten × ten) + 0 (ten) + 0 ones	1 (twelve × twelve × twelve) + 0 (twelve × twelve) + 0 (twelve) + 0 ones	1 (five × five × five) + 0 (five × five) + 0 (five) + 0 ones
34 = 3(10) + 4	3 (base) + 4 ones	3 (ten) + 4 ones	3 (twelve) + 4 ones	3 (five) + 4 ones
4302 = $4(10^3)$ + $3(10^2)$ + 0(10) + 2	4 (base × base × base) + 3 (base × base) + 0 (base) + 2 ones	4 (ten × ten × ten) + 3 (ten × ten) + 0 (ten) + 2 ones	4 (twelve × twelve × twelve) + 3 (twelve × twelve) + 0 (twelve) + 2 ones	4 (five × five × five) + 3 (five × five) + 0 (five) + 2 ones

In Fig. 2–10 the symbols **10, 100, 1000, 34,** and **4302** are interpreted for any base, for base ten, for base **twelve,** and for base **five.** It should be studied very carefully, as it carries significant implications for work not only in base ten but in whatever base one might choose to use.

Exercises

1 Use the indicated base to write the numeral which tells how many letters there are in the English alphabet: (*a*) **verto;** (*b*) **six;** (*c*) **seven;** (*d*) **eight;** (*e*) **two.**

2 Why are these equivalent numerals?

   (*a*) **2314—five** and ⊥ △ I □; (*b*) **302—five** and △0⊥.

3 First use base **five,** then base **twelve,** then base **eight,** and finally base **two** to count and record the number of words in each of the following quotations:

   (*a*) ... *mathematics may be defined as the subject in which we never know what we are talking about, nor whether what we are saying is true.* BERTRAND RUSSELL

   (*b*) *Pure mathematics is a collection of hypothetical, deductive theories, each consisting of a definite system of primitive,* un-*defined, concepts or symbols and primitive,* unproved, *but self-consistent assumptions (commonly called axioms) together with their logically deducible consequences following by rigidly deductive processes without appeal to intuition* . . . .
   G. D. FITCH

   (*c*) *The grandest achievement of the Hindoos and the one which, of all mathematical investigations, has contributed most to the general progress of intelligence, is the invention of the principle of position in writing numbers.* F. CAJORI

   (*d*) *Arithmetic has a very great and elevating effect, compelling the soul to reason about abstract number, and if visible or tangible objects are obtruding upon the argument, refusing to be satisfied.* PLATO

   (*e*) *Leibniz saw in his binary arithmetic the image of creation. He imagined that Unity represented God, and zero the void; that the Supreme Being drew all beings from the void, just as unity and zero express all numbers in his system of numeration.* LAPLACE

4 Since twelve dozen = one gross and twelve gross = one great gross, what symbol in base **twelve** could be used to indicate each of the following?

(a) Eight dozen, four
(b) Ten gross
(c) Five great gross, three gross, two
(d) Two great gross, eleven gross, ten dozen, nine
(e) Ten great gross, eleven gross, ten dozen, eleven
(f) Eleven great gross
(g) Ten great gross, ten dozen

5 Use the duodecimal system of numeration to record each of these measures:

(a) Two feet, three inches
(b) Eight feet, ten inches
(c) Four feet
(d) Eleven feet, eleven inches

6 Explain why **23104** means

$$2(10^4) + 3(10^3) + 1(10^2) + 0(10) + 4(1)$$

in any system of numeration with a base larger than four.

7 Write the symbol in base **five**:

(a) For the number of fingers you have on both hands
(b) For the total number of fingers and toes you have on both hands and both feet

8 Explain why 10—ten means the same as **20—five**.

9 (a) What symbol in a vigesimal scale might be used to express "three score years and ten"?
(b) What is the symbol in the numeration system used by the Maya Indians?

10 In a sexagesimal scale what might be the symbol for:

(a) Five hours, six minutes, four seconds
(b) Eight hours
(c) Ten hours, eleven minutes, five seconds
     (*Hint:* All digits must be one-figure symbols.)
(d) Forty-five hours, thirty minutes, fifty seconds

11 If **b** is the base of a given numeral system, how many digital symbols will be necessary if we assume that place value is to be used in writing all numerals?

12 What are some of the relative advantages and disadvantages in using ten, **twelve, twenty,** and **sixty** as bases in systems of numeration?

INVITATIONS TO EXTENDED STUDY

1   Contrast the modern Chinese system of numeration with ours. What are the distinguishing characteristics?   Which seems to be the more efficient?   Why?

2   Look up information on the numeration systems used by different tribes of early American Indians.   What reasons would you give as to why some one of these systems did not prevail over the Hindu-Arabic system?

3   Look into the history of the evolution of the shape of our numerals and our number names.   Why do differences still exist?

4   Investigate the use of two as a base in electronic computers.

5   If any number **b** is used as the base for a system of numeration, distinct number names are needed for the digital symbols $0, 1, 2, 3, \ldots,$ $b - 1$ and for the various powers of **b**, namely, $b, b^2, b^3, b^4, \ldots$.   How many different number names would be needed to name all the numerals from zero up to and including the numeral equivalent to 1,000—ten in the respective numeration systems for **b = two, five, eight, twelve, twenty,** or **sixty?**   For example, if **b** = ten, we need names for 0, 1, 2, 3, 4, 5, 6, 7, 8, 9, 10, 100, and 1,000.

the natural number system

GUIDELINES FOR CAREFUL STUDY

We have now constructed a context within which to undertake a careful study of the number systems that serve as the foundation upon which the structure of elementary mathematics is built. The natural number system is the simplest and most fundamental of these number systems. Its basic concepts and principles are the concern of Chap. 3. Guidelines for the study of this chapter are:

1 Do you have a clear understanding of the concept of a cardinal, or counting, number?
2 What is a mathematical system, and, in particular, what is meant by a number system?
3 What is the basic distinction between the techniques of determining the cardinal number of the union of two sets when the two sets are disjoint and when they are not disjoint?
4 What are the basic functions of the operations of addition and multiplication?

5　What are the basic properties which experience seems to identify as the characteristics of these two operations?

6　Can you use the words *closure, commutative, associative, distributive,* and *identity* intelligently?

7　When is an operation upon the elements of a set said to be well-defined?

8　How does place value simplify the algorithms which have evolved for the use of the operations of addition and multiplication?

9　What are some of the effective checks of addition and multiplication?

10　What are the properties which characterize the relation of equality?

11　Which of the properties of equality do not hold for the relations $<$ and $>$?

12　What are the basic properties of the natural number system?

13　What is an implication?

14　What is a theorem?　What are its hypothesis and its conclusion?

15　What is a deductive proof?

16　What is the distinction between a *valid* conclusion and a *true* conclusion?

17　What is meant by a converse of a theorem?

18　Why is it that a numeral such as 1234 has no meaning until it is given orientation in the context of a pattern of grouping to be used as the base for the system of numerals?

19　How can multiplication be used as a technique for converting a numeral oriented in a system with a specified base into an equivalent numeral in some different base?

INTRODUCTION

The concept of the cardinality of a set is an important capstone in the structure of modern civilization. Answers to such questions as How many?, How much?, How far?, and How long? are found by means of counting, the technique of determining the cardinal numbers of identifiable sets of objects. Thus the counting numbers have evolved as a natural means to aid civilized man to comprehend and communicate quantitative ideas. For the more efficient use of these numbers certain combinatorial operations have been defined. Intuition and experience have combined to formulate certain operational characteristics into fundamental properties or laws. Using these fundamental properties as a foundation, one may employ the techniques of logic to derive other properties, relations, and principles of operation which may be combined with them to shape the basic structure of the natural number system.

3–1   THE NATURAL NUMBERS

Legend has it that Leopold Kronecker (1823–1891) made the statement, "Die ganzen Zahlen hat Gott gemacht, alles andere ist Menschenwerk."† Herein lies the foundation of the philosophy that associates the concept of natural numbers with the numbers 1, 2, 3, 4, 5, 6, 7, 8, 9, 10, 11, . . . , which are felt to have an existence independent of man. As was noted in Chap. 1, each such number n is the cardinal number of some clearly identifiable set of n elements, as well as of all other sets which can be put in one-to-one correspondence with it.

Natural numbers

In the use of these numbers man has observed certain fundamental characteristics which he has accepted on a purely intuitive basis. Since 1 is the cardinal number of the set $\{1\}$ and

Characteristics of the set of natural numbers

$$\{1\} \subset \{1,2\} \subset \{1,2,3\} \subset \{1,2,3,4\} \subset \cdots \subset \{1,2,3,4, \ldots , n\}$$

it seems intuitively acceptable to say that 1 is a natural number and that each natural number (except 1) follows a natural number. Let us say this another way by stating that each natural number has a successor (a number which follows it) and that each natural number (except 1) is the successor of another natural number. Two other statements about natural numbers which are as readily acceptable as those already mentioned are (1) if two natural numbers a and b have successors which are equal, then $a = b$; (2) if a set S contains the natural number 1 and also contains the successor of any one of its members, which may be selected arbitrarily, then it contains all the natural numbers.

Principle of finite induction

This last statement is known as the *principle of finite induction*. The above statements are adapted from a list of five statements about natural numbers known as Peano's postulates. They were originally stated by G. Peano (1858–1932) and used as a basis for a critical study of the natural numbers and their properties.

3–2   THE NATURE OF A NUMBER SYSTEM

Structure of a number system

A number system consists of (1) a nonempty set of elements (defined or undefined); (2) at least one well-defined operation‡ upon these elements; (3) a set of postulates (acceptable assumptions) which govern the use of the operation, or operations; and (4) all the valid statements,

---

† "God made the whole numbers, all the rest is the work of man."
‡ An operation is said to be *well defined* for a set of elements if, no matter to what elements of the set the operation is applied, the result obtained has these two characteristics: (1) it is an element of the set; (2) it is clearly and uniquely identifiable.

or properties, which can be derived as consequences of the postulates and any previously derived statements.

The title of this chapter, The Natural Number System, indicates our intention to examine now the set of natural numbers $N = \{1,2,3,4, \ldots \}$, along with certain operations to be defined and postulates to be stated, in terms of its fundamental structure as a mathematical system. In the preceding section we have at least hinted at a basis for setting up a list of postulates. There still remains the necessity for specifying "at least one well-defined operation" and for providing a pattern for deriving all the consequential valid statements, or properties. For the natural number system there are two operations: *addition* and *multiplication*. We now need to define clearly what is meant by each of these two operations.

3–3   WHAT IS ADDITION?

Addition is defined in the usual sense. It is the operation we use when we desire to find the cardinal number of the union of *two* disjoint sets of objects in order to determine how many objects there are all together. In other words, for two disjoint sets A and B, $n(A \cup B) = n(A) + n(B)$. The table of basic addition facts, which may be learned through the process of counting, then completes the definition of addition. It is for this reason that we think of addition as a short form of counting. For example, if the cardinal number of set A is 3 and that of set B is 5, and if A and B are disjoint sets of objects, then $n(A \cup B) = n(A) + n(B) = 3 + 5 = 8$. For natural numbers, then, addition is a *binary* operation which combines two numbers to give a *sum*, or *total*.

Union of two disjoint sets

Addition is a binary operation

3–4   NAMES AND SYMBOLS USED IN ADDITION

In the annals of history there are to be found many different names for the process which we call addition. Some of the more frequently used names are *aggregation, summation, composition,* and *collection*. In fact, nowadays in some phases of more advanced mathematics the term *summation process* is used to indicate that addition is taking place.

The terms to be added are called *addends*. This name is derived from the Latin *numeri addendi*, meaning "numbers to be added." Interestingly enough, this name has been used frequently in the past to apply to all the numbers in a column to be added except one, which was called

Addend

the *augend,* the number to be augmented. The word "augend" dropped from popular usage for a long period of time, but is appearing again in current literature relative to electronic computation.†

Two words were used rather generally by early writers to indicate the result of adding a group of numbers. These words were "sum," which applied only to addition, and "product," which apparently was used to represent the result of any form of computation.‡ Although other words and phrases were used, these two seemed to be the most popular. Usage has established "sum" as the name for the result obtained by the process of addition. The word "total" is also used fairly generally today.

In the oldest known mathematical writing, the Ahmes papyrus (ca. 1650 B.C.), the symbol Λ (representing a pair of legs walking forward) was used to indicate the process of addition. In the writing of unit fractions (fractions with one as the numerator) the Egyptians used juxtaposition to indicate addition. For example, $\dfrac{1}{2}\dfrac{1}{18}$ represented $\dfrac{1}{2} + \dfrac{1}{18}$. This practice of using juxtaposition to indicate addition was also used in certain early Greek and Arab manuscripts. It is one which we still follow today in writing mixed numbers; for example, $4\frac{1}{3}$ is used to represent $4 + \dfrac{1}{3}$.

During the latter part of the fifteenth century the sign $\tilde{p}$ was introduced to indicate addition; it remained as an important symbol among Italian writers during the sixteenth century. A cross, much like our + sign, appeared in the Bakhshālī manuscript as a symbol to indicate subtraction. In 1429, Widman first used the + sign in print, and it was used to indicate addition. By the early part of the seventeenth century the use of the symbol "+," in the sense in which we use it today, had become rather well established. Some of the problems given by Widman, however, seem to indicate that the symbol might have been used in warehouses to denote excess weights. It apparently was used also as an abbreviation for "and," or to indicate error in computation involving the *rule of false position.* There is also evidence that the symbol might have found its origin in variations of the word *et* in Latin manuscripts.§ Attention should be called to the fact that, in the early use of the symbol, it seemed to be employed quite frequently as a descriptive label (as we use it today in directed numbers) rather than as a symbol of operation.

Margin notes: Sum · Total · Symbols used to indicate addition · The symbol +

---

† See, for example, C. B. Tompkins, Computing Machines and Automatic Decisions, *Twenty-third Yearbook of the National Council of Teachers of Mathematics,* p. 381, Washington, 1957.

‡ David Eugene Smith, "History of Mathematics," vol. II, pp. 89–90, Ginn and Company, Boston, 1925.

§ F. Cajori, "A History of Mathematical Notations," vol. I, pp. 229–236, The Open Court Publishing Company, La Salle, Ill., 1928.

3-5   THE ADDITION ALGORITHM

Just as our number system evolved out of a struggle for simplicity, compactness, and effectiveness in the recording of quantitative experience,
so did our computational algorithms emerge from a desire for speed,
accuracy, and efficiency in carrying out numerical calculations. The
concept of place value has made fully as significant a contribution to the
refinement of computation as it has to the simplification of number
symbolism.

*Place value as
an aid in com-
putation*

The numerals of the ancients did not adapt themselves very readily
to calculation. For this reason different races, of necessity, had to de-
vise computational aids to make up for their notational deficiencies.
Three principal mechanical aids, all variants of the abacus, were used.
They were the dust board, the table with loose counters, and the table
with counters fastened to lines. It is of interest to note that these
primitive "computing machines," which were based on the concept of
place value, were used by races of people whose number notation had
no semblance of the concept. The abacus is still an important aid to
computation in some countries, and a high degree of proficiency in its
use is developed.

*Early devices
used in addi-
tion*

The process of adding two or more numbers is so elementary that one
would not expect in the course of time to find much change in its techniques. The principal variations, particularly since the general acceptance of the Hindu-Arabic numerals, have been in the forms of recording
the results. The Hindus seem to have used two methods: one was the
method we now use, while the other, which they called the *inverse* or
retrograde, consisted in adding from the left and recording the result
for each column, blotting out (canceling in the illustration) as it was
necessary to "carry" from one column to the next. Figure 3–1 shows

*Retrograde
method of
addition*

FIGURE 3–1   Retrograde addition

	2,642		2,642
	1,756		1,756
	803		803
Step 1	3̶	2 + 1 = 3	3̶,1̶9̶1
Step 2	2̶1̶	6 + 7 + 8 = 21; record 1	520
Step 3	5	Replace 3 by 3 + 2 = 5	
Step 4	9̶	4 + 5 = 9	
Step 5	1̶1	2 + 6 + 3 = 11; record 1	
Step 6	20	9 + 1 = 10; record 0	
Step 7		Replace 1 by 1 + 1 = 2	

The sum is 5,201

the step-by-step analysis of this form of addition in finding the sum 2,642 + 1,756 + 803. The colored numerals show the complete analysis of each step, with each result being recorded in the colored block. On the right the algorithm is shown as actually used, except that the auxiliary digits 3, 1, and 9 would not have shown. Only the sum 5,201 would have shown in the end, as the canceled digits 3, 1, and 9 would have been blotted out as they were replaced.

In the sixteenth century Gemma Frisius introduced a method of addition which is still used by some today, particularly in the addition of long columns of numbers. This method is illustrated in Fig. 3–2. Note that he wrote the largest addend first, recorded the sum of each column in order from right to left, as shown by the colored numerals, and then added the partial sums.

A review of the variations in addition forms used by different races and individuals impresses one with the fact that the major source for differences and difficulties was an inadequate comprehension of the full significance of place value in a system of numeration. Our system is a decimal system; consequently, any natural number symbol is to be interpreted in terms of ones, tens, hundreds, thousands, and higher powers of 10. Hence, in any addition problem, place value becomes a very effective guide in arranging the addends so that it becomes rather simple to make sure that we are *combining* disjoint sets of like things, ones with ones, tens with tens, hundreds with hundreds, etc. It also serves very effectively as a guide in recording the sum. The sum of the ones column in Fig. 3–3 is 13, which by the form in which it is written means $1(10) + 3$. Therefore, we record the 3, since that is the only group of ones we have, and then we do the natural thing of combining the 1 ten with the other tens we have. The sum of the tens gives us 25 tens, which we recognize as 2 hundreds and 5 tens. The 5 tens are recorded in the tens column. The total number of hundreds is found to be 24, which we write as 2 thousands and 4 hundreds. When the thousands are totaled we obtain 13 thousands and think of it as 1 ten

Significance of place value in addition

	8,762
	3,256
	783
	652
Step 1	13
Step 2	24
Step 3	2 2
Step 4	11
Step 5	13,453

FIGURE 3–2   Algorithm of Gemma Frisius. Sums are recorded by columns from right to left.

FIGURE 3–3   Use of place value in addition

	Step 4	Step 3	Step 2	Step 1
8,762	$8(1{,}000)$	$+\,7\,(100)$	$+\,6\,(10)$	$+\,2\,(1)$
3,256	$3(1{,}000)$	$+\,2\,(100)$	$+\,5\,(10)$	$+\,6\,(1)$
783		$7\,(100)$	$+\,8\,(10)$	$+\,3\,(1)$
652		$6\,(100)$	$+\,5\,(10)$	$+\,2\,(1)$
13,453	$1(10{,}000) + 3(1{,}000)$	$+\,4\,(100)$	$+\,5\,(10)$	$+\,3\,(1)$

thousand and 3 thousands. Our sum is thus 13,453. If one thinks in terms of the full significance of place value in number symbolism, the process of addition loses virtually all its major aspects of difficulty.

3–6   PROPERTIES OF THE NATURAL NUMBERS UNDER ADDITION

As the operation of addition has evolved for the set of natural numbers, the set has been observed to satisfy certain laws under this operation. If two natural numbers are added, the sum is a unique natural number. For this reason, the set of natural numbers is said to have the property of *closure*, or the set of natural numbers is closed under addition. From the fact that $A \cup B = B \cup A$ for any two sets, whether disjoint or not (see Exercise 12a, page 11), we have strong intuitive support for assuming that the order in which two natural numbers are added has no effect on the sum obtained   The sum of 3 and 5 is 8 regardless of whether we think of adding 5 to 3 or 3 to 5; $3 + 5 = 5 + 3$. Since this is true for any two natural numbers, addition of natural numbers is said to be *commutative*.

Closure under addition

Addition is a binary operation, that is, it is a process that operates only on two numbers. Because of this fact there is a question as to how one might proceed to find the cardinal number $n(A \cup B \cup C)$, call it $a + b + c$, where A, B, and C are three disjoint sets. From the definition of addition $n(A \cup B)$ is $n(A) + n(B)$, which is a natural number by the closure property. If $a = n(A)$ and $b = n(B)$, then the cardinal number $n(A \cup B)$ is the natural number $(a + b)$. It thus follows that, if $c = n(C)$, $n(A \cup B) + n(C)$ is the natural number $(a + b) + c$. By a similar argument it follows that $n(A) + n(B \cup C)$ is the natural number $a + (b + c)$. Furthermore, it has been shown (see Exercise 12c, page 11) that $(A \cup B) \cup C = A \cup (B \cup C)$, which supports the assumption that in the addition of any three natural numbers a, b, and c,

The commutative property of addition

the same sum $a + b + c$ is always obtained whether the grouping is $a + (b + c)$ or $(a + b) + c$. Hence addition of natural numbers is said to be *associative*.

The associative property of addition

These three properties which hold for the set N under the operation of addition have such far-reaching significance that it is important that they be listed for emphasis.

Properties of the natural numbers under addition

Under the operation of addition the set $N = \{1,2,3,4,\dots\}$ satisfies these properties:

A-1   Closure   For $a, b \in N$, it is true that $a + b$ is a unique element of N.

A-2   Commutative   For $a, b \in N$, it is true that $a + b = b + a$.

A-3   Associative   For $a, b, c \in N$, it is true that $(a + b) + c = a + (b + c)$.

Analysis of the addition process

Example   Figures 3–4 to 3–6 complete the definition of addition for number systems whose numerals are written in the respective bases of ten, **two**, and **six**. In Fig. 3–4 the basic addition facts are recorded for a numeral system with ten as a base. As an example of how the table is to be used we find, in the row with 4 at the extreme left, the numeral 12 in the column headed by 8. This tells us that $4 + 8 = 12$. Similarly, 12 is found opposite 8 and under 4. Thus $8 + 4 = 12$. Opposite 9 and under 8 we find 17; so $9 + 8 = 17$. In the same manner the sum of any two one-digit numbers, with numerals written in base ten, can be read from the table.

Figure 3–5 may be used in a corresponding manner for numerals written in base **two**. The basic addition facts are few in this system. $0 + 0 = 0; 1 + 0 = 0 + 1 = 1;$ and $1 + 1 = 10.$

+	0	1	2	3	4	5	6	7	8	9
0	0	1	2	3	4	5	6	7	8	9
1	1	2	3	4	5	6	7	8	9	10
2	2	3	4	5	6	7	8	9	10	11
3	3	4	5	6	7	8	9	10	11	12
4	4	5	6	7	8	9	10	11	12	13
5	5	6	7	8	9	10	11	12	13	14
6	6	7	8	9	10	11	12	13	14	15
7	7	8	9	10	11	12	13	14	15	16
8	8	9	10	11	12	13	14	15	16	17
9	9	10	11	12	13	14	15	16	17	18

FIGURE 3–4   Basic addition facts (base ten). In the row headed by 6 on the left we find 13 in the column headed by 7 above; thus $6 + 7 = 13$. Similarly, $7 + 6 = 13$.

FIGURE 3–5   Basic addition facts (base **two**). In the row headed by **1** on the left we find **10** in the column headed by **1** above; thus $1 + 1 = 10$—**two**.

+	0	1
0	0	1
1	1	10

In Fig. 3–6 we have the addition facts for a numeral system using **six** as a base. Opposite **4** and under **2** we find **10**, which tells us that $4 + 2 = 10$. Opposite **5** and under **4** we find **13**; so $5 + 4 = 13$.

Each table contains only numerals representing numbers from the set of counting numbers as written in the particular system specified, and serves as an illustration of the closure property: The sum of two counting numbers is a counting number. We assume that this would continue to be true if each table could be extended to contain the sum of any two counting numbers of that particular system.

Examination of each table reveals the fact that the table has symmetry with respect to the dotted line which is a diagonal of the particular diagram (the same numerals are seen in corresponding positions on each side of the diagonal). This fact illustrates that addition in each system is commutative. As in the case of closure, we assume that this characteristic would continue to be true if each table could be extended to contain the sum of any two counting numbers.

As an illustration of the associative property we raise the question of what is the sum of the four numbers $3 + 0 + 1 + 4$ if the numerals represent numbers written in base **six**. Since addition is a binary operation we must group these numbers in such a way that we can combine them two at a time. We might have any one of four groupings.

1 $(3 + 0) + (1 + 4)$, base **six**

From Fig. 3–6, first we have $3 + 0 = 3$ and $1 + 4 = 5$; then $3 + 5 = 12$—**six**.

2 $3 + (0 + 1) + 4$

First we have $0 + 1 = 1$, and the desired sum becomes $3 + 1 + 4$. This sum may be found by the grouping $(3 + 1) + 4 = 4 + 4 = 12$—**six** or by $3 + (1 + 4) = 3 + 5 = 12$—**six**.

FIGURE 3–6   Basic addition facts (base **six**). In the row headed by **3** on the left we find **11** in the column headed **4** above; thus $3 + 4 = 11$—**six**. Similarly, $4 + 3 = 11$.

+	0	1	2	3	4	5
0	0	1	2	3	4	5
1	1	2	3	4	5	10
2	2	3	4	5	10	11
3	3	4	5	10	11	12
4	4	5	10	11	12	13
5	5	10	11	12	13	14

3 3 + (0 + 1 + 4), base **six**

To find this sum we first must determine a sum for 0 + 1 + 4 which may be grouped either as (0 + 1) + 4, giving the sum 1 + 4 = 5, or as 0 + (1 + 4) = 0 + 5 = 5. Then 3 + (0 + 1 + 4) = 3 + 5 = 12—six.

4 (3 + 0 + 1) + 4, base **six**

First we have 3 + 0 + 1 = (3 + 0) + 1 = 3 + 1 = 4, or 3 + 0 + 1 = 3 + (0 + 1) = 3 + 1 = 4, whence it follows that (3 + 0 + 1) + 4 = 4 + 4 = 12—six.

It will be informative at this point to observe to just what extent these properties enter into finding the sum of any set of addends, for example, those in the illustrations of the preceding section. Rather than use the large addends of those illustrations it will suffice to analyze the process of finding the sum 57 + 83. This analysis, which is given in the following example, will be simpler to follow if the addition is accomplished with the numbers in horizontal rather than vertical array, although the details of the operation are the same. The steps are given in the left column, with their respective reasons given directly opposite in the right column.

Example   Find the sum of 57 and 83, base ten.

1   57 + 83 = (50 + 7) + (80 + 3)   Place value

2   (50 + 7) + (80 + 3) = 50 + (7 + 80) + 3   Associative property

3   50 + (7 + 80) + 3 = 50 + (80 + 7) + 3   Commutative property

4   50 + (80 + 7) + 3 = (50 + 80) + (7 + 3)   Associative property

5   (50 + 80) + (7 + 3) = 130 + 10   Addition

6   130 + 10 = 140   Addition

7   57 + 83 = 140   The justification for this last step is found in a certain property E-3 of equality, which is listed later.

Up to this point we have, on occasion, used the symbol = to express the relation of equality between two sets or two numbers. It is used to mean "is the same as." For example, in step 7 of the preceding example we have 57 + 83 is the same as 140. When we are dealing with numbers, this relation has five properties which distinguish it from other relations which may exist between numbers. In this context the numbers with which we are concerned are natural numbers. However, these properties of equality hold for the numbers of any of the number systems discussed in this text. They will, therefore, be stated in that context.

The relation of equality between any two elements of the set $S = \{a,b,c, \ldots \}$ has these properties:

E-1   Reflexive $a = a$. **Any number is equal to itself.**

E-2   Symmetric   **If** $a = b$, **then** $b = a$. **It is immaterial whether we read an equality from left to right or from right to left.**

This is not always true for a relation between two numbers. For example, it is a true statement to say that 2 is less than 4, but it is not a true statement to say that 4 is less than 2.

E-3   Transitive   **If** $a = b$ **and** $b = c$, **then** $a = c$.

This is the property which justifies the statement in step 7 of the preceding example. The reader should make sure that he can trace the five applications of this property necessary in the illustration before the statement $57 + 83 = 140$ can be made. Frequently this property is referred to by the phrase "by substitution." In other words, by property E–3, a can be substituted for c or c for a, where the hypotheses of the property hold.

E-4   Additive   **If** $a = b$, **then** $a + c = b + c$.

E-5   Multiplicative   **If** $a = b$, **then** $ac = bc$.

This last property, of course, has significance only in the context of the definition of multiplication, as stated later. (See pages 58 to 66.)

It should be clearly understood that the properties of the set N under addition (A–1 to A–3) have not been derived by any process of formal reasoning. They are postulates, or assumed statements, which have resulted from centuries of observation of the results obtained from performing the operation of addition on natural numbers. No counterexample has ever occurred to prove that any one of the assumptions does not hold. This, however, does not prove the utter impossibility of discovering that they do not all hold. Mathematicians are quite firmly convinced that no such occasion will occur as far as natural numbers are concerned. It is possible, however, to define a mathematical system, not necessarily purely artificial, which will not obey properties A–2 and A–3 under addition, as defined in that system. Whatever the definition of such a system might be, it would take care to preserve property A–1. Closure is of great importance to any mathematical system. We shall see later that there are operations defined for the natural numbers for which properties A–2 and A–3 do not hold (Exercise 18, Sec. 4–5, and Exercise 19, Sec. 5–11). The desire for closure will lead to interesting results.

Addition has been defined as an operation by means of which the cardinal number of the union of two disjoint sets may be obtained. It was stated in the preceding chapter that the cardinal number of a set is a property of the set only, and is *independent* of the count used to derive it. Thus, it follows that the addition of two natural numbers is *unique*. It is a well-defined operation under which this set has the closure, commutative, and associative properties, and results in a sum concerning which there is no ambiguity.

Addition is unique and well-defined

3–7   CHECKING ADDITION

The surest check for the accuracy of an addition is to combine the addends in the reverse order to that used in finding the sum. If the sum is found by "adding down" the columns, then the check is established by "adding up," and vice versa. The commutative and associative properties of addition assure us that the two sums thus obtained must be the same.

Commutative property provides a check

Probably the most easily used of the simple checks is that known as *casting out nines*. If the digits of a number are added and, if this sum is more than a one-digit number, the process is repeated until a one-digit number is obtained then the one-digit number so obtained is called the *excess of nines* in the original number. For example, in Fig. 3–7 the sum of the digits in 4,823 is $4 + 8 + 2 + 3 = 17$, and the sum of the digits in 17 is $1 + 7 = 8$. From this it follows that the excess of nines is 4,823 is 8. This simply means that if 4,823 is divided by 9 there will be a remainder of 8. Why this works we shall leave as an open question to return to at a later time (Sec. 7–4). The process of casting out nines can be made still simpler. Look at the digits in a number and discard any group whose sum is 9. Then add the remaining digits. For example, in 4,823, $4 + 2 + 3 = 9$. When these digits are discarded, the digit 8 is left. It is less than 9 and is the excess of nines in the number. In 4,736 the sum of the digits 3 and 6 is 9, so they are discarded. Then $4 + 7 = 11$ and $1 + 1 = 2$, the excess of nines in 4,736.

Casting out nines

4,823	$4 + 8 + 2 + 3 = 17$	$1 + 7 = 8$		
4,736	$4 + 7 + 3 + 6 = 20$	$2 + 0 = 2$		
2,591	$2 + 5 + 9 + 1 = 17$	$1 + 7 = 8$		
3,425	$3 + 4 + 2 + 5 = 14$	$1 + 4 = 5$		
			23	$2 + 3 = 5$
15,575	$1 + 5 + 5 + 7 + 5 =$		23	$2 + 3 = 5$

FIGURE 3–7
Casting out nines is a quick check. It is not perfect, however, since transposition of digits will not change their sum.

5 000
5 000
3 000
3 000
16 000

FIGURE 3–8   Approximation can help determine whether an obtained sum is in the right order of magnitude.

The check of casting out nines in addition then is in accordance with the following statement, which will be proved later (Sec. 7–4):

The excess of nines in the sum of two or more numbers is the same as the excess in the sum of the excesses of each of the numbers.

In the example of Fig. 3–7 the excess of nines in the sum 15,575 is 5. The sum of the excesses in each of the numbers is 23, in which the excess is 5.

The check of addition by casting out nines is by no means an absolute check.   If the excesses in the two sums indicated are not the same, then one knows there is an error somewhere.   However, errors can be made and not detected by this process.   For example, suppose that either of the incorrect sums 15,665 or 15,755 had been obtained in the example.   In either case the excess of nines is 5, so the check would fail. In spite of this weakness, this method of checking is recognized as worthy of use because of its simplicity.

Another quick and effective check, especially against the making of absurd errors, is the method of estimating the answer by approximation. *Estimating the* For example, in Fig. 3–8 each of the first two addends of Fig. 3–7 rounds *answer* to 5,000, and the other two to 3,000.   Thus a quick approximation to the sum is 16,000.

Exercises

1   Give a brief description of the use of the abacus in addition.
2   What is meant by the statement that addition of natural numbers is a well-defined process?
3   What is the basis of the procedure called "carrying" in addition?
4   Use the following sums to illustrate the importance of place value in addition:

(a) 75	(b) 2,519	(c) 295
203	3,420	76
42	4,032	80
56	5,678	304

+	0	I	⊥	△	□
0	0	I	⊥	△	□
I	I	I	△	□	10
⊥	⊥	△	□	10	II
△	△	□	10	II	I⊥
□	□	10	II	I⊥	I△

FIGURE 3–9 Addition facts for verto system. In the row headed by △ on the left we find I⊥ in the column headed by □ above. △ + □ = I⊥. Similarly, □ + △ = I⊥.

5   Use the three addition checks suggested in the text for checking the three sums of Exercise 4.

6   The addition facts for the **verto** system are given in Fig. 3–9. How does an examination of the table illustrate the fact that the **verto** system is closed under addition?

7   Does an examination of Fig. 3–9 illustrate that addition in the **verto** system is commutative? Why?

8   Find these sums:

   (a) (⊥ + □) + I; ⊥ + (□ + I)
   (b) (△ + △) + □; △ + (△ + □)
   (c) (⊥I + △□) + △⊥; ⊥I + (△□ + △⊥)

9   What property of addition does each pair of sums illustrate for the **verto** system?

10   Find these sums:

   (a) I⊥△ + □0⊥ + △⊥□
   (b) △△△ + ⊥I□ + ⊥0⊥
   (c) 10△□ + ⊥△I□ + △□I□

11   Construct addition tables for base **five** and base **eight**.

12   How can the tables of Exercise 11 be used to argue that addition in each of the respective number systems has the properties of closure and commutativity?

13   Construct examples based on each table of Exercise 11 to illustrate the associative property for addition with each of the respective bases.

14   Find these sums in base **five:**

   (a) 14 + 23 + 31 + 40
   (b) 2003 + 4103 + 2142 + 4404
   (c) 102 + 321 + 413 + 204 + 34
   (d) 2340 + 4100 + 1024 + 3124

15   Find these sums in base **eight:**

   (a) 14 + 23 + 31 + 40
   (b) 321 + 475 + 402 + 135
   (c) 7643 + 1025 + 347 + 6045

(d) 1004 + 2746 + 3124 + 5407
(e) 5204 + 7162 + 1035 + 2172
(f) 45 + 3023 + 712 + 1070 + 2064

16   Use the table for base **two** (page 51) to find these sums:

(a) 101 + 110 + 11 + 101 + 111
(b) 11011 + 10010 + 1001 + 11001 + 111
(c) 101010 + 111 + 111111 + 1001 + 11011
(d) 101 + 110111 + 10 + 1101 + 101101 + 10011

17   Use the table for base **six** (page 51) to find these sums:

(a) 123 + 204 + 512 + 343
(b) 4012 + 3145 + 2300 + 1005
(c) 3421 + 50243 + 101 + 3542 + 45
(d) 5435 + 10035 + 341 + 2030 + 52034

18   Construct examples based on Exercises 16 and 17 to show how the commutative property provides an effective means for checking addition.
19   Construct addition tables for bases **seven, eleven,** and **twelve.**
20   Find these sums in base **seven.** Use the commutative property to provide a check for each sum.

(a) 16 + 52 + 30 + 44 + 6 + 12
(b) 204 + 312 + 451 + 325
(c) 2106 + 5432 + 610 + 4002
(d) 41003 + 31260 + 52361 + 41021
(e) 123 + 4602 + 36 + 50231 + 6120

21   Find these sums in base **eleven:**

(a) 189 + 34 + 708 + 259
(b) 6089 + 7182 + 3002 + 9019
(c) 561 + 8190 + 99 + 7002
(d) 4002 + 8060 + 7100 + 329

22   Why is casting out **fives** in base **six** similar to casting out nines in base ten?
23   Check each sum of Exercise 17 by casting out **fives.**
24   Casting out what numbers in bases **seven** and **eleven** is similar to casting out nines in base ten?
25   Use the techniques of Exercise 24 to check the sums in Exercises 20 and 21.
26   Find these sums in base **twelve:**

(a) 14 + 23 + 31 + 40
(b) 52 + 78 + 67 + 83
(c) 709 + 234 + 189 + 480

(d) $402 + 569 + 3te + e0e + t0e$
(e) $1078 + te82 + ette + 30te$
(f) $e00e + 8102 + t0t0 + tete$

27   Use the sum $87 + 72 + 58$ in base ten to illustrate how the associative and commutative laws are used in finding such sums.

3-8   WHAT IS MULTIPLICATION?

Multiplication is a short form of addition

Fundamentally, multiplication of natural numbers is a short form of addition. It is the process which is used when we desire to determine how many objects there are in several disjoint sets when the sets all have the same cardinal number. For example, suppose we desire to know how many letters of the alphabet there are in the three sets $A = \{a,b,c,d\}$, $B = \{e,f,g,h\}$, and $C = \{i,j,k,l\}$. These are disjoint sets and, by the definition of addition, $n(A \cup B \cup C) = n(A) + n(B) + n(C) = 4 + 4 + 4 = 12$. Since $n(A) = n(B) = n(C) = 4$, the answer to this problem can be found by the process of multiplication. Thus $n(A \cup B \cup C)$ is the product 3×4. The table of basic multiplication facts, which complete the definition of the operation, makes it possible for us to know that the result of the indicated multiplication 3×4 is the *product* 12. As in the case of addition, each fact of the table may be established by counting or, even better for multiplication, by addition.

Multiplication is unique

Just as the sum in addition is unique, so is the product in multiplication unique.

A less restricted interpretation of the process of multiplication may be obtained from the following consideration. The three sets A, B, and C of the preceding paragraph are represented in Fig. 3–10 by the three rows (A, B, and C) of pigeonholes. The pigeonholes are to be used, let us say, for sorting letters of the alphabet. There are four pigeonholes in each row because we wish to have four letters in each set when the sorting is finished. How many letters will it take to accomplish this

FIGURE 3–10   Row distribution pattern.

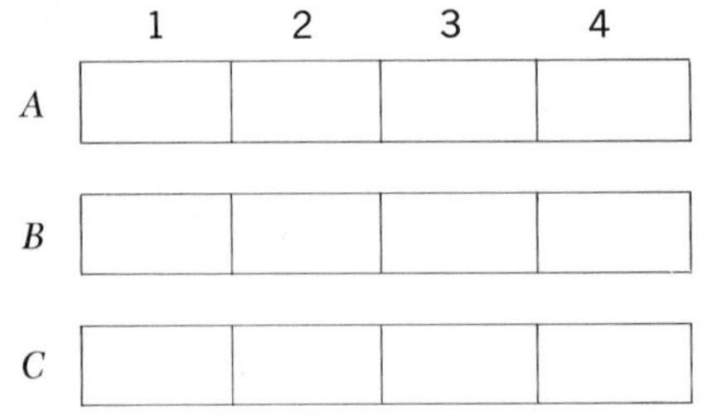

FIGURE 3–11   Key for row distribution.

$A-1$	$A-2$	$A-3$	$A-4$
$B-1$	$B-2$	$B-3$	$B-4$
$C-1$	$C-2$	$C-3$	$C-4$

purpose? If the rows of pigeonholes are arranged so that the holes are also in vertical array, it will be simple to indicate where each letter will be placed. For example, the symbol B-3 can be used to indicate that the row B has been selected first and a letter is to be placed in pigeonhole 3 of this row. With this understanding the distribution of the letters will then be as indicated in Fig. 3–11, where each symbol represents a letter. Note that the order of arrangement is significant. Each symbol is an ordered pair of two individual symbols which indicates by its arrangement that, in this selection, the horizontal row was chosen first and then the vertical array. Referring to a pair of elements (x,y) as an *ordered pair* simply calls attention to the fact that the individual elements are arranged in order. Here x is the first element and y the second element of the ordered pair (x,y).

Ordered pair

By actual count there are 12 letters required, or by multiplication $3 \times 4 = 12$. This illustration has counted the pigeonholes in each specified row. It is significant to note that in each vertical array of pigeonholes there is a hole for each row. In other words, the symbol 3-B could be used to indicate that the vertical array 3 has been selected first and a letter is to go in the pigeonhole in row B of this array. Following the same agreement as that followed for Fig. 3–10, the ordered pairs which display the pattern for this second selection of pigeonholes are shown in Fig. 3–12. With this method of counting there would be 4 vertical arrays of 3 rows each, or 4×3 letters would be required. By actual count this can be established as 12. Regardless of which method of selection is used, the result is the same: the number of letters required is the same.

The preceding paragraph can be summarized effectively by considering the two sets $R = \{A,B,C\}$ and $C = \{1,2,3,4\}$. If each element of R is paired with one and only one element of C, the cardinal number of the resulting set of ordered pairs is called the product of the cardinal numbers of the given sets.

This illustration affords the basis for a more general definition of multiplication. This new concept of multiplication not only is equivalent

More general concept of multiplication

FIGURE 3–12   Key for column distribution.

$1-A$	$2-A$	$3-A$	$4-A$
$1-B$	$2-B$	$3-B$	$4-B$
$1-C$	$2-C$	$3-C$	$4-C$

to the one already given for natural numbers but also offers opportunities for significant interpretation in more general situations.

Cartesian product of two sets

Definition 3-1 If $P = \{p_1, p_2, p_3, \dots\}$ and $Q = \{q_1, q_2, q_3, \dots\}$ and $P \times Q$† represents the set of all ordered pairs of elements in which an element from P is paired with one and only one element from Q, then $n(P \times Q) = n(P) \times n(Q) = n(Q) \times n(P) = n(Q \times P)$.

One of the immediate advantages of this definition of multiplication lies in the fact that, while it is equivalent to the definition given for the case in which P and Q are disjoint sets, it no longer requires that the sets be disjoint. In fact, it allows for the product in the extreme case in which $P = Q$. For example, consider $A = \{1,2\}$ and $B = \{1,2\}$. The set of ordered pairs $A \times B$ is the set $\{(1,1),(1,2),(2,1),(2,2)\}$, and it is evident that $n(A \times B) = n(A) \times n(B)$. Incidentally, an important point implied by the above discussion is the fact that when the product of two natural numbers is obtained, the order in which they are multiplied is immaterial. In other words, it seems intuitively acceptable to assume that *multiplication of natural numbers is commutative.* Attention is also called to the fact that centuries of experience in the use of the mul-tiplication process have given mathematicians strong intuitive back-

Multiplication is commuta-tive and associative

ground for asserting that *multiplication of natural numbers is associa-tive as well as commutative.* In symbols we say that for all natural numbers a, b, and c it is true that $(a \times b) \times c = a \times (b \times c)$. For example, $(2 \times 3) \times 5 = 6 \times 5 = 30$, and $2 \times (3 \times 5) = 2 \times 15 = 30$. Thus $(2 \times 3) \times 5 = 2 \times (3 \times 5)$.

Multiplication of natural numbers is thus a well-defined binary opera-tion which gives a unique result known as a product.

3–9   NAMES AND SYMBOLS USED IN MULTIPLICATION

Names used in multiplication

The terms *multiplicand, multiplier,* and *product* come from the Latin expressions *numerus multiplicandus* (number to be multiplied), *numerus multiplicans* (multiplying number), and *numerus productus* (number produced). Since the word *numerus* was dropped occasion-ally by Latin writers, the terms finally became the single words in technical translations. As was pointed out in an earlier section, the word "product" was rather generally used to indicate the result ob-tained from any form of computation, although in recent years it has been used almost exclusively to indicate the result obtained from the

---

† This symbol may be read *P cross Q* and represents what is called the *cartesian product of the sets P and Q.* Other than in this set, symbol $\times$ means multiplication in the usual sense.

process of multiplication. In more modern usage the two words "multiplier" and "multiplicand" are being replaced by the one word "factor." This is due to the fact that multiplication is commutative and any two factors combine to give the same product, independent of which is considered as the multiplier and which as the multiplicand. Thus, a *factor* of a natural number n is any one of two or more natural numbers whose product is n.

Factor

The symbol $\times$, most commonly used in arithmetic to indicate multiplication, was developed in England in the early seventeenth century. Cajori is of the opinion that the first use of "the St. Andrew's cross" as a symbol for multiplication is to be attributed to W. Oughtred.[†] Other methods of indicating multiplication include the practice of Diophantus of using no symbol at all, juxtaposition in the Bakhshālī manuscripts, the dot of Bhāskara, ideograms by the Babylonians and Egpytians, and the use of M by such mathematicians as Stifel, S. Stevin, and Descartes.[‡] Although some of the Bhāskara manuscripts contained an unexplained use of the dot as a symbol for multiplication and similar unexplained uses occurred in. manuscripts of Thomas Harriot (1631) and Thomas Gibson (1655), the actual introduction of the use of this symbol is attributed to G. W. Leibniz (1646–1716), who, in writing to John Bernoulli, stated: "I do not like $\times$ as a symbol in multiplication, as it is easily confounded with x, . . . often I simply relate two quantities by an interposed dot and indicate multiplication by $ZC \cdot LM$."[§] Modern notation uses both symbols to indicate multiplication.

The symbol $\times$

3–10   THE MULTIPLICATION ALGORITHM

Little is known about the multiplication algorithm used in ancient times. There is rather strong evidence, however, that the Egyptians and many generations of their successors used the method of duplation (doubling). This method is used in Fig. 3–13 to find the product 43×23. The multiplicand 23 is written opposite the number 1. As 1 is doubled, so is 23. This process is repeated, as shown by the colored numerals, until the next double in the column headed by 1 would be greater than 43. Then the numbers in this column whose sum is 43 are found and checked ($\sqrt{\ }$) along with the numbers opposite them. The sum of these corresponding numbers (those checked) in the column headed by 23 gives the desired product. It is to be noted that this process reduces the necessary multiplication facts down to only those in which 2 is the

Method of doubling

[†] F. Cajori, *op. cit.*, p. 251.
[‡] *Ibid.*, p. 250.
[§] *Ibid.*, p. 267.

$$
\begin{array}{lll}
1\ \checkmark & \checkmark\ 23 & \\
2 \times 1\ = 2\ \checkmark & \checkmark\ 46 = 2 \times 23 & \text{Step 1} \\
2 \times 2\ = 4 & 92 = 2 \times 46 & \text{Step 2} \\
2 \times 4\ = 8\ \checkmark & \checkmark\ 184 = 2 \times 92 & \text{Step 3} \\
2 \times 8\ = 16 & 368 = 2 \times 184 & \text{Step 4} \\
2 \times 16 = 32\ \checkmark & \checkmark\ 736 = 2 \times 368 & \text{Step 5}
\end{array}
$$

$$1 + 2 + 8 + 32 = 43$$

$$23 + 46 + 184 + 736 = 989 = 43 \times 23$$

FIGURE 3–13   Multiplication by doubling. In each step both multiplier and multiplicand are doubled.

$$
\begin{array}{lll}
\checkmark\ 43 & 23\ \checkmark & \\
\checkmark\ 21 & 46\ \checkmark & \text{Step 1} \\
10 & 92 & \text{Step 2} \\
\checkmark\ \ 5 & 184\ \checkmark & \text{Step 3} \\
2 & 368 & \text{Step 4} \\
\checkmark\ \ 1 & 736\ \checkmark & \text{Step 5} \\
& 989 &
\end{array}
$$

FIGURE 3–14   Multiplication by doubling and halving. In each step the multiplicand is doubled but the multiplier is halved; remainders are discarded.

multiplier. It results from the following generalized definition of multiplication which is of historical significance:

Multiplication is the process of finding a third number related to one of two given numbers in the same ratio as the second number is related to 1.

Basically similar to the duplation method is the technique of finding a product sometimes referred to as the "Russian peasant method." In this method duplication is accompanied by mediation (halving), as illustrated in Fig. 3–14. Both the multiplier and multiplicand are written down. As the multiplicand is doubled, the multiplier is halved. In the halving process any remainder is discarded. Thus, the process will terminate ultimately with 1 in the multiplier column. To get the product, add those numbers in the multiplicand column which correspond to the odd numbers in the multiplier column. Note that the same numbers are checked in the multiplicand column in Figs. 3–13 and 3–14.

The forms used through the ages have varied so greatly that it would be tedious to present all of them. The number receiving significant attention had increased to eight by the time Pacioli published his "Suma" in 1494.† Of these eight, only four are of interest to us in this discussion. They picture something of the evolution of form through which the multiplicative process passed in the struggle for the most

† David Eugene Smith, *op. cit.*, p. 107.

effective use of place value to produce efficiency of operation. Interestingly enough, one of the forms is the one which we use today, with the slight variations shown in the example (Fig. 3–15). It is rather evident that the extra lines were drawn as an aid in keeping the digits aligned.

The *scacchera* (chessboard) method was quite popular for many years. There were variations in the relative positions of the two factors and the partial products. Two distinct forms of this particular method are illustrated in Fig. 3–16, in which we find the same product, 36 × 759.

The *gelosia* method, so called because of the resemblance of its framework to latticework, simplifies multiplication in that it records the result of each multiplication and thus does away with adding unseen numbers in obtaining the partial products. One of its several different forms is illustrated in Fig. 3–17 in finding the product 269 × 8,075. After each product is recorded in its proper block, the final product is then found by summing along each diagonal, starting at the extreme right. This product is 2,172,175.

The *repiego* method broke the multiplier down into simple factors and then multiplied the multiplicand by these factors in order. For example, to find the product 36 × 759, first multiply 759 by 9 and then multiply this result by 4. Multiplication is *associative:* (4 × 9) ×

FIGURE 3–15   Early form of multiplication.

	7 5 9			
	3 6			
4 5 5 4	= 6 × 759		Step 1
2 2 7 7	= 30 × 759		Step 2
2 7 3 2 4	= 4554 + 22770		Step 3

FIGURE 3–16   Scacchera method of multiplication.

Step 1	5 4	= 6 × 9
Step 2	2 7	= 30 × 9
Step 3	3 0	= 6 × 50
Step 4	1 5	= 30 × 50
Step 5	4 2	= 6 × 700
Step 6	2 1	= 30 × 700
Step 7	2 7 3 2 4	= Total

	7 5 9	
6 × 759 =	4 5 5 4/6	Step 1
30 × 759 =	2 2 7 7/3	Step 2
Total =	2 7 3 2 4	Step 3

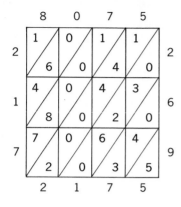

FIGURE 3–17   Gelosia (lattice) multiplication.   In each square, the colored line separates the tens digit from the ones.   For example in the lower right corner 45 = 9 × 5.   The adding is along diagonals: 0 + 4 + 3 = 7; 0 + 3 + 2 + 6 + 0 = 11, and the 1 ten is added to the numbers in the next diagonal array; 1 + 1 + 4 + 4 + 0 + 0 + 2 = 12.

234		
456		
1 404 =	6 × 234	Step 1
11 70 =	50 × 234	Step 2
93 6 =	400 × 234	Step 3
106,704 =	93,600 + 11,700 + 1,404	Step 4

FIGURE 3–18   Algorithm used today.

$759 = 4 \times (9 \times 759)$.   Of course, other factors could be used.   This is an effective method for oral multiplication.†

Each of these algorithms depends heavily on a property which multiplication has when used in conjunction with addition.   This new property, called the *distributive* property, states that for any three natural numbers (a,b,c) it is true that $a \times (b + c) = (a \times b) + (a \times c)$. For example, $5 \times (8 + 2) = (5 \times 8) + (5 \times 2)$.   This property, which is easily verified in this case since $5 \times 10 = 50$ and $40 + 10 = 50$, is displayed as a property relating multiplication and addition of natural numbers which is intuitively acceptable.   This is used in the method of multiplication by duplation, as shown in Figure 3–13.   Since $43 = 1 + 2 + 8 + 32$, the product 43×23 is written as $(1 + 2 + 8 + 32) \times 23$, which is the same as $23 \times (1 + 2 + 8 + 32) = (23 \times 1) + (23 \times 2) + (23 \times 8) + (23 \times 32)$.   Each of these products was found by doubling so that $23 \times 43 = 23 + 46 + 184 + 736 = 989$.

The algorithm which we use today also depends on the distributive property.   In the product shown in Fig. 3–18, the partial products are placed in their respective positions due to place value and the distributive property of multiplication.   The colored numerals illustrate the fact that the product is found by taking the product $234 \times (400 + 50 + 6)$.

Multiplication is distributive over addition

† *Ibid.*, pp. 106–128.

Thus the 1,170 is in reality 11,700, since it is the product 234×50. Likewise, 936 actually represents $234 \times 400 = 93,600$. Place value makes it unnecessary to write the zeros. What other properties of multiplication are used in finding this product?

3–11 PROPERTIES OF NATURAL NUMBERS UNDER MULTIPLICATION

Attention has been called already to the fact that multiplication of natural numbers is associative, is commutative, and also is distributive over addition. It also has the property of closure and one additional property, the existence of an identity, not yet mentioned.

Properties of the natural numbers under multiplication

The set $N = \{1,2,3,4, \ldots \}$ of natural numbers satisfies these properties under the operation of multiplication.

M-1 *Closure* For $a, b \in N$ it is true that $a \times b$ is a unique element of N.

M-2 *Commutative* For $a, b \in N$ it is true that $a \times b = b \times a$.

M-3 *Associative* For $a, b, c \in N$ it is true that $(a \times b) \times c = a \times (b \times c)$.

M-4 *Distributive* For $a, b, c \in N$ it is true that $a \times (b + c) = (a \times b) + (a \times c)$.

M-5 *Identity* 1 is the unique natural number such that $1 \times a = a$ for any natural number a.

The property M–4 states that multiplication distributes over addition; that is, in any case of a product involving the multiplication of a sum of two natural numbers by a third natural number, one may either add first and then multiply or multiply first and then add. The identification of 1 as the identity element for multiplication will increase in significance as we work further with natural numbers and later as we extend our considerations to other number systems.

3–12 CHECKING MULTIPLICATION

One of the surest checks in multiplication is to interchange multiplicand and multiplier and redetermine the product. As in addition, the method of casting out nines is an effective simple check. The rule in this case is:

Commutative property provides a check

Casting out nines

The excess of nines in the product is equal to the excess in the product of the excesses in the multiplicand and multiplier.

For example, the excess of nines in 872 (see Fig. 3–19) is 8, while the excess in 425 is 2. The product of the excesses is 16, in which the excess is 7. Also, the excess in the product 370,600 is 7. As in addition, the check by casting out nines is in no sense an absolute check; its principal value lies in the ease and simplicity of its use. Another check, valuable because of its simplicity, is that of estimating the answer. In the example of Fig. 3–19, 872 is near 900 and 425 is near 400, so a very satisfactory check on the reasonableness of the answer is $400 \times 900 = 360,000$.

3–13 CONVERSION TO DIFFERENT BASES BY MULTIPLICATION

In Chap. 2 the observation was made that the symbol representing the number of letters in the English alphabet is 26—ten, **22—twelve,** or **101—five.** These are equivalent numerals all representing the same number. This fact suggests that it is possible to change from a numeral in a given base to an equivalent numeral in some other base. This can be done by multiplication.

Equivalent numerals in different bases

Example Use multiplication to change **22—twelve** to its equivalent numeral in base ten.

The symbol **22** means $2(10) + 2(1)$ in any base. Since we are given that the symbol is in base **twelve,** $2(10) + 2(1)$ means 2 twelves and 2

FIGURE 3–19   Casting out nines to check multiplication.

872	$8 + 7 + 2 = 17$	$1 + 7 = 8$	Step 1
425	$4 + 2 + 5 = 11$	$1 + 1 = 2$	Step 2
4 360		$8 \times 2 = 16$	
17 44		$1 + 6 = 7$	Step 3
348 8			
370,600	$3 + 7 + 0 + 6 + 0 + 0 = 16$	$1 + 6 = 7$	Step 4

Twelve	Ten
22 =	
2(10) + 2(1) ⟶	$2(12) + 2(1)$
	$= 24 + 2$
	$= 26$

FIGURE 3–20   Conversion from base **twelve** to base ten.   **10—twelve = 1 twelve** = 1 ten + 2 ones = 12.

Twelve	Five
22 = **2(10) + 2(1)** ──▶	**2(22) + 2(1)** **= 44 + 2** **= 101**

FIGURE 3–21   Conversion from base **twelve** to base **five.**   **10—twelve = 1** twelve = **2** fives + **2** ones = 22.

×	0	1	2	3	4	5
0	0	0	0	0	0	0
1	0	1	2	3	4	5
2	0	2	4	10	12	14
3	0	3	10	13	20	23
4	0	4	12	20	24	32
5	0	5	14	23	32	41

FIGURE 3–22   Multiplication: Base **six.**   In the row headed by **3** on the left we find **20** in the column headed by **4** above.   Thus **3 × 4 = 20—six.**

ones.   When this is translated into base ten it becomes $2(12) + 2(1)$. The arrow ($\longrightarrow$) of Fig. 3–20 means "translates into."   Thus the equivalent numeral is 26—ten.   Notice that in the figure the computation is done in base ten, because at the arrow the thinking was translated from base **twelve** to base ten.

Example   Use multiplication to change **22—twelve** to its equivalent numeral in base **five.**   In Fig. 3–21 the multiplication and addition are all done in base **five.**   Note that **22—twelve** is *not* the same as **22—five.**   **22—twelve** converts into **101—five.**

Example   Use multiplication to change the numeral 268—ten to its equivalent numeral in base **six.**
Before we can make this conversion it is necessary to be able to multiply in base **six.**   Figure 3–22 gives all the basic multiplication facts for base **six.**
NOTE: The digits 6—ten and 8—ten become two-figure numerals in base **six,** since they are each larger than five and smaller than thirty-six (see Fig. 3–23).

The most difficult part of the computation is finding the product $2(14^2)$.   It is necessary to compute in base **six:**

$$14 \times 14 = 14 \times (10 + 4)$$
$$= (14 \times 10) + (14 \times 4) \qquad \text{Why?}$$
$$= 140 + 104$$
$$= 244$$
$$2 \times (14^2) = 2 \times 244 = 532\text{—six}$$

FIGURE 3-23   Conversion from base ten to base **six**.

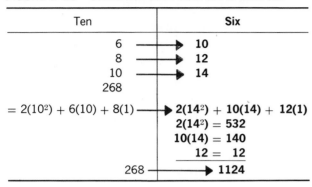

The addition is then carried out in base **six**. 268—ten converts into 1124—**six**.

It should be obvious that any such conversion can be checked by multiplication. In this example the check is to convert **1124**—**six** to its equivalent numeral in base ten.

$$1124 = 1(10^3) + 1(10^2) + 2(10^1) + 4(1)\text{—six}$$
$$= 1(6^3) + 1(6^2) + 2(6^1) + 4(1)\text{—ten}$$
$$= 216 + 36 + 12 + 4\text{—ten}$$
$$= 268\text{—ten}$$

Exercises

1   What is meant by the statement that multiplication of natural numbers is a well-defined process?

2   How are addition and multiplication related to each other?

3   What is the basis of the procedure called "carrying" in multiplication?

4   Use the following products to illustrate the importance of place value in multiplication:

(a) 48
     32

(b) 407
     546

(c) 8,105
     723

5   Use the three methods suggested in the text for checking multiplication to check each of the products of Exercise 4.

6   Construct the table of basic multiplication facts for base ten, base **verto**, base **eight**, and base **twelve**.

7   What do the tables of Exercise 6 illustrate about the properties of closure and commutativity in each system?

8 Construct examples based on the tables of Exercise 6 to illustrate the fact that multiplication in each system is associative.

9 Find these products and check:

(a) ΙΔ
   Δ⊥

(b) □Ι⊥
   Δ0□

(c) ΔΙ□⊥
   ⊥ΔΙ□

10 Use the duplation method to find the product 77×29. Explain how this illustrates the distributive law of multiplication.

11 Use the duplation and mediation method to find the product 45×95.

12 Use the repiego method to find each of these products:

(a) 63×36 (b) 85×28 (c) 272×54

13 How are the products of Exercise 12 illustrations of the associative property of multiplication?

14 Use the gelosia method to find each of these products:

(a) 839
    76

(b) 3,624
    805

(c) 7,536
    873

15 Find each of these products in base **eight:**

(a) **24 × 72**   (b) **506 × 327**   (c) **746 × 2056**

16 Find each of these products in base **twelve:**

(a) **tt**
   ee

(b) **t0te**
   30e

(c) **ette**
   t89t

17 Use these products to illustrate the property that multiplication is distributive over addition. Compute in base ten.

(a) 236
    74

(b) 3,024
    507

(c) 2,526
    370

18 Consider the numeral 5266—ten. Use multiplication to convert to an equivalent numeral in base **twelve,** base **eight,** base **verto,** and base **six.** Check each conversion.

19 Consider the numeral □⊥0ΙΔ—**verto.** Use multiplication to convert to an equivalent numeral in base ten, base **eight,** base **twelve,** and base **six.** Check each conversion.

20 Consider the numeral **7326—eight.** Use multiplication to convert to an equivalent numeral in base ten, base **verto,** base **twelve,** and base **six.** Check each conversion.

21 Consider the numeral **etet—twelve.** Use multiplication to convert to an equivalent numeral in base ten, base **eight,** base **verto,** and base **six.** Check each conversion.

22   Use each of these products to show in detail how the associative, commutative, and distributive properties of addition and multiplication are used:

(a) 24×63 (b) 315×408

3–14   THE POSTULATES OF THE NATURAL NUMBER SYSTEM

Postulates of the natural number system

The set of natural numbers $N = \{1,2,3,4, \ldots \}$, for which we now have two well-defined operations, addition $(+)$ and multiplication $(\times)$, satisfies the following postulates.

For any a, b, $c \in N$:

N-1   Closure   If $a + b = x$ and $a \times b = y$, then x and y are unique elements of N.

N-2   Associative $(a + b) + c = a + (b + c)$; $(a \times b) \times c = a \times (b \times c)$.

N-3   Commutative $a + b = b + a$; $a \times b = b \times a$.

N-4   Distributive $a \times (b + c) = (a \times b) + (a \times c)$.

N-5   Multiplicative Identity   There exists a natural number 1 such that $1 \times a = a$ for any $a \in N$.

N-6   Trichotomy   For any two elements a and b of N we have $a = b$, $a + c = b$, or $a = b + c$ for some $c \in N$.

N-7   Cancellation   If $a + c = b + c$, then $a = b$; if $a \times c = b \times c$, then $a = b$.

N-8   Finite Induction   If $P \subseteq N$ such that
   1    $1 \in P$, and
   2    $(k + 1) \in P$ whenever $k \in P$

then $P = N$.

Postulates N–1 to N–5 will be recognized as those which have been listed as satisfied by the set N under addition (A–1 to A–3) and multiplication (M–1 to M–5). Postulate N–6 is frequently referred to as the

The law of trichotomy

law of trichotomy and sets the stage for a basic definition and related theorem concerning an important relation existing between natural numbers.

Definition 3-2   If, for a, $b \in N$, it is true that $a + c = b$ for some $c \in N$, then a is said to be less than b ($a < b$), or b is greater than a ($b > a$).

From postulate N–6 and Definition 3–2 we have as an immediate consequence the following theorem.

Theorem 3–1 **If a and b are any two natural numbers, then $a = b$, $a < b$, or $a > b$.**

The natural numbers are ordered

It will be demonstrated later that the two statements incorporated in N–7 are, respectively, converse statements to the additive property (E–4) and the multiplicative property (E–5) of equality (see page 73). Since the principle of finite induction (N–8) is of great significance in the study of the natural number system, it is listed here for completeness. In the development of this text we shall have only limited occasion to refer to it.

These eight postulates can be shown to be equivalent to the Peano postulates mentioned earlier. From them and the postulates of equality (page 53), all the remaining properties of natural numbers can be derived.†

3–15 THE NATURE OF PROOF

The process used in deriving the properties of natural numbers from the basic postulates is that of *deduction*, which is the process of reasoning by *implication*. If we have two propositions, represented by the symbols p and q, which are so related to each other that it is absolutely impossible for q to be false if p is true, then we say that p implies q $(p \rightarrow q)$. By a "proposition" we shall mean a sentence which is stated so precisely that it has the property of being either true or false. No effort will be made here to go beyond the intuitively acceptable connotations of the terms "true" and "false." Furthermore, there is no requirement that we must know which of the labels applies to the sentence in order to be able to classify it as a proposition.

Deduction and the nature of implication

What is a proposition?

Example Consider these sentences:

1 Christmas Day fell on Tuesday in 1962.
2 Christmas Day fell on Tuesday in 1963.
3 Christmas Day will fall on Tuesday in 2963.
4 Christmas Day will fall on Tuesday.

The first two sentences make statements which can be checked readily by reference to the appropriate calendars. Statement (1) is

† Howard Eves and Carroll V. Newsom, "An Introduction to the Foundations and Fundamental Principles of Mathematics," pp. 194–203, Holt, Rinehart and Winston, Inc., New York, 1958.

true and statement (2) is false. While the truth or falsity of statement (3) cannot be so readily checked, the statement does have the property of being either true or false. These three sentences are, therefore, bona fide propositions. Statement (4), however, does not meet the conditions necessary to qualify as a proposition. Although the sentence makes a complete statement, there is no way in which its truth or falsity may be judged.

Nature of a deductive system   In any deductive system there are (1) undefined terms; (2) defined terms; (3) assumed propositions (*postulates* or *axioms*); and (4) derived propositions (*theorems*). In the natural number system we have undefined terms such as *set* and *number* which we use to build a vocabulary of such terms as *addition, multiplication, closure, associative, commutative, distributive, identity, equal, is less than,* and *is greater than.* The postulates of the system are the propositions listed as N–1 to N–8 and E–1 to E–5. We are to use all this information as the context within which all the remaining properties of natural numbers can be derived as provable propositions (theorems). Within the limitations of this book we shall not be able to exhaust the possibilities of all such theorems. We shall prove a few and state as exercises a few others for the reader to prove.

All theorems follow a pattern of statement which is of the form "if p then q," where p and q are propositions. This form of statement is synonymous with "p implies q" ($p \rightarrow q$), since the statement "if p then q" is simply saying that if proposition p is assumed or known to be true, then it must follow that proposition q is true. Thus every theorem has two distinct parts: (1) the *hypothesis,* or that which is given as true, and (2) the *conclusion,* or the proposition which follows as a logical consequence of the hypothesis.

p implies q

Hypothesis and conclusion

Actually, in a deductive pattern of reasoning we are not so much concerned with whether the propositions involved are true or false; rather, we are concerned with whether or not the argument is a valid one. In other words, we are concerned not so much with whether the conclusion we can draw is true as with the fact that it is valid. A *valid conclusion* is one which follows through a chain of implications from hypothesis. Whether a conclusion is true or false is most frequently determined by a check against experience or previously established knowledge.

Valid conclusion

True conclusion

Cancellation property contains two theorems   In the cancellation property, N–7, there are two distinct theorems stated: (A) If a, b, $c \in N$ and $a + c = b + c$, then $a = b$; (M) if a, b, $c \in N$ and $a \times c = b \times c$, then $a = b$. For each of these theorems there are two hypotheses and one conclusion. For example, for Theorem A we have hypothesis 1: a, b, $c \in N$; hypothesis 2: $a + c = b + c$; conclusion: $a = b$.

If property E–4 is stated specifically for natural numbers it will have the form hypothesis 1: a, b, $c \in N$; hypothesis 2: $a = b$; conclusion: $a + c = b + c$.

When Theorem A and property E–4 are compared, it becomes evident that hypothesis 2 of one theorem is the conclusion of the other and that the conclusion of one is hypothesis 2 of the other. For this reason Theorem A is said to be a *converse theorem* of E–4, and E–4 is a converse theorem of Theorem A. Similarly, Theorem M and E–5 are conversely related.

In any theorem the hypothesis and the conclusion may each incorporate more than one proposition. Here each hypothesis incorporated two propositions and each conclusion only one.

Definition 3-3 **A converse of a particular theorem may be obtained by interchanging any number of conclusions with a corresponding number of hypotheses.**

Converse of a theorem

It is important to keep in mind that it *does not necessarily* follow that a converse of a theorem is true when the theorem is true. It is simply another theorem to be investigated.

Example A theorem which can be proved easily is: If a natural number has 4 as a factor, then it is an even number. This follows as an immediate consequence of the definition of an even number as a number which has 2 as one of its factors. If a number has 4 as a factor, then it certainly has 2 as a factor since 2 is a factor of 4.

A converse of the above theorem is: If a natural number is an even number, then it has 4 as a factor. One counterexample will suffice to show that this theorem is not necessarily true. The natural number 2 is an even number which does not have 4 as a factor.

3–16 SOME DERIVED PROPERTIES OF THE NATURAL NUMBER SYSTEM

On page 71 the statement was made that Theorem 3–1 follows as an immediate consequence of postulate N–6 and Definition 3–2. The theorem is restated here and examined in the light of the preceding section.

Theorem 3-1 **If a and b are any two natural numbers, then $a = b$, $a < b$, or $a > b$.**

Derived theorem about order

Hypothesis $a, b \in N$.

Conclusion $a = b$, $a < b$, or $a > b$.

What are the full implications of the hypothesis? Since $a, b \in N$ it follows that all the properties N–1 to N–8 hold for a and b.

Which of these properties might be helpful in the argument of this theorem? When we examine the conclusion we wish to be able to draw, we see that it is concerned with three possible relationships between any two natural numbers a and b. This suggests, at least, that the law of trichotomy might be helpful.

Proof

Statements	Reasons
$a, b \in \mathrm{N}$	Hypothesis
$a = b$ or there exists a natural number c	
such that $a + c = b$ or $b + c = a$	N–6
$a = b, a < b$, or $a > b$	Definition 3–2

A few more properties will be derived merely for illustrative purposes.

Extension of the multiplicative property

Theorem 3-2 **If c and d are any two natural numbers such that $c = d$, then $b \times c = b \times d$ for any natural number b.**

Hypothesis $b, c, d \in N$ and $c = d$.

Conclusion $b \times c = b \times d$.

Proof

Statements	Reasons
1 $c = d$	Hypothesis
2 $c \times b = d \times b$	E–5
3 $b \times c = c \times b;\ d \times b = b \times d$	N–3
4 $b \times c = b \times d$	E–3; steps 2 and 3

It is to be noted that bc and $b \times c$ are used to mean the same product, that obtained with b and c as the factors. It may seem unusual to say that this theorem needs to be proved since we have the equality postulate E–5. Attention is called to the fact that the key to the argument is postulate N–3, as can be observed from step 3. There are mathematical systems where the commutative law does not hold. In such systems it would not necessarily follow that $bc = bd$ just because $cb = db$. That is the reason for the necessity for proving Theorem 3–2 for natural numbers.

Derived theorem about multiplication

Theorem 3-3 **If a, b, c, and d are natural numbers such that $a = b$ and $c = d$, then $ac = bd$.**

Hypothesis $a, b, c, d \in N$ such that $a = b$ and $c = d$.

Conclusion $ac = bd$.

Proof

Statements	*Reasons*
1 $a = b$	Hypothesis
2 $ac = bc$	E–5
3 $c = d$	Hypothesis
4 $bc = bd$	Theorem 3–2
5 $ac = bd$	Steps 2 and 4; E–3

This theorem has established the property which you probably recognize as "If equal numbers are multiplied by equal numbers, the products are equal."

Theorem 3–4   If a, b, c are **natural numbers and** $a < b$, **then** $a + c < b + c$.

Extension of additive property to inequality

Hypothesis $a, b, c \in N$ and $a < b$.

Conclusion $a + c < b + c$.

Proof

Statements	*Reasons*
1 $a < b$	Hypothesis
2 For k a natural number, $a + k = b$	Definition 3–2
3 $(a + k) + c = b + c$	Step 2; E–4
4 $(a + c) + k = (a + k) + c$	N–2 and N–3
5 $(a + c) + k = b + c$	Steps 3 and 4; E–3
6 $a + c < b + c$	Definition 3–2

These four theorems are presented merely to illustrate the fact that the properties of natural numbers can be developed as logical consequences of the basic postulates stated.   The set N of natural numbers, the well-defined operations of addition and multiplication, the set of postulates N–1 to N–8, and all the properties of natural numbers which follow as logical consequences from the definitions and these eight postulates constitute the number system we call the *natural number system.*

Exercises

1   The relations "less than" ($<$) and "greater than" ($>$) are called *in-equalities* because they do not have all the properties E–1 to E–5 of equality.   Which of these properties do these relations not have?

2   *Prove Theorem 3–5:* If a, b, c are natural numbers such that $a < b$ and $b < c$, then $a < c$. This proves that the relation "less than" is transitive.

3   *Prove Theorem 3–6:* If c and d are any two natural numbers such that $c = d$, then $b + c = b + d$ for any natural number b.

4   *Prove Theorem 3–7:* If a, b, c, $d \in N$ such that $a = b$ and $c = d$, then $a + c = b + d$.

5   *Prove Theorem 3–8:* If a, b, c, $d \in N$ such that $a < b$ and $c < d$, then $a + c < b + d$.

6   *Prove Theorem 3–9:* If a, b, $c \in N$ such that $a < b$, then $ac < bc$.

For the natural numbers a, b, c, d, and e, state the four theorems each of which has one of the following propositions as its conclusion. Prove each theorem.

7   $(a + b) + (c + d) + e = (a + c) + b + (e + d)$.

8   $(a + b)(c + d) = (ac + ad) + (bc + bd)$.

9   $(a + b)(c + d + e) = (ae + be) + (c + d)(a + b)$.

10 When $a > b$, then $ac + ad > bc + bd$.

INVITATIONS TO EXTENDED STUDY

1   What is meant by the contrapositive or the inverse of a given theorem?

2   Why is proving the contrapositive of a theorem equivalent to proving the theorem?

3   What are the basic differences between a direct proof and an indirect proof?

4   Make a study of the the truth tables of symbolic logic.

Prove these three theorems.

5   If a, $b \in N$ and $a < b$, then $a^2 < b^2$.

6   If a, b, c, $d \in N$ and $a < b < c$, then $a + d < b + d < c + d$.

7   If $n \in N$, there exists no natural number k such that $k + n = n$.

Use the principle of finite induction to prove these two theorems.

8   If n is a natural number, then $1 \leq n$.

9   The sum of the first n natural numbers is $\dfrac{n(n + 1)}{2}$.

10 Given the definitions $a^1 = a$ and $a^{n+1} = a^n \cdot a$ for all natural numbers a and n, use the principle of finite induction to prove the following properties of exponents.

(a) If a is a natural number, then a^k is a natural number for all numbers k.

(b) $1^k = 1$ for all natural numbers k.

(c) If $a, b, n \in N$, then $(ab)^n = a^n b^n$.

(d) If $a, m, n \in N$, then $a^m \cdot a^n = a^{m+n}$.

(e) If $a, m, n \in N$, then $(a^m)^n = a^{mn}$.

11 It has been previously stated that electronic computing machines are based on a binary number scale. These machines make use of the processes of duplation and mediation in their computations. Use the product $35 \times 1,246$ to give an example of the justification of this procedure. (*Hint:* Convert the multiplier 35 to an equivalent numeral in the binary scale.)

12 By using multiplication it is rather simple to see that **37—twelve** converts into 43—ten. An interesting technique which gives this same result is as follows:

(a) Observe the fact that in base **twelve** 2 more digital symbols are required than are needed in base ten.

(b) Multiply this number by the digit 3, which is the base position in the given numeral. $(3 \times 2 = 6.)$

(c) Consider the original numeral as if it were a numeral in base ten and add it to the product found in step (b). The result obtained is the required equivalent numeral in base ten. 37—ten + 6—ten = 43—ten.

Why does this scheme work? Generalize the procedure and show that it will convert any two-digit numeral in any arbitrary base to its equivalent numeral written in any other arbitrary base.

CHAPTER 4
the domain of integers

GUIDELINES FOR CAREFUL STUDY

The word "structure" is a name which is ascribed to a very important concept in mathematics. You should take stock at this point to see whether or not you have clearly in mind just what is meant by the structure of a number system. You should also have in mind a clear concept of the natural number system. This chapter will point out some shortcomings of this particular system and make extensions necessary to remove some of them. It will be very important for you to acquire a competent understanding of just what these shortcomings are and what are the legitimate procedures that must be followed in making the desirable extensions.

The following questions will be very helpful as guidelines for the careful study of Chap. 4.

1   What is meant by a number system?
2   What are the basic postulates of the natural number system?

3 What are the definitions of addition and multiplication? Why are they called binary operations?

4 Do you have the theorems of Chap. 3 in mind for ready and effective use?

5 Why should the property of closure be given so much importance in the study of number systems?

6 What is the definition of subtraction?

7 Why is subtraction said to be inversely related to addition?

8 What is an integer?

9 What is meant by "additive identity" and "additive inverse"?

10 When two integers k and l are found, by any valid reasoning, to be so related that $k + l = 0$, what can be said about k and l?

11 What is the full significance to be attached to the terms "digit value" and "place value" when applied to the digital symbols used in any numeral?

12 What is the new interpretation of the law of trichotomy introduced in this chapter?

13 Do you have a clear understanding of the extensions of the operations of addition and multiplication to the set of integers?

14 In what way is the set of postulates of the natural number system modified to obtain the set of postulates of the domain of integers? Do you understand clearly why this modification is made?

15 What is the fundamental theorem of arithmetic and why is it considered to be of such great importance?

16 What is the basic distinction between an indirect proof and a direct proof?

INTRODUCTION

In the preceding chapter the binary operations of addition and multiplication were defined for natural numbers. Certain properties which intuition and experience have identified as basically characteristic of these operations were then accepted and listed as the postulates of the natural number system. From these properties other properties were derived by means of the techniques of logical deduction. Still other derivable properties characteristic of natural numbers under these two operations were indicated by exercises and suggestions. There is a great deal of operational flexibility and effectiveness possible within this familiar system. However, it has definite restrictions and limitations which necessitate important extensions in order to make possible the further study of number systems that are significant in the structure of elementary mathematics. The consequences of these extensions constitute the subject matter of this and subsequent chapters.

4–1   THE CONCEPT OF INTEGER

In the preceding chapter emphasis was placed on closure as a significant property of the natural number system.   Recall that for addition the closure postulate (N–1) states that if a and b are any two natural numbers such that $a + b = c$, then c is also a natural number.   Contemplation and use of this property leads very naturally to the question, Is it true that for any two natural numbers a and b there exists a natural number d such that $a + d = b$?   One counterexample is sufficient to establish the fact that the answer to this question is No.   If a is the natural number 8 and b is the natural number 3, there exists no natural number d such that $8 + d = 3$.   The difficulty occurs only when a is greater than or equal to b $(a \geq b)$, for when $a < b$ there does exist, by Definition 3–2, a natural number d such that $a + d = b$.   When the natural number d does exist, it is called the *difference* between b and a in accordance with this definition.

Inadequacy of the natural number system — margin note

Definition 4–1   **For any two numbers a and b, the *difference* between b and a is said to be d $(d = b - a)$ if and only if $a + d = b$.   The process of finding the difference between two numbers is called *subtraction*.**

Difference and subtraction — margin note

While this definition is stated and holds for any numbers, whether they are natural numbers or not, at present it has significance only if a and b are natural numbers and $a < b$.   It is this same situation which exists in the early primary grades, where the number system used is essentially the natural number system, and the process of subtraction is limited to the subtraction of a smaller number from a larger number. In the later grades this restriction grows more and more artificial.   In order to give more freedom of interpretation and use not only to addition and multiplication but also to the new operation of subtraction, we find it necessary and desirable to extend our number system so that the new system will have closure under all three operations.   In any such extension it is desirable that the postulates of the old system be valid in the new system.   Also, the definitions, operations, and derived properties of the new system must include the definitions, operations, and derived properties of the old system as special cases.   This, of course, implies that the associative, commutative, and distributive properties must be preserved in the extension of the definitions of addition and multiplication.   Furthermore, these extensions must be such that, when the operations are restricted to the natural numbers, the new definitions will conform to those already established.

Need to extend the number system — margin note

We shall postulate the existence of these new numbers and then proceed to investigate the significant characteristics of the new number system to which they lead.

Postulate 4-1 For any two natural numbers a, b, there exists a number i such that $a + i = b$. The number i is called an *integer*.

Existence of integers

When $a < b$ we have, by Definition 3–2, that the integer i is a natural number. Thus, if $Z = \{i | i$ is an integer$\}$ and $N = \{n | n$ is a natural number$\}$, it follows that $N \subset Z$. Furthermore, we shall retain the operations of addition and multiplication as they were defined for natural numbers and investigate their implications for integers. Our problem thus resolves itself into the determination of what implications the relation $a + i = b$ of Postulate 4–1 has for the integer i when $a = b$ and when $a > b$.

4–2 THE ADDITIVE IDENTITY

When $a = b$, whether they are elements of the set Z or of the subset N, the relation $a + i = b$ takes the form $a + i = a$. Under this hypothesis the integer i is such that, when it is added to any integer a, the resultant sum is a. It is then called the *additive identity* and given the symbol 0. Under these conditions Postulate 4–1 may be restated for this special case of integers as follows:

Additive identity

Postulate 4-2 There exists one and only one integer 0, called the *additive identity*, such that $a + 0 = a$ for any integer a.

Zero is an integer

In the definition of the additive identity, zero (0) is defined as an integer which serves the same purpose for addition that the integer 1 serves for multiplication. (Why is it that now we can call 1 an integer as well as a natural number?)

4–3 THE ADDITIVE INVERSE

Since, by definition, $a + 0 = a$ for any natural number a, we shall say that $a > 0$ and follow the pattern of Definition 3–2 to state the following definition for integers.

Definition 4-2 If, for two integers a and b, it is true that $a + c = b$ for some integer $c > 0$, then $a < b$, or $b > a$.

It follows from this definition and Definition 4–1 that $b > a$ if $b - a = c$, where c is an integer greater than zero.

The natural numbers now have been identified as that proper subset of the set $Z = \{i | i$ is an integer$\}$ for which $i > 0$. In other words, the two phrases "a natural number" and "an integer greater than zero" now may be used interchangeably.

From the preceding discussion we now have an interpretation for the symbol i in the relation $a + i = b$ of Postulate 4–1 for $a \leq b$, where a and b are integers greater than zero. When $a < b$, i is an integer greater than zero; when $a = b$, i is the integer 0. In order to arrive at an interpretation for i when $a > b$, there are two cases to consider, namely, $b = 0$ and $b \neq 0$.

Case I When $b = 0$, does there exist an integer i such that $a + i = 0$? We know that if a person earns \$5 and then spends \$5, his net earning from this experience is 0 dollars. If we symbolize this by letting 5 represent the money earned and -5 the money spent, we have $5 + (-5) = 0$ as the representation of the combination of the two experiences. If a person, starting on a 50-mile trip north from his home, drives 2 miles north and then recalls something he has left behind and drives 2 miles south, the combined result of his traveling is 0 miles north, $2 + (-2) = 0$. The reader can construct many other similar examples. From such experiences we have the intuitive background for this special version of Postulate 4–1.

Postulate 4–3 **There exists one and only one integer $-a$, called the** ***additive inverse*** **of a, such that $a + (-a) = 0$ for every integer a.**

The symbol $-a$, in addition to being read "additive inverse of a," is also read "negative a" or "minus a." With the extension of our number system to include the additive identity and the additive inverses of all natural numbers, the elements of the set Z of all integers have been clearly defined; they are the infinite set $\{\ldots, -5, -4, -3, -2, -1, 0, 1, 2, 3, 4, 5, \ldots\}$, sometimes described as the set containing 0 and all positive and negative integers. The natural numbers then are identified as "positive integers" in contrast to the "negative integers." The set of nonnegative integers $\{0, 1, 2, 3, 4, \ldots\}$ was defined in Chap. 1 as the set of counting numbers. Some writers are inclined to call it the "set of *whole numbers*." Since $a > 0$ for any natural number a, it follows that, where desirable, we can identify an integer i as being positive by specifying $i > 0$. Similarly, a negative integer k can be identified by specifying $k < 0$. When it is desirable in any discussion to distinguish between the positive integer and the natural number, the symbol $+$ will be used to identify the positive integer. For example, $+4$ indicates the positive integer, 4 is the natural number, and -4 the negative integer. When there is no confusion as to the context of the use of the symbol, 4 will have the same significance as $+4$. We may write Z as the set $\{0, \pm 1, \pm 2, \pm 3, \ldots\}$, where the symbol ± 3 is to be read "plus or minus 3" and means that both $+3$ and -3 are to be included. It is important to note that 0 is its own additive inverse $(0 + 0 = 0)$; also, it is the only integer i for which it is true that $+i = -i$ $(0 = -0)$. Furthermore, the relation $a + (-a) = 0$ identifies not only $-a$ as the additive inverse of a but also a as the additive inverse of $-a$ $[a = -(-a)]$. Attention is called to the fact that $-a$ is not necessarily a negative integer. For example, since -5 is an integer, its additive inverse is $+5$ since $5 + (-5) = 0$. The symbol for the additive inverse of -5 is $-(-5)$.

0 is its own additive inverse

Case II When $b \neq 0$ and $a > b$, does there exist an integer i such that $a + i = b$? The answer to this question is found in Theorem 4–6, but before it can be answered it is necessary to determine how the definitions of addition and multiplication are to be interpreted as applying to the extended number system, which now includes not only the natural numbers but also 0 and the additive inverses of the natural numbers. In this extension it must be kept in mind that not only must the operations have meaning for the new numbers, but also they must retain the properties they have for natural numbers, since the natural numbers are also integers.

We know what the result is when any integer is added to its own additive inverse $a + (-a) = 0$. But what does it mean to add to an integer a the additive inverse of some other integer? What is the interpretation of $a + (-b)$ when $a \neq b$ (a is not equal to b)? If $b = 0$, the answer to the question is simple since the additive inverse of 0 is 0 and $a + 0 = a$. Theorem 4–1 answers the question when $b \neq 0$.

Theorem 4-1 If a and b are integers, then $a + (-b) = a - b$.

The meaning of $a + (-b)$

Hypothesis a, b are integers.

Conclusion $a + (-b) = a - b$.

What are the implications of the hypothesis? We are given that a and b are integers. We know how to find the sum of two integers which are natural numbers; of an integer and its own additive inverse; of an integer and the additive identity. We also know that addition of integers must be both associative and commutative. We can use these properties if they are helpful.

The conclusion we wish to draw states that the sum of one integer a and the additive inverse of another integer b is the same as the difference, $a - b$, between a and b. Definition 4–1 tells us that, in order to show this, we must be able to establish that $b + [a + (-b)] = a$. If this can be established, then we can draw the conclusion that $a + (-b)$ is the difference between a and b, or $a + (-b) = a - b$. We shall therefore attempt to show that this can be established.

Proof

Statements	*Reasons*
1 $-b$ is an integer	Postulate 4–3
2 Let $x = a + (-b)$, then $x \in Z$	Closure
3 $x + b = [a + (-b)] + b$	E–4
4 $= a + [(-b) + b]$	Associative property
5 $= a + 0$	Commutative property; Postulate 4–3
6 $= a$	Postulate 4–2
7 $x + b = a$	Steps 3 to 6; E–3
8 $x = a - b$	Definition 4–1
9 $a + (-b) = a - b$	Steps 2 and 8; E–2 and E–3

The meaning of
$(-a) + (-b)$

Theorem 4-2   If a and b are integers, then $(-a) + (-b) = -(a + b)$.

The proof for this theorem is very similar to that for Theorem 4–1. Let $x = (-a) + (-b)$ and x is an integer. Then show first that $x + b = -a$, from which it follows that $x + (b + a) = 0$. The commutative property and Definition 4–1 then lead immediately to the desired conclusion.

In the proofs of each of the above theorems the familiar properties for addition were used and were imposed on both the new and the old numbers. As a result of this discussion the definition of addition has been extended to the set of all integers.

It is well, at this point, to call attention to the fact that, in the proof of Theorem 4–1 and the suggestions for the proof of Theorem 4–2, the closure, associative, commutative, and distributive properties for addition were cited as justification for certain steps. This is in accordance with the stipulation that the extended definitions of addition and multiplication must be consistent with these properties. They are, therefore, assumed to hold for integers as well as for natural numbers, as are the remaining properties, N–5 through N–8. There are two significant restrictions, however, that must be kept in mind. While the postulates N–1 through N–6 are accepted as true for all integers, a slight modification is required for postulate N–7, and postulate N–8 remains restricted to the natural numbers. An immediate consequence of great significance derives from these stipulations. It is the fact that all theorems and other derived properties of the natural number system can be established as derivable properties of integers. They will hold for all integers except in those cases, such as postulate N–8, where the conditions of the hypothesis restrict the application only to the positive integers. Thus it follows that the theorems of Chap. 3—both those proved and those stated as exercises to be proved—can also be proved for integers. Because of space limitations we shall dispense with the formality of restating these theorems in the language of integers. They will be cited as authority in cases where needed, and the reader will need only to replace the words "natural numbers" by the word "integers." It could be an instructive exercise to the reader to make this substitution and construct the proof for each theorem as stated specifically for integers.

As a consequence of the previously mentioned "slight modification" of postulate N–7, the cancellation law, as stated for integers, becomes:

Cancellation Law for Integers   If a, b, c are integers such that $ac = bc$ and $c \neq 0$, then $a = b$.

Note that there is no cancellation law stated for addition of integers. The reason for this is not that it is no longer a true statement. It is true, but it can be proved as a theorem by using the postulates of the domain of integers (see Exercise 13, page 102). Also it is now necessary to state an additional hypothesis for the cancellation law for multiplication. The multiplier must be nonzero ($c \neq 0$). This condition was not necessary for natural numbers, since $0 \in N$. The law is not true for integers if $c = 0$. For example, $8 \cdot 0 = 3 \cdot 0$ since each product is equal to zero (Theorem 4–3), but $8 \neq 3$.

Theorem 4–3   **For any integer a it is true that $a \times 0 = 0$.**   Zero in multiplication

Hypothesis a is any integer.

Conclusion $a \times 0 = 0$.

Since by hypothesis a is an integer, this means that we may use the properties of integers to obtain the conclusion. As an immediate consequence of the closure property we have that $a \times 0$ is an integer.

The conclusion we are asked to draw is that $a \times 0 = 0$. This means that we are asked to show that the integer $a \times 0$ can serve as the additive identity. In other words, we want to show that we can find a situation in which the sum of $a \times 0$ and some other integer, say k, is k. If this can be done, then we shall have exhibited that $a \times 0$ is the additive identity 0, since Postulate 4–2 tells us that the additive identity is unique. An important question now is, How can we place our thinking in the context of the additive identity? An immediate answer is that we know that $a + 0 = a$. How can we get multiplication in the picture? The multiplicative property of equality is worth a try.

Proof

Statements	*Reasons*
1 $a + 0 = a$	Postulate 4–2
2 $a \times (a + 0) = a \times a$	Theorem 3–2
3 $(a \times a) + (a \times 0) = a \times (a + 0)$	Distributive property
4 $(a \times a) + (a \times 0) = a \times a$	Steps 2 and 3; E–3
5 $a \times 0 = 0$	Postulate 4–2

An immediate consequence of this theorem is the following corollary.

Corollary   If a and b are nonzero integers, then $a \cdot b \neq 0$.

Hypothesis $a, b \in Z$ and $a \neq 0$, $b \neq 0$.

Conclusion $a \cdot b \neq 0$.

Nature of indirect proof and direct proof

In the proof of this corollary we shall use a form of argument known as *indirect proof,* which is quite different in nature from the *direct* type of proof used in all previous theorems of this book.   Prior to this point, in the proof of each theorem the argument has started with the hypothesis of the particular theorem and proceeded by direct implication to the desired conclusion.   Recall that $p \to q$ (p implies q) means that it is absolutely impossible for q to be false if p is true.   Also recall that a statement or proposition is always either true or false.   If it is not true then it must be false; or, conversely, if it is not false then it must be true.   One pattern of indirect proof consists in assuming that the desired conclusion.is false.   By using this assumption either as an additional hypothesis or as a substitute hypothesis, the argument proceeds to investigate the implications which follow from it.   If they lead to a conclusion which contradicts either the hypothesis of the theorem being investigated or some fact known to follow as a direct implication from this hypothesis, the assumed falsity of the conclusion cannot hold as long as the hypothesis is accepted as true.   From this fact it then follows that the conclusion, as stated in the theorem, must be accepted as true.

Proof

Statements	*Reasons*
1 b is a nonzero integer	Hypothesis
2 $0 = 0 \cdot b$	Theorem 4–3; commutativity
3 Assume $a \cdot b = 0$	The contradiction of the conclusion
4 $a \cdot b = 0 \cdot b$	Steps 2 and 3; E–3
5 $a = 0$	Cancellation law for integers since $b \neq 0$

The conclusion of step 5 is implied by the assumed statement $a \cdot b = 0$. The hypothesis of the theorem states that $a \neq 0$. Since $a = 0$ and $a \neq 0$ cannot both be true, we have reached a contradiction. This fact assures us that the assumption that $a \cdot b = 0$ is false. It therefore follows that $a \cdot b \neq 0$, and the theorem is proved.

Theorem 4-4 If a and b are integers, then $a \times (-b) = -(a \times b)$. The meaning of $a \times (-b)$

Hypothesis a, b are integers.

Conclusion $a \times (-b) = -(a \times b)$.

The hypothesis states that a and b are integers, so we have the properties of integers at our disposal.

To prove that $a \times (-b) = -(a \times b)$ means that we must show that the integer $a \times (-b)$ is the additive inverse of the integer $a \times b$. In other words, we must attempt to prove that $(a \times b) + [a \times (-b)] = 0$. When this has been accomplished, the desired conclusion can be drawn.

Proof

Statements	Reasons
1 $-b$ is an integer	Postulate 4–3
2 $(a \times b) + [a \times (-b)] = a \times [b + (-b)]$	Distributive property
3 $\qquad\qquad\qquad\quad = a \times 0$	Postulate 4–3
4 $\qquad\qquad\qquad\quad = 0$	Theorem 4–3
5 $(a \times b) + [a \times (-b)] = 0$	Steps 2 to 4; E–3
6 $a \times (-b) = -(a \times b)$, the additive inverse of $a \times b$	Postulate 4–3

Corollary If a and b are integers, then $(-a) \times b$ is the additive inverse of $a \times b$.

Theorem 4-5 If a and b are integers, then $(-a) \times (-b) = a \times b$. The meaning of $(-a) \times (-b)$

Hypothesis a and b are integers.

Conclusion $(-a) \times (-b) = a \times b$.

Proof

Statements	Reasons
1 $-a, -b$ are integers	Postulate 4–3
2 $[(-a) \times (-b)] + [(-a) \times b]$ $= (-a) \times [(-b) + b]$	Distributive property
3 $\qquad = (-a) \times 0$	Commutative property; Postulate 4–3

Statements   *Reasons*

4   $= 0$ Theorem 4–3
5   $[(-a) \times (-b)] + [(-a) \times b] = 0$ Steps 2 to 4; E–3
6   $(-a) \times (-b) = a \times b$, the   Corollary to
    additive inverse of $[(-a) \times b]$ Theorem 4–4

The operations of addition and multiplication have now been extended so that they are well-defined operations for the set Z of all integers.

Case II   We are now ready to investigate the interpretation of the relation $a + i = b$ of Postulate 4–1 when $a > b$ and $b \neq 0$. It is taken care of by Theorem 4–6.

General inter-
pretation of
$a + i = b$ **Theorem 4-6**   **If a, b, and i are integers such that $a + i = b$, and $a > b$, $b \neq 0$, then $i = -(a - b)$.**

Hypothesis a, b, and i are integers and $a + i = b$, $a > b$, $b \neq 0$.

Conclusion $i = -(a - b)$.

We are given that a, b, and i are integers such that $b \neq 0$; $a > b$; and $a + i = b$. This means that i cannot be a natural number since $a > b$.

To prove that $i = -(a - b)$ we must be able to prove that $(a - b) + i = 0$; in other words, i is the additive inverse of $a - b$. Since $a > b$ we know from Theorem 4–1 that $a - b = a + (-b)$. This means that, as an aid in the proof of this theorem, we can use $a + (-b)$ in place of $a - b$. Since this is the case, we can direct our thinking toward using the given relation $a + i = b$ and the properties of integers to see whether we can derive the relation $[a + (-b)] + i = 0$. From this relation the desired conclusion can be drawn.

Proof

Statements   *Reasons*

1   $-b$ is an integer   Postulate 4–3
2   $a + i = b$ Hypothesis
3   $(a + i) + (-b) = b + (-b)$ E–4
4   $a + [i + (-b)] = b + (-b)$ Associative property
5   $a + [(-b) + i] = b + (-b)$ Commutative property
6   $[a + (-b)] + i = b + (-b)$ Associative property
7   $[a + (-b)] + i = 0$ Postulate 4–3
8   $(a - b) + i = 0$ Theorem 4–1
9   $i = -(a - b)$, the additive
    inverse of $(a - b)$ Postulate 4–3

Attention should be called to the fact that, in the argument of this theorem, the principle of substitution has been used. This makes possible a more compact form of argument than that possible when, in each case, the steps to justify the substitution are detailed. For example, $a + [i + (-b)] = (a + i) + (-b)$, by the associative property of addition. This fact, combined with step 3 of the proof and property E–3 of equality, justifies step 4. It should be evident from this detail why the associative property is cited as the authority for step 4. Similar patterns of reasoning justify steps 5 to 8 of the proof.

Example   This example is constructed for the purpose of calling attention to the fact that although Theorem 4–6 was proved to take care of the interpretation of the symbol i in $a + i = b$ of Postulate 4–1 when $a > b$ and $b \neq 0$, it can be used to provide interpretations also when $a > b$ and $b = 0$ and when $a \leq b$. This should be evident from the fact that, in the proof of the theorem, there is no condition whatsoever imposed on the relation between a and b. In the previous interpretations of the cases $a < b$, $a = b$, and $a > b$ when $b = 0$ we used simpler techniques which were readily available. Of course these interpretations should be the same as those which Theorem 4–6 provides.

1   When $a < b$, the previous interpretation required $i > 0$. For example, for $a = 3$, and $b = 8$, $i = 5$ since $3 + 5 = 8$. By Theorem 4–6, $i = -(a - b) = -(3 - 8) = -(-5)$. In other words, in this case, i is the additive inverse of -5. This is 5 since $5 + (-5) = 0$.

2   When $a = b$, the previous interpretation required $i = 0$. For example, when $a = 3$ and $b = 3$ then $i = 0$ since $3 + 0 = 3$ by Postulate 4–2. By Theorem 4–6, $i = -(a - b) = -(3 - 3) = -0 = 0$.

3   When $a > b$ and $b = 0$, that is, when $a > 0$, the previous interpretation (Case I) required that i be the additive inverse of a. For example, when $a = 3$ and $b = 0$, then $i = -3$ since $3 + (-3) = 0$ by Postulate 4–3. By Theorem 4–6, $i = -(a - b) = -(3 - 0) = -3$.

4   Finally, the only interpretation we have when $a > b$ and $b \neq 0$ is that provided by Theorem 4–6. If $a = 8$ and $b = 3$, then $i = -(8 - 3) = -5$. In other words, $8 + (-5) = 3$. This is checked by Theorem 4–1, which states that $8 + (-5) = 8 - 5 = 3$.

4–4   THE NATURE OF SUBTRACTION

Historically there have been four distinct processes which, at one time or another through the years, have been used to characterize the process of subtraction. They are (1) *decomposition,* breaking down a number into component parts; (2) *deduction,* taking away a part of a number

Characteristics of subtraction

and retaining the rest, or remainder; (3) *diminution,* decreasing the size of a number; and (4) *comparison,* finding how much larger or how much smaller one number is than another. While each of these interpretations of subtraction places emphasis on an important computational function of the operation, no one of them lends emphasis to its significance in the basic structure of a number system.

In the natural number system, addition and multiplication are well-defined operations. These definitions have now been extended to the set of integers. Subtraction has been defined in terms of addition (Definition 4–1), and Theorem 4–1 establishes the fact that the subtraction of any integer b from another integer a can be accomplished by adding to a the additive inverse of b. [$a - b = a + (-b)$.] It should also be clear that another equally valid interpretation of Theorem 4–1 is that the addition of one integer, d, to another, a, can be accomplished by subtracting its additive inverse from a. [$a + d = a - (-d)$.]

Subtraction is the inverse of addition

These facts lay the foundation for the statement that *subtraction is defined as the inverse of the process of addition.* This fact is made more convincing by Theorem 4–7, which shows that each operation, addition or subtraction, cancels the effect of the other; they are inverse operations.

Theorem 4-7   For any two integers a and b: $(a + b) - b = a$; $(a - b) + b = a$.

Hypothesis a and b are integers.

Conclusion   Case I $(a + b) - b = a$.

Proof

Statements	*Reasons*
1 a and b are integers	Hypothesis
2 $a + b$ is an integer	Closure
3 $(a + b) - b = (a + b) + (-b)$	Theorem 4–1
4 $\quad\quad\quad\quad = a + [b + (-b)]$	Associative property
5 $\quad\quad\quad\quad = a + 0$	Postulate 4–3
6 $\quad\quad\quad\quad = a$	Postulate 4–2
7 $(a + b) - b = a$	Steps 3 to 5; E–3

Conclusion   Case II $(a - b) + b = a$.

1 $a - b$ is an integer	Definition 4–1; Postulate 4–1
2 $(a - b) + b = [a + (-b)] + b$	Theorem 4–1
3 $\quad\quad\quad\quad = a + [(-b) + b]$	Associative property

Statements		Reasons
4	$= a + 0$	Commutative property; Postulate 4–3
5	$= a$	Postulate 4–2
6	$(a - b) + b = a$	Steps 2 to 5; E–3

How do the facts presented here show that the addition tables you constructed previously can also be used as subtraction tables?

Just as in the case of addition, there have been many different names used for what we today call "subtraction." In addition to *subtraction* (to subtract), some of the more important of these terms are *diminution* (to diminish), *extraction* (to extract), *detraction* (to detract), and *subduction* (to subduce or subtray). We get the words *minuend* and *subtrahend* from the Latin phrases *numerus minuendus* (number to be diminished) and *numerus subtrehendus* (number to be subtracted), respectively. Since subtraction is more clearly understood in the context of its definition as the inverse operation of addition, the words "minuend" and "subtrahend" are no longer considered as very significant words even in the vocabulary of elementary mathematics. As a consequence, they are being dropped from current usage. Our terms *difference* and *remainder* seem to date from Latin and English writers of the sixteenth century.†

The earliest symbols for subtraction came from the Babylonians and Egyptians. In writing their numerals, the Babylonians made use of the subtractive principle and used the symbol $\triangledown \triangleright$ to indicate subtraction. In the Ahmes papyrus, the symbol $\wedge$, indicating a pair of legs walking away, was used. In the manuscript of the Hindu writer Bhāskara (ca. 1150), we find three forms for indicating which of two numbers is the subtrahend: a circle or dot placed over the number, as in $\overset{\circ}{4}$ or $\overset{\bullet}{4}$, or the enclosure of the number in a circle, ④. Just as in the case of the signs $\tilde{p}$ and $+$, the two signs $\tilde{m}$ and $-$ were in sharp competition during the fifteenth and sixteenth centuries. There are many different hypotheses as to the origin of the minus sign ($-$), none of which seems supported by very strong evidence. The first occurrence in print of this sign, along with the plus sign, was in Widman's arithmetic published in 1489. In spite of the simplicity of the minus sign as a symbol for subtraction, there have been several variations that were popular for a time. There were three in particular which were used fairly widely: $\div$, $\div\div$, and the two or three successive dots . . . used by Descartes and others.‡ Just as the earliest use of the plus sign seems to have been to show excess, so the minus sign seems to have been used first as a label denoting deficiency rather than as a symbol to indicate the process of subtraction.

Symbols used to indicate subtraction

The symbol —

† David Eugene Smith, "History of Mathematics," vol. II, pp. 94–95, Ginn and Company, Boston, 1925.
‡ F. Cajori, "A History of Mathematical Notations," vol. I, pp. 229–236, The Open Court Publishing Company, La Salle, Ill., 1928.

4–5   THE SUBTRACTION ALGORITHM

Some writers in the past have claimed to identify nine, twelve, and even thirty distinct operational patterns for subtracting one integer from another. The variations lie in different details of procedure and different techniques for capitalizing on the significance of place value. For convenience we might categorize these variations within these four classifications: *decomposition take-away, decomposition additive, equal additions take-away, equal additions additive.*

The decomposition methods

Both *decomposition* methods are based on the idea of breaking a number down into what might be called its component parts. For example, the colored numerals of Fig. 4–1 show the analysis of the process used in finding the difference between 5,032 and 1,687. We first discover that we cannot subtract 7 ones from 2 ones. We then proceed to use one of the 3 tens and convert it to 10 ones, which are combined with the 2 ones to give 12 ones. Since there are only 2 tens remaining in the minuend and there are 8 tens to be subtracted, it now becomes necessary to use one of the 5 thousands to convert to 10 hundreds, of which one may be converted into 10 tens to be combined with the 2 tens to give 12 tens. The process of subtraction then becomes:

Decomposition

Take-away	*Additive*
7 from 12 = 5	7 and 5 make 12
8 from 12 = 4	8 and 4 make 12
6 from 9 = 3	6 and 3 make 9
1 from 4 = 3	1 and 3 make 4

Either method of decomposition is at times referred to as a "borrowing method." It is likely that this concept is traceable back to the language of abacal reckoning. In using the abacus, the computer

FIGURE 4–1   Decomposition method of subtraction.

				Step 1	3 ten = 2 tens + 10 ones
	9			Step 2	10 ones + 2 ones = 12 ones
4	1̷0̷	12		Step 3	12 ones − 7 ones = 5 ones
		2̷	12	Step 4	5 thousands = 4 thousands + 10 hundreds
5̷	0	3̷	2̷	Step 5	10 hundreds = 9 hundreds + 10 tens
				Step 6	10 tens + 2 tens = 12 tens
1	6	8	7	Step 7	12 tens − 8 tens = 4 tens
3	3	4	5	Step 8	9 hundreds − 6 hundreds = 3 hundreds
				Step 9	4 thousands − 1 thousand = 3 thousands

literally takes the subtrahend away from the minuend. Thus whenever a line or column has an insufficient number of beads to make the subtraction possible, beads are borrowed from the next higher column.

The *equal additions* methods are both based on the fact that addition and subtraction are inverse processes (see Theorem 4–7). For example, in Fig. 4–1, since 7 cannot be subtracted from 2, we add 10 ones to the 2 ones to obtain 12 ones. Since 10 ones have been added, we must subtract 10 ones, or 1 ten. We combine this 1 ten with the 8 tens to be subtracted. This procedure is followed in each step. The subtraction process then becomes:

The equal additions methods

Equal Additions

Take-away	*Additive*
7 from 12 $=$ 5	7 and 5 make 12
9 from 13 $=$ 4	9 and 4 make 13
7 from 10 $=$ 3	7 and 3 make 10
2 from 5 $=$ 3	2 and 3 make 5

The estimation of a difference is an effective and worthwhile check on the reasonableness of an answer in subtraction. While the check of casting out nines is also adaptable to this process, it is of minor significance because it is just about as simple, and much more effective, to add the difference to the subtrahend to obtain the minuend.

Checking subtraction

Exercises

1   What is meant by saying that addition and subtraction are inverse processes? Illustrate.

2   In what way are the words "decomposition," "deduction," "diminution," and "comparison" descriptive of the process of subtraction?

3   For what purposes do we subtract?

4   Answer the following questions about the set $\{1,0,-1\}$. Give reasons for your answers.
    (*a*) Is the set closed under addition?
    (*b*) Is the set closed under subtraction?
    (*c*) Is the set closed under multiplication?

5   Answer the questions of Exercise 4 about the set $\{a,0,-a\}$ where *a* is any natural number.

6   Prove that the odd integers are not closed either under addition or under subtraction.

7   Construct a rule for using the process of casting out nines as a check for subtraction.

8 First find each of these sums and then use the process of subtraction to check each sum.

   (a) 157   (b) 2,034   (c)   25
       456   9,022   413
       203   5,681   1,062
       821   403   67

9 Use each of the four methods of subtraction described in this book to find each of these differences:

   (a) 2,654   (b) 4,326   (c) 5,072
     1,231   2,348   1,986

10 Use the examples of Exercise 9 to point out the significance of place value in the process of subtraction.

11 Find these differences in base **twelve:**

   (a) **6784 − 2341**   (b) **5682 − 1378**   (c) **5082 − 2598**
   (d) **8te4 − 6e95**   (e) **t04e − 9372**   (f) **8007 − 2ete**

12 Find these differences in base **five:**

   (a) **432 − 112**   (b) **314 − 132**   (c) **302 − 204**
   (d) **400 − 124**   (e) **403 − 342**   (f) **201 − 13**

13 Find these differences in base **eight:**

   (a) **742 − 345**   (b) **1504 − 672**   (c) **3605 − 2716**
   (d) **4003 − 1276**   (e) **7002 − 6724**   (f) **5000 − 4765**

14 Find these differences:

   (a) **⊥△□ − I△⊥**   (b) **△△I − ⊥⊥△**
   (c) **△00 − I⊥□**   (d) **△0I△ − I⊥△□**

15 Use each of the four methods of subtraction described in this book to find each of these differences:

   (a) **4725—eight**   (b) **8e0t3—twelve**   (c) **□⊥I△**
      2467—eight   **6t2e4—twelve**   **I△⊥I**

16 Construct a subtraction table for base **nine.**

17 Use the table of Exercise 16 to find these differences in base **nine:**

   (a) **2078**   (b) **5681**   (c) **6001**
      1325   **4723**   **3504**

18 Illustrate the fact that integers are neither associative nor commutative under subtraction. What about natural numbers?

4-6   PROPERTIES OF THE DOMAIN OF INTEGERS

For the set of integers $Z = \{0, \pm1, \pm2, \pm3, \pm4, \pm5, \pm6, \ldots\}$ we now have two well-defined operations, addition and multiplication. The set Z satisfies the following postulates:

Properties of the domain of integers

For $a, b, c \in Z$:

D-1   Closure   If $a + b = x$ and $a \times b = y$, then x, y are unique elements of Z.

D-2   Associative $a + (b + c) = (a + b) + c$;
$$a \times (b \times c) = (a \times b) \times c.$$

D-3   Commutative $a + b = b + a$; $a \times b = b \times a$.

D-4   Distributive $a \times (b + c) = (a \times b) + (a \times c)$.

D-5   Additive Identity   There exists an integer 0, called the *additive identity*, such that $a + 0 = a$ for every integer a.

D-6   Additive Inverse   For every integer a there exists an integer $(-a)$ such that $a + (-a) = 0$. The integer $(-a)$ is called the *additive inverse* of a.

D-7   Multiplicative Identity   There exists an integer $1 \neq 0$, called the *multiplicative identity*, such that $1 \times a = a$ for every integer a.

D-8   Cancellation   If $ac = bc$ and $c \neq 0$, then $a = b$.

From these eight postulates, and the five postulates of equality, all the remaining properties of integers may be derived. In fact, while this mathematical system has been defined under the restricted hypothesis that its elements belong to the set Z of integers, this is not necessary. We might have merely specified that we have a set of elements $(a,b,c,d, \ldots)$, with addition and multiplication as the well-defined operations, which satisfies the eight given postulates. There are sets of numbers other than the integers (as we shall see later) which do meet these conditions. The mathematical system defined in any such case would be an integral domain. For our general purposes it will be sufficient to restrict ourselves at this point to the integral domain whose elements are the integers of the set Z.

Notice that postulates D–1 to D–4 and D–7 are the same as postulates N–1 to N–5 for the natural number system. Attention has been called to the fact that D–8, the cancellation property for integers, differs slightly from N–7, the cancellation property for natural numbers. In D–7 there is the assumption that the multiplicative identity differs from the additive identity $(1 \neq 0)$. This is necessary to eliminate the possibility that any trivial cases, such as a set consisting of only the element

0, may be considered as an integral domain. Postulate 4–2 specified that the additive identity is unique. Similarly, Postulate 4–3 specified uniqueness for the additive inverse. The assumptions of uniqueness were for clarity of development at the point where used. Neither is a necessary assumption, and neither is incorporated in the corresponding postulates D–5 and D–6 of the domain of integers. This is due to the fact that the property of uniqueness can, in each case, be derived as a consequence of the stated postulates. The case for the additive identity is established in Theorem 4–8; that for the additive inverse is left as an exercise for the reader (see Exercise 20, page 102).

Uniqueness of the additive identity

Theorem 4-8 **If there exists an element i of the set Z such that $a + i = a$ for every element a in Z, then $i = 0$.**

Hypothesis   The integer i is such that $a + i = a$ for every integer a.

Conclusion $i = 0$.

Proof

Statements	*Reasons*
1 0 is an integer	Postulate 4–2
2 $0 + i = 0$	Hypothesis since 0 is an integer
3 $i + 0 = 0 + i$	D–3
4 $i = i + 0$	D–5
5 $i = 0$	Steps 2 to 4; E–3

The integers are ordered

The integers of the set Z can be arranged in the usual order of increasing size . . . , $-5, -4, -3, -2, -1, 0, 1, 2, 3, 4, 5, \ldots$. This arrangement is accomplished by the test implied by Definition 4–2, namely, $a < b$ if $b - a$ is a positive integer.

Example

1 $8 < 12$ since $12 - 8 = 4$.
2 $-5 < -4$ since $(-4) - (-5) = (-4) + [-(-5)] = (-4) + (5)$
     $= 5 + (-4) = 5 - 4 = 1$.

Supply the reasons for each statement in this continued equality. Why does it follow that $(-4) - (-5) = 1$?

Furthermore, the positive integers $1, 2, 3, 4, \ldots$ of the set Z have these three properties:

Closure for positive integers

1 *Addition*   The sum of two positive integers is a positive integer.
2 *Multiplication*   The product of two positive integers is a positive integer.

3   Trichotomy   For any given integer a, one and only one of the
following three relations holds: a is positive $(a > 0)$, $a = 0$, or $-a$ is
positive $(-a > 0)$.

The law of
trichotomy for
integers

The set N of natural numbers has been identified previously with the
set of positive integers.   We shall therefore use the symbol N interchangeably to indicate either of the two sets.

At this point it is necessary to restate Theorems 3–4 and 3–9 specifically for integers.   The restatement of Theorem 3–4 is:

Theorem 4-9   If a, b, c are integers and $a < b$, then $a + c < b + c$.

A bit of investigation will verify that this theorem is true for any integers which satisfy the condition $a < b$.

The restatement of Theorem 3–9 is not quite so simple.   In fact,
there are three cases to consider, depending on whether the multiplier
c is such that $c = 0$, $c > 0$, or $c < 0$.

Case I $c = 0$ From Theorem 4–3 and D–3 it follows that $a \times 0 =
0 \times a = 0$.   It thus should be evident that multiplication of an in-
equality by zero changes the inequality into a trivial equality.

Case II $c > 0$ In this case c can be identified as a natural number
and Theorem 3–9 may be restated as:

Theorem 4-10   If a, b, c are integers such that $a < b$ and $c > 0$, then
$ac < bc$.

The argument of this theorem is essentially the same as that for
Theorem 3–9.

Case III $c < 0$ The theorem covering this case is quite different from
Theorem 3–9.   The difference lies in the fact that the inequality rela-
tion "less than" is changed into the inequality relation "greater than."
In such cases the *sense of the inequality* is said to be changed.

Sense of an
inequality

Theorem 4-11   If a, b, c are integers such that $c < 0$ and $a < b$, then
$ac > bc$.

Hypothesis a, b, c are integers, $c < 0$, and $a < b$.

Conclusion $ac > bc$.

In the argument of this theorem we shall attempt to prove that since
$a < b$ and $c < 0$ it follows that $bc + k = ac$, where k is a positive
integer.

Proof

Statements	Reasons
$a + d = b$ where d is a positive integer	Hypothesis; Definition 4-2
$(a + d)c = bc$	E-5
$ac + dc = (a + d)c$	Commutative and distributive properties
$ac + dc = bc$	E-3
$-dc$ is an integer	Closure
$(ac + dc) + (-dc) = bc + (-dc)$	E-4
$ac + [dc + (-dc)] = (ac + dc) + (-dc)$	Associative property
$ac + 0 = ac + [dc + (-dc)]$	Additive inverse
$ac = ac + 0$	Additive identity
$ac = bc + (-dc)$	E-3
$-dc = d(-c)$	Theorem 4-4
Since c is a negative integer, its additive inverse $-c$ is a positive integer.	Definition of additive inverse; trichotomy
$d(-c)$ is positive	Closure for positive integers
$ac > bc$	Definition 4-2

There are many subsets of the set Z which are of interest and significance. In particular, there are two sets of subsets of Z which are of interest to us in this development. In each of these cases the subsets of Z are disjoint sets.

Composite number and integral factors

1   *The prime numbers and the composite numbers.* If an integer a can be written in the form bc where b and c are both integers other than 1 or 0, it is called a *composite number.* The integers b and c are said to be *integral factors* of a.

Prime number

A prime number is any integer greater than 1 which has no positive integral factors other than itself and 1.

Example   Numbers such as 12, 30, and 210 are composite numbers. $12 = 2 \times 2 \times 3$; $30 = 2 \times 3 \times 5$; $210 = 2 \times 3 \times 5 \times 7$. Numbers such as 2, 3, 5, 7, 11 are prime numbers. The above composite numbers 12, 30, and 210 have been *factored* into their prime factors. Upon examination it is evident that 2 is a common factor of the three numbers, and 3 is also a common factor. From this it follows that $2 \times 3 = 6$ is a common factor. In fact, we may write $12 = 2 \times 6$, $30 = 5 \times 6$, and $210 = 35 \times 6$. Thus 6 is the largest integer which is a common factor of the three integers. It is their *greatest common factor.*

Greatest common factor (g.c.f.)

Definition 4-3   The *greatest common factor (g.c.f.)* of two or more integers is the largest integer which is a factor of each of the given integers.

Two integers which have no common factor other than 1 are said to be *relatively prime*. Thus 33 and 70 are relatively prime, since $33 = 3 \times 11$ and $70 = 2 \times 5 \times 7$, and it is evident that they have no common factor other than 1.

Relatively prime integers

The elements of Z may be separated into the three disjoint subsets {1}, {all prime numbers}, {all composite numbers}. Many of the considerations of mathematicians center around the elements of these sets, and many properties have been established both for composite numbers and for prime numbers. Three fundamental theorems, which are of significance to this development, will be stated here as postulates, since their proofs are of a rather abstract nature.

Postulate 4-4   There are infinitely many primes.

Postulate 4-5   The Fundamental Theorem of Arithmetic   Except for the ordering of the factors, any integer greater than 1 may be written as the product of primes in one and only one way.

Example   The composite number 105 may be factored into primes as $3 \times 5 \times 7$, $3 \times 7 \times 5$, $5 \times 3 \times 7$, $5 \times 7 \times 3$, $7 \times 3 \times 5$, or $7 \times 5 \times 3$. While these are six different arrangements, they are of the same three primes 3, 5, and 7.

The prime number 17 has no factors other than itself and 1; so it has only one prime factor, namely, 17.

Postulate 4-6   If the prime p is a factor of the composite number ab, then it must be a factor of either a or b and, if a and b are relatively prime, p is a factor of exactly one of them.

Example   If by any means one knows that 17 is a factor of 1,615 and also that $1,615 = 5 \times 323$, then by Postulate 4-6 it follows that 17 is a factor of 323 since it is not a factor of 5. On the other hand, if one knows that 12 is a factor of 1,020 and also that $1,020 = 6 \times 170$, it does not follow that 12 must divide 170 since it does not divide 6. The difference lies in the fact that 17 is a prime number while 12 is not.

The theory of prime numbers and its applications have occupied an important place in the world of mathematics and still do. Mathematicians have engaged in a great deal of research and expended a vast amount of effort in search of techniques which will discover primes. One of the first and simplest of all such techniques is the sieve of Eratosthenes (ca. 230 B.C.). This is a scheme to select all primes less than a selected integer n. In Fig. 4-2 it is used to select all primes less than 40. All integers beginning with 2 and up to the selected number (40) are written in an array such as the rectangular array of Fig. 4-2. Then starting from 2, strike out every second number thereafter; next start with 3 and strike out every third number; then with 5, the next number not al-

Sieve of Eratosthenes

FIGURE 4-2   Eratosthenes sieve.

	2	3	4̸	5	6̸	7	8̸	9̸	1̸0̸
11	1̸2̸	13	1̸4̸	1̸5̸	1̸6̸	17	1̸8̸	19	2̸0̸
2̸1̸	2̸2̸	23	2̸4̸	2̸5̸	2̸6̸	2̸7̸	2̸8̸	29	3̸0̸
31	3̸2̸	3̸3̸	3̸4̸	3̸5̸	3̸6̸	37	3̸8̸	3̸9̸	4̸0̸

/ indicates a number with 2 as a factor
— indicates a number with 3 as a factor
\ indicates a number with 5 as a factor

ready stricken, and strike every fifth number; then repeat the process with 7, and so on. Continue until there are no further numbers less than n to be stricken. The numbers which remain will be all the primes less than n. From Fig. 4–2 it is seen that the primes less than 40 are 2, 3, 5, 7, 11, 13, 17, 19, 23, 29, 31, 37.

This process soon becomes very cumbersome and unwieldy. In the present day of the rapid computing machine, remarkable success is being achieved in determining prime numbers and in the factorization of composite numbers of tremendous size.

Even and odd numbers   2   *The even positive integers and the odd positive integers.*   If an integer has 2 as one of its factors, then that integer is said to be an *even number;* otherwise it is an *odd number.* Thus the set N may be separated into the two following disjoint subsets:

1   The set O of odd positive integers:

$O = \{1,3,5,7,9,11,13, \dots \}$

2   The set E of even positive integers:

$E = \{2,4,6,8,10,12,14,16, \dots \}$

There are many occasions in which these two subsets of N have significance. They are cited here to illustrate an interesting and important

$2n$	n	$2n - 1$
2	1	1
4	2	3
6	3	5
8	4	7
10	5	9
12	6	11
14	7	13
16	8	15
18	9	17

FIGURE 4-3   Correspondence between sets of integers.

property of infinite sets. We may describe the two subsets O and E of N by the set selectors

$O = \{2n - 1 | n$ is a positive integer$\}$
$E = \{2n | n$ is a positive integer$\}$

The table of Fig. 4–3 shows how to each positive integer n there corresponds one and only one element in each of the sets O and E as determined by their respective set selectors, and to each element in either O or E there corresponds one and only one element of N. Thus we have not only a one-to-one correspondence between the elements of O and the elements of E but also a one-to-one correspondence between the elements of either of these sets and the elements of N. In other words, the elements of N can be put into one-to-one correspondence with the elements of a subset of N other than N itself. This is a property of infinite sets which does not hold for finite sets. For example, suppose we consider the set $A = \{$the set of all letters of the English alphabet$\}$. There are 26 elements in this set; it is a finite set. No subset of A, except A itself, can be selected such that its elements can be placed in one-to-one correspondence with the elements of A. This property of infinite sets was first observed by Galileo and pointed out in a work published in 1638. It is used today as a characteristic property which distinguishes infinite sets from finite sets.

Characteristic of an infinite set of elements

Exercises

1 Answer these questions for each of the sets O and E of the last section. Give reasons for your answers.

   (a) Is the set closed under addition?
   (b) Is the set closed under subtraction?
   (c) Is the set closed under multiplication?

2 Which, if any, of these sets, with addition and multiplication, is an integral domain?

   (a) All even integers
   (b) All odd integers
   (c) All positive integers

3 Given the set $B = \{0,1\}$ with addition and multiplication defined by these tables. (Note that the only unusual thing about the operations is that $1 + 1 = 0$.) Is this system an integral domain?

+	0	1
0	0	1
1	1	0

×	0	1
0	0	0
1	0	1

Exercise 3

4   Use Eratosthenes' sieve to find all prime numbers less than 100.

5   Why is 2 the only even prime number?

6   What is the greatest common factor of 15 and 77? What are these two numbers called?

7   What is the greatest common factor of any two prime numbers? Why?

In Exercises 8 to 11, first factor each number into its prime factors, then determine the greatest common factor of all the numbers in the set.

8   24, 28, 100

9   192, 108, 234

10 13, 17, 23

11 78, 105, 110

12 Let the symbol (a,b) mean "find the greatest common factor of a and b," where a and b are in the set N of natural numbers.

   (*a*) Is N closed under the operation (,)?
   (*b*) Is the operation (,) commutative over N?
   (*c*) Is the operation (,) associative over N?

In Exercises 13 to 21, the letters a, b, c, u represent integers. Prove each of the theorems stated.

13 If $a + c = b + c$, then $a = b$. This is the cancellation law for addition.

14 $0 + a = a$.

15 $a \times 1 = a$.

16 If there exists an integer u such that $au = a$ for all nonzero integers a, then $u = 1$.

17 $-(-a) = a$.

18 If a and b are integers, then $-(a - b) = b - a$.

19 $-a = (-1)a$.

20 If $a + b = 0$, then $b = -a$.

21 If $a < b$, then $-a > -b$.

22 Complete the proof for Theorem 4–2.

23 Prove the corollary to Theorem 4–4.

24 Prove Theorem 4–9.

25 On a sheet of paper construct a table similar to that in the figure. Use the letters n, o, and e to indicate whether the given numerals represent *no* number (*n*), an *odd* number (*o*), or an *even* number (*e*). As an illustration, the table is marked for the numeral 31.

26 On a sheet of paper construct another table for the same set of bases used in Exercise 25. Use the numerals 2, 10, 11, 23, 32, 47, 54 as the given numerals, and indicate which of them represent *no* number (*n*), which represent a *prime* number (*p*), and which represent a *composite* number (*c*).

	Base					
Numeral	**two**	**three**	**five**	**seven**	**ten**	**twelve**
1						
2						
10						
11						
31	n	n	e	e	o	o
43						
44						
555						

Exercise 25

INVITATIONS TO EXTENDED STUDY

Prove these two theorems.

1   If $a, b, c \in Z$, then $a + (b - c) = (a + b) - c$.

2   If $a, b, c \in Z$, then $a - (b - c) = (a - b) + c$.

3   Why are 5 and 2 the only prime numbers whose difference is 3?

4   List all the prime numbers less than 1,000.

5   Why will any composite number which is the square of a prime number have three and only three factors?

6   How many distinct factors will a number have if it is the product of three prime numbers?

7   A *perfect number* is a number which is the sum of all its factors except the number itself.   For example, 6 is a perfect number since $6 = 1 + 2 + 3$.   A formula for finding perfect numbers is $2^{n-1}(2^n - 1)$ where n is a positive integer and $2^n - 1$ is a prime number.   Find two more perfect numbers and check them by finding the sum of their factors.

8   Show that, if the formula $2^n - 1$ is to give a prime number, n must be a prime.

9   If the factors of 220, other than the number itself, are added, the sum is 284.   Similarly, if the factors of 284, other than the number itself, are added, the sum is 220.   For this reason these two numbers are called *amicable numbers*.   Verify the above statement concerning the sums of the factors of these two numbers.

10   Verify that 1,184 and 1,210 is another pair of amicable numbers.

CHAPTER 5

the field
of rational
numbers

GUIDELINES FOR CAREFUL STUDY

With the domain of integers the structure of the number system of elementary mathematics is only partially complete. Extensions of the foundation structure of the natural number system were made possible through the introduction of the concepts of additive identity and additive inverse. This led to the identification of the additive identity as the integer zero, the natural numbers as positive integers, and their additive inverses as negative integers. With the introduction of subtraction as the inverse operation to addition a complete facility of operational procedure was established with respect to addition. There still remain limitations and restrictions in the use of multiplication. It is the purpose of Chap. 5 to extend this operation by introducing the notion of a multiplicative inverse, which enables us to enlarge our number system to include the field of rational numbers.

The following questions will be very helpful as guidelines for the careful study of Chap. 5.

1 What is meant by a number system?

2 What are the basic postulates of the natural number system? Of the domain of integers?

3 What are the definitions of addition, subtraction, and multiplication?

4 Why are addition and subtraction said to be inverse operations?

5 Do you have sufficient command of the properties, concepts, and theorems of Chaps. 3 and 4 to be able to use them in the study of division?

6 What is the definition of division?

7 Why are multiplication and division said to be inverse operations?

8 What is a rational number?

9 What is meant by the multiplicative inverse of a nonzero number?

10 When two nonzero numbers a and b, by any process of valid reasoning, are found to be so related that $a \times b = 1$, what can be said about the two numbers?

11 What are the definitions of equality, greater than, less than, addition, subtraction, and multiplication as applied to rational numbers?

12 Why are addition, subtraction, multiplication, and division referred to as rational operations or field operations?

13 What is the division algorithm, and how does place value contribute to better understanding of the algorithm and greater facility in its use?

14 What is the euclidean algorithm, and how is it used in finding the greatest common divisor of two or more numbers?

15 How may division be used to convert a numeral in a given base to an equivalent numeral in another base?

16 What is a number field?

17 What are the properties of the field of rational numbers?

18 What are some of the basic distinctions in the use of a common fraction as the representation of a rational number and as a ratio?

19 Do you have a clear understanding of the terminology of fractions?

20 How does the use of decimal fractions introduce a simplification into the use of fractions?

21 Why can the set of all decimal fractions be considered as a proper subset of all fractions? What are the implications of this fact?

22 Do you have a clear understanding of the terminology of decimal fractions?

23 Can you analyze any common fraction and tell into what kind of decimal fraction it will convert?

24 Can you convert any repeating infinite decimal or any finite decimal into its equivalent common fraction in its lowest terms?

25 Can you operate efficiently using common and decimal fractions?

26   Why can the set of all per cents be considered as a proper subset of decimal fractions? What implications does this relation have toward the study of the topic of percentage?

27   Can you use the percentage formula intelligently as an aid in the analysis and solution of percentage problems?

28   What are some of the precautions that must be observed in using per cents?

INTRODUCTION

In the preceding chapter a more liberal interpretation of the closure property for addition led to the extension from the natural number system to the domain of integers. Since the set of natural numbers (positive integers) is a proper subset of the set of all integers, it was desirable that all characteristics of the old system should be retained in the new. The properties which had characterized addition and multiplication as binary operations of the natural number system thus became guides in the extension of the definitions of the two operations, so that they not only accommodated the demands of the new system but also retained all significant attributes of the old.

As a number system, the domain of integers provides for much less restricted operational procedures than does the natural number system. In spite of this fact, in the domain of integers there still remain limitations on the computational efficiency that is desirable for an adequate number system. In the present chapter a more liberal interpretation of the closure property, as it applies to multiplication, will lead to a further extension of the number system. The new system will provide more freedom and greater efficiency in operational procedure than either the natural number system or the domain of integers and yet will retain all the significance of both systems.

5-1   THE CONCEPT OF RATIONAL NUMBER

In Chaps. 3 and 4 a great deal of emphasis was given to the significance of closure as a fundamental property of the integers under multiplication. If $a \times b = c$, postulate N–1 states that c is a natural number if a and b are natural numbers, and postulate D–1 states that c is an integer if a and b are integers. One is led rather naturally in this case to a question analogous to the question asked on page 80 with reference to addition of natural numbers, namely: Is it true that for any two integers a and b there exists an integer q such that $q \times b = a$? One counter-example will suffice to show that the answer to this question is No. If $a = 3$ and $b = 8$ there exists no integer q such that $q \times 8 = 3$. There are, however, integers a and b such that the integer q does exist. For example, if $a = 16$ and $b = 8$, then $q = 2$ since $2 \times 8 = 16$. When the number q does exist, it is called the *quotient of a divided by b* in accordance with this definition.

Definition 5-1   For any two numbers a and b the ***quotient*** of a di-vided by b $(a \div b)$ is said to be q if and only if $q \times b = a$. The process of finding the quotient is called *division.*

<small>Definition of quotient</small>

In seeking an interpretation of this definition there are two significant cases to consider.

Case I $b = 0$ As a consequence of Theorem 4–3 we know that $q \times 0 = 0$ for *any integer q*. It follows that, under this hypothesis, the only way $q \times b = a$ can be a true statement is for a also to be zero, in which case q can be any integer whatsoever. There is thus no way of determining a unique value for q such that $q \times b = a$ where $b = 0$. It is for this reason that we say that *division by zero is an undefined process.*

Case II $b \neq 0$ At present, under this hypothesis, the definition has significance only where a is a composite number one of whose factors is q. In order to have more freedom of interpretation and use both for multiplication and for the newly defined operation of division, it be-comes necessary to make a further extension of our number system. This extension is to be made not only so that the set of all integers will be a subset of the extended set of numbers but also so that in the new system we shall have closure not only under multiplication and division but also under addition and subtraction. This, of course, means that the definitions of addition, subtraction, and multiplication will have to be extended to apply to the new numbers. Furthermore, these exten-sions will have to be such that, when the operations are restricted to the subset of integers and, further, even to the subset of natural numbers, the new definitions will conform to those already established.

We shall postulate the existence of these new numbers and then pro-ceed to investigate the significant characteristics of the new number system to which they lead.

Postulate 5-1   For any two integers a and b $(b \neq 0)$ there exists a number q such that $q \times b = a$. The number q is called a *rational number.*

We may now combine the concepts of Definition 5–1 and Postulate 5–1 to get a clearer idea of just what is meant by a rational number. In the definition q is identified as the quotient of $a \div b$. Another accepted, and very useful, form for expressing this concept is the fraction $\dfrac{a}{b}$. Postulate 5–1 restricts the existence of such quotients to only those cases in which $b \neq 0$. This fraction is recognizable as the means of expressing a quotient between the integers a and b. Thus we might formulate the explicit definition of a rational number as follows:

Rational number

Definition 5–2   A *rational number* is a number which can be expressed in the form of the quotient of two integers $\dfrac{a}{b}$ where $b \neq 0$.

Note that the definition does not state that the number *must* be, but only that it *can* be, expressed as the quotient of two integers. A specific illustration is the fact that the integers are rational numbers since each integer can be expressed in the form of the quotient of two integers. For example,

$$3 = \frac{3}{1} \qquad -5 = \frac{-5}{1} \qquad 1{,}000 = \frac{1{,}000}{1} \qquad -600 = \frac{-600}{1}$$

Integers a proper subset of the rational numbers   Thus the set of integers and the set of natural numbers are proper subsets of the set of rational numbers. A slightly more involved illustration of the nature of a rational number is

$$\frac{3 - 3\sqrt{3}}{2 - 2\sqrt{3}} = \frac{3(1 - \sqrt{3})}{2(1 - \sqrt{3})} = \frac{3}{2}$$

The given number is certainly not in the form of the quotient of two integers, but it can be put in that form. Such illustrations can be given largely at will.

It has been established that the set of natural numbers is a proper subset of the set of integers, which is a proper subset of the set of rational numbers. From this it follows that whatever might be the definitions of addition, subtraction, and multiplication for the set of rational numbers, they must be such that they conform to the definitions and properties already established for integers (D–1 to D–8, page 95) and for natural numbers (N–1 to N–8, page 70). The properties of equality (E–1 to E–5, page 53) also apply. As an immediate consequence we have that all postulates previously assumed and all theorems previously proved may be restated for rational numbers except in those cases where the intrinsic nature of any hypothesis is such that it restricts the conclusions either to integers or to natural numbers. An illustration of such a situation is the postulate of finite induction (N–8). The nature of this postulate is such that it relates *only* to natural numbers. Thus, in the domain of integers or the field of rational numbers, it applies only to the subset of positive integers. Space limitations prevent formal restatement of these postulates and theorems in the specific context of rational numbers. They will be used, however, in appropriate places as established authority for deductions made, leaving to the reader the substitution of "rational numbers" for "natural numbers" or "integers" as the case may be.

Definition 5-3   Two rational numbers $\frac{a}{b}$ and $\frac{c}{d}$ are said to be equal if   Equality

and only if $ad = bc$.

Example   The rational numbers $\frac{3}{4}$ and $\frac{15}{20}$ are equal since $3 \times 20 = 60$ and $4 \times 15 = 60$.

The rational numbers $\frac{3}{4}$ and $\frac{5}{7}$ are not equal, since $3 \times 7 = 21$ and $4 \times 5 = 20$, and $21 \neq 20$.

The equality of rational numbers involves a concept of equality which is basically different from that used in dealing with natural numbers and integers. For two natural numbers or two integers, $a = b$ carries the meaning "a is the same as b." For two rational numbers this is not the case. For example, $\frac{3}{4}$ and $\frac{15}{20}$ are two distinct rational numbers. So $\frac{3}{4} = \frac{15}{20}$ cannot be read "$\frac{3}{4}$ is the same as $\frac{15}{20}$"; but the definition of equality states that they are equal since $3 \times 20 = 4 \times 15$, or since the integer 3×20 is the same as the integer 4×15. Thus, for rational numbers, equality carries the meaning of *equal in value*, or *equivalence*, and not that of identity of symbols.

Under this concept of equality, rational numbers may be grouped   Equivalence
into *equivalence classes*, that is, sets of rational numbers which are   classes
all equal in value, such as

$$\left\{ \frac{1}{2}, \frac{2}{4}, \frac{3}{6}, \frac{4}{8}, \cdots \right\}$$

$$\left\{ \frac{3}{4}, \frac{6}{8}, \frac{9}{12}, \frac{12}{16}, \frac{15}{20}, \cdots \right\}$$

Thus $\frac{3}{4}$ and $\frac{15}{20}$ belong to the same equivalence class.

Definition 5-4   If $bd > 0$, the rational number $\frac{a}{b}$ is said to be greater   Order

than $\frac{c}{d}$, $\frac{a}{b} > \frac{c}{d}$, if and only if $ad > bc$. Similarly, for $bd > 0$, $\frac{a}{b} < \frac{c}{d}$ if and only if $ad < bc$.

In the example, $\frac{3}{4} > \frac{5}{7}$ since $3 \cdot 7 > 4 \cdot 5$.

Although Definition 5–4 might seem to imply that rational numbers can be ordered only if their denominators have the same sign, this is not the case. The definition is adequate for the ordering of all rational numbers, since any rational number may be written so that its denominator is positive (see page 111).

These definitions obviously meet the requirement of conformity for integers and natural numbers.

Addition   **Definition 5–5**   The sum of the rational numbers $\frac{a}{b}$ and $\frac{c}{d}$ is $\frac{ad + bc}{bd}$.

$$\left(\frac{a}{b} + \frac{c}{d} = \frac{ad + bc}{bd} \right).$$

This definition guarantees closure since $ad + bc$ and bd are integers. Why? Also $bd \neq 0$. Why? Furthermore, if $\frac{a}{b}$ and $\frac{c}{d}$ should be the integers $\frac{a}{1}$ and $\frac{c}{1}$, this definition gives $\frac{a + c}{1}$ as their sum. This is equivalent to the definition of addition of integers as given in Chap. 4.

Addition is commutative. By definition, $\frac{c}{d} + \frac{a}{b} = \frac{cb + da}{db}$. Since a, b, c, and d are integers, it follows that $cb + da = bc + ad = ad + bc$, and $db = bd$. Why? Therefore

$$\frac{c}{d} + \frac{a}{b} = \frac{a}{b} + \frac{c}{d} \qquad \text{Why?}$$

While it is a bit longer, it is not a very involved argument to show that the associative property holds under this definition of addition.

Occasionally the sum of two fractions (rational numbers) is obtained by the incorrect formula $\frac{a}{b} + \frac{c}{d} = \frac{a + c}{b + d}$. It is interesting to note that even with this incorrect definition, addition of rational numbers would have the properties of closure, associativity, and commutativity. The definition, however, does not meet two other very important restrictions on the definitions of the operations to be applied to any set of numbers.

1   The definition of an operation must result in a well-defined operation. As an illustration that this incorrect definition does not meet this condition, consider the two sums $\frac{2}{3} + \frac{5}{7}$ and $\frac{4}{6} + \frac{5}{7}$. Since $\frac{2}{3} = \frac{4}{6}$ it follows that, if the operation of addition is well-defined, the two sums must be equivalent. However, by the incorrect definition, we get

$$\frac{2}{3} + \frac{5}{7} = \frac{2+5}{3+7} = \frac{7}{10} \quad \text{and} \quad \frac{4}{6} + \frac{5}{7} = \frac{4+5}{6+7} = \frac{9}{13} \qquad \frac{7}{10} \neq \frac{9}{13}$$

since $7 \times 13 \neq 10 \times 9$. The correct definition gives equivalent sums.

2   *The definition of any given operation must not introduce inconsistencies in working with numbers.* Attention has been called to the fact that the correct definition of addition applied to the rational numbers $\frac{a}{1} + \frac{c}{1}$ gives for the sum $\frac{a+c}{1}$. This is in agreement with the result expected for the sum of the integers a and c. The incorrect definition being discussed gives the sum $\frac{a}{1} + \frac{c}{1} = \frac{a+c}{1+1} = \frac{a+c}{2}$, thus introducing an inconsistency which cannot be tolerated.

Definition 5-6   The product of the rational numbers $\frac{a}{b}$ and $\frac{c}{d}$ is $\frac{ac}{bd}$.   Multiplication $\left(\frac{a}{b} \times \frac{c}{d} = \frac{ac}{bd}\right).$

Definition 5-7   Subtraction of two rational numbers is the inverse   Subtraction operation to the addition of two rational numbers. $\frac{a}{b} - \frac{c}{d} = \frac{e}{f}$ if and only if $\frac{a}{b} = \frac{c}{d} + \frac{e}{f}$.

By analogy with integers, $-\frac{c}{d}$ is the symbol for the additive inverse   The additive inverse of $\frac{c}{d}$. Since $\frac{c}{d} + \left(\frac{-c}{d}\right) = \frac{cd + d(-c)}{d \cdot d} = \frac{d[c + (-c)]}{d \cdot d} = 0$, $\frac{-c}{d}$ will be used interchangeably with $-\frac{c}{d}$. It can now be proved, just as in the case of integers (Theorem 4–1), that $\frac{a}{b} - \frac{c}{d} = \frac{a}{b} + \left(\frac{-c}{d}\right)$. It thus follows that the difference obtained by subtracting $\frac{c}{d}$ from $\frac{a}{b}$ may be symbolized by the formula $\frac{a}{b} - \frac{c}{d} = \frac{ad - bc}{bd}$.

We are now in a position to examine a bit more carefully the process of division and the rational number q, presented in Definition 5–1 and Postulate 5–1. From the postulate there exists a rational number q such that $q \times b = a$ where b and a are integers with $b \neq 0$. From the definition this number is the quotient of $a \div b$. Also recall that another symbol introduced to represent this quotient is the fraction $\frac{a}{b}$. We shall use $a \div b$ and $\frac{a}{b}$ interchangeably at times.   There are two distinct cases to consider.

Case I $a = b$ Under this hypothesis $q \times b = a$ becomes $q \times a = a$. Since, by the commutative property, $q \times a = a \times q$, we have by properties E–2 and E–3 that $a \times q = a$.   It follows from this fact by Exercise 16 (page 102) that $q = 1$.   Incidentally, note that this identifies the integer 1 as a rational number.   It may be expressed as the quotient $\frac{a}{a}$ where a is any integer $\neq 0$.

Case II $a \neq b$ Here there are two hypotheses on a which we must examine.

Hypothesis 1 $a = 1$ Under this condition $q \times b = a$ becomes $q \times b = 1$.   Such familiar considerations as "two halves make a whole" $(2 \times \frac{1}{2} = 1)$, "three thirds make a whole" $(3 \times \frac{1}{3} = 1)$, and "four fourths make a whole" $(4 \times \frac{1}{4} = 1)$ furnish a strong intuitive background for the acceptance of the following special version of Postulate 5–1.

The multiplicative inverse

Postulate 5–2   **For every rational number $b \neq 0$ there exists a rational number $\frac{1}{b}$ such that $b \times \frac{1}{b} = 1$.   The number $\frac{1}{b}$ is called the *reciprocal* of b, or the *multiplicative inverse* of b.   Another symbol frequently used instead of $\frac{1}{b}$ is b^{-1}.**

Notice, incidentally, that in this case $q = \frac{1}{b}$ is indeed the quotient of $1 \div b$, as stated in Definition 5–1, since $q \times b = \frac{1}{b} \times b = b \times \frac{1}{b} = 1$. Furthermore, $\frac{1}{b} \neq 0$.   For, if $\frac{1}{b} = 0$ then $b \times \frac{1}{b} = b \times 0 = 0$ by Theorem 4–3.   This is impossible since $b \times \frac{1}{b} = 1$ by Postulate 5–2.

Hypothesis 2 $a \neq 1$ Under this condition we can appeal to the properties of multiplication to assist us in getting an interpretation of $q = a \div b$.

Division

Theorem 5–1   If a and b are two integers such that $b \neq 0$, then
$$a \times \frac{1}{b} = a \div b.$$

Hypothesis a, b are integers; $b \neq 0$.

Conclusion $a \times \dfrac{1}{b} = a \div b$.

Since a and b are integers and $b \neq 0$ we know that $a, b, \dfrac{1}{b}$, and $\dfrac{a}{b}$ are rational numbers. This means that we can use the properties of integers or rational numbers in dealing with a and b and the properties of rational numbers with $\dfrac{a}{b}$ and $\dfrac{1}{b}$.

We are to prove that the product of the integer a by the multiplicative inverse of the nonzero integer b is the rational number $\dfrac{a}{b}$, or the quotient of $a \div b$. From Definition 5–1 we know that any number q can be the quotient of $a \div b$ if and only if $q \times b = a$. This means that if we are to be able to prove that $a \times \dfrac{1}{b}$ is the quotient $a \div b$, we must be able to establish that $\left(a \times \dfrac{1}{b} \right) \times b = a$.

Proof

Statements	*Reasons*
The rational number $\dfrac{1}{b}$ exists	Postulate 5–2
$a \times \dfrac{1}{b}$ is a rational number	Closure
$\left(a \times \dfrac{1}{b} \right) \times b = a \times \left(\dfrac{1}{b} \times b \right)$	Associative property
$\left(a \times \dfrac{1}{b} \right) \times b = a \times 1$	Multiplicative inverse
$\left(a \times \dfrac{1}{b} \right) \times b = a$	Multiplicative identity

Since $a \times \dfrac{1}{b}$ is a rational number q such that

$q \times b = a$, it follows that $a \times \dfrac{1}{b} = a \div b$ Definition 5–1

Corollary   If a, b and c are any three integers such that $c \neq 0$, then $(a + b) \div c = (a \div c) + (b \div c)$.

Theorem 5–2 is proved as an important illustration of the possibility of extending to rational numbers theorems previously proved for integers. It is to be noted that the only essential difference in the statements and proofs of Theorems 5–1 and 5–2 is the replacement of "integers" by "rational numbers."

Theorem 5-2 If r and s are any two rational numbers such that $s \neq 0$, then $r \times \dfrac{1}{s} = r \div s$.

Hypothesis r and s are rational numbers; $s \neq 0$.

Conclusion $r \times \dfrac{1}{s} = r \div s$.

Proof

Statements	*Reasons*
The rational number $\dfrac{1}{s}$ exists	Postulate 5–2
$r \times \dfrac{1}{s}$ is a rational number	Closure
$\left(r \times \dfrac{1}{s} \right) \times s = r \times \left(\dfrac{1}{s} \times s \right)$	Associative property
$\left(r \times \dfrac{1}{s} \right) \times s = r \times 1$	Multiplicative inverse
$\left(r \times \dfrac{1}{s} \right) \times s = r$	Multiplicative identity
Since $\left(r \times \dfrac{1}{s} \right)$ is a rational number q such that $q \times s = r$, it follows that $r \times \dfrac{1}{s} = r \div s$	Definition 5–1

These two theorems are indeed the authority for the familiar rule of elementary arithmetic: In division you invert the divisor and multiply.

Just as subtraction was defined as the inverse operation of addition, now division is defined as the inverse operation of multiplication. If $\dfrac{a}{b}$ and $\dfrac{c}{d}$ are any two rational numbers such that $\dfrac{c}{d} \neq 0$, then

$$\left(\frac{a}{b} \times \frac{c}{d} \right) \div \frac{c}{d} = \frac{a}{b} \qquad \text{and} \qquad \left(\frac{a}{b} \div \frac{c}{d} \right) \times \frac{c}{d} = \frac{a}{b}$$

The proof of these facts is left as an exercise (see Exercise 20, page 115). How do the facts presented here emphasize the fact that the multiplication tables you constructed in previous chapters can be used as tables giving the basic division facts?

Exercises

In Exercises 1 to 9, use the rational numbers $\dfrac{2}{3}, \dfrac{4}{5}$, and $\dfrac{6}{7}$ to illustrate the principles stated for rational numbers.

1   The rational numbers are closed under addition.
2   The rational numbers are closed under multiplication.
3   Addition of rational numbers is associative.
4   Addition of rational numbers is commutative.
5   Multiplication of rational numbers is associative.
6   Multiplication of rational numbers is commutative.
7   For rational numbers multiplication is distributive over addition.

8   If $\frac{a}{b}$ is any rational number, then $\frac{-a}{b}$ is its additive inverse.

9   If $\frac{a}{b}$ is any rational number other than 0, then $\frac{b}{a}$ is its multiplica-

   tive inverse.

10–18   Use the symbols $\frac{a}{b}$, $\frac{c}{d}$, and $\frac{e}{f}$ where $b \neq 0$, $d \neq 0$, and $f \neq 0$,

   to prove that the statements of Exercises 1 to 9 are true for all rational numbers.

19   Use $\frac{2}{3}$ and $\frac{5}{7}$ to illustrate the two statements

$$\left(\frac{a}{b} \times \frac{c}{d}\right) \div \frac{c}{d} = \frac{a}{b} \quad \text{and} \quad \left(\frac{a}{b} \div \frac{c}{d}\right) \times \frac{c}{d} = \frac{a}{b}$$

20   Prove the general statement: If $\frac{a}{b}$ and $\frac{c}{d}$ are any two rational num-

   bers with $\frac{c}{d} \neq 0$, then

$$\left(\frac{a}{b} \times \frac{c}{d}\right) \div \frac{c}{d} = \frac{a}{b} \quad \text{and} \quad \left(\frac{a}{b} \div \frac{c}{d}\right) \times \frac{c}{d} = \frac{a}{b}$$

21   Show that the rational numbers, with addition and multiplication
   as defined here, form an integral domain.

22   Show that each of the numbers 0, 5, and $\frac{2}{3}$ can be written as a

   rational number in infinitely many ways.

5–2   THE NATURE OF DIVISION

Division has been defined as the process of finding a number q such
that $q \times b = a$ for any two numbers a and b with $b \neq 0$. This definition is general in its connotation in that it applies to all numbers—
natural numbers, integers, rational numbers, and other types to be
introduced later.   Furthermore, it emphasizes the important inverse
relationship of division to multiplication and also incorporates the
simpler and more concrete concepts of finding how many times one
integer is contained as a factor in another integer; of finding a number
which is contained in the dividend as many times as unity is contained

in the divisor; of separating a large group into a number of groups of equal size; of finding how many smaller groups of equal size are contained in a larger group; of finding how many times a smaller number may be subtracted from a larger number; or of finding a number which has the same relation to unity that the dividend has to the divisor.

Terms used in division

The terms *dividend* and *divisor* come from the Latin expressions *numerus dividendus* (number to be divided) and *numerus divisor* (dividing or divider number). As in the cases of addition, subtraction, and multiplication, the word *numerus* gradually disappeared through technical usage and translation. In early practice the word "result" was used to indicate the answer to the actual division process. Other terms used at one time or another are "product," "part," "exiens," "outcome," and "quotient," with "quotient" finally winning general approval.† The term "remainder," used to designate that part left over in cases of uneven division, has likewise won general approval over such words as *numerus residuus* and *residuus*.‡ The symbol ÷ was first used as a symbol to indicate subtraction.§ The early symbols for division were varied just as were the symbols for multiplication. Abbreviations, words, literal symbols, a straight horizontal or slanting line, one dot, a colon, one or two parentheses, as in 6)30 or 6)30(, and variations of the form $6\overline{)30}$, have been some of the more popular symbols used to indicate division. Of these we have retained the following: the symbol ÷, the colon, both the horizontal and the slanting line, the parentheses, and the form $\overline{)}$. The colon is used primarily to emphasize the ratio concept of division, and the horizontal or slanting line to emphasize the fractional aspect.

5–3 THE DIVISION ALGORITHM

The division process, historically, has been the most difficult of the elementary computational processes. This fact is not hard to comprehend, for in the words of Pacioli,¶ "if a man can divide well, everything else is easy, for all the rest is involved therein." From the struggle for efficiency in operation our present algorithm has evolved as the one which seems to combine most effectively the benefits of place value with simplicity in recording the results of the incidental operations necessary to carry out the division.

† David Eugene Smith, "History of Mathematics," vol. II, p. 130, Ginn and Company, Boston, 1925.
‡ *Ibid.*, p. 132.
§ F. Cajori, "A History of Mathematical Notations," vol. I, pp. 240–244, The Open Court Publishing Company, La Salle, Ill., 1928.
¶ David Eugene Smith, *op. cit.*, p. 132.

The simplest of all methods of historical significance is the one we use today as a shortcut in cases of division with one-digit and simple two-digit divisors (formerly referred to as short division). The basic techniques of this method have remained the same, and there has been only slight change in form. The oldest form of division is probably that of the Egyptians in which they used an adaptation of duplation and mediation for multiplication. Another method of interest with a limited amount of merit is the repiego method. As in the case of multiplication, this method employs the principle of decomposition of one of the numbers—in this case the divisor—into simple factors. For example, the quotient of $2,212 \div 28$ can be obtained very simply by thinking of 28 as 7×4 and then considering either the continued division of $(2,212 \div 7) \div 4$ or that of $(2,212 \div 4) \div 7$. The merit of this method lies in the possibility of reducing to simple oral division a problem which otherwise would require the recording of incidental steps in arriving at the desired result.

Prior to the seventeenth century the most popular form for division seemed to be that known as the galley, *batello*, or scratch method. It is illustrated by the example of Fig. 5–1. The exercise is one of finding that $10,282 \div 75$ gives a quotient of 137 with a remainder of 7. The complete algorithm is at the extreme right. This is a three-step division, and each step is presented and analyzed from the left. The partial quotients as well as the complete quotient are shown in color. The divisor (75) is written directly under the first partial dividend (102). The quotient (1) for this step is then determined and written in the place provided at the right. Then we have $1 \times 7 = 7$, which is subtracted from 10. The 7 and the 10 are then scratched and 3, the remainder of $10 - 7$, is recorded directly above the stricken 10. Next, $1 \times 5 = 5$; the 5 is subtracted from 32 and the 32 and the 5 are

FIGURE 5–1   The galley (scratch) method.

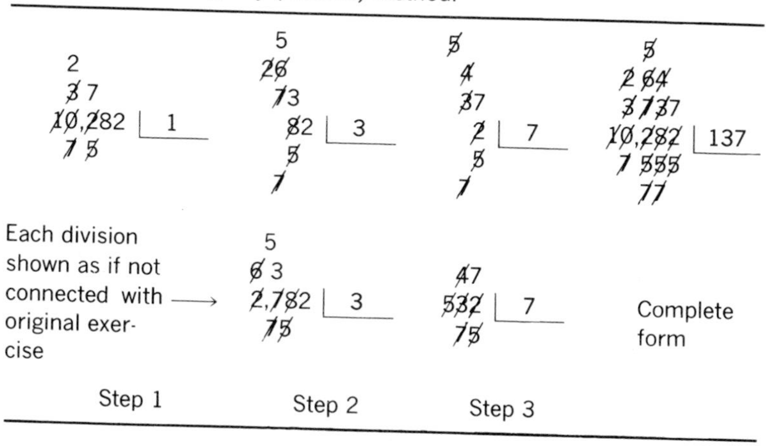

Each division shown as if not connected with ⟶ original exercise

Step 1   Step 2   Step 3

```
        137                       137
  75 | 10,282            75 | 10,282
       7                       7 5
       3 2                     2 7
         5                     2 78
       2 78                    2 25
       2 10                      53
         68                     532
         15                     525
        532                       7
        490
         42
         35
          7

      Form A               Form B
                          (a danda)
```

FIGURE 5-2   Early variations of modern method.

scratched as the remainder 27 is recorded. If all scratched numbers are removed and the process repeated for the resultant dividend (2,782), the second step will take the form shown. Here we have $3 \times 7 = 21$, $27 - 21 = 6$; $3 \times 5 = 15$, $68 - 15 = 53$. The dividend for step 3 is then 532. Then $7 \times 7 = 49$, $53 - 49 = 4$; $7 \times 5 = 35$, $42 - 35 = 7$. The algorithm derived its popularity from its effective adaptation to both sand reckoning and abacal computation.

Historians have been unable to fix an exact date for the origin of the algorithm we use today. The first appearance in printed form seems to have been in an arithmetic, by Calandri, published in 1491.† Two forms bearing strong resemblance to it are illustrated in Fig. 5–2 by carrying out the same division as that used to illustrate the scratch method. Form A, used in the fourteenth century by Maximus Planudes, might be described as a variation of the scratch method in which the numbers used were not scratched. Form B, which dates to the fifteenth century, is known as the *a danda* (by giving) method. It derives its name from the fact that, at each step, an additional digit from the dividend is "given" to the remainder to derive a new partial dividend for the succeeding step. This form is definitely recognizable as a forerunner of the form we use today, the only difference being that the remainder at each step is copied before the new digit is "given" to it. An abbreviated form of the *a danda* method is illustrated in Fig. 5–3. The abbreviation is due to the fact that all partial products are omitted. This modification, which requires somewhat more mental effort than the form we use, seems to be in current use in some South American countries.

† *Ibid.*, p. 141.

```
          137
    ┌─────────
75 │ 10,282
    │  2 78
    │    532
    │      7
```

FIGURE 5–3   South American method.

These forms are but a selected few of the many different patterns which have been of historical significance in the struggle to overcome the difficulties incident to the implication of the division algorithm. In fact, an examination of arithmetic texts in current use in the United States will reveal variations, each carrying some argument in its favor over the others in use.

The division algorithm guarantees that division by an integer different from zero can always be accomplished. While this all-important theorem can be proved, its proof would carry us beyond the scope of this text. We shall, therefore, state it as a postulate.

Postulate 5–3   The Division Algorithm   For any given integers a and b, with $b > 0$, there exist unique integers q and r such that $a = qb + r$ and $0 \leq r < b$.

The division algorithm

In this algorithm a is called the *dividend,* b is the *divisor,* q is the *quotient,* and r the *remainder.* The condition $0 \leq r < b$ simply states that the remainder may be 0, in which case we have what we call an *exact* or *even division;* or it may be greater than 0, in which case it will be less than b. Attention should be called at this point to an incorrect interpretation of the remainder, sometimes found in elementary texts. The division algorithm ensures the existence of an *integral* remainder which may be greater than or equal to 0. At times one will find in elementary texts instructions worded somewhat after this pattern: Find the quotient $8 \overline{)189}$ and express the remainder as a fraction. There is nothing essentially incorrect in the statement of this exercise. The error is in the implications as to the answer expected, as inferred from supplementary instructions and illustrations. In the division of Fig. 5–4 the answer expected for the result, under the above instructions, is $23\frac{5}{8}$.

```
          23
    ┌─────────
 8 │ 189
    │  16
    │  ─────
    │   29
    │   24
    │   ───
    │    5
```

FIGURE 5–4

The fraction $\frac{5}{8}$ is supposed to be "the remainder expressed as a fraction." It is not. The remainder is the integer 5. It can be expressed in fraction form as $\frac{5}{1}$, or some element of its equivalence class such as

The complete quotient

$\frac{10}{2}$ or $\frac{15}{3}$, but not as $\frac{5}{8}$. The number $23\frac{5}{8}$ is the *complete quotient* obtained by dividing 189 by 8 since $8 \times 23\frac{5}{8} = 189$.

It is also significant that the two basic functions of the division process are to partition a large group into smaller groups and to compare the sizes of groups. In *partition division* the problem is to determine how many objects there will be in each of several small groups when a large group is broken up. "There are 27 people who plan to make a trip and there are 6 cars to accommodate them. On an average, how many people will there be to each car?" $27 \div 6 = 4$ with a remainder of 3. This answer is to be interpreted as meaning there will be an average of 4 people to a car with 3 people left over, which means that at least one car will have to accommodate more than the average share. In *meas-*

Two forms of division

urement division, the sizes of two groups are compared. "There are 27 people who plan to make a trip and only 6 people can be accommodated by one car. How many cars will be needed?" Here the result of the division is to be interpreted as meaning that there are 4 carloads with 3 people left over, so an additional car will have to be secured if all people are to make the trip.

5-4   THE EUCLIDEAN ALGORITHM

In Chap. 4 you were introduced to the concept of the greatest common factor (g.c.f.) of two or more integers. It is the largest integer which is a common factor of the given integers. As a consequence of Definition 5-1, any factor of an integer is recognized as a divisor of the integer. Thus the concept of *greatest common divisor (g.c.d.)* is synonymous with that of greatest common factor (g.c.f.). The procedure used in Chap. 4 for finding the greatest common factor of two numbers a and b consisted in breaking each number down into its prime factors and then selecting all those factors which were common to both a and b. The product of these common factors then was the sought-for g.c.f. For example, the g.c.f. of 390 and 462 is 6 since $390 = 2 \times 3 \times 5 \times 13$ and $462 = 2 \times 3 \times 7 \times 11$. Thus $6 = 2 \times 3$ is the g.c.f. This scheme works very well for small numbers whose prime factors are readily recognizable, but not so well in other cases. In a later chapter (pages 182–187) we shall discover means for recognizing certain cases of factorability.

Example   Find the g.c.f. of 2,958 and 3,162.

The primes 2 and 3 are rather easily recognizable as factors of each of the given integers.

$2,958 = 2 \times 3 \times 493$
$3,162 = 2 \times 3 \times 527$

There is no simple way of determining whether 493 and 527 are prime numbers or, if not prime, whether they have any common factors. Actually they are factorable and each has 17 as a factor. Thus the complete factorization of the two numbers is

$2,958 = 2 \times 3 \times 17 \times 29$
$3,162 = 2 \times 3 \times 17 \times 31$

From Eratosthenes' sieve 17, 29, and 31 are seen to be primes. Therefore the g.c.f. of 2,958 and 3,162 $= 2 \times 3 \times 17 = 102$.

In cases, such as that of this example, where prime factorization is difficult, the division algorithm offers a simple means of finding the g.c.f. of any two integers. The process used is known as the *euclidean algorithm*, which we shall postulate. Since division, rather than factorization, is the process used, the result is called the greatest common divisor (g.c.d.) rather than the greatest common factor (g.c.f.).

Postulate 5-4   The Euclidean Algorithm   **To find the greatest common divisor of two positive integers, divide the larger integer by the smaller one. Use the remainder of this division as the new divisor and the former divisor as the new dividend. Continue this process of dividing the old divisor by the new remainder until the remainder is zero. The last divisor used is the g.c.d. of the given integers.**   The euclidean algorithm

The division algorithm is the authority for this process, which is illustrated in Fig. 5–5, where we find the g.c.d. of the two integers 2,958

	Step 1	Step 2	Step 3
	1		
	2,958 ⟌ 3,162		
	2,958	14	
	204	2,958	
		2 04	
		918	
		816	2
		102	204
			204
			0

FIGURE 5-5   The euclidean algorithm.

and 3,162 of the previous example. In the first step, for example, $3,162 = 1 \times 2,958 + 204$. It is not difficult to see upon inspection here that any common divisor of 204 and 2,958 will also be a divisor of 3,162. Therefore, the g.c.d. of 204 and 2,958 will also be the g.c.d. of 2,958 and 3,162. In the second step $2,958 = 14 \times 204 + 102$. The same reasoning exhibits that the g.c.d. of 102 and 2,958 is also the g.c.d. of 204 and 2,958, which has already been established as the g.c.d. of 2,958 and 3,162. The remainder in the next division is 0. Therefore, $204 = 2 \times 102$. Thus 102 is the g.c.d. of the given numbers 2,958 and 3,162.

5-5   CONVERSION TO DIFFERENT BASES BY DIVISION

In Chap. 3 attention was given to the technique of converting, by multiplication, from numerals in one base to equivalent numerals in another base. The division algorithm provides a means for making similar conversions by using division as the technique.

First, recall that in base **b**, the digital symbols used in writing any numeral are $0, 1, \ldots, b - 1$. Secondly, as a consequence of the division algorithm, these same numerals represent the only possible remainders when any integer is divided by the integer b. These two facts combine to give us the technique for conversions to a new base by division, which is illustrated by the following example.

Example   Use division to carry out these three conversions:

1   Convert **11004—five** to its equivalent numeral in base ten.

2   Convert the resulting numeral in base ten to its equivalent numeral in base **twelve**.

3   Check the entire process by converting the resultant numeral in base **twelve** to its equivalent numeral in base **five**.

Each of these conversions is carried out in Fig. 5–6. The computations are all in the base in which the numeral is given. In the left column, the question is basically: How many tens are there in **11004?** Since the numeral is written in base **five** it is necessary to divide in this base. Hence the divisor, ten, is written as **20**, since ten is 2 fives + 0 ones. The division shows that in **11004** there are **300** tens with a remainder of **4**. This remainder thus becomes the digital symbol in ones position in the numeral in base ten. The division is continued to determine how many tens there are in **300—five**. There are **12** tens with a remainder of **10**. Since the computation is in base **five**, **10** means "1 five." Therefore **10—five → 5—ten**, which becomes the digital symbol in tens position in the numeral in base ten. Similarly, **12—five**

→ 7—ten, which is the digital symbol in hundreds position in the numeral in base ten.

Observation of the process reveals that the division is carried out until the final quotient figure is zero, each remainder being recorded in the notation of the new base. Then the numeral in the new base is obtained by reading the remainders in the reverse order to that in which they were obtained.

This same process is repeated in each of the two remaining bases, ten and **twelve.**

Since one can convert from any given base to any other base either by multiplication or by division, either process may be used to check the other. Also, as in the example, any conversion may be checked by the same process as that used in the conversion.

FIGURE 5–6   Conversion of numerals to different bases.   In each column the computation is carried out in the base indicated at the top of the column.   The arrows which connect two columns are to be read "transforms into."   For example, in the conversion from base **five** to base ten we have 4—**five** transforms into 4—ten; **10—five** transforms into 5—ten; and **12—five** transforms into 7—ten.

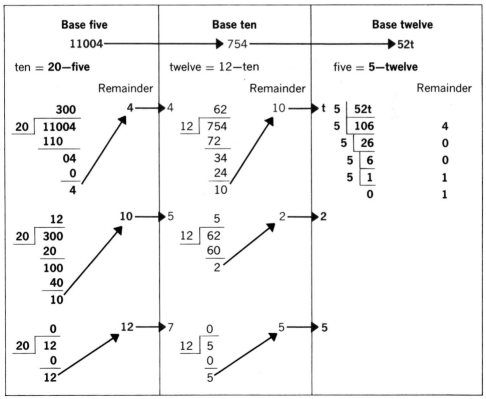

Example   Use division to convert 2,158—ten into its equivalent numeral in base **twelve**. Check the work by using multiplication to convert the resultant numeral into its equivalent numeral in base ten.

The necessary computation for this example is outlined in Fig. 5–7. The reader should make sure that the details of each operation are understood and can be supplied. It should be recognized that there are other combinations of the two processes by which such a conversion and its check can be accomplished.

Exercises

1   When and for what purposes do we divide?
2   Why is division by zero an undefined process?
3   How are multiplication and division related?
4   Why can the multiplication tables you constructed in Chap. 3 be used also as tables of the basic division facts?

FIGURE 5–7   Conversion from base ten to base **twelve**.
Step 1: $2,158 \div 12 = 179$ with remainder 10 which transforms into **t—twelve**
Step 2: $179 \div 12 = 14$ with remainder $11 \longrightarrow$ **e—twelve**
Step 3: $14 \div 12 = 1$ with remainder $2 \longrightarrow$ **2—twelve**
Step 4: $1 \div 12 = 0$ with remainder $1 \longrightarrow$ **1—twelve**
Step 5: To check—**12et—twelve** $\longrightarrow 1(12^3) + 2(12^2) + 11(12) + 10$—ten
Step 6: To get the numeral in base ten the indicated operations are performed in base ten

Base ten		Base **twelve**
	Remainder Digit symbol	
Step 1 12 $\lfloor$2,158		The symbol in
Step 2 12 $\lfloor$179	10 $\longrightarrow$ t	base **twelve** is
Step 3 12 $\lfloor$14	11 $\longrightarrow$ e	**12et**; read "one-
Step 4 12 $\lfloor$1	2 $\longrightarrow$ 2	two-e-te"
0	1 $\longrightarrow$ 1	

2,158—(ten) $\longrightarrow$ **12et—(twelve)**

Check

Base ten	Base **twelve**
	12et means:
Step 5 $1(12^3) + 2(12^2) + 11(12) + 10 = \longleftarrow 1(10^3) + 2(10^2) + e(10) + t$	
Step 6 $\begin{cases} 1(1,728) + 2(144) + 11(12) + 10 = \\ 1,728 + 288 + 132 + 10 = 2,158 \end{cases}$	
2,158—(ten) $\longleftarrow$ **12et = (twelve)**	

5 Use the division algorithm as a guide in constructing a rule for checking the result of any division.

6 Carry out these divisions and then use the rule of Exercise 5 to check each one.

(a) $35\overline{)2{,}467}$ (b) $117\overline{)24{,}531}$ (c) $403\overline{)71{,}245}$

7 Construct a scheme for checking division by casting out nines. (*Hint:* Use Exercise 5 as a guide.)

8 Check each of the divisions of Exercise 6 by casting out nines.

9 How can division be checked by using subtraction?

10 Carry out these divisions and then check each one by subtraction.

(a) $52\overline{)164}$ (b) $315\overline{)1{,}375}$ (c) $508\overline{)1{,}339}$

11 Use the repiego method to find each of these quotients orally:

(a) $1{,}248 \div 24$ (b) $2{,}205 \div 21$ (c) $3{,}735 \div 45$

12 Use these examples to illustrate the importance of place value in division:

(a) $6{,}798 \div 33$ (b) $9{,}672 \div 18$ (c) $41{,}935 \div 321$

13 Express the results of Exercise 12 in the form of the division algorithm.

14 Break each of the given integers into its prime factors and then find the greatest common divisor in each example.

(a) 20, 35, 75   (b) 42, 56, 70
(c) 66, 150, 210, 300   (d) 132, 165, 231, 297

15 Use the euclidean algorithm to find the greatest common divisor of each pair of integers.

(a) 1,785, 2,590   (b) 3,927, 7,161
(c) 9,666, 206,745   (d) 22,134, 32,538

16 Use the euclidean algorithm to find the greatest common divisor in each set of integers.

(a) 814, 1,295, 1,517
(b) 29,172, 30,420, 185,484
(c) 2,565, 7,315, 11,115, 21,615
(d) 8,283, 9,789, 21,335, 38,905

17 How can the euclidean algorithm be used to determine whether or not two integers are relatively prime?

18 Find these quotients in base **twelve:**

(a) **724** $\div$ **42**   (b) **6028** $\div$ **3t**   (c) **t4e7** $\div$ **e3**

19 Find these quotients in base **verto:**

(a) $\triangle\square\perp \div \perp I$ (b) $\perp I 0 \square \div \square \triangle$ (c) $\square\perp\perp\triangle \div I\perp\triangle$

20   Find these quotients in base **eight:**

(*a*) **3456 ÷ 21**   (*b*) **7065 ÷ 57**   (*c*) **70204 ÷ 316**

21   Make each of the following conversions by division. Check each conversion by division.

(*a*) 3,043—ten to an equivalent symbol in base **twelve**
(*b*) **5122**—twelve to an equivalent symbol in base ten
(*c*) **5122**—twelve to an equivalent symbol in base **five**
(*d*) **5122**—eight to an equivalent symbol in base **twelve**
(*e*) 4,023—ten to an equivalent symbol in base **verto**
(*f*) ⊥0□△l—**verto** to an equivalent symbol in base **eight**

22   Construct a division table for base **seven** and then use it to convert each of the following symbols as indicated. Check each conversion by multiplication.

(*a*) **5264**—seven to base ten, base **five**, and base **twelve**
(*b*) **30515**—seven to base **verto**, base **eight**, and base **twelve**

23   Use multiplication to convert 5,122—ten to its equivalent numeral in base **verto**. Check your work by using division to convert the numeral from base **verto** to base ten.

24   Show that ⊥⊥△l△—**verto** and **tee**—twelve are numerals which represent the same number by converting each into its equivalent numeral in base ten.

25   Show that □ll—**verto** and **1101010**—two are numerals which represent the same number by converting each into its equivalent numeral in base **eight.**

5-6   DEFINITION OF A NUMBER FIELD

With the definition of division as the inverse operation to multiplication and the extension of the number system to include rational numbers, a number system has been obtained which retains all the operations and properties of an integral domain and which also has the property of closure under the newly defined operation of division with nonzero divisors. Such a number system is called a *number field* in accordance with this definition.

Definition 5-8 **A number field is a set *F* of numbers, with two well-defined binary operations, addition and multiplication, which satisfy the following postulates:**

For *a*, *b*, *c*, in *F*:

F-1   Closure   If $a + b = x$ and $a \times b = y$, then x and y are unique elements of F.

F-2   Associative $(a + b) + c = a + (b + c)$; $a \times (b \times c) = (a \times b) \times c$.

F-3   Commutative $a + b = b + a$; $a \times b = b \times a$.

F-4   Distributive $a \times (b + c) = (a \times b) + (a \times c)$

F-5   Additive Identity   There exists a number 0 in F, called the *additive identity*, such that $a + 0 = a$ for every number a in F.

The field properties

F-6   Additive Inverse   For every a in F there exists a number $-a$ in F such that $a + (-a) = 0$. The number $-a$ is called the *additive inverse* of a.

F-7   Multiplicative Identity   There exists a number $1 \neq 0$ in F, called the *multiplicative identity*, such that $1 \times a = a$ for every number a in F.

F-8   Multiplicative Inverse   For every nonzero number a in F there exists a number $\dfrac{1}{a}$, or a^{-1}, in F such that $a \times \dfrac{1}{a} = 1$. The number $\dfrac{1}{a}$ is called the *multiplicative inverse* of a.

Justify this definition of a field:

A number field is an integral domain in which each nonzero element has a multiplicative inverse.

Just as in the case of the integers, the rational numbers can be arranged in order of increasing size. This ordering of the rational numbers is, in fact, dependent upon the ordering of the integers. By Definition 5–2, a, b, c, and d of the two rational numbers $\dfrac{a}{b}$ and $\dfrac{c}{d}$ are integers, and by convention b and d are both positive. The criterion of Definition 5–4 then states that $\dfrac{a}{b} < \dfrac{c}{d}$ if and only if $ad < bc$ or, by Definition 4–2, if and only if $bc - ad$ is a positive integer.

Order

Example

1   $\dfrac{3}{4} < \dfrac{5}{6}$ since $3 \cdot 6 < 4 \cdot 5$. This last statement is true because $20 - 18 = 2$, which is a positive integer.

2   $-\dfrac{8}{7} < -\dfrac{2}{3}$ since $(-8) \cdot 3 < 7(-2)$. This last statement is true because $(-14) - (-24) = (-14) + 24 = 10$, which is a positive integer.

Definition 5–4 also yields the corresponding criterion: $\frac{a}{b} > \frac{c}{d}$ if and only if $ad > bc$ or, equivalently, if and only if $ad - bc$ is a positive integer.

Example

1    $\frac{10}{4} > \frac{3}{2}$ since $10 \cdot 2 > 4 \cdot 3$. $20 - 12 = 8$, which is a positive integer.

2    $-\frac{15}{2} > -\frac{25}{3}$ since $(-15)(3) > (2)(-25)$. $(-45) - (-50) = (-45) + 50 = 5$, which is a positive integer.

The positive rational numbers also have in common with the positive integers the important properties expressed in the following postulates:

Properties of positive rational numbers

1   Addition   The sum of two positive rational numbers is a positive rational number.

2   Multiplication   The product of two positive rational numbers is a positive rational number.

3   Trichotomy   For a given rational number q, one and only one of the following properties holds: q is positive, $q = 0$, or $-q$ is positive.

It thus follows, just as in the case of integers, that a positive rational number q can be identified by the relation $q > 0$. Similarly, if q is such that $-q$ is positive, we say that q is a negative rational number and identify it by one or the other of the two equivalent relations $-q > 0$ or $q < 0$.

Since the set of rational numbers has the property of closure under the operations of addition, subtraction, multiplication, and division by nonzero divisors, these operations are at times referred to as the *four rational operations.* They are also called the *four field operations,* since any set of numbers which has the property of closure under these four operations constitutes a number field. In other words, in any field the two equations $a \div b = c$ and $a \times b = c$, with $b \neq 0$, can always be interpreted. This is equivalent to saying that in a field, there always exists a solution for the general linear equation in one unknown

Field operations

$$ax + b = c \qquad a \neq 0$$

If a, b, and c are numbers of a given number field F, then x is also in F.

The eight field properties (page 127), the two additional properties of addition and multiplication, and the property of trichotomy (above), constitute the postulates of an *ordered field.* The field of rational numbers and the field of real numbers (see Chap. 6) are the ordered fields that shape the structure of elementary algebra and are thus significant in the study of mathematics.

Ordered field

5–7   RATIONAL NUMBERS AS FRACTIONS

One of the very important interpretations of rational numbers is that of a fraction expressing the quotient of two integers $a \div b = \frac{a}{b} (b \neq 0)$.
This is by no means, however, the complete significance of the concept of fraction.

Early in man's dealing with the quantitative demands of his environment he came in contact with concepts which the integers could not describe adequately. Such concepts as a broken spear, a part of a day, one shepherd's flock of sheep which was not an exact multiple of another shepherd's flock, or a certain distance which was more than 1 day's journey but not as much as 2 days' journey led to the necessity of finding a way to give expression to parts of a whole or parts of a group. The concept of equal parts was not necessarily incorporated in this early idea of fraction but quite possibly was a much later refinement. Our word "fraction" is a derivative of the Latin word *frangere* (to break). Thus, etymologically at least, we continue the tradition that the idea implied by the use of the word "fraction" has to do with a "broken unit."

Through the ages the concept of fraction and the problems connected with its proper use have presented several confusing paradoxes. It has been a concept which (1) represents parts of a unit or is an entity within itself; (2) is a quotient or is not a quotient; (3) expresses a relationship between two numbers or merely expresses a partitioning; (4) has many of the characteristics of integers yet came into being because of their inadequacy. While the desire for clarification in computation has not removed all the confusing contrasts, the cumbersome symbolism, and the involved computational processes associated with the unit fractions of the early Egyptians, it has led to the more precise interpretations and more facile operational procedures of the present.

5–8   UNIT FRACTIONS

The largest and most famous work on Egyptian mathematics is the Ahmes (or Rhind) papyrus, which was written about 1550 B.C. Its rather complete treatment of fractions gives evidence that prior to this early date unit fractions had already passed through a long period of development.† A *unit fraction* is a fraction with 1 as the numerator. To indicate a fraction the Egyptians used the symbol $\bigcirc$, or in some

† David Eugene Smith, *op., cit.* p. 210.

cases a mere dot. Thus, with the two exceptions of symbols for the fractions $\frac{1}{2}$ and $\frac{2}{3}$, all the Egyptian fractions took on the appearance of being mere reciprocals of the corresponding natural number. The symbols ⌒⌒ and ⌒⌒, for example, represented $\frac{1}{3}$ and $\frac{1}{5}$, respectively, while ⊂ and ⌒ represented $\frac{1}{2}$ and $\frac{2}{3}$, respectively.[†]

Computation with such fractions was, indeed, a rather involved process. The Ahmes papyrus gives a table of values for the respective ratios of 2 to each of the numbers 5 through 101. For example,

$$\frac{2}{5} = \frac{1}{3}\,\frac{1}{15} \quad \text{and} \quad \frac{2}{17} = \frac{1}{12}\,\frac{1}{51}\,\frac{1}{68}$$

are two of the entries. In our modern notation these entries would read

$$\frac{2}{5} = \frac{1}{3} + \frac{1}{15} \quad \text{and} \quad \frac{2}{17} = \frac{1}{12} + \frac{1}{51} + \frac{1}{68}$$

The values found in the table are merely the values of the doubles of the corresponding unit fractions to be used as aids in the process of doubling, or Egyptian multiplication. Cajori, however, points out that the table can be used as an aid in decomposing a fraction with numerator greater than 2 provided "there is a fraction in the table having the same denominator *it* has."[‡] Historians have made various speculations as to what rules were used in arriving at these unit fraction decompositions.[§]

Although such unit fractions seem rather artificial and awkward, there are instances in which we make rather simple use of them today:

1 The concept of the reciprocal. For example, the reciprocal of 5 is $\frac{1}{5}$.

2 The unit used to express the fineness of gold is a *carat*. In this sense it means "a twenty-fourth part" $\left(\frac{1}{24}\right)$. For example, 18-carat gold means 18 parts of pure gold and 6 parts of alloy $\left(\frac{18}{24} + \frac{6}{24} = \frac{24}{24}\right)$.

3 Precision workers in various types of manufacturing use tolerances quoted in terms of $\frac{1}{16}$, $\frac{1}{32}$, or $\frac{1}{64}$ inch or, at times, even smaller units.

† F. Cajori, *op. cit.* p. 14.
‡ F. Cajori, "A History of Mathematics," p. 12, The Macmillan Company, New York, 1919.
§ Howard Eves, "An Introduction to the History of Mathematics," pp. 39–40, 45–46, Holt, Rinehart and Winston, Inc., New York, 1959.
Otto Neugebauer, "The Exact Sciences in Antiquity," Princeton University Press, Princeton, N. J., 1952.
David Eugene Smith, *op. cit.*, pp. 210–211.

4   The method of making change is essentially that of using unit fractions. Suppose you make a purchase for 19 cents and give the clerk a 50-cent piece. As she makes your change, you will probably hear these words: "nineteen, twenty, twenty-five, fifty" as she starts with the amount of the purchase and then places one cent, one nickel, and one quarter in your hand. In essence what she has said to you is that

$$\frac{1}{100} + \frac{1}{20} + \frac{1}{4} = \frac{31}{100}$$

5–9   GENERAL FRACTIONS

Through their interest in astronomy the Babylonians and Greeks made use of sexagesimal fractions (fractions with denominators expressed in terms of powers of 60). The Greeks also made extensive use of such fractions in their study of geometry. While these fractions did not use one fixed number in the same sense as the unit numerator of the Egyptian fraction, all denominators were related to the one number, 60. The numerators could vary just as did the denominators of the Egyptian fractions. Today we use sexagesimal fractions in our time units. One minute $= \frac{1}{60}$ of an hour (originally called *pars minuta prima*), and one second $= \frac{1}{60}$ of a minute, or $\frac{1}{(60)^2} = \frac{1}{3,600}$ of an hour (*pars minuta secunda*).

The Romans went to extensive effort to avoid the use of fractions through the use of submultiples in their dealing with money, weights, and measures. They created new units in terms of twelfths, twenty-fourths, etc., of an accepted unit. Today we use some of these submultiples: 1 inch instead of $\frac{1}{12}$ of a foot, 1 ounce (Troy weight) instead of $\frac{1}{12}$ of a pound, 1 month instead of $\frac{1}{12}$ of a year, and so on.

While, in addition to the sexagesimal fractions, the Greeks developed and used a system of fractions much like the fractions we use, it was the Hindus—the originators of our number system along with place value and the use of 10 as a base—who developed a pattern for the general fraction which seemed to capture all the specifics of the various other forms in the generality of its notation. Difficulties of printing caused variations in the mechanics of form which produced, for example, such symbols as $\frac{2}{3}$, $\frac{2}{3}$, 2:3, 2/3, and $\frac{2}{3}$ as ways of writing two-thirds. The last three are used today as accepted variations of the symbol.

When a fraction is used to represent the number of equal parts into

Fraction as
a rational
number

which a whole has been divided, one of the equal parts into which a group has been divided, or a quotient of one number divided by another, it is used as a number. It is indeed a rational number for which the four field operations of addition, subtraction, multiplication, and division are well-defined processes.

5-10 FRACTION AS A RATIO

Official Greek mathematics did not contain fractions. According to Plato, "the experts in this study" could readily accept the concept of visible things being divisible (or broken), but not mathematical units. Thus, while merchants might operate with fractions, mathematicians made use of *ratios of integers*.† This confusing dichotomy in the use of the fraction symbol continues into the modern age. Confusion can be expected when the same symbol is used to represent a number, as in a partitioning, or to represent not a number but merely a relationship between two numbers. The symbol $\frac{3}{4}$ can be used, for example, to represent 3 of the equal fourths of a unit or merely to say that one group of objects when compared with another group of objects is found to be so related to it that for each 3 objects in the one group there are 4 in the other. The symbol $\frac{3}{4}$ thus may represent a number and be used as such (as in the first part of the illustration), or not represent a number at all but be merely a convenient symbol for recording the quantitative

Fraction as a
ratio

specifics of a relationship. As a ratio, $\frac{3}{4}$ means that the relationship under consideration is such that for each 3 of a group there are 4 of another. It is frequently written as 3:4 and read "three to four." Thus, if there are 7 marbles of exactly the same size and smoothness in a bag and 3 of them are red while 4 are blue, then the chances are 3:4 that a blindfolded person in lifting a single marble from the bag would select a red one. This means that there are 3 chances out of 7 of the marble's being red and 4 chances out of 7 of its being blue.

A *proportion* is an expression of equality between two ratios which are equal. Thus, "3 is to 4 as 75 is to 100" $\left(\frac{3}{4} = \frac{75}{100}\right)$ states a true pro-

Proportion

portion, since, when 75 is compared with 100, it is found that the ratio is the same as 3 to 4 because there are 3 twenty-fives in 75 and 4 twenty-fives in 100. This latter ratio is frequently read as 75 *per* 100, or 75 per cent. Herein lies the justification for the use of the terminology *rate*

† B. L. Van der Waerden, "Science Awakening," p. 49, Groningen, Netherlands, Erven P. Noordhoff, NV, 1954.

per cent. It means *ratio to one hundred.* Similarly, it is a true proportion to state that the ratio of 3 to 4 is the same as that of the fractional part $\left(\frac{3}{4}\right)$ to the whole, or $\frac{3}{4}:1$. Just as the ratio of $2:1$ may be associated with the numerical concept of 2, so the ratio of $\frac{3}{4}:1$ (three-fourths to one) may be associated with the numerical concept of $\frac{3}{4}$ (three-fourths).

If two groups are so related that the ratio of group A to group B is $2:1$, we can say that the size of group A is two times that of group B. Similarly, if the ratio is $\frac{3}{4}:1$, we can say that the size of group A is three-fourths the size of B. It is in this concept that we find justification for use of the same symbolism to represent "a fractional part" or "a ratio."

5–11   THE VOCABULARY OF FRACTIONS

The fractions which were used in the commerce of ancient times were distinguished from the sexagesimal fractions used in astronomy. The terminology used for this distinction has come down to us through the Latin *fractiones vulgares* (the vulgar fractions of the English) to give us the expression *common fractions.* The contrast, however, is no longer with sexagesimal fractions (those with powers of 60 as denominators), but with *decimal* fractions (those with powers of 10 as denominators). All common fractions may be grouped into two distinct classes: *proper fractions* (those whose numerator $<$ the denominator) and *improper fractions* (those whose numerator $\geq$ the denominator). Any improper fraction may be converted into a *mixed number* (a whole number and a proper fraction) or into a whole number.

Types of fractions

The parts of a fraction are called *terms.* The upper number is called, after the Latin custom, the *numerator* (or numberer) while the lower number is called the *denominator* (namer). With the different interpretations of a fraction the numerator and denominator take on different meanings. When the fraction is thought of as a part of a whole, the denominator tells the number of equal parts into which the whole has been divided while the numerator tells how many parts have been taken. When the fraction is thought of as a fractional part of a group, the denominator tells the number of equal parts into which the group has been divided while the numerator tells the number in the group. When the fraction is thought of as a quotient, the denominator is the divisor while the numerator is the dividend. In this sense the fraction is sometimes thought of as an "expressed division." When the fraction is thought of as a ratio, the denominator simply gives quantitative expression to one of the groups being compared while the numerator gives quantitative expression to the other.

When the numerator and denominator of a fraction are multiplied or divided by the same nonzero number, another fraction is obtained whose value is the same as that of the first fraction. For this reason they are called *equivalent fractions*. Fractions with a common (like) denominator are called *like fractions*, and those with unlike denominators are called *unlike fractions*. Two unlike fractions such as $\frac{5}{6}$ and $\frac{3}{8}$ may be changed to like fractions by using as a common denominator a number which has both given denominators as factors and converting the two fractions to equivalent fractions, both having this same denominator. In this case, 24 is the smallest number which has both 6 and 8 as factors.

Equivalent fractions

$$\frac{5}{6} = \frac{5 \times 4}{6 \times 4} = \frac{20}{24}, \quad \text{and} \quad \frac{3}{8} = \frac{3 \times 3}{8 \times 3} = \frac{9}{24}$$

It is usually best, though not necessary, that this common denominator be the smallest possible common denominator, or *least common denominator*. The fact that both terms of a fraction can be multiplied or divided by the same nonzero number without changing the value of the fraction has been called the Golden Rule of Fractions.[†] Its validity is established, of course, because of the inverse relationship that exists between multiplication and division. For example, by multiplying and dividing $\frac{5}{6}$ by 4, it is changed to the equivalent fraction $\frac{20}{24}$. Through the application of this rule, fractions may easily be reduced to *lower*, or even *lowest, terms* and changed to *higher terms*. A fraction is considered to be in its lowest terms when its numerator and denominator are relatively prime integers.

Least common denominator

In the reduction of fractions to lower terms a technique known as cancellation is sometimes used. For example, $\frac{6}{8} = \frac{\not{2} \times 3}{\not{2} \times 4} = \frac{3}{4}$. The validity of this technique is justified by two facts: (1) a fraction may be considered as the expressed quotient of the numerator divided by the denominator; and (2) multiplication and division are inverse processes, so one process neutralizes or annuls the effect of the other. In the above example, one may consider that $\frac{6}{8}$ can be obtained from $\frac{3}{4}$ by multiplying by 2 and dividing by 2. The order in which the two operations are performed is immaterial; the net effect is to produce *no change in the value of the fraction*. $\frac{3}{4}$ and $\frac{6}{8}$ are equivalent fractions. The

---

[†] F. F. Potter, "The Teaching of Arithmetic," p. 208, Sir Isaac Pitman & Sons, Ltd., London, 1930.

word "cancel" means "to annul or destroy; to neutralize or counter-balance." The "canceling" of a factor common to both numerator and denominator of a fraction is the mere physical act of indicating the fact that one factor destroys the effect of the other. Since addition and sub-traction are inverse processes, the same device can at times be used to advantage in simplifying computations involving these two operations. For example, $8 - \not{5} + \not{5} = 8$. Such a technique can be used *only* in computing the result of inversely related operations. In the simplifica-tion of the expression $\dfrac{5 + 4}{4}$, the 4's cannot be canceled, because addi-tion and division are not inversely related operations and one operation does not annul or destroy the effect of the other.

At more advanced levels of mathematical discussion, the term *fraction* is used to represent *any* type of algebraic expression which has both a numerator and a denominator. The types of fraction we have been discussing—namely, those with integral numerators and denomi-nators—are then called *rational fractions*.

Exercises

1 How many illustrations can you find of modern usage of the con-cept of unit fractions?

2 What is meant by the statement: A fraction may be thought of as representing a number?

3 Give various illustrations of each of the following concepts of a fraction: (*a*) part of a unit; (*b*) part of a group; (*c*) quotient; (*d*) ratio; (*e*) number.

4 Explain the meanings to be given the terms "numerator" and "denominator" in each of the uses of fraction given in Exercise 3.

5 Criticize the number $5\frac{2}{7}$ given as an answer to the request: Find the quotient of $37 \div 7$ and express the remainder as a fraction.

6 What rule is sometimes called the Golden Rule of Fractions? Ex-plain why it works.

7 Why do the concept of equality and the processes of addition, subtraction, multiplication, and division have to be defined for fractions?

8 The introduction of rational numbers is necessary to give a set of numbers which will have the property of closure with respect to what operation?

9 The set of positive rational numbers has closure with respect to what operations?

10 Arrange these fractions in order from largest to smallest with the largest fraction on the left: $\dfrac{2}{3}, \dfrac{5}{5}, \dfrac{1}{2}, \dfrac{3}{4}, \dfrac{5}{8}, \dfrac{3}{7}$.

11   Explain why finding the sum of two rational numbers by applying Definition 5–5 is equivalent to finding the sum of two common fractions by first changing the fractions to fractions with common denominators and then adding their numerators.

12   Show that the associative and commutative laws hold for these sums: $(a)\ \dfrac{3}{4} + \dfrac{5}{6} + \dfrac{1}{2}$; $(b)\ \dfrac{7}{5} + \dfrac{2}{3} + \dfrac{8}{15}$. Why does this *not* prove that these two laws hold for the addition of fractions?

13   Show that the commutative law does not hold for finding the difference of two fractions. Use the fractions $\dfrac{3}{4}$ and $\dfrac{7}{8}$. Why does this prove that the commutative law does not hold for the subtraction of fractions?

14   Explain why one does not have to change fractions to a common denominator before they can be multiplied or divided.

15   Would it be necessarily incorrect to change two fractions to fractions with common denominators before finding their product or the quotient of one divided by the other?

16   Show that the commutative law holds for these products: $(a)\ \dfrac{3}{4} \times \dfrac{8}{27}$; $(b)\ \dfrac{5}{6} \times \dfrac{7}{9}$. Why does this *not* prove that multiplication of fractions is commutative?

17   Why would the practice of finding common denominators in multiplication and division of fractions be, in general, undesirable procedure?

18   Develop a rationalization of the process of inverting the divisor and multiplying when dividing by a fraction:
(a) Through the use of unit fractions
(b) Through the use of the concept of measurement division

19   Use the fractions $\dfrac{5}{6}, \dfrac{2}{3}$, and $\dfrac{3}{4}$ to construct examples which show that rational numbers are neither associative nor commutative under division. Does this statement hold true also for integers? For natural numbers?

20   Use each set of numbers to illustrate each of the three fundamental laws of arithmetic: associative, commutative, and distributive.

(a) 5, 7, 12 (b) 3, 4, 6, 9 $(c)\ \dfrac{1}{2}, \dfrac{3}{4}, \dfrac{2}{3}$

$(d)\ \dfrac{5}{6}, \dfrac{4}{9}, \dfrac{7}{25}$ $(e)\ 3\frac{1}{2}, 2\frac{1}{4}, 5\frac{1}{3}$ $(f)\ -\dfrac{3}{5}, \dfrac{1}{2}, -\dfrac{4}{7}$

21   Explain why you can use cancellation in the reduction of each of these fractions to lower terms, and then reduce each fraction to its lowest terms.

$(a)\ \dfrac{15}{20}$ $(b)\ \dfrac{7}{21}$ $(c)\ \dfrac{52}{28}$ $(d)\ \dfrac{16}{24}$

22 Explain why you cannot use cancellation in each of these fractions:

(a) $\dfrac{8 + 3}{8}$ (b) $\dfrac{5 - 2}{2}$ (c) $\dfrac{8}{3 + 2}$ (d) $\dfrac{10}{5 - 4}$

23 Explain how cancellation may be used to reduce each of these fractions to lower terms, and then reduce each fraction to its lowest terms.

(a) $\dfrac{6 - 4}{8}$ (b) $\dfrac{9 + 12}{3}$ (c) $\dfrac{5}{22 - 7}$ (d) $\dfrac{8}{20 + 4}$

24 In what way do the postulates of a field differ from those of an integral domain?

25 Why is it that a set of numbers with the ordinary definitions of addition and multiplication which satisfy the postulates for an integral domain do not necessarily constitute a number field?

26 Why is it that a set of numbers with the ordinary definitions of addition and multiplication which satisfy the postulates of a field do necessarily satisfy the postulates for an integral domain?

5–12   DECIMAL FRACTIONS

The concept of place value, so important in the structure of our numeral system, places great significance on the decimal fraction. The basic principle of place value is that each position in a numeral has a significance of its own. Since ten is the base of our system, this meaning is interpreted in terms of powers of 10. The value of any position in a numeral should thus be obtainable by *starting from ones position* and counting positions moved to the right or left, the number of the position thus indicating the power of 10 to be used in finding the value of the position. Because counting to the right from ones place calls for division by powers of 10, it is evident that the efficiency of our numeral system was seriously restricted until the introduction of the concept of decimal fractions by Simon Stevin in 1585. With the introduction of this concept, positional values such as tenth $\left(0.1 = \dfrac{1}{10}\right)$, hundredth $\left(0.01 = \dfrac{1}{100} = \dfrac{1}{10^2}\right)$, and thousandth $\left(0.001 = \dfrac{1}{1,000} = \dfrac{1}{10^3}\right)$ have just as much significance as do ten (10), hundred (10^2), and thousand (10^3). With such flexibility of positional value and the 10 digital symbols (0, 1, 2, 3, 4, 5, 6, 7, 8, 9) we have the means to write any numeral no matter how large or how small. (Review Sec. 2–6, pages 32–33.)

5-13   READING AND WRITING DECIMALS

Too frequently, the decimal point receives undue emphasis. It is merely a device used to indicate the ones place and is not usually used if the numbers are whole numbers, because, in such cases, it is easy to recognize the ones place at the extreme right-hand position. Ones place is the center (so to speak) of our notational scheme. There are still some differences in the device to be used for what we call the decimal point. The decimal which in the United States we write as 3.14 is written as $3 \cdot 14$ in England, while in other countries it may appear as 3,14 or 3_{14}. Even in the United States, many people in writing a check for three dollars and fourteen cents would write it \$3$\frac{14}{}$. In each of the above numbers, however, the positional value of the 1 in the number is $\frac{1}{10}$ the value of the ones place, and that of the 4 is $\frac{1}{100}$ the value of the ones place.

There are decimals which have only a fraction part and there are others which have a whole-number part as well as a fraction part.

Types of decimals

Decimal fractions which have only a fraction part are called *pure decimals*. There may be two kinds of pure decimals, as shown in Fig. 5-8. They may either end in a common fraction (*complex decimal*) or not (*simple decimal*). Pure decimal fractions correspond to proper common fractions; their numerators are smaller than their denominators.

In decimal fractions there is no exact counterpart of the improper common fraction. The *mixed decimal* 3.14, mentioned previously, can be written as the equivalent improper fraction $\frac{314}{100}$ or as the equivalent mixed number $3\frac{14}{100}$. In reading any mixed decimal the word "and" should be used to bridge the decimal point. Thus, 3.14 is read as three *and* fourteen hundredths. This is exactly the same way that the symbol $3\frac{14}{100}$ is read. The word "and" should not be used in reading numerals in any way other than that indicated here. Frequently in business and industry a short method for reading decimals is used. In such cases 3.14 is read "three-point-one-four."

As is indicated in Fig. 5-8, mixed decimals can also be either simple

FIGURE 5-8   Kinds of decimals.

	Pure	Mixed
Simple	0.25	2.5
Complex	0.16$\frac{2}{3}$	1.6$\frac{2}{3}$

or complex. The mixed complex decimal of the figure is read "one and six-and-two-thirds tenths." In any such case, whether decimals are used or not, the common fraction indicates a fractional part of the value of the position to which it is attached $\left(0.00\frac{1}{4}\right.$ is read as one fourth of one hundredth; its value may be written as the common fraction $\left.\frac{1}{400}\right).$

All the decimal fractions we have used up to this point are called *finite*, or *terminating*, decimals. These two words mean the same thing about the decimal. They tell us that when we start writing the fraction we come to a stopping place. In Fig. 5–8, for example, the decimal fractions are all finite decimals; the writing stops after two digits have been written. There is a slight exception in the case of the common fraction of the complex decimals, but, even here, the writing stops with the writing of the common fraction.

There are decimal fractions for which the above is not true. Such decimals are called *infinite*, or *nonterminating*. They do not stop. If we should wish to write a finite decimal fraction which would be equal to $\sqrt{2}$, we could not do so (see Fig. 6–2, page 159). In the expression $\sqrt{2} = 1.41421\cdots$ the three dots mean that there are digits omitted from the decimal. If we multiply 1.41421 by itself we get a number which is very close to 2 in value, but we do not get 2. It is not possible to fill in enough decimal places to give a number which when multiplied by itself will give the value 2. We might say that $\sqrt{2}$ is approximately equal to 1.41421. Note that the three dots after the decimal are missing. In this case 1.41421 is a finite decimal which is an approximation to the positive square root of 2. Since 1.41421 is a rational number, it is also called a rational approximation to the positive square root of 2.

There are two types of nonterminating, or infinite, decimals. There are some like $0.333\cdots$, which just keep on repeating the same digits in the same pattern. They are called *repeating decimals*. The decimals $0.142857142857\cdots$ and $0.1666666\cdots$ are two other repeating decimals. The standard notation used to indicate repeating decimals is a bar over the repetend (the part which repeats):

$0.142857142857\cdots = 0.\overline{142857}$
$0.333\cdots \qquad\qquad = 0.\overline{3}$
$0.16666\cdots \qquad\quad\; = 0.1\overline{6}$

Infinite decimals such as $1.41421\cdots$ representing $\sqrt{2}$ can be proved never to follow a pattern of repetition. They are called *nonrepeating decimals*.

5–14   USING DECIMALS

The concept of decimal fraction does not necessitate another extension of our number system.   In fact, when we restrict our considerations to decimal fractions we are, indeed, simplifying our operations with fractions.   Heretofore, we have been dealing with fractions for which any integers might serve as denominators.   Now, we are dealing with fractions whose denominators can be only powers of 10.   No new definitions are needed to tell us how to operate with decimals.   The definitions for equality, less than, greater than, and the fundamental operations that were given previously for fractions are sufficient here.

Two finite decimals are equal if they are composed of identically the same digits, each with identically the same place value.   This means that, if these decimals were written as common fractions, they would be like fractions with the same numerators.   In comparing two decimals, remember that one unit in any position is equal to 10 units of the next position to its right.   For this reason, the decimal 2.64 is larger than the decimal 2.639; in fact, 2.64 would still be the larger decimal regardless of how many 9's might be annexed to 2.63.   Such statements can be checked by noting, for example, that 2.64 and 2.639 can be written as the following like common fractions: $\dfrac{2,640}{1,000}$ and $\dfrac{2,639}{1,000}$.   There is an essential point that must be observed in this connection.   The fraction $\dfrac{2,640}{1,000}$, written as a decimal, becomes 2.640, which can be obtained from 2.64 by annexing a zero to the right.   Frequently, the statement is made that "annexing a zero to the right of the decimal point does not affect the decimal fraction."   This is an incorrect statement.   The value of the decimal fraction is not changed, but as we shall see in a later chapter (see Sec. 9–8), the significance of the fraction is changed considerably.

In the addition and subtraction of finite decimals a very convenient practice to follow as a guide for getting digits of like positional value aligned is to align the decimal points.   This is by no means a necessary practice; it is merely an accepted crutch that is very convenient to use.   The actual process of adding is then carried out as if the members were all integers.

Computing
with decimal
fractions

There is nothing new in the processes of multiplication and division with decimals except the proper placing of the decimal point in the results.   The details of the operations are exactly the same as those for whole numbers.   The rationalization of the placing of the decimal point in multiplication can be accomplished by different methods, two of which are illustrated in the following example.

Example Find the product 3.63×27.9.

1 Find the product of the two integers 363×279. Place the decimal point in the product so that there will be as many decimal places as there are in both the multiplier and the multiplicand. The rationalization of this scheme can be accomplished by writing both multiplier and multiplicand as common fractions and carrying through the detail of finding such a product.

$$3.63 \times 27.9 = \frac{363}{100} \times \frac{279}{10} = \frac{363 \times 279}{100 \times 10} = \frac{101{,}277}{1{,}000} = 101.277$$

2 Estimate the product:

3.63 is approximately equal to 4. $\quad 3.63 \approx 4$
$27.9 \approx 28$
$3.63 \times 27.9 \approx 4 \times 28 = 112$

The estimate not only provides a rough check on the product but also tells us that there will be three places *to the left* of the decimal point. Now multiply as if the two numbers were integers and then place the decimal point three places from the left.

The above illustration has been chosen deliberately so that attention may be called to a seeming difficulty with the second suggested technique.

Compare the second method of the example with the same technique applied to finding the product 2.63×37.9 (Fig. 5–9). This time the product is approximately $3 \times 38 = 114$. The actual product, however, has only two places, rather than three, to the left of the decimal.

This difficulty is easily taken care of by remembering that the value at which a number changes from a two-figure number to a three-figure number is 100. If the final product has the digit 1 to the extreme left, there will be *three* digits to the left of the decimal; otherwise there will be *only two*.

This same ᵢ recaution will have to be kept in mind when the products are near any transition point (10; 100; 1,000; 10,000; etc.).

FIGURE 5–9

37.9	$\approx$	38
2.63	$\approx$	3
1 137		114
22 74		
75 8		
99.677		

```
6.28 | 0.2826
        becomes
            .045
   628 | 28.260
        25 12
         3 140
         3 140
```

FIGURE 5–10   Division by decimal.

Probably the simplest pattern for division of decimals is to multiply both divisor and dividend by the power of 10 necessary to convert the divisor into a whole number. After this has been done, the only new problem that remains is that of placement of the decimal point in the quotient. The actual mechanics of division are the same as if one were dividing one whole number by another. Here again custom has evolved, as in the case of addition and subtraction of decimals, a "rule without authority." The rule states: When dividing a decimal by a whole number, place the decimal point in the quotient directly over the decimal point of the dividend. This is in no sense a bona fide rule or law that must of necessity be followed. It is no more than a crutch of convenience to assist in placing the digits of the quotient in their respective places of value. A meaningful procedure for placing the decimal point in the quotient is illustrated in the example that follows:

Example   Find the quotient of $0.2826 \div 6.28$.

Rewrite the exercise as $28.26 \div 628$ (see Fig. 5–10).

By inspection observe that $0.1 \times 628 = 62.8$, which is larger than the dividend 28.26. On the other hand, $0.01 \times 628 = 6.28$, which is smaller than the dividend 28.26. It therefore follows that the quotient is smaller than 0.1 but larger than 0.01, so the first figure of the quotient must be placed in the hundredths position.

Now the placing of the decimal point in the quotient directly over the decimal point in the dividend becomes a convenient device for making sure that the figures of the quotient will be in their proper relative positions. This makes it possible to place the first quotient figure in the hundredths place by merely writing it directly above the figure in the hundredths place in the dividend. In this particular division it is necessary to use a placeholder in the tenths place. Why? Since we are seeking only the numerical value of the quotient, zeros may be annexed to the dividend if it is desirable in carrying out the division. Later (Sec. 9–11) we shall see that, under certain conditions, there are precautions that must be observed in such practice.

5–15   CONVERTING COMMON FRACTIONS TO DECIMALS

Any common fraction will convert into a simple decimal which is either finite or repeating. The division algorithm affords a simple explanation of why this is so. The fraction $\frac{a}{b}$ may be considered as synonymous with the expressed division in which a is the dividend and b is the divisor. By the division algorithm, $a = bq + r$ where $0 \le r < b$.

Thus, in the conversion of the fraction $\frac{a}{b}$, the only possible remainders in the division are the numbers $0, 1, 2, 3, \ldots, b - 1$. At any point in the process when 0 is obtained as a remainder, the division terminates and the fraction has been converted into a finite decimal. When this does not occur, there are only $b - 1$ distinct remainders. Therefore, if it does not occur sooner, repetition will have to take place after $b - 1$ divisions.

The fraction $\frac{3}{4}$ will convert into the finite decimal 0.75 (see Fig. 5–11). To see why this is true, let us examine what takes place.

$$\frac{3}{4} = \frac{3 \times 10 \times 10}{4 \times 10 \times 10} = \frac{3 \times \overset{5}{\cancel{10}} \times \overset{5}{\cancel{10}}}{\cancel{2} \times \cancel{2} \times 10 \times 10} = \frac{3 \times 5 \times 5}{100} = \frac{75}{100} = 0.75$$

The fraction $\frac{3 \times 10 \times 10}{4 \times 10 \times 10}$ can be written in the form $\frac{3.00}{4}$. Each zero in the numerator represents a multiplication by 10. Each decimal place in the numerator represents a division by 10. The quotient is not changed if both dividend (numerator) and divisor (denominator) are multiplied by the same number. But why use two 10's, no more and no less? Notice that the denominator $4 = 2 \times 2$. These two 2's are to be removed from the divisor if the division is to terminate. $10 = 2 \times 5$, so one 10 will take care of one 2. Why will it take three decimal places before $\frac{3}{8}$ will terminate when converted to a decimal? How many decimal places will be required to convert $\frac{5}{16}$ into a deci-

Common fractions equivalent to finite decimals

```
        0.75
   4 | 3.00
       2 8
       ----
         20
         20
       ----
```

FIGURE 5–11   Decimal conversion of $\frac{3}{4}$.

mal fraction?   Why will it take only one decimal place for $\dfrac{2}{4}$ to terminate and two places for $\dfrac{2}{25}$ to terminate?

Each 10 used as a multiplier in the numerator of a fraction will remove one and only one 2 and one and only one 5 from the denominator. When a fraction *which is in its lowest terms* is converted to a decimal, the fraction will produce a terminating decimal if and only if each prime factor of the denominator is a 2 or a 5.   It will require as many decimal places as there are either 2's or 5's, whichever occurs the larger number of times.   For example,

$$\frac{3}{200} = \frac{3}{2 \times 2 \times 2 \times 5 \times 5}$$

There are three 2's and only two 5's in the denominator; so this fraction will convert into a three-place terminating decimal.

What about $\dfrac{1}{3}$?   Since 10 does not contain 3 as a factor, there is no way the division of the numerator by the denominator can terminate. Also, since 3 is the divisor, and the division cannot come out even, there are only two possible remainders that can be obtained: 1 and 2.   An examination of the division in Fig. 5–12 shows that actually only the 1 is obtained.   So this division gives a repeating quotient: $\dfrac{1}{3} = 0.\overline{3}$. When a common fraction $\dfrac{a}{b}$ in its lowest terms converts into a repeat-

```
      0.33 ...
   ┌─────────
 3 │ 1.00
     9
    ──
    1 0
      9
    ──
      1
```

FIGURE 5–12   Decimal conversion of $\frac{1}{3}$.

```
       0.1136 ...
    ┌──────────
 44 │ 5.0000
      4 4
     ──
      60
      44
     ──
      160
      132
     ───
       280
       264
      ───
        16
```

FIGURE 5–13   Decimal conversion of $\frac{5}{44}$.

ing decimal, we can say that the quotient will have no more than $b - 1$ digits in the repetend. For example, $\dfrac{5}{7}$ can have no more than six digits in the part that repeats; $\dfrac{7}{13}$ can have no more than twelve; etc. We cannot say exactly how many digits there will be without dividing.

Common fractions equivalent to repeating decimals

Now consider a fraction such as $\dfrac{5}{44} = \dfrac{5}{4 \times 11}$. In the denominator there are two 2's, which can be removed by two 10's, and one 11, which cannot be removed. This fraction, when converted to a decimal, will go two places before it starts the repeating pattern and there will be no more than 10 places in the repetend. Why? Actually there are only two (see Fig. 5–13). The fraction $\dfrac{9}{56}$ will go three decimal places before starting the repeating pattern. Why will $\dfrac{7}{75}$ go two places before starting the repeating pattern, and $\dfrac{14}{36}$ only one?

When investigating any common fraction to determine into what type of decimal it will convert, it is first desirable to reduce the fraction to its lowest terms.

5–16   CONVERTING DECIMALS TO COMMON FRACTIONS

It is a very simple matter to convert any terminating decimal to a common fraction in its lowest terms. All that is necessary is to use the proper power of 10 as the denominator and to use the numerator of the decimal as the numerator, then reduce.

Finite decimals equivalent to common fractions

$$0.075 = \frac{75}{1,000} = \frac{3}{40}$$

The technique for converting repeating decimals, while intuitively acceptable, really calls for proof. It will not be given here. There are two types of repeating decimals to consider, namely, those like $0.\overline{6}$, which have nothing but a repeating pattern, and those like $0.1\overline{6}$ or $3.2\overline{25}$, which have both a nonrepeating part and a repeating part.

Case I   Repeating decimals which have only a repeating part

1   Multiply by the power of 10 sufficient to move one *repetend* (one group of digits which repeat) to the left of the decimal point.

2   Subtract the repeating decimal from the newly obtained mixed decimal.

3   Solve the resulting equation for the value of the repeating decimal.

4   Reduce the common fraction to its lowest terms.

Example   Convert $0.\overline{6}$ to a common fraction in its lowest terms (Fig. 5–14).

1   There is one digit in the repetend, so the fraction is multiplied by 10 to move one repetend to the left of the decimal point.

2   The repeating decimal is subtracted from the newly obtained mixed decimal.

3   The resulting equation is solved for the value of the repeating decimal.

4   The common fraction is reduced to its lowest terms.

Case II   Repeating decimals which have both a repeating part and a nonrepeating part

1   Multiply by the power of 10 sufficient to move the nonrepeating part to the left of the decimal.   The fraction part of the obtained mixed decimal will thus have only a repeating part.

2   Use Case I to convert the mixed decimal into an improper common fraction in its lowest terms.

3   Solve the resulting equation for the value of the repeating decimal.

Example   Convert $0.01\overline{6}$ to a common fraction in its lowest terms.

1   There are two digits in the nonrepeating part; so the fraction is multiplied by 100 to obtain $1.\overline{6}$, a mixed decimal whose fraction part contains only the repeating part of the given fraction (see Fig. 5–15).

2   By Case I, $1.\overline{6} = 1\frac{2}{3}$, which may be expressed as the improper common fraction $\dfrac{5}{3}$.

3   When the equation is solved and the resulting fraction is reduced to its lowest terms, we have $0.01\overline{6} = \dfrac{1}{60}$.

$$10(0.\overline{6}) = 6.\overline{6} \qquad (1)$$
$$\underline{1(0.\overline{6}) = 0.\overline{6}}$$
$$9(0.\overline{6}) = 6 \qquad (2)$$
$$0.\overline{6} = \tfrac{6}{9} \qquad (3)$$
$$0.\overline{6} = \tfrac{6}{9} = \tfrac{2}{3} \qquad (4)$$

FIGURE 5–14   Fractional conversion of $0.\overline{6}$.

$$100(0.01\overline{6}) = 1.\overline{6}$$
$$= 1\tfrac{2}{3} = \tfrac{5}{3}$$
$$0.01\overline{6} = \tfrac{5}{300} = \tfrac{1}{60}$$

FIGURE 5–15   Fractional conversion of $0.01\overline{6}$.

There is a very simple rule which can be followed for the ready conversion of any repeating decimal of the type of Case I. While this rule
can be developed in a rigorous manner, we shall merely state it for
use here.

Conversion Rule for Repeating Decimals A repeating decimal, containing only the repeating part, can be converted to a common fraction
by writing one complete repetend as the numerator and then writing
as the denominator a number composed of as many 9's as there are
digits in the numerator.

$$0.\overline{6} = \frac{6}{9} = \frac{2}{3} \qquad 0.\overline{063} = \frac{63}{999} = \frac{7}{111}$$

Repeating decimals equivalent to common fractions

In summary, the discussion of this last section has illustrated in a
great deal of detail the truth of a very important theorem in mathematics. The proof of this theorem is beyond the scope of this book, but
since it is of such fundamental significance, it will be stated here as a
postulate.

Postulate 5-5 Any rational number $\frac{a}{b}$ $(b \neq 0)$ may be expressed
either as a finite decimal or as an infinite repeating decimal. Conversely, any finite or infinite repeating decimal may be expressed as a
rational number.

Rational numbers expressed in decimal form

In many mathematical discussions it is desirable to express a finite
decimal in the form of an infinite repeating decimal. For example, 0.5
might be expressed either as $0.5\overline{0}$ or as $0.4\overline{9}$ (see Exercise 8, page 152).
The latter form is the one which is more generally used when this pat-
tern of representation is used.

5-17 PERCENTAGE

In discussing percentage no really new topic is being considered. The
first concern of this discussion was with common fractions, i.e., fractions for which any integer might serve as a numerator and any nonzero
integer might serve as a denominator. It was necessary to define the
processes for comparing and operating with these new numbers.
Secondly, decimal fractions were discussed, i.e., fractions for which
only powers of 10 can serve as denominators. Now the discussion is
directed to the use of per cents, decimal fractions for which only the

Per cents as decimal fractions

second power of 10, or 100, can serve as a denominator. No new definitions are needed to make it possible for us to use per cents in making computations. All the rules for the use of fractions apply.

The words *per cent* are derived from the Latin *per centum.* They mean *by the hundred.* Thus a per cent, or *rate per cent,* is always the ratio of some number to 100. Herein lies the great importance of percentage as an individual topic of elementary mathematics. The concept of the ratio of two integers is very basic to the practices of business, industry, and everyday living. Since this is so generally true it is very desirable to be able to express all such ratios in terms of some convenient denominator. The fact that our number system is decimal in nature makes some power of 10 a very natural choice for this denominator. The first power of 10, or 10, is too small to allow for desirable flexibility in making comparisons. The third power of 10, or 1,000, while desirable for certain types of comparisons—baseball standings, for example—is larger than is necessary for general practice. Thus the second power of 10, or 100, has been selected as the basis for making such comparisons.

5–18   USING PER CENTS

Since per cents are fractions with a common denominator, the comparisons for equality, greater than, and less than reduce to the simple comparisons of integers. Thus 35% is larger than 20% because $35 > 20$. Here, as in dealing with all fractions, certain precautions are necessary. Although the number $\frac{3}{4}$ is larger than $\frac{1}{2}$, it still is quite possible that $\frac{3}{4}$ of one apple might be much smaller than $\frac{1}{2}$ of another. Similarly, $\frac{3}{4}$ of 20 is much smaller than $\frac{1}{2}$ of 60. In like manner, while 75% is larger than 50% in an abstract sense, it is absolutely essential that the objects or groups to which the per cents are applied be taken into consideration before intelligent comparisons can be made (75% of 40 is 30, while 50% of 90 is 45, and $30 < 45$).

Per cents are always "like fractions" since they always have a common denominator. Thus, they technically meet the conditions for addition or subtraction. Here again it is essential that the base be taken into consideration. There are similar essential considerations of the base in problems involving per cents and the processes of multiplication and division. The following example illustrates a basic error that is frequently made, namely, that of averaging per cents.

Example Mr. Thomas was able to invest four sums of money for 1 year as follows: $4,000 at 3.5%; $1,400 at 5%; $3,600 at 2.5%; and $1,000 at 3%. What average per cent did he realize on his investment?

The total yield for the year on the total investment of $10,000 was $330 (see Fig. 5–16). Thus the average rate per cent is 3.3%. The average of the per cents given is 3.5%. If the interest on each amount is computed at 3.3%, the total yield is found to be $330, as would be expected. If the interest on each amount is computed at 3.5%, the total yield found is $350, giving an error of $20. Of course, if Mr. Thomas had invested exactly the same amounts at each of the four different rates of interest, then the average of the per cents, 3.5%, would have been correct.

In dealing with per cents it is frequently desirable either to convert from the per cent form to the fraction form or vice versa. Conversion in either direction is a simple process if one only remembers that any per cent represents a decimal fraction with two decimal places, or a common fraction with 100 as the denominator.

Example

$$25\% = 0.25 = \frac{25}{100} = \frac{1}{4}$$

$$37\tfrac{1}{2} = 0.37\tfrac{1}{2} = \frac{37\tfrac{1}{2}}{100} = \frac{75}{200} = \frac{3}{8}$$

$37\tfrac{1}{2}\%$ may also be written as 37.5%, which is to be interpreted as $\frac{37.5}{100} = \frac{375}{1,000} = 0.375$.

FIGURE 5–16   Average per cent on investment.

3.5% of $4,000 = $140	3.5%
5.0% of $1,400 = 70	5.0%
2.5% of $3,600 = 90	2.5%
3.0% of $1,000 = 30	3.0%
$10,000 $330	4 ⎮ 14.0%
	3.5%

Average per cent	Average yield
3.5% of $4,000 = $140	3.3% of $4,000 = $132.00
3.5% of $1,400 = 49	3.3% of $1,400 = 46.20
3.5% of $3,600 = 126	3.3% of $3,600 = 118.80
3.5% of $1,000 = 35	3.3% of $1,000 = 33.00
$350	$330.00

5-19   THE PERCENTAGE FORMULA

One of the basic relationships that pervades all mathematics, and particularly arithmetic, is the product relationship, in which one number is the product of two other numbers. In this relationship one number serves as the number upon which the relationship is based. We call it the multiplicand or, better, the *base*. A second number serves as the *multiplier* which operates on the base to give the *product*. In formula form

$$\text{Product} = \text{multiplier} \times \text{base} \qquad \text{or} \qquad p = m \times b = mb$$

In the language of percentage, the multiplier is the rate per cent (r) and the product is the percentage (p). The percentage formula is therefore

$$p = rb$$

In such product relationships there are three numbers involved, and there are three associated relationships between these three numbers. For the numbers of percentage these relationships are

Three forms of the percentage formula

$$p = rb \qquad b = \frac{p}{r} \qquad r = \frac{p}{b}$$

If any two of these numbers are known, the third one can be determined. If the unknown number is the product number (or percentage), then multiplication is the operation necessary to find this unknown number. This fact is expressed in the first form of the percentage formula given above. If one of the two known numbers is the product number (percentage), then division is the expressed operation necessary to find the unknown number. This fact is expressed in the other two forms of the percentage formula.

If p and r are known, then $b = \dfrac{p}{r}$

If p and b are known, then $r = \dfrac{p}{b}$

Thus, $p = rb$ states that there is a certain unknown number which is a given per cent of a given number; $b = \dfrac{p}{r}$ states that there is a certain unknown number of which a given number is a given per cent; and $r = \dfrac{p}{b}$ states that one given number is a certain unknown per cent of another given number.

Any problem in percentage can be stated not only in the language of percentage but also as a problem that uses common or decimal fractions:

1   $p = rb$: What number is 25% of 600?

   What number is $\frac{1}{4}$ of 600?

   What number is 0.25 of 600?

2   $b = \frac{p}{r}$: 150 is 25% of what number?

   150 is $\frac{1}{4}$ of what number?

   150 is 0.25 of what number?

3   $r = \frac{p}{b}$: 150 is what per cent of 600?

   150 is what fractional part of 600?
   (Give the answer as a common fraction and also as a decimal fraction.)

Since rate per cent always implies a ratio, all per cents can be stated in the form of proportions. The proportion form combines all three types of problems into one, a single proportion in which one number is unknown. The basic proportion is

$$\frac{p}{b} = \frac{r}{100}$$

The above problems expressed in this proportion form are as follows:

1   What number is 25% of 600? $\dfrac{p}{600} = \dfrac{25}{100}$

2   150 is 25% of what number? $\dfrac{150}{b} = \dfrac{25}{100}$

3   150 is what per cent of 600? $\dfrac{150}{600} = \dfrac{r}{100}$

It is thus evident that the whole topic of percentage is merely a consideration of a very special type of fraction, namely, a decimal fraction consisting of two decimal places or a common fraction with 100 as the denominator. Furthermore, it should be evident that the frequently-referred-to three problems of percentage are by no means three distinct and unrelated problems. They are merely three related aspects of a basic arithmetical relationship; there are three numbers so related that one is the product of the other two, and the problem is to find one of the numbers when the other two are known.

Exercises

1   Give examples of each of the following types of decimals: (*a*) pure simple; (*b*) mixed complex; (*c*) mixed simple; (*d*) pure complex.

2   Distinguish between terminating and repeating decimals.

3   What is the basic reason for aligning decimal points in the addition and subtraction of decimals?

4   First estimate each product and then find the true product:

(*a*) 5.73×46.34 (*b*) 0.0342×0.823
(*c*) 69.21×18.3 (*d*) 58.4×16.7

5   Convert each of these fractions to a terminating decimal. First state how many places will be necessary before each terminates.

(*a*) $\dfrac{5}{8}$ (*b*) $\dfrac{7}{125}$ (*c*) $\dfrac{9}{2,500}$ (*d*) $\dfrac{6}{32}$

(*e*) $\dfrac{15}{75}$ (*f*) $\dfrac{9}{72}$ (*g*) $\dfrac{60}{250}$ (*h*) $\dfrac{49}{560}$

6   Why will these fractions not convert into terminating decimals? Convert each fraction to a decimal.

(*a*) $\dfrac{3}{7}$ (*b*) $\dfrac{5}{6}$ (*c*) $\dfrac{9}{54}$

(*d*) $\dfrac{11}{56}$ (*e*) $\dfrac{6}{36}$ (*f*) $\dfrac{12}{450}$

7   Convert each of these decimals to common fractions in their lowest terms:

(*a*) 0.045 (*b*) $0.04\overline{5}$ (*c*) $0.0\overline{45}$ (*d*) $0.\overline{045}$

8   Show that $0.5\overline{0} = \dfrac{1}{2} = 0.5$; also that $0.4\overline{9} = \dfrac{1}{2} = 0.5$.

9   Arrange these numbers in order from left to right with the smallest number on the left: $0.\overline{6}$, 31%, 0.032, $\dfrac{2}{5}$, 0.403, 0.3%, $\dfrac{3}{4}$, 0.3, $\dfrac{2}{7}$, 0.430, $\dfrac{1}{2}\%$, 0.302, $\dfrac{3}{5}$, 0.285, $\dfrac{3}{7}$.

10 (*a*)   What is the numerical error in using 0.667 to represent $\dfrac{2}{3}$?

   (*b*)   What is the approximation to $\dfrac{2}{3}$ that has an error which is $\dfrac{1}{100}$ of the error in 0.667?

11 Write each of these percentage problems as an exercise in proportion:

Exercise 12   Records of daily attendance.

| A. FIVE GRADES FOR ONE DAY | | | | B. ONE GRADE FOR FIVE DAYS | | | |
GRADE	ENROLL-MENT	ATTEND-ANCE	PER CENT	DAYS	ENROLL-MENT	ATTEND-ANCE	PER CENT
4	80	72	90	Mon.	80	72	90
5	70	28	40	Tues.	80	32	40
6	100	70	70	Wed.	80	56	70
7	90	90	100	Thurs.	80	80	100
8	40	20	50	Fri.	80	40	50
Total	380	280		Total	400	280	

(a) 13 is 15% of what number?
(b) 13 is what per cent of 15?
(c) 13% of 15 is what number?

12 The figure above gives hypothetical data relative to two situations of daily attendance in school. Note that the per cents are identical in both situations. The average of these per cents is 70%.

(a) Show that this is correct for the average per cent of attendance in situation B but incorrect in situation A. Why is this so?
(b) If 70% is used as the average per cent of attendance in situation A, what is the error in number of pupils?
(c) Compute the average per cent of attendance in situation A correct to the nearest tenth per cent.
(d) Prove that your answer gives the correct representation.

INVITATIONS TO EXTENDED STUDY

1 Restate for rational numbers and prove Theorems 4–1 to 4–5.

2 Show that the rational number $\frac{a}{b}$ can be written as a rational number in infinitely many ways.

3 Prove that if r is a rational number then r^2 and r^3 are rational numbers.

4 The greatest common divisor of 3,450 and 5,775 is 75; symbolically $(5,775; 3,450) = 75$. It can be shown that 75 can be expressed in the form $75 = 3 \cdot 5,775 - 5 \cdot 3,450$ or, in equivalent form, $(5,775; 3,450) = 3 \cdot (5,775) + (-5) \cdot 3,450$. Verify this last statement. Now use the euclidean algorithm to find $(5,775; 3,450)$ and show how the integral multipliers 3 and -5 can be computed from the results obtained in the steps of the algorithm.

This exercise illustrates a very important property of numbers, namely, if d is the greatest common divisor of the positive integers a and b, then there exist integers p and q such that $d = pa + qb$.

5   Find $(63{,}973; 6{,}105)$ and determine the integers p and q such that $(63{,}973; 6{,}105) = p \cdot 63{,}973 + q \cdot 6{,}105$.

6   Use the fact that $\dfrac{1}{3} = 0.\overline{3}$ to establish that the integer 1 may be written as the periodic decimal $0.\overline{9}$.

7   Show that any rational number of the form $\dfrac{a}{2^m 5^n}$ where a is a non-zero integer and m and n are nonnegative integers may be written as a decimal fraction in two essentially distinct forms.

8   If a, b, and c are positive integers and $b > c$, which of the following is the true statement: $\dfrac{a}{b} = \dfrac{a}{c}$; $\dfrac{a}{b} < \dfrac{a}{c}$; $\dfrac{a}{b} > \dfrac{a}{c}$?

9   If, in exercise 8, a is a negative integer, which of the relations is the true statement?

the number
field of
elementary
mathematics

GUIDELINES FOR CAREFUL STUDY

The field of rational numbers provides the basic number structure sufficient for the intelligent servicing of a variety of the demands for quantitative inquiry and computational performance. This number field is characterized by a great amount of operational freedom due to the fact that the set of rational numbers is closed under each of the four operations addition, subtraction, multiplication, and division by non-zero divisors. In spite of this fact there still remain a few restrictions which prevent the exercise of complete procedural freedom. These restrictions will be considered in this chapter.

The following questions will serve as helpful guidelines for the careful study of Chap. 6.

1 What is the definition of a field?
2 In what decimal forms may rational numbers be expressed?
3 What is meant by the word "factor"?
4 What is meant by raising to a power?
5 What does a positive integer used as an exponent indicate?

6   What is meant by the extraction of a root?

7   What is the essential difference between a direct proof and an indirect proof?

8   What is an irrational number?

9   How may an irrational number be expressed as a decimal fraction?

10   What is the process for rounding approximate numbers?

11   What is a real number?

12   What is a number line and how may one be constructed?

13   What is meant by the absolute value of a real number?

14   What is a general condition that may be used for placing any two real numbers in their proper order with respect to each other?

15   What is the imaginary unit?

16   What is a complex number?

17   Why may the set of real numbers be considered as a proper subset of all complex numbers?

18   What are the definitions of equality, addition, and multiplication for complex numbers?

19   What are the additive and multiplicative identities for complex numbers?

20   What are the essential differences between these number fields: rational numbers, real numbers, complex numbers?

21   Can you, without reference to the book, construct the diagram of the number systems of elementary mathematics?

INTRODUCTION

In Chap. 4, when subtraction was introduced and defined as the inverse operation to addition, it became necessary to extend the natural number system to embrace the integers. This extension gave us the domain of integers, which was closed not only under addition and multiplication but also under the newly defined operation of subtraction. A further extension to the field of rational numbers (Chap. 5) became necessary to provide closure under the operation of division with nonzero divisors, defined as the inverse of multiplication.

The closure property, as applied to multiplication, has still other consequences which need to be investigated. A special form of multiplication occurs when all the factors in a given product are the same. We call this form of multiplication *raising to powers* (*involution*), and we use an exponential form of notation to indicate the product. For example, $2 \cdot 2 \cdot 2$ would be written as 2^3, where the positive integer 3 is the exponent which indicates the power to which 2 is to be raised. If the exponent is a positive integer, we know that an integer raised to any

Involution

such power will produce an integer ($2^3 = 2 \cdot 2 \cdot 2 = 8$), and a rational number raised to any such power will produce a rational number $\left[\left(\frac{3}{4}\right)^2 = \frac{3}{4} \cdot \frac{3}{4} = \frac{9}{16}\right]$. This is due to the fact that both integers and rational numbers are closed under multiplication.

Since the set of all integers is a proper subset of the set of rational numbers, the preceding paragraph may be summarized in these words: If we are given the fact that $a^n = b$ where a is a rational number and n is a positive integer, then we know that b is necessarily a rational number. Does it also follow that if b is a rational number and n is positive integer, then a is necessarily a rational number? From the examples of the preceding paragraph it is evident that if $a^3 = 8$, then $a = 2$, or if $a^2 = \frac{9}{16}$, then $a = \frac{3}{4}$. Another form in which to make these last two statements is to use radicals to indicate the *extraction of roots* (*evolution*). For example $\sqrt[3]{8} = 2$ is read "a cube root of 8 is 2," and $\sqrt{\frac{9}{16}} = \frac{3}{4}$ is read "the positive square root of $\frac{9}{16}$ is $\frac{3}{4}$." The difference in the wording of the two statements enclosed within quotation marks is not a matter of too great concern here. There are two square roots of $\frac{9}{16}$, one positive $\left(\frac{3}{4} \cdot \frac{3}{4} = \frac{9}{16}\right)$ and one negative $\left[\left(-\frac{3}{4}\right) \cdot \left(-\frac{3}{4}\right) = \frac{9}{16}\right]$ (Theorem 4–5, page 87). That there are cube roots of 8 other than 2 will be demonstrated later (see Exercise 7, page 174). The symbol $\sqrt[3]{8}$ may also be interpreted in the form of the question: What is a number which used 3 times as a factor will give 8 as the product? Similarly, the symbol $\sqrt{\frac{9}{16}}$ may be interpreted as the question: What positive number used 2 times as a factor will give $\frac{9}{16}$ as the product? In each of these two examples we were given a rational number b and asked to find a number a which when raised to a positive integral power would give b. In both cases we were able to find a rational number a that satisfied the equality $a^n = b$. That this is not always the case will be established in the next section.

Evolution

6–1   THE CONCEPT OF IRRATIONAL NUMBER

In order that the number system shall have closure under the operation of extraction of roots, an extension again becomes necessary. One illustration of the necessity of such extension is established by Theorem 6–1. In the proof of this theorem we shall use an indirect pattern of argument similar to that used in the proof of the corollary to Theorem 4–3 (page 86). We shall assume that there does exist a rational number whose square is 2, which is a contradiction of the desired conclusion. The argument will then show that this assumption implies a conclusion which contradicts a statement that must be true if the hypothesis of the theorem is true. Since this is an impossible situation, the assumption must be false. It then follows that the stated conclusion of the theorem is true.

Theorem 6–1   **There exists no rational number whose square is 2.**

Hypothesis   There exists the set of all rational numbers.

Conclusion   The square of no rational number is 2.

Proof

Statements	*Reasons*
1 There exists the rational number $\frac{a}{b}$ where a and b are relatively prime integers and $b \neq 0$	Hypothesis and the reduction of fractions
2 Assume $\frac{a^2}{b^2} = 2$	The assumed contradiction of the conclusion
3 $a^2 = 2b^2$	E–5 (multiply both sides by b^2)
4 Since 2 is a factor of the square of a, it must be a factor of a	The odd integers are closed under multiplication. (See Exercise 1-c, page 101.)
5 $a = 2m$, where m is an integer and $a^2 = 4m^2$	Definition of factor
6 $4m^2 = 2b^2$	Substitution in step 3
7 $2m^2 = b^2$	E–5 $\left(\text{multiply both sides by } \frac{1}{2}\right)$
8 $b = 2k$, where k is an integer	Same reasoning as in steps 4 and 5
9 a and b have a common factor 2, which contradicts step 1	Steps 5 and 8
10 Therefore 2 cannot be expressed as the square of a rational number	

While there exists no rational number whose square is 2, the pythagoreans exhibited the fact that there does exist such a number. It expresses the value of the ratio of the diagonal of a square to the length of a

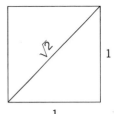

FIGURE 6-1   A pythagorean discovery.

side (see Fig. 6–1). Such numbers, which are not rational numbers, are called *irrational numbers*.† Many other types of irrational numbers exist. In addition to a few square roots and cube roots, the only such numbers significant here are π, the ratio of the circumference of a circle to its diameter, and the values of a few ratios related to triangles.‡

Irrational
numbers

6-2   DECIMAL REPRESENTATION OF IRRATIONAL NUMBERS

We have seen how every rational number may be expressed uniquely either as a finite decimal or as an infinite repeating decimal (Postulate 5–5). Similarly, we shall postulate a provable theorem concerning irrational numbers.

Postulate 6-1   **Every irrational number may be expressed in one and only one way as an infinite nonrepeating decimal.**

Irrational num-
bers as infinite
decimals

Although techniques exist for determining the successive digits in the decimal representation of irrational numbers, they do not submit to simple explicit formalization as in the case of rational numbers. In Fig. 6–2 two step-by-step approximations to the positive square root of 2 are given.

† The "ir" of the word "irrational" is a derivative from the Latin prefix "in," which means *not;* so the word "irrational" means simply "not rational."
‡ To prove that π is an irrational number is a much more involved process than to prove that $\sqrt{2}$ is irrational. That π is irrational was first shown by J. H. Lambert in 1767, and later supported by F. Lindeman in 1882.

FIGURE 6-2   Approximation to the positive square root of 2.

$$1^2 = 1 < 2 < 4 = 2^2$$
$$(1.4)^2 = 1.96 < 2 < 2.25 = (1.5)^2$$
$$(1.41)^2 = 1.9881 < 2 < 2.0164 = (1.42)^2$$
$$(1.414)^2 = 1.999396 < 2 < 2.002225 = (1.415)^2$$
$$(1.4142)^2 = 1.99996164 < 2 < 2.00024449 = (1.4143)^2$$
$$(1.41421)^2 = 1.9999899241 < 2 < 2.0000182084 = (1.41422)^2$$

Not any of the rational numbers exhibited in Fig. 6–2 gives 2 when squared. Each is a rational approximation to the square root of 2. From the last line we have that 1.41421 is a rational approximation to $\sqrt{2}$, correct to five decimal places. As can be seen, its square differs from 2 by a very small amount and by a smaller amount than does the square of 1.41422.

The chronology of π

The chronology[†] of π is an interesting and eventful story dating from the first scientific efforts of Archimedes (ca. 240 B.C.) to the modern age of the electronic computer. It has been given distinctive character by Biblical edict,[‡] efforts at state legislation,[§] the peculiar peregrinations of circle squarers,[¶] and inquiring research of competent mathematicians using the techniques of infinite series and, in recent years, the facilities of electronic computers. The most recent such computation gives the value of π correct to 100,000 decimal places.[††]

As with the square root of 2, rational approximation of the value of π can be given correct to any desired number of decimal places. Probably the most familiar approximations used are $\frac{22}{7}$, $3\frac{1}{7}$, 3.14, and 3.1416.

Many mnemonics have been given from time to time to aid in quoting a value of π correct to a specified number of decimal places.

It should be quite evident that, in the use of irrational numbers, it frequently becomes necessary to round the decimal representation of a given number to some selected number of decimal places. This means that all digits to the right of a chosen position in the decimal representation are to be dropped. The question then naturally arises of how to obtain the best approximation to the irrational number, within the selected number of decimal places.

Example   What is the best approximation, to three decimal places, to $\sqrt{2}$?

From Fig. 6–2 it is evident that $\sqrt{2}$ lies between 1.414 and 1.415. Therefore, one or the other of these two numbers is the answer to the question posed. $(1.414)^2 = 1.999396$, which differs from 2 by the

---

[†] Howard Eves, "An Introduction to the History of Mathematics," pp. 90–96, Holt, Rinehart, and Winston, Inc., New York, 1953.

H. C. Schipler, The Chronology of Pi, *Mathematics Magazine*, January–February, 1950, pp. 165–170; March–April, 1950, pp. 216–228; May–June, 1950, pp. 279–283.

[‡] "Then he made the molten sea; it was round, ten cubits from brim to brim, and five cubits high, and a line of thirty cubits measured its circumference." (I Kings 7:23 and II Chronicles 4:2.)

[§] House Bill No. 246 of the Indiana State Legislature (1897): "Be it enacted by the General Assembly of the State of Indiana: It has been found that a circular area is to the square on a line equal to the quadrant of the circumference, as the area of an equilateral rectangle is to the square on one side . . . ." (Eves, *ibid.*)

[¶] Among the more ambitious of such efforts are the voluminous writings of one author in support of the claim that the value of π is given exactly by the rational number $3\frac{13}{81}$.

[††] Daniel Shanks and John W. Wrench, Jr., Calculation of π to 100,000 Decimal Places, *Math. Computation*, **16** (January, 1962):76–99.

amount of 0.000604, and $(1.415)^2 = 2.002225$, which differs from 2 by the amount 0.002225. The difference 0.002225 is much larger than the difference 0.000604, so 1.414 is a closer approximation, correct to three decimal places, to $\sqrt{2}$ than is 1.415.

Example From Fig. 6–2 it is also seen that 1.41421 is a better approximation to $\sqrt{2}$ than is 1.41422. Notice that in order to obtain 1.414 from 1.41421, the digits 21 at the extreme right are dropped and nothing is done to the digits retained.

The value of π, correct to eight decimal places, is 3.14159265. One of the most frequently used approximations is 3.1416, which is correct to four decimal places. Note that in this case the digits to the right of the indicated position, the fourth decimal place, are dropped, but this time the extreme right-hand digit of those retained is increased by 1, from 5 to 6.

The illustrations of the two examples demonstrate the important technique of *rounding numbers*. Similar practices are followed in rounding the repeating decimal representation of rational numbers. For example, $\frac{1}{3} = 0.\overline{3}$, which is closely approximated to three decimal places by 0.333; and $\frac{1}{6} = 0.1\overline{6}$ which, correct to three decimal places, is 0.167. They also illustrate applications of the rule to be followed.

Rounding numbers

Rule for Rounding Numbers If the extreme left digit of those being dropped is 5 or more, increase by 1 the extreme right digit of those being retained. If the extreme left digit is less than 5, make no change in the digits retained.

Attention should be called to the fact that, when whole numbers are rounded, zeros are required as placeholders for the digits dropped in order to maintain the relative place value for the digits which are not dropped. This is neither necessary nor desirable when fractions are rounded. For example, if 28,672 were rounded to retain only two non-zero digits, it would become 29,000, while 0.28672 would become 0.29.

Other rules are sometimes given. The results from all rules are essentially the same, and this rule submits itself to concise and simple statement. Whatever rule is given, the basic idea is to balance that which is dropped in a given computation with that which is retained. In electronic computation, or any pattern of computation which involves a sequence of operations with approximations, this problem becomes a very serious one in which more careful refinements are necessary than are possible to investigate here.

6-3   THE CONCEPT OF REAL NUMBER

In each of the previous extensions—from natural numbers to integers, from integers to rational numbers—it has been fairly simple to extend the definitions of the basic operations to accommodate the new numbers. This has not been the case with the extension to real numbers. In fact, a good many centuries marked the time between the disturbing discovery of the existence of irrational numbers by the pythagoreans (ca. 540 B.C.) and the refinement of their definition late in the nineteenth century by Georg Cantor (1845–1918), Richard Dedekind (1831–1916), and Karl Weierstrass (1815–1897). These and subsequent researches have led to further refinements, all of which have given a sound philosophical basis for the generalization from the field of rational numbers of the operations of addition, subtraction, multiplication, and division as well as the relations of "equal to," "less than," and "greater than." All the properties which characterized these operations and relations in the field of rational numbers are retained under this new extension. Unlike the rational numbers, however, the irrational numbers are not closed under these operations. One counterexample in each case will suffice to establish the truth of this statement:

1   Addition $\sqrt{2} + (-\sqrt{2}) = 0$; definition of additive inverse.
2   Subtraction $\sqrt{2} - \sqrt{2} = \sqrt{2} + (-\sqrt{2}) = 0$; definition of subtraction.
3   Multiplication $\sqrt{2} \times \sqrt{2} = 2$; definition of square root.
4   Division $\sqrt{2} \div \sqrt{2} = 1$, since $\sqrt{2} \times 1 = \sqrt{2}$; definition of division.
The numbers 0, 1, and 2 are not irrational numbers.

Rational numbers as a proper subset of real numbers   The set of all rational numbers and the set of all irrational numbers are disjoint sets and their union is the set of all *real numbers*. Since every irrational number can be expressed uniquely as an infinite nonrepeating decimal (Postulate 6–1), we may state the following postulate concerning real numbers.

Postulate 6-2   **Every real number may be expressed in one and only one way either as a finite decimal, an infinite repeating decimal, or an infinite nonrepeating decimal.**

On page 147 the statement was made that, at times, mathematicians prefer to think of finite decimals as infinite repeating decimals. In Exercise 8, page 152, you were asked to show that the rational number $\frac{1}{2}$ can be expressed as an infinite repeating decimal in either of the two forms $0.5\bar{0}$ or $0.4\bar{9}$. Likewise, 0.43 can be expressed as $0.43\bar{0}$ or $0.42\bar{9}$.

(As an exercise you might prove this.)   A similar statement can be proved about any rational number.   For certain good reasons the mathematician prefers to use the succession of 9's rather than the succession of 0's.   If it is agreed that any finite decimal will be written as an infinite repeating decimal in a form such as $0.5 = 0.4\bar{9}$ or $0.43 = 0.42\bar{9}$, Postulate 6–2 may be written in the equivalent, but simpler, language:

Postulate 6–2′ **Every real number may be expressed uniquely as an infinite decimal.**

Real numbers
as infinite
decimals

Postulate 6–2, or its simplified form, provides the background for the proof of an important property of real numbers which will be postulated here.

Postulate 6–3 **There exists a one-to-one correspondence between the set of all real numbers and the set of points on a line; that is, to each real number there corresponds one and only one point, and to each point there corresponds one and only one real number.**

The real
number line

This correspondence on the *number line* may be set up in a manner described in the six steps:

1   On a line of infinite extent, mark a reference point, O in Fig. 6–3, and place it in correspondence with the real number 0.   This point will be referred to as the *origin* or *point of reference.*

2   Choose a positive direction on the line, to the right in Fig. 6–3. The opposite direction (to the left) then will be the negative direction on the line.

3   Mark a second point, A in Fig. 6–3, and place it in correspondence with the real number 1. OA then becomes a unit to be applied to the line.

4   Assume that this unit can be applied indefinitely along the line, as it were, without loss of identity.   By such application to the right from O, points are selected which are in one-to-one correspondence with the positive integers.   Application to the left from O will select the points in correspondence with the negative integers.

5   Points can now be placed in correspondence with the rational fractions, by constructing the appropriate fractional parts of the unit length OA and applying them in the proper intervals between integers. The rational number $2\frac{1}{2}$ can be placed in correspondence with the point

FIGURE 6–3
The real number
line.

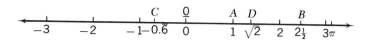

B, which is one-half unit distance more than 2 units to the right of O. The rational number $-0.\overline{6}$ can be placed in correspondence with the point C, which is two-thirds unit distance to the left of O.

By the technique outlined in these five steps a unique point can be found on the number line to correspond to any rational number. Such points are referred to as *rational points*. An interesting and important observation to make here is that for any two distinct rational points, no matter how close together they may be located, there always exists at least one rational point which lies between them. For example, if a and b are distinct rational numbers then their average $\left(\dfrac{a+b}{2}\right)$ is a rational number c which is between a and b. (See Exercise 10 at the end of this chapter.) The rational point c (the point on the number line which corresponds to c) will be located between the rational points a and b. This fact, which seems intuitively correct, will be accepted here without formal argument. Similarly, the rational point $\dfrac{a+c}{2}$ will be located between the rational points a and c, hence between the rational points a and b. This can be continued indefinitely to exhibit an infinite number of rational numbers between any two given rational points a and b. Because of this fact and the fact that the set of rational numbers is a subset of the real numbers, the rational numbers are said to be *dense* in the reals. Synonymously, the rational points are said to be dense in the number line.

Density of rational numbers

Example   In Fig. 6–4 the rational points 1 and 3 are shown. The rational point $2 = \dfrac{1+3}{2}$ is located between them. The point $\dfrac{3}{2} = \dfrac{1+2}{2}$ is between 1 and 2 and, therefore, between 1 and 3. Similarly, $\dfrac{5}{4} = \dfrac{1+\frac{3}{2}}{2}, \dfrac{9}{8} = \dfrac{1+\frac{5}{4}}{2}, \dfrac{17}{16} = \dfrac{1+\frac{9}{8}}{2}$ are all between 1 and 3. The process can be continued indefinitely to exhibit an infinite number of rational points between 1 and 3.

6   Points on the line can also be found to correspond to irrational numbers. We shall see later (Sec. 8–7) how the pythagorean theorem applied to right triangles such as triangle OAD of Fig. 6–5 establishes the fact that $\overline{OD}$ is $\sqrt{2}$ units in length if $\overline{OA}$ and $\overline{AD}$ are each 1 unit in

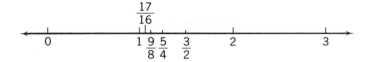

FIGURE 6–4
Rational points on
the real number
line.

FIGURE 6-5   The pythagorean property.

length.   The length of $\overline{OD}$ has been measured on the number line, and
the point D is placed in correspondence with the real number $\sqrt{2}$.   This
is but one illustration.   The techniques for finding other irrational points
would not all be so simple as this illustration.

With this correspondence established the real numbers may be identified with distances measured from the point of reference on the number line.   A real number a is then said to be *less than* a real number   Order
b (that is, $a < b$) if and only if the point which corresponds to a on the
number line is to the left of the point which corresponds to b.   If the
point corresponding to a is to the right of the one corresponding to b,
then a is said to be *greater than* b $(a > b)$.   If the two points coincide,
then $a = b$.   Thus a positive real number a is one whose corresponding
point on the number line is to the right of the reference point O and can
be identified by the symbol $a > 0$.   By like token a negative real number b is one whose corresponding point is on the number line to the left
of the reference point O.   It may be identified by $b < 0$, in which case
$-b > 0$.

6-4   THE FIELD OF REAL NUMBERS

With the definitions of the fundamental operations extended to apply
to irrational numbers as well as rational numbers, the set of real numbers satisfy the field postulates F-1 to F-8 (page 127).   As was pointed
out in the 'ast paragraph of the preceding section, the real numbers can
be ordered in increasing order of magnitude in terms of their relative
position on the number line.   This is equivalent to the previous techniques for ordering the integers and the rational numbers.   In fact, for
real numbers which are integers or, more generally, for rational numbers, either the previously developed tests or that presently mentioned
may be used.

Example

1 $8 > 5$ since the point which corresponds to 8 is on the number line
to the right of the point which corresponds to 5.   This is equivalent
to saying that $8 - 5 = 3$, a positive integer.

2   $-\dfrac{15}{4} < -\dfrac{7}{3}$ since the point which corresponds to $-\dfrac{15}{4}$ is on the

number line to the left of the point corresponding to $-\dfrac{7}{3}$.   This is

equivalent to saying that $(-15)(3) < 4(-7)$, the test for rational numbers.

3   $\sqrt{2} > \dfrac{1}{2}$ since the point which corresponds to $\sqrt{2}$ is on the number

line to the right of the point which corresponds to $\dfrac{1}{2}$.   Another

method for comparing two such numbers is by means of their decimal expansions.

Properties of positive real numbers

The field of real numbers is an ordered field since the positive real numbers share with the positive integers and positive rational numbers the following three important postulated properties:

1   *Addition*   The sum of two positive real numbers is a positive real number.

2   *Multiplication*   The product of two positive real numbers is a positive real number.

3   *Trichotomy*   For any given real number a, one and only one of the following three relations holds: a is positive ($a > 0$), $a = 0$, or $-a$ is positive ($-a > 0$).

In many situations one may be concerned merely with the numerical value of a number, and not whether it is positive or negative.   If one person loses \$5 and another gains \$5, the amount of money is the same.   True, for any given individual, it might make considerable difference whether he gains or loses the \$5, but that does not alter the fact that the numerical value of the money involved is \$5.   If we symbolize the loss of \$5 by -5, the gain of \$5 by $+5$, and the numerical value involved by $|-5|$ or $|+5|$, as the case may be, we can make this evidently true statement: $|-5| = |+5| = 5$.   This is an illustration of a very important concept in dealing with real numbers.

Absolute value

Definition 6-1   The *numerical,* or *absolute value* of the real number a is such that

$$|a| = a \qquad \text{if } a \geq 0$$

$$|a| = -a \qquad \text{if } a < 0$$

Note that, in the definition, *numerical value* and *absolute value* are used synonymously.   Mathematicians, for good reasons which are not pertinent here, give preference in most instances to the phrase "absolute value" over "numerical value." In the context of this discussion, they may be used interchangeably.

Example

1 The condition $a \geq 0$ simply means that the real number is either positive or equal to zero. If a is $+9$, then $|a| = |+9| = 9$. If a is 0, then $|a| = |0| = 0$.

2 The condition $a < 0$ means that a is negative, that is, it is located on the number line to the left of the reference point O. If $a = -6$, then $|a| = |-6| = -(-6)$ by definition. From Exercise 17, page 102, it follows that $-(-6) = 6$.

In Fig. 6–6 the portion of the number line from -2 to $+2$ has been indicated. Any portion of the number line thus specifically designated may be referred to as an *interval*. Several points in this interval have been labeled by the real numbers to which they correspond. The two points labeled in color to correspond to -2 and 2, respectively, are each two units' distance from the origin. Each of the other points of the interval is less than two units' distance from the origin. This means that each of the points labeled in black is to the right of the point labeled -2; that is, -2 is less than each of the corresponding

Interval on the number line

numbers. (For example, $-2 < -\sqrt{2}$; $-2 < -1$; $-2 < -\frac{1}{2}$; $-2 < 0$; $-2 < \frac{1}{2}$; and $-2 < \frac{5}{3}$ are a few specific illustrations.) Similarly, each of these numbers is less than 2. (Thus, $-\sqrt{2} < 2$; $-1 < 2$; $-\frac{1}{2} < 2$; $0 < 2$; $\frac{1}{2} < 2$; $\frac{5}{3} < 2$.) We may combine these two statements about the numbers in the interval into this one statement: Each number of the interval is greater than -2 but less than 2. (In symbols, $-2 < -\sqrt{2} < 2$; $-2 < -1 < 2$; $-2 < -\frac{1}{2} < 2$; $-2 < 0 < 2$; $-2 < \frac{1}{2} < 2$; $-2 < \frac{5}{3} < 2$.) If we use some symbol, say x, to represent any number in the interval, then we may state this fact by the symbol $-2 < x < 2$, which may be read either of two ways: x is greater than -2 but less than 2; or -2 is less than x, which is less than 2. The symbol $|x| < 2$ also means the same thing. [For example, $|-\sqrt{2}| = -(-\sqrt{2}) = \sqrt{2} < 2$; $|-1| = -(-1) = 1 < 2$; $\left|-\frac{1}{2}\right| = -\left(-\frac{1}{2}\right) =$

FIGURE 6–6   The interval $-2 \leq x \leq 2$.

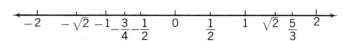

$\frac{1}{2} < 2$; $|0| = 0 < 2$; $\left|\frac{1}{2}\right| = \frac{1}{2} < 2$; $\left|\frac{5}{3}\right| = \frac{5}{3} < 2$.] If we wish to indicate that both -2 and $+2$ are possible values of x, then the two symbols should be written $-2 \leq x \leq 2$ (-2 is less than or equal to x, which is less than or equal to 2); $|x| \leq 2$ (the absolute, or numerical, value of x is less than or equal to 2).

Example   Express each of these inequalities in the equivalent form $a \leq x \leq b$: (1) $|x| \leq 5$; (2) $|x + 3| \leq 2$.

1 $|x| \leq 5$ means that the numerical value of x is a number less than 5 or at most equal to 5. This means that $-5 \leq x \leq 5$.

2   As in item 1, $|x + 3| \leq 2$ means $-2 \leq x + 3 \leq 2$. Since Theorem 3–4 (page 75) holds for real numbers as well as natural numbers, we may add -3 to each member of these inequalities to get

$$
\begin{array}{ccc}
-2 \leq & x + 3 & \leq 2 \\
-3 & -3 & -3 \\
\hline
-5 \leq & x & \leq -1
\end{array}
$$

Over the field of real numbers it is always possible to solve linear equations of the form $ax + b = c$, where a, b, and c are real numbers with $a \neq 0$. While there are also equations of higher degree with real coefficients which can be solved over the field of real numbers, there are other such equations for which solutions do not exist until a further extension of the number system is made. As a simple illustration of this fact, consider the equation $x^2 = -4$. To solve this equation is to find a real number which multiplied by itself will give -4. Because the proposition of Theorem 4–5 (page 87) can be extended to real numbers there exists no negative real number whose square is a negative real number. Furthermore, positive real numbers are closed under multiplication. Therefore, there exists no real number whose square is a negative real number.

6–5   THE FIELD OF COMPLEX NUMBERS

The needed extension of the number field to make possible the solution of such equations as $x^2 = -4$ calls for the introduction of a new unit. In the real field the unit is 1. We now define a new unit $i = \sqrt{-1}$, called the *imaginary unit*, which is such that $i^2 = -1$. With the introduction of this new unit we also postulate the existence of the set of complex numbers.

The imaginary unit

Complex numbers

Postulate 6–4   There exist complex numbers of the form $a + bi$ where a and b are real numbers and $i = \sqrt{-1}$ is such that $i^2 = -1$.

For complex numbers we then state these definitions:

Definition 6-2 Two complex numbers $a + bi$ and $c + di$ are equal   Equality
if and only if $a = c$ and $b = d$.

Definition 6-3 The sum of the two complex numbers $a + bi$ and   Addition
$c + di$ is the complex number $(a + c) + (b + d)i$.

Definition 6-4 The product of the two complex numbers $a + bi$ and   Multiplication
$c + di$ is the complex number $(ac - bd) + (ad + bc)i$.

Just as in the case of real numbers, subtraction of complex numbers
is the inverse of addition, and division is the inverse of multiplication.

Under these definitions of addition and multiplication the closure,
associative, commutative, and distributive properties can be shown to
hold for complex numbers. The additive identity exists and is the complex number $0 + 0i$ since $(a + bi) + (0 + 0i) = (a + 0) + (b + 0)i =$
$a + bi$ by the field properties of real numbers. Similarly, the multipli-   Field of com-
cative identity is $1 + 0i$ since   plex numbers

$$(a + bi) \cdot (1 + 0i) = (a \cdot 1 - b \cdot 0) + (a \cdot 0 + b \cdot 1)i = a + bi$$

by the field properties of real numbers. Finally, additive and multiplicative inverses can be shown to exist. Hence the set of all complex
numbers with addition and multiplication, as defined above, satisfy the
field properties F-1 to F-8 (page 127).

The additive inverse of $a + bi$ is the complex number $(-a) + (-b)i$,   The additive
or more simply $-a - bi$. For proof of this statement see exercise 16,   inverse
page 173. It may be verified as follows:

$$(a + bi) + [(-a) + (-b)i] = [a + (-a)] + [b + (-b)i]$$
$$= 0 + 0 \cdot i$$

Similarly, exercise 9 (page 174) calls for proof of the fact that the
multiplicative inverse of $a + bi$ is the complex number $\dfrac{a}{a^2 + b^2} -$ The multiplica-
$\dfrac{b}{a^2 + b^2} i$. Of course this inverse does not exist if both a and b are 0.   tive inverse
As verification we have

$$(a + bi) \cdot \left(\frac{a}{a^2 + b^2} - \frac{b}{a^2 + b^2} i \right) = \left(\frac{a^2}{a^2 + b^2} + \frac{b^2}{a^2 + b^2} \right)$$
$$+ \left(\frac{-ab}{a^2 + b^2} + \frac{ab}{a^2 + b^2} \right) i$$
$$= \frac{a^2 + b^2}{a^2 + b^2} + 0 \cdot i$$
$$= 1 + 0 \cdot i$$

The inverse relation between multiplication and division in the field of real numbers continues to hold for complex numbers. It thus follows that the quotient $(a + bi) \div (c + di)$ can be obtained by multiplying $a + bi$ by the multiplicative inverse of $c + di$.

$$(a + bi) \div (c + di) = (a + bi) \cdot \left(\frac{c}{c^2 + d^2} - \frac{d}{c^2 + d^2}i \right)$$

Example   Find the quotient $\dfrac{2 + 3i}{1 + 2i}$.

The multiplicative inverse of $1 + 2i$ is the complex number $\dfrac{1}{1 + 4} - \dfrac{2}{1 + 4}i = \dfrac{1}{5} - \dfrac{2}{5}i$. Therefore

$$(2 + 3i) \div (1 + 2i) = (2 + 3i)\left(\frac{1}{5} - \frac{2}{5}i \right)$$

$$= \left(\frac{2}{5} + \frac{6}{5} \right) + \left(\frac{-4}{5} + \frac{3}{5} \right)i$$

$$= \frac{8}{5} - \frac{1}{5}i$$

Check: $(1 + 2i) \cdot \left(\dfrac{8}{5} - \dfrac{1}{5}i \right) = \left(\dfrac{8}{5} + \dfrac{2}{5} \right) + \left(\dfrac{-1}{5} + \dfrac{16}{5} \right)i$

$$= 2 + 3i$$

In this field there exists a number x such that $x^2 = -4$. There are indeed two values of x which meet the conditions of this equation. If $x = 2i$, then $x^2 = (2i)(2i) = (0 + 2i)(0 + 2i)$. From the definition of multiplication we have

$$(0 + 2i)(0 + 2i) = (0 \cdot 0 - 2 \cdot 2) + (0 \cdot 2 + 2 \cdot 0)i = -4 + 0i = -4$$

whence $x^2 = -4$. This multiplication can be accomplished in a much simpler way if we recall that the definition of multiplication for complex numbers is such that it is both associative and commutative. From this fact we have $x^2 = (2i)(2i) = (2 \cdot 2)(i \cdot i) = 4i^2 = 4(-1) = -4$. Similarly, $x = -2i$ is a solution, since

$$x^2 = (-2i)(-2i) = (-2)(-2)(i \cdot i) = 4i^2 = 4(-1) = -4$$

Numbers such as $2i$ or $-2i$, which are of the form bi, are called *pure imaginary numbers*.

Not only are simple quadratic equations of this type solvable in the field of complex numbers, but no further extensions of our number system are necessary to solve any algebraic equations of the form

$$ax^n + bx^{n-1} + cx^{n-2} + \cdots + d = 0$$

where n is a positive integer, and a, b, c, d, ... are complex numbers.

6-6   THE NUMBER SYSTEMS OF ELEMENTARY MATHEMATICS

In each of the number systems, two requisites that have persisted are that the previously established set of numbers must be a subset of the newly defined set and that the newly defined operational processes must give results consistent with previously established definitions. These conditions are met in the extension from the field of real numbers to the field of complex numbers. The real number a may be represented as the complex number $a + 0i$, and thus the set of real numbers is a proper subset of the set of complex numbers. Furthermore, from the definition of the sum of two complex numbers, we have

Real numbers as a proper subset of complex numbers

$$(a + 0i) + (b + 0i) = (a + b) + (0 + 0)i = (a + b) + 0i$$

which is the representation of the real number $a + b$. This is the sum of the two real numbers a and b in accordance with the definition of addition of real numbers. Similarly, the product

$$(a + 0i)(b + 0i) = (ab - 0 \cdot 0) + (a \cdot 0 + 0 \cdot b)i = ab + 0i$$

which is the representation of the real number ab.

The outline of the entire discussion of Chaps. 3 to 6 is presented briefly, but significantly, in the diagram of Fig. 6–7.

The number experiences of the elementary school are confined to the field of real numbers. In fact, with the exception of the irrational number π and a few square roots, these experiences are restricted to the field of rational numbers. That these should be tremendously significant mathematical experiences is emphasized by the diagram of Fig. 6–7 since it places the field of real numbers and its subfield of rational numbers in their proper orientation in the structure of the complex number system, which is the self-sufficient number system of elementary mathematics. The diagram also lends emphasis to the fact that the surety of structure and the firmness of understanding in any extension of the number system not only are dependent upon the soundness of all substructure but also are essential to the strength and elegance of all superstructure.

Exercises

1   Give three illustrations each of the operations of involution and evolution. Explain how these two operations are inverse operations to each other.
2   Distinguish between rational and irrational numbers.
3   Is 0 a rational number or an irrational number?

FIGURE 6–7   The number systems of elementary mathematics.

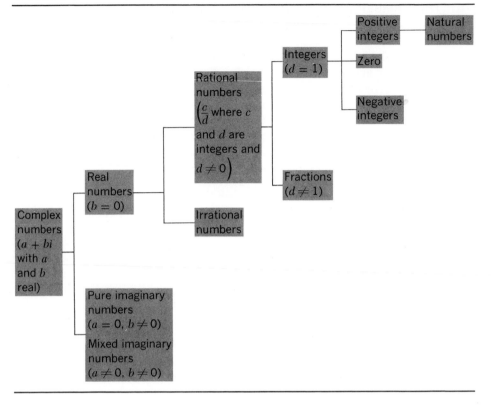

4   Prove that $\sqrt{3}$ is an irrational number.

5   Follow the pattern of Fig. 6–2 to exhibit two approximations to the positive square root of 3. (*Hint:* Use a table of squares and square roots and build the approximation correct to the nearest ten-thousandth.)

6   Is the set of all irrational numbers with the usual definitions of addition and multiplication a field?

7   Express each of these real numbers as an infinite decimal:

(a) $\dfrac{5}{7}$ (b) $\dfrac{7}{8}$ (c) $\dfrac{2}{3}$ (d) $7\frac{1}{2}$

8   Draw a number line and mark a point on it to correspond to each of these rational numbers: 5, $-\frac{1}{2}$, $3\frac{1}{2}$, -6, 0.5, $0.\overline{3}$, 0.125, $-1.\overline{6}$.

9   Find four rational numbers between $3\frac{1}{4}$ and $3\frac{1}{2}$.

10   *Prove Theorem 6–2:* If a and b are rational numbers such that $a < b$, then $a < \dfrac{a+b}{2} < b$. $\left(\textit{Hint:}\ \dfrac{a+b}{2} = \dfrac{a}{2} + \dfrac{b}{2}.\right)$

11   On the number line drawn for Exercise 8, mark a point to correspond to each of these irrational numbers: $\sqrt{2}$, $\sqrt{3}$, $\sqrt[3]{4}$, $-\sqrt[3]{2}$,

$\pi = 3.1415\cdots$. (*Hint:* Use a table of square roots and cube roots. Round each number correct to the nearest tenth and use this approximation as the representation to be marked on the number line.)

12 Arrange these numbers in ascending order from left to right: $\sqrt[3]{3}$, -2, -1.25, 0.857, $-1.2\overline{5}$, $-\sqrt[3]{2}$, 1.4, 1.414, $0.85\overline{7}$, $\dfrac{6}{7}$.

13 Express each absolute value in its equivalent form using inequalities of the form $-a < x < a$ or $-a \leq x \leq a$.

(a) $|x| < 3$ (b) $|x| \leq \dfrac{1}{2}$

(c) $|x + 2| \leq 4$ (d) $|x - 1| \leq 3$

14 Express each inequality in its equivalent form using absolute value:

(a) $-1 \leq x \leq 1$ (b) $3 \leq x \leq 5$
(c) $-5 < x < 5$ (d) $-\sqrt{3} \leq x \leq \sqrt{3}$

15 Find the sum and product of each pair of complex numbers:

(a) $2 + i, 3 + 2i$ (b) $1 + i, 1 - i$
(c) $i, 2 + 4i$ (d) $3 - i, 4 - i$
(e) $-4i, 3i$ (f) $4, 2 + 3i$

(g) $\sqrt{2} + \sqrt{3}i, \sqrt{2} - \sqrt{3}i$ (h) $\dfrac{1}{2} + \dfrac{\sqrt{3}}{2}i, \dfrac{1}{2} + \dfrac{\sqrt{3}}{2}i$

(i) $\dfrac{1}{2} + \dfrac{\sqrt{3}}{2}i, \dfrac{1}{2} - \dfrac{\sqrt{3}}{2}i$ (j) $\dfrac{\sqrt{3}}{2} + \dfrac{1}{2}i, 2 - i$

16 Prove that the complex number $-a - bi$ is the additive inverse of $a + bi$.

17 Write the additive and multiplicative inverse of each of these complex numbers.

(a) $1 + i$ (b) $3 + 4i$
(c) $5 - 12i$ (d) $-\sqrt{2} + \sqrt{3}i$
(e) $-1 - i$ (f) $-2 - \sqrt{3}i$

18 Find these quotients.

(a) $\dfrac{3 + i}{1 - i}$ (b) $\dfrac{2 - 3i}{3 + 4i}$

(c) $\dfrac{6 + 5i}{2 - 3i}$

19 Follow the diagram of the number system of elementary mathematics (Fig. 6–7) and give the most restricted classification of each of these numbers: 6, $-\dfrac{7}{8}$, $\sqrt[3]{2}$, -1.5, -4, π, $\sqrt{9}$, $2i$, $3 - 4i$.

(*Hint:* 6 is a natural number, π is an irrational number.)

INVITATIONS TO EXTENDED STUDY

1   Prove that $\sqrt[3]{4}$ is an irrational number.

2   Prove that the multiplicative inverse of an irrational number is also irrational.

3   Prove that $\sqrt{6}$ is an irrational number.

4   Prove that $\sqrt{2} + \sqrt{3}$ is an irrational number.

5   Show that numbers of the form $a + b\sqrt{2}$ where a and b are rational numbers form a field.

6   Prove that the set of all complex numbers is closed under addition; under multiplication; under subtraction; under division.

7   Use the definition of multiplication for complex numbers to show that both $-1 + \sqrt{3}i$ and $-1 - \sqrt{3}i$ are cube roots of 8.

8   The *conjugate* of the complex number $a + bi$ is $a - bi$. Use this definition to prove that the product of any complex number (other than the additive identity) by its conjugate is always a positive real number.

9   The multiplicative inverse of $a + bi$ (when $\neq 0 + 0i$) may be written in the reciprocal form $\dfrac{1}{a + bi}$. Show that this multiplicative inverse may be written as the complex number $\dfrac{a}{a^2 + b^2} - \dfrac{b}{a^2 + b^2}i$ where $\dfrac{a}{a^2 + b^2}$ and $\dfrac{b}{a^2 + b^2}$ are real numbers.

10   Prove that, for complex numbers, addition, and subtraction are inverse operations; also that multiplication and division are inverse operations.

11   Show that numbers of the form $a + b\sqrt{3}$, where a and b are integers, satisfy the properties of an integral domain.

12   Show that the complex numbers $a + bi$, where a and b are integers, satisfy the properties of an integral domain. Such numbers are called *Gaussian integers*.

CHAPTER 7
modular arithmetic

GUIDELINES FOR CAREFUL STUDY

In previous chapters the emphasis has been on the structure of our number system and the characteristics of a number field. In particular, we have been interested in the rational, real, and complex number fields. While the complex number field has been exhibited as the only self-sufficient number field of elementary mathematics, actually the field of real numbers, and in many cases the field of rational numbers, suffices to provide for all normal quantitative needs at the elementary level.

There are many other types of mathematical systems, some more involved and some much simpler than those we have studied. It is not the purpose of this book to pursue the study of the structure of mathematical systems to any greater extent than that already accomplished. Our attention now will be directed to the study of some of the basic concepts and principles of position, shape, size, and functional relationship. Before making this departure, however, it will be both instructive and interesting to examine briefly one of the simpler yet more important number systems. This is the purpose of this chapter.

The following questions will serve as helpful guidelines to the careful study of Chap. 7.

1   What is meant by a well-defined binary operation?
2   What are the basic properties of a field?
3   What is the definition of a group? An abelian group?
4   What is meant when one integer is said to be congruent to another integer?
5   What is meant by the modulus of a particular congruence?
6   What is modular arithmetic?
7   What is meant by "addition modulo m"?
8   What is meant by "multiplication modulo m"?
9   What are the simple tests of divisibility, and how can the concept of congruency of integers be used in developing them?

INTRODUCTION

Each of the number systems so far studied has been characterized, along with other properties, by two well-defined binary operations. One of the patterns used for constructing simpler number systems is to shape a structure based on only one well-defined binary operation. We shall draw our discussion of number systems to a close with a brief examination of one such system which is of great significance in the study of mathematics. Although most of the real significance of this system is beyond the scope of this book, we shall have the opportunity to view it in the simplicity of its structure and to examine some of its applications.

7-1   THE CONCEPT OF GROUP

Among the simplest of all mathematical systems is the *group*, which consists of a set of elements and one well-defined operation which has certain characteristic properties in accordance with this definition.

Definition of
a group

Definition 7-1   **A *group* consists of a set of elements $G = \{a,b,c, \ldots \}$ and one well-defined operation (*) such that the set satisfies the following postulates under the given operation:†**

† The symbol *, call it "star," is used to represent an unspecified operation. For specific types of groups the operation * will be translated into the appropriate operational symbol. For example, for an *additive group* * will be interpreted as $+$, the sign for addition.

G-1   Closure   If $a * b = x$, then x is in G.

G-2   Associative $a * (b * c) = (a * b) * c$.

G-3   Identity   There exists in G an element i, called the identity element, such that $i * a = a$ for each a in G.

G-4   Inverse   For each element a in G there exists in G an element a^{-1}, called the inverse of a, such that $a^{-1} * a = i$.

If, in addition to these four properties, the set G also satisfies the commutative property under the operation $(*)$, the group is said to be a *commutative*, or *abelian*, *group*.

Abelian group

G-5   Commutative $a * b = b * a$.

Example   Given the set $G = \{a,b\}$ and the operation $(*)$ defined by the table of Fig. 7–1, show that the system is a group.
  The table is read: $a * a = a$; $a * b = b$; $b * a = b$; and $b * b = a$.

1   An examination of the table reveals that the set has closure under the given operation since a and b are the only elements seen in the table, and they are both elements of the set.
  2   One example will be given of the associative property:

$$a * (b * a) = a * b = b \qquad \text{from Fig. 7–1}$$
$$(a * b) * a = b * a = b$$

It thus follows that $a * (b * a) = (a * b) * a$.
  To establish this property for the system would call for the verification of all such possible groupings.

3   From the first row we see that $a * a = a$ and $a * b = b$, which exhibits a as the identity element.
  4   From the fact that $a * a = a$ and $b * b = a$ it is evident that each element is its own inverse.
  5   This system is, in fact, an abelian group since $a * b = b * a$.

Example   Does the set of all real numbers with the usual definition of multiplication† form a group?

1   The set of real numbers, under the operations of addition and multiplication, is a field, so that the system is necessarily closed with respect to multiplication.

† Here the operation $*$ is defined to be multiplication, $\times$.

$*$	a	b
a	a	b
b	b	a

FIGURE 7–1   Operational table for $G = \{a,b\}$.

2 Multiplication of real numbers is associative.

3 The real number 1 is the identity element.

4 The number 0 is a real number and there does not exist a multiplicative inverse for 0.

This system is not a group, since it does not have the property that for every element of the system there exists an inverse with respect to multiplication.

Example Does the set of all real numbers with the usual definition of addition as the given operation form a group?

1 The system is closed with respect to addition.

2 The addition of real numbers is associative.

3 The real number 0 is the additive identity.

4 For every real number there does exist an additive inverse.

This system is a group. Furthermore, it is an abelian group. Why?

7–2 CALENDAR ARITHMETIC

Suppose you were asked the question: What day of the week will it be 90 days from today? Whatever pattern of thinking you might use in arriving at an answer to the question, it would in one way or another involve determining the number of weeks in 90 days and the number of extra days. The simplest way to determine these facts is to divide 90 by 7. The quotient will indicate the number of weeks and the remainder will be the number of extra days: $90 \div 7 = 12$ with 6 as a remainder. There are 12 weeks and 6 days in 90 days. After this has been determined the 12 may be discarded, since any number of weeks from a given day in the week is that same day. All that is necessary to determine the answer to the question is to use the remainder 6 and count that number of days from the given day. For example, assume the "today" of the question to be Wednesday. Twelve weeks from Wednesday will be Wednesday, and 6 days more will be Tuesday of the next week. So if the original question had been "What day of the week will it be 90 days from Wednesday?" the answer would be "Tuesday."

It is to be noticed that the answer would be the same if the 90 days were changed to 20, 41, 76, 370, or any other number of days which yields the remainder 6 when divided by 7. ($20 = 2 \times 7 + 6$; $41 = 5 \times 7 + 6$; $76 = 10 \times 7 + 6$; $370 = 52 \times 7 + 6$.) In other words, for this computation we are not concerned with the quotient in the division by 7, but are interested only in the remainder.

This problem can be simplified still further in the following manner:

1 Associate each day of the week with a number in this manner:

Sunday 0, Monday 1, Tuesday 2, Wednesday 3, Thursday 4, Friday 5, and Saturday 6. Note that the numbers used are the only possible remainders when 7 is used as a divisor.

2 Since Wednesday is the day of the week involved in the question, we take its associated number 3 and add it to 90. (90 + 3 = 93.)

3 Divide 93 by 7 and discard the quotient, and the remainder will be the number associated with the day which is 90 days from Wednesday. $93 \div 7 = 13$ with a remainder of 2. This is the number associated with Tuesday, the day already determined as the answer to the question.

Example

1 What day of the week will it be 21 days from Friday? The number associated with Friday is 5. Then $21 + 5 = 26$; $26 \div 7 = 3$ with a remainder of 5, so 21 days from Friday is Friday. This, of course, checks with the fact that 21 days is the same as 3 weeks. The division shows this since $21 \div 7 = 3$ with 0 as a remainder.

2 What day of the week will it be 38 days from Sunday? The number associated with Sunday is 0. Then $38 + 0 = 38$, and $38 \div 7$ leaves a remainder of 3. Since $0 + 3 = 3$, Wednesday, the day associated with 3, is the day of the week 38 days from Sunday.

The fact that the remainder of the division is the only result of concern in this type of arithmetic affords a means for further simplification of the problem. This simplification is the result of a notation which discards the quotient and indicates only the remainder of a particular division.

The divisor is called a *modulus,* usually abbreviated to *mod;* and the symbol $\equiv$, which is read "is congruent to," is used to indicate the remainder. From the division algorithm (page 119) we know that for any given integers a and b, with $b > 0$, there exist integers q and r such that $a = qb + r$ and $0 \le r < b$. With the new notation this equality may be replaced by $a \equiv r \pmod{b}$. This is read "a is congruent to r modulo b." It means that r is the remainder when a is divided by b. For comparison, the numbers mentioned previously in this section are listed in the symbolism of the division algorithm and also the new symbolism of congruency.

Modulus

$90 = 12 \times 7 + 6$	$90 \equiv 6 \pmod 7$
$20 = 2 \times 7 + 6$	$20 \equiv 6 \pmod 7$
$41 = 5 \times 7 + 6$	$41 \equiv 6 \pmod 7$
$76 = 10 \times 7 + 6$	$76 \equiv 6 \pmod 7$
$370 = 52 \times 7 + 6$	$370 \equiv 6 \pmod 7$
$93 = 13 \times 7 + 2$	$93 \equiv 2 \pmod 7$
$21 = 3 \times 7 + 0$	$21 \equiv 0 \pmod 7$
$26 = 3 \times 7 + 5$	$26 \equiv 5 \pmod 7$
$38 = 5 \times 7 + 3$	$38 \equiv 3 \pmod 7$

Modular
arithmetic

These are merely examples of the symbolism and the type of computation in a very convenient and useful form of arithmetic known as *modular arithmetic*. In this type of arithmetic the computations of the previous examples would be carried out in a manner illustrated in this example.

Example What day of the week will it be (1) 90 days from Wednesday, (2) 21 days from Friday, and (3) 38 days from Sunday?

1 $90 \equiv 6$ (mod 7). 3 is the number associated with Wednesday. $6 + 3 = 9$. $9 \equiv 2$ (mod 7), so Tuesday is the day of the week 90 days from Wednesday.

2 $21 \equiv 0$ (mod 7). 5 is associated with Friday. $0 + 5 = 5$, and $5 \equiv 5$ (mod 7). Friday is the day of the week 21 days from Friday.

3 $38 \equiv 3$ (mod 7). 0 is associated with Sunday. $3 + 0 = 3$, and $3 \equiv 3$ (mod 7). Wednesday is the day of the week 38 days from Sunday.

7–3 CONGRUENCE MODULO m

A more general concept of the congruence of two integers is that given by the following definition.

Congruent
modulo m

Definition 7-2 Two integers a and b are said to be congruent modulo m if and only if they leave the same remainder upon division by the integer m.†

Properties of
congruence

There are three theorems which are of fundamental importance to the brief development of modular arithmetic which is to be pursued here. They will be stated without proof. They might be proved as exercises by the interested student. (See Exercises 19, 20, 22, 23, page 188.)

These theorems are stated for integers, so all symbols occurring are used to represent integers.

Theorem 7-1 $a \equiv b$ (mod m) if and only if $a - b$ is divisible by m.

Corollary $a \equiv b$ (mod m) if and only if $a = km + b$.

It follows as an immediate consequence of this corollary that the concept of congruence of the previous section is a special case of the more general definition, 7–2.

† This definition was given in 1801 by Gauss (1777–1855). See E. T. Bell, "Development of Mathematics," pp. 175–176, McGraw-Hill Book Company, New York, 1940.

Theorem 7-2   If $a \equiv b$ (mod *m*) and $c \equiv d$ (mod *m*), then $a + c \equiv b + d$ (mod *m*).

Theorem 7-3   If $a \equiv b$ (mod *m*) and $c \equiv d$ (mod *m*), then $ac \equiv bd$ (mod *m*).

Example   Show that $221 \equiv 5$ (mod 3) by first showing that $221 \equiv 2 + 2 + 1$ (mod 3).

$$221 = 200 + 20 + 1 = 2(10^2) + 2(10) + 1$$

Since $2 \equiv 2$ and $10 \equiv 1$ it follows from Theorem 7–3 that

$$10^2 = 10 \times 10 \equiv 1 \times 1 = 1 \qquad \text{or} \qquad 2(10^2) \equiv 2 \times 1 = 2$$

Also $2(10) \equiv 2 \times 1 = 2$.   (All congruencies are mod 3.)   It then follows from Theorem 7–2 that

$$221 = 2(10^2) + 2(10) + 1 \equiv 2 + 2 + 1 = 5 \text{ (mod 3)}$$

In modular arithmetic there are interesting examples of groups.   In such an arithmetic with *m* as a modulus the only elements to be considered are the possible remainders in any division involving an integral dividend and the integer *m* as the divisor, namely, the integers $0, 1, 2, 3, \ldots, m - 1$.   Before considering any such systems it is necessary to define the operations to be used.

Definition 7-3   Addition modulo *m* means that ordinary addition is used, but the results are all reduced to the remainders upon division by *m*.

Addition modulo m

Definition 7-4   Multiplication modulo *m* means that ordinary multiplication is used, but the results are all reduced to the remainders upon division by *m*.

Multiplication modulo m

Example   Find the sum and product of the integers 5 and 6 (mod 7).

$$5 + 6 = 11 \equiv 4 \text{ (mod 7)}$$
$$5 \times 6 = 30 \equiv 2 \text{ (mod 7)}$$

Example   Show that the set of integers $\{0,1,2,3,4\}$ with addition mod 5 is a group.

Before proceeding with the test, be sure that you understand how the addition table is derived.   As an example, in the row labeled 4 at the left these sums are recorded in order from left to right (see Fig. 7–2): $4 + 0 = 4 \equiv 4$; $4 + 1 = 5 \equiv 0$; $4 + 2 = 6 \equiv 1$; $4 + 3 = 7 \equiv 2$; $4 + 4 = 8 \equiv 3$.   (All congruencies are mod 5.)

1   Closure   Only the elements of the set, i.e., the integers 0, 1, 2, 3, 4, are seen in the table.

+	0	1	2	3	4
0	0	1	2	3	4
1	1	2	3	4	0
2	2	3	4	0	1
3	3	4	0	1	2
4	4	0	1	2	3

FIGURE 7–2   Addition modulo 5.

×	1	2	3
1	1	2	3
2	2	0	2
3	3	2	1

FIGURE 7–3   Multiplication modulo 4.

2 Associative   The addition involves only integers, and addition of integers is associative.

3 Identity   The identity element is 0. This can be seen to be true by looking at the sums in the row or column headed by 0.

4 Inverse   The identity element 0 is seen once and only once in each row and column. This means that each element has an additive inverse. For example, 1 is the inverse of 4 and 4 is the inverse of 1 since $1 + 4 = 4 + 1 = 0$.

Is this group an abelian group?   Why?

Example   Show that the set of integers $\{1,2,3\}$ with multiplication modulo 4 does not form a group. The multiplication table is given in Fig. 7–3.

This set does not have closure under the given operation, because $2 \times 2 = 4 \equiv 0 \pmod 4$, and 0 is not in the given set. Hence the set is not a group.

Can you determine another reason why this system is not a group?

7–4   TESTS FOR DIVISIBILITY

In the reduction of fractions to lower terms, in the finding of greatest common divisors of two or more numbers, and in many other forms of division exercises, it is very desirable to be able to test large numbers for divisibility by smaller numbers. The techniques of congruence afford very simple means for testing any number for divisibility by 2, 3, 4, 5,

6, 8, 9, 11, and composite numbers of which these numbers are the only factors.

Recall that any integer may be written in the form

$$a(10^n) + b(10^{n-1}) + \cdots + c(10) + d$$

where the coefficients represented by $a, b, \ldots, c, d$ are one-digit, non-negative integers and n is any positive integer. This fact, combined with Theorems 7–1 to 7–3, provides the means for establishing the tests. In each case a specific number will be used for convenience of illustration; the reader should make sure that the general application is understood.

Divisibility by 2 Consider the number 3,472. This number may be written: $3(10^3) + 4(10^2) + 7(10) + 2(1)$. Since $10 \equiv 0 \pmod{2}$, it follows, by Theorem 7–3, that $10^2 \equiv 0$ and $10^3 \equiv 0$. Again by Theorem 7–3, $3(10^3) \equiv 1 \times 0 = 0$, $4(10^2) \equiv 0 \times 0 = 0$, $7(10) \equiv 1 \times 0 = 0 \pmod{2}$. By Theorem 7–2, since $2 \equiv 0$ and $1 \equiv 1 \pmod{2}$, $3,472 = 3(10^3) + 4(10^2) + 7(10) + 2 \cdot 1 \equiv 0 + 0 + 0 + 0 = 0 \pmod{2}$. Since $3,472 \equiv 0 \pmod{2}$, it follows from Theorem 7–1 that 3,472 is divisible by 2.

An analysis of this example will reveal that, since $10^n \equiv 0 \pmod{2}$ for any positive integer n, the test for divisibility by 2 is:

An integer is divisible by 2 if and only if the digit in ones place is divisible by 2.   Divisibility by 2

Divisibility by 4 Since $10 \equiv 2$ and $10^2 \equiv 0 \pmod{4}$, it follows that $10^n \equiv 0 \pmod{4}$ if $n \geq 2$. These facts may be used to give two tests for divisibility by 4.

1 An integer is divisible by 4 if and only if twice the tens digit plus   Divisibility by 4
the ones digit is a number which is divisible by 4.

2 An integer is divisible by 4 if and only if the last two digits form a number divisible by 4.

Example Test 3,472 for divisibility by 4.

1 $3,472 = 3(10^3) + 4(10^2) + 7(10) + 2(1)$
$\equiv (3 \times 0) + (4 \times 0) + (7 \times 2) + (2 \times 1) \qquad \text{mod } 4$
$= 14 + 2 = 16 \equiv 0 \qquad \text{mod } 4$

(Only powers of 10 have been reduced in order to illustrate the statement of test 1.) Therefore 3,472 is divisible by 4.

2 $3,472 = 3,400 + 72 = 34(100) + 72$. $100 = 10^2 \equiv 0 \pmod{4}$. This means that any number of hundreds is divisible by 4. Therefore, in 3,472, we only need to examine 72. Since $72 = 18 \times 4$ it follows that 3,472 is divisible by 4.

Divisibility by 8   Argument similar to that used for 4 will give two tests for divisibility by 8.

1   **An integer is divisible by 8 if and only if 4 times the hundreds digit + 2 times the tens digit + the ones digit is a number divisible by 8.**

2   **An integer is divisible by 8 if and only if the last three digits form a number which is divisible by 8.**

The reader should derive these two tests.   (See Exercise 26 at the end of this section.)

Divisibility by 5 and powers of 5   Since $10 = 2 \times 5$, the tests for divisibility by 5 and powers of 5 (25, 125, 625, and so on) are similar to those for 2 and powers of 2 (4, 8, 16, and so on).   (See Exercises 28 to 31, page 188.)

Divisibility by 3   Since $10 \equiv 1 \pmod{3}$, it follows that $10^n \equiv 1 \pmod{3}$.   Thus if Theorems 7–2 and 7–3, with $m = 3$, are applied to any number, the result will be the sum of the digits in the number.   For example, $3{,}472 = 3(10^3) + 4(10^2) + 7(10) + 2(1)$. If we reduce *only* the powers of 10, we then have

$$3{,}472 = 3(10^3) + 4(10^2) + 7(10) + 2(1)$$
$$\equiv (3 \times 1) + (4 \times 1) + (7 \times 1) + (2 \times 1) \qquad \mathrm{mod}\ 3$$
$$= 3 + 4 + 7 + 2$$

Thus, the question of whether or not the number 3,472 is divisible by 3 has been reduced to the question of whether or not the sum of the digits gives a number which is divisible by 3.   The sum in this case is 16 and $16 \equiv 1 \pmod{3}$.   Therefore, 3,472 is *not* divisible by 3.   In fact, $3{,}472 = 1{,}157 \cdot 3 + 1$ and the 1 of the test is exhibited as the remainder of the division.

Theorem 7–2 provides a shortcut to this addition by making it possible to drop any digit, or sum of digits, which is congruent to 0 (mod 3), so we have the same result as before: The sum of the digits $\equiv 1 \pmod{3}$.

An integer is divisible by 3 if and only if the sum of its digits is a number divisible by 3.

Divisibility by 9   Since $10 \equiv 1 \pmod{9}$, the test for divisibility by 9 is similar to that for 3.

An integer is divisible by 9 if and only if the sum of its digits is a number divisible by 9.

The same shortcut as that used in the test for 3 can be used in the test for 9.   Of course 9 replaces 3.

This is the property needed to validate the checks of addition and multiplication by casting out nines presented on pages 54 and 66. There are three principles to be established.

Principle I   The excess of nines in any given integer is the excess in the sum of its digits.

The excess of nines

The truth of this statement follows immediately from the fact that $10^n \equiv 1$ (mod 9) where n is any positive integer.   Furthermore, this excess is, of course, the remainder obtained upon dividing the given number by 9.

Example   The excess of nines in 7,642 is 1, since

$$7{,}642 = 7(10^3) + 6(10^2) + 4(10) + 2(1)$$
$$\equiv (7 \cdot 1) + (6 \cdot 1) + (4 \cdot 1) + (2 \cdot 1) \qquad \text{mod } 9$$
$$= 7 + 6 + 4 + 2 \equiv 1 \qquad \text{mod } 9$$
$$7{,}642 = 849 \cdot 9 + 1$$

Principle II   The excess of nines in the sum of two integers is the same as the excess in the sum of their respective excesses.

Proof   By the division algorithm the integers l and m may be written in the form $l = 9 \cdot r + a$ and $m = 9 \cdot s + b$ where a and b are the excesses of nines in l and m, respectively.   Hence $l \equiv a$ and $m \equiv b$ (mod 9), and by Theorem 7–2

$$l + m \equiv a + b \qquad \text{mod } 9$$

This statement is equivalent to the statement of Principle II.   The principle can be extended to apply to the sum of any number of integers.

Principle III   The excess of nines in the product of two integers is equal to the excess in the product of their respective excesses.

Proof   From the argument for Principle II, $l \equiv a$ and $m \equiv b$ (mod 9). By Theorem 7–8 it then follows that $lm \equiv ab$ (mod 9).   Thus the excess of nines in the product lm is exhibited as being equal to the excess in ab.   This principle can be extended to apply to the product of any number of integers.

Divisibility by 6   Any number which is divisible by 6 must also be divisible by both 2 and 3.   Conversely, any number which is divisible by both 2 and 3 is divisible by 6.   For these reasons the test for divisibility by 6 is a combination of the tests for 2 and 3.

Example   Is the integer 346,752 divisible by 6?
Since the ones digit is divisible by 2, the number is divisible by 2.

The sum of the digits is $3 + 4 + 6 + 7 + 5 + 2 = 27 \equiv 0 \pmod 3$. Therefore 346,752 is divisible by 6.

The shortcut suggested in Theorem 7–2 can be applied very effectively in this case by noting that $3 + 6 = 9 \equiv 0$; $4 + 5 = 9 \equiv 0$; $7 + 2 = 9 \equiv 0 \pmod 3$.

Divisibility by 11 Since $10 = 0 \cdot 11 + 10$ or $10 = 1 \cdot 11 + (-1)$, we may use either of the congruences $10 \equiv 10 \pmod{11}$ or $10 \equiv -1 \pmod{11}$. From these facts we have the following table of values mod 11: $1 \equiv 1$, $10 \equiv -1$; $10^2 = 10 \times 10 \equiv (-1) \times (-1) = 1$; $10^3 = 10 \times 10^2 \equiv (-1) \times (1) = -1$; $10^4 = 10 \times (10^3) \equiv (-1) \times (-1) = 1$; and so on with alternating values of 1 and -1. From this we derive the test for divisibility by 11, which is best stated in three steps.

Divisibility by 11

For any given integer:

1 Add the digits in the odd places, starting with the ones digit. Call this sum S.
2 Add the digits in the even places, starting with the tens digit. Call this sum T.
3 Subtract T from S.

If $S - T$ is a number which is divisible by 11, then the given integer will be divisible by 11, and the converse will also be true.

Example Test the number 382,349 for divisibility by 11.

$S = 9 + 3 + 8 = 20$
$T = 4 + 2 + 3 = 9$
$S - T = 20 - 9 = 11 \equiv 0$ mod 11

Therefore, 382,349 is divisible by 11.

NOTE: If $T > S$ and one wishes to avoid negative numbers, there may be added to S any multiple of 11 sufficient to make $S - T \geq 0$.

Example Test the integer 968,874 for divisibility by 11.

$S = 4 + 8 + 6 = 18$
$T = 7 + 8 + 9 = 24$
$T > S$ so 11 will be added to S
$S + 11 = 29$ $29 - 24 = 5$

Since 5 is not divisible by 11, it follows that 968,874 is not divisible by 11. In fact, $968,874 = 88,079 \cdot 11 + 5$, and the 5 of the test is exhibited as the remainder of the division.

As the preceding note indicated, this procedure is followed only if one wishes to avoid negative numbers. It is not necessary. In this particular example $S - T = 18 - 24 = -6$, and -6 is not divisible by 11. From this it follows that 968,874 is not divisible by 11. Just as $968,874 = 88,079 \cdot 11 + 5$, it is also true that $968,874 = 88,080 \cdot 11 - 6$.

The test for divisibility by 6 serves as an example for determining tests for divisibility by simple composite numbers. The number must be broken down into factors which are relatively prime. For example, the test for divisibility by 12 would resolve into the tests for divisibility for 3 and 4, since $12 = 3 \times 4$. It is to be noted, however, that 12 may also be factored as 2×6, but tests for 2 and 6 would not suffice, since any number which is divisible by 6 is also divisible by 2. The number 6 itself will serve as a counterexample since it is divisible by both 6 and 2, but it is not divisible by 12. The number 18 is another number divisible by both 6 and 2, but not by 12. What is a test for divisibility by 18?

Divisibility tests for composite numbers

No test for divisibility by 7 has been derived. It is possible to follow the procedures used above, including 11, and derive such a test. It is not a simple one, and because of this fact it is usually simpler to proceed to divide by 7 rather than apply the test. It is also possible to derive tests for other prime numbers such as 13, 17, 19, but the difficulty of the test supersedes the practicality of its use. In fact, the size of the dividend enters into the determination of the practicality of the use of any of the tests devised.

Exercises

Which of the systems in Exercises 1 to 17 are groups?

1 The set of all nonzero real numbers with multiplication.
2 The set of all nonzero real numbers with addition.
3 The set of all nonnegative integers with addition.
4 The set of all integers with addition.
5 The set of all nonzero integers with multiplication.
6 The set of all nonzero rational numbers with multiplication.
7 The set of all irrational numbers with multiplication.
8 The set $\{1, -1, i, -i\}$ with multiplication defined as in the table of Fig. 7-4.

$\times$	1	-1	i	$-i$
1	1	-1	i	$-i$
-1	-1	1	$-i$	i
i	i	$-i$	-1	1
$-i$	$-i$	i	1	-1

FIGURE 7-4   Multiplication table for the set $\{1, -1, i, -i\}$.

9 The set of all even integers with addition.
10 The set of all odd integers with addition.
11 The set {0,1} with multiplication modulo 2.
12 The set {0,1} with addition modulo 2.
13 The set {1} with multiplication modulo 2.
14 The set {0,1,2,3,4,5} with addition modulo 6.
15 The set {1,2,3,4,5} with multiplication modulo 6.
16 The set {0,1,2,3,4,5,6} with addition modulo 7.
17 The set {0,1,2,3,4,5,6} with multiplication modulo 7.
18 The set {1,2,3,4,5,6} with multiplication modulo 7.
19 Prove Theorem 7-1.
20 Prove the corollary to Theorem 7-1.
21 Show why the concept of congruence of page 179 is a special case of Definition 7-2.
22 Prove Theorem 7-2.
23 Prove Theorem 7-3.
24 Prove: If $a \equiv b$ (mod m), then $ac \equiv bc$ (mod m). (*Hint:* Use Theorem 7-1.)
25 Give one counterexample to show that the fact that $ac \equiv bc$ (mod m) does not necessarily imply that $a \equiv b$ (mod m).
26 Derive the two tests for divisibility by 8.
27 Derive two tests for divisibility by 16.
28 Derive the test for divisibility by 5.
29 Derive one test for divisibility by 25.
30 Derive one test for divisibility by 125.
31 Derive one test for divisibility by 625.
32 What are tests for divisibility by 15, 18, 22, 24?
33 Why are there not two distinct tests for divisibility by 25, 125, and 625, as there are for 4, 8, and 16?

Test each of the numbers in Exercises 34 to 42 for divisibility by 2, 3, 4, 5, 6, 8, 9, 11, 12, 15, 18, 22, 24.

34	55,692	35	4,740	36	180,840
37	36,036	38	79,460	39	1,665,158
40	213,240	41	60,720	42	3,526,740

43 Derive tests for divisibility by **2** and **4** in base **five.**
44 Derive tests for divisibility by **2, 3, 4,** and **5** in base **six.**
45 Derive tests for divisibility by **2, 3, 4, 6,** and **8** in base **nine.**

INVITATIONS TO EXTENDED STUDY

1 For the set of integers {0,1,2,3,4,5,6,7,8,9,10}, construct the addition table for addition modulo 11.

2   For the set of integers $\{1,2,3,4,5,6,7,8,9,10\}$, construct the multiplication table for multiplication modulo 11.

3   For the set of integers $\{0,1,2,3,4,5,6,7,8,9,10,11\}$, construct the addition table for addition modulo 12.

4   For the set of integers $\{1,2,3,4,5,6,7,8,9,10,11\}$, construct the multiplication table for multiplication modulo 12.

5   Which of the systems of exercises 1 to 4 are groups and which are not?

6   For the set of integers $\{0,1,2,3,4\}$, construct the addition and multiplication tables modulo 11 in base five.

7   For the set of integers $\{1,2,3,4\}$, construct the addition and multiplication tables modulo 12 in base five.

8   Which of the systems of exercises 6 and 7 are groups and which are not?

9   Use the above exercises as a guide in arguing this theorem: Any set of integers with multiplication modulo m is not a group if m is a composite number.

10   Construct a test for divisibility by 7.   (*Hint:* $1 \equiv 1$, $2 \equiv 2$, $3 \equiv 3$, $4 \equiv -3$, $\dot{5} \equiv -2$, $6 \equiv -1$, all mod 7.)

For the remaining exercises, use the elements of the set G in Definition 7-1 to prove the theorems.

11   If a, b, $c \in G$ and $a * c = b * c$, then $a = b$.

12   For any element a in G it is true that $i * a = a * i = a$.

13   If there exists any element u in G such that $a * u = a$, for $a \in G$, then $u = i$.

14   For any a in G it is true that $(a^{-1})^{-1} = a$.

15   For each element $a \in G$ it is true that $a^{-1} * a = a * a^{-1} = i$.

16   If for any given $a \in G$ there exists another element $x \in G$ such that $a * x = i$, then $x = a^{-1}$.

CHAPTER 8

the concepts of position, shape, and size

GUIDELINES FOR CAREFUL STUDY

In our study of number systems we were at all times dealing with sets of numbers. Complex numbers were defined in terms of real numbers and a new unit which we called the imaginary unit; real numbers, in terms of rational numbers and a set of new numbers which we called irrational numbers; rational numbers, in terms of integers; and integers, in terms of natural numbers and a new number which we called zero, or the additive identity. No effort was made to define natural numbers; rather, we accepted them as the numbers used in counting—undefined concepts for which we could establish acceptable intuitive perceptions through the technique of one-to-one correspondence between sets of objects. Our familiarity with these undefined elements was of such a nature that we were able to postulate a set of basic properties which controlled their use within the demands of certain well-defined operations and relations. From these basic assumptions other properties were derived to give structure to the natural number system. Upon this system as a foundation we were then able to build the other systems.

In the study of geometry we shall follow a somewhat similar pattern except that, for this development, the undefined element will be "point" rather than "number." The universal set will be the set of all points, and it will be called "space." Subsets of this space in which we shall be interested are such familiar geometric configurations as lines, planes, angles, polygons, circles, prisms, pyramids, cylinders, cones, and spheres. Fundamental properties and relations which characterize such sets of points will constitute the subject matter of this chapter.

The following questions will serve as helpful guidelines to careful study of Chap. 8.

1   What is meant by the union of two sets? The intersection of two sets?

2   What is the null set?

3   What is meant by the term *space*?

4   What is the basic distinction between a straight line and a curved line?

5   What are the distinctions between line, line segment, and ray?

6   What is the distinction between parallel lines, skew lines, intersecting lines, and perpendicular lines?

7   When is a set of points said to be collinear?

8   When is the point *C* said to be between the points *A* and *B*?

9   What is a half line? A half plane? A half space?

10   What is the distance between two points on a number line?

11   When are two line segments said to be congruent? Two angles?

12   What are conditions which determine a plane?

13   What is the intersection of two planes?

14   When are two planes parallel?

15   When are points or lines said to be coplanar?

16   What is a plane angle? A dihedral angle?

17   What is meant by the interior and exterior of a plane angle? Of a dihedral angle?

18   What is meant by vertical angles? Adjacent angles? Complementary angles? Supplementary angles?

19   What is meant by a cartesian frame of reference?

20   What are the names of the different axes in a cartesian frame of reference in space? In a plane?

21   What are circles of longitude and latitude?

22   What is the prime meridian? The international date line?

23   What is a simple closed curve? A circle? A polygon? A regular polygon?

24   How may triangles be classified according to angles? According to sides?

25   How may quadrilaterals be classified?

26   What is a sphere? A prism? A pyramid? A cone?

27   What are the regular polyhedrons?

28   When are two geometric figures said to be similar?

29 When are two geometric figures said to be congruent?

30 What are the conditions for congruence of two triangles?

31 When is a plane region said to be symmetric with respect to a point? An axis?

32 What is meant by a euclidean construction?

INTRODUCTION

During our earlier study of number systems no effort was made to give a logically structured definition of number. Instead, we accepted the intuitive concept we have of number and its basic characteristics as sufficiently convincing and firm to serve as a foundation for the development of the systems which provide for its efficient use. In the study of geometry a similar situation exists concerning *points*. We shall make no effort to define the concept of "point." We shall assume, however, an intuitive familiarity with the concept sufficient to serve as an acceptable basis for the definition and discussion of different sets of points. For these sets of points we shall then proceed to formulate clear-cut ideas. Just as was the case in the study of number, some properties and relations will be postulated or merely described, while others will be examined in somewhat more detail. One major difference between the two developments will be that we shall restrict our interests much more severely here than in the study of number. We shall be concerned primarily with those basic concepts and principles of geometry which are acceptable on a purely intuitive or experimental basis. This subject matter, though quite restricted in nature, constitutes a body of geometrical content which is of great significance not only to elementary mathematics but to mathematics in general.

"Point" is undefined

8-1 THE CONCEPT OF POINT

The cardinal number of any set of objects which can be placed in one-to-one correspondence with the set of fingers on any normal hand is "five." If we wish to record this number we do so by means of the symbol 5. This symbol is not the number. Similarly, when we wish to identify a point we usually do so by a dot (.), maybe with a letter attached. This dot is not a point; it is merely a convenient symbol acceptable as the representation of a point. A point has no size. It has only *position*, and a dot, or any equivalent symbol, is only a recognized symbol for indicating such position. For example, this dot (.) indicates

A point has position

a different position from that of the dot previously used. They thus represent two different points within the context of this discussion. The set of all points is what we shall call *space*. We shall see later (Sec. 8–5) that there is a very simple, yet effective, technique for locating in space any particular point, or points, pertinent to a given discussion. The configurations of geometry are subsets of the points of space. Thus each different configuration is a particular set of points identified by a specific nonambiguous characterization.

The universal set

8–2   THE CONCEPT OF LINE

One of the most familiar and the simplest of the sets of points is that of the configuration we call a *line*. There are essentially two different types of lines: (1) the *straight line* (or *line*), which may be drawn continuously without changing directions, as illustrated in Fig. 8–1*a*; and (2) the *curved line* (or *curve*), no part of which is straight, so that, when drawn, it continuously changes direction, as illustrated in Fig. 8–1*b*. If a person is driving in a straight line along a highway, he is maintaining the same direction at all points along his line of travel. On the other hand, if he is driving along a curve, he is changing direction at all points along his line of travel.

Line is a set of points

As we proceed in our discussion we shall use the words "straight line" and "line," "curved line" and "curve," synonymously. A ruler or straightedge may be used to draw the representation of a line. In Fig. 8–1*a* the two arrowheads indicate that the line represented extends indefinitely in either direction. We shall designate such a line by a small letter, such as the letter *l*, or by the symbol $\overleftrightarrow{AB}$, using two points of the line. This latter designation finds its justification in the following basic assumption about points and lines.

Postulate 8–1   For any two distinct points in space there exists one and only one straight line which contains these two points.

By Definition 1–6 the *intersection* of two sets is the set of elements common to both sets. As we have seen, such an intersection may be

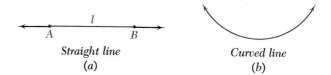

FIGURE 8–1   Two kinds of line.

Straight line
(a)

Curved line
(b)

either nonempty or empty (see the example on page 8). When the sets are lines (sets of points) it is convenient to speak of *intersecting* or *nonintersecting lines,* depending on whether they do or do not have points in common.

Intersecting
lines

Definition 8-1   Intersecting lines are lines which have at least one point in common.

As an immediate consequence of Postulate 8–1 we have this property of intersecting lines.

Theorem 8-1   **If two distinct lines intersect, they have one and only one point in common.**

Hypothesis   Lines *s* and *t* are distinct lines which intersect (Fig. 8–2).

Conclusion   The two lines have one and only one point in common.

From the hypothesis we have two distinct sets of points, the lines *s* and *t* which intersect. We can thus use the properties of lines and of intersection of sets. This means that the two lines have at least one point in common.

We are to prove that they can have only one point in common since they are distinct. The immediate question which arises is: Under what conditions will it be impossible for two lines to be distinct? This question brings Postulate 8–1 to mind.

Proof

Statements	*Reasons*
Lines *s* and *t* are nonempty sets of points.	Definition of line
s ∩ *t* is nonempty and hence contains at least one point.	Hypothesis; Definition 1–6
s and *t* are distinct lines.	Hypothesis
s and *t* cannot have more than one point in common.	Postulate 8–1

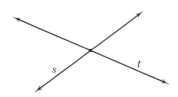

FIGURE 8–2   Intersecting lines.

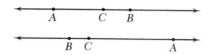

FIGURE 8-3   Betweenness.

Any two points with fixed positions on a line, such as the points A and B in Fig. 8–1a, determine a measurable portion of the line, called a *line segment*, which is designated $\overline{AB}$. It is frequently advantageous to think of a line segment as a set of points in accordance with this definition:

Definition 8-2 The line segment $\overline{AB}$ consists of two points A and B on a straight line and all points between them. The points A and B are called end points of the segment.

Line segment

In this definition, and previously in the discussion of the number line (page 164), the undefined concept of "between" has been used. One thing that both usages have in common is the fact that the points with which the concept of "betweenness" was associated were all on the same straight line. It is very familiar usage and a clearly under-stood statement to say that three points A, B, and C are situated so that C is *between* A and B if the three points are on a straight line in one of the two patterns of Fig. 8–3. Also the points A, B, and C of the figure are said to be collinear in accordance with this definition.

Betweenness

Definition 8-3 A set of points is said to be *collinear* if and only if all points of the set are contained in the same straight line. Otherwise they are said to be *noncollinear*.

On line l of Fig. 8–4a a point P has been marked. This point divides the line l into two *half lines*. The point P is not a point of either half line but is the *boundary* of each. Since the two half lines have no point in common, they do not intersect. On line r of Fig. 8–4b a segment $\overline{OM}$ has been marked. The point P has been placed on the line so that M is between O and P. These three points may be used as an aid in defin-ing the *ray* $\overrightarrow{OP}$ as the union of the points of the line segment $\overline{OM}$ and of the set of all points P such that M is between O and P. The arrow of the figure indicates that the ray $\overrightarrow{OP}$ consists of the point O and all points of the line to the right of O. The point O is called the end point of the

Half line

Ray

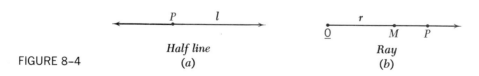

FIGURE 8-4

Half line
(a)

Ray
(b)

ray. While the ray $\overrightarrow{OP}$ may have any direction, the arrow of the symbol is always drawn from left to right. Note that, in Fig. 8–4a, the set of points consisting of P and either of the two half lines defines a ray. Similarly, the point C of either of the two lines of Fig. 8–3 may be considered as the end point of either of the two rays $\overrightarrow{CA}$ or $\overrightarrow{CB}$. On each line the two rays have opposite directions from C. In such a case the rays are said to be *oppositely directed* or, more simply, *opposite rays*.

The number line of Chap. 6 (page 163) used the concept of a measurable line segment in the designation of "a unit to be applied to the line." This unit, whether considered as some specified standard unit of measure (Sec. 9–6) or merely as an unspecified unit, may be used as in Sec. 6–3 to set up a one-to-one correspondence between the set of real numbers and the set of points on a line. For example, in Fig. 8–5, whatever the unit may be, the point A is 1 unit removed from the reference point O and is located to the right of O; the point D is $3\frac{3}{4}$ units to the right of O; and the point E is 5 units to the right of O. Similarly, the point F is 2 units removed from O, the minus sign $(-)$ simply indicates that the 2 units are measured to the left of the reference point O; the point G is $2\frac{1}{2}$ units to the left of O; and H is 5 units to the left of O.

There is at least one other familiar and important concept implied by the discussion of the preceding paragraph. Not only is the number 5 associated with the position of the point E on the line of Fig. 8–5, but also it is associated with the line segment $\overline{OE}$ in that it indicates the length of the segment, or the *distance* between the two points O and E. Whatever the unit of measure may be, the length of the segment $\overline{OE}$ is 5 units; or, synonymously, the distance from the point O to the point E is 5 units. Supporting argument should not be necessary for the statement that, since the distance from O to E is 5 units, it follows immediately that the distance from E to O is also 5 units. Likewise the distance from O to H, or from H to O, is 5 units. The minus sign used with each of the numbers to the left of the reference point O has nothing to do with the distance each point is from O. The sign merely indicates that the point is located on the line to the left of O at a distance designated by each respective real number. Similarly, the distance CE,† or the length of the segment $\overline{CE}$, is given by the number $3 = 5 - 2$. The number 5 corresponds to the point E, and the number 2 corresponds to the point C; and the distance corresponds to the number 3, which is the difference between the numbers 5 and 2. By analogy, the distance EC would correspond to the difference $2 - 5 = 2 + (-5) = -3$. This seems to contradict what we expected to find,

---

† At this point it is well to call attention to the need for careful distinction of notation: $\overleftrightarrow{AB}$ represents a line which extends indefinitely in either direction, as indicated by the double arrow; $\overrightarrow{AB}$ is the ray whose end point is A and extends indefinitely in one direction from A; $\overline{AB}$ is the line segment whose end points are A and B; AB represents the length of the line segment $\overline{AB}$, the distance from A to B along the line joining them.

FIGURE 8–5   Distance on the number line.

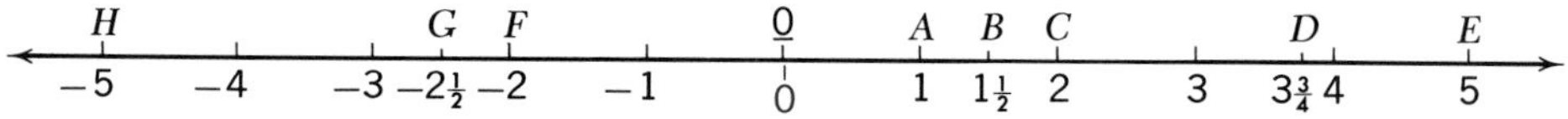

namely, that the length of segment $\overline{EC}$ = the length of segment $\overline{CE}$. Such possibilities of conflict and contradiction in the concepts of "distance between two points" and "length of a line segment" are removed by these two definitions.

Definition 8-4   The *distance* between two points on a number line is the absolute value of the difference between their corresponding numbers.

Definition 8-5   The *length* of a line segment is the distance between its two end points.

Length of a line segment

The assumption in step 4 of the discussion of the number line (page 163) is equivalent to the following distance postulate.

Postulate 8-2   To every pair of distinct points on a number line there corresponds a unique positive real number, called the *measure* of the length of the line segment joining the two points.

Example   If the points P and Q correspond to the real numbers p and q, respectively, then the length of the line segment $\overline{PQ}$ is given by the formula

$PQ = |p - q| = |q - p|$

In Fig. 8–5

$CE = |5 - 2| = 3 = |2 - 5| = EC$
$OE = |5 - 0| = 5 = |0 - 5| = EO$
$OH = |(-5) - 0| = 5 = |0 - (-5)| = HO$
$HE = |5 - (-5)| = 10 = |(-5) - 5| = EH$

To review the meaning of $|a|$, where a is a real number, see Definition 6–1 (page 166).

In this example note that $OE = OH = 5$. These two line segments are said to be *congruent*. Since the point O divides the line segment $\overline{HE}$ into two congruent segments it is said to be the *midpoint* of $\overline{HE}$.

Definition 8-6   Two line segments of the same length are said to be *congruent*.

Congruent line segments

If $\overline{AB}$ and $\overline{CD}$ are congruent line segments, we may indicate this fact in either of two equivalent forms:

$AB = CD$ length of $\overline{AB}$ = length of $\overline{CD}$
$\overline{AB} \cong \overline{CD}$ segment $\overline{AB}$ *is congruent to* segment $\overline{CD}$

Midpoint of a line segment

Definition 8-7 If the point R is located between the points P and Q so that $PR = RQ$, then R is the *midpoint* of the line segment $\overline{PQ}$. The point R is said to *bisect* the line segment $\overline{PQ}$.

Attention is called to the fact that Definition 8–4 allows for the concept of zero distance. If, in the example, the numbers p and q are equal, then the points P and Q are the same point and $PQ = |p - p| = 0$.

8-3   THE CONCEPT OF PLANE

Plane is a set of points

Another very important set of points is that of a *flat surface,* or *plane,* of which a table top, a windowpane, and a room floor are familiar illustrations. An accepted test to apply to a surface to determine whether or not it is a plane is to select arbitrary pairs of points anywhere on the surface and fit a straightedge or ruler to these pairs of points. If, in every case, the straight line represented by the edge of the instrument lies wholly within the surface then it may be said to be a flat surface, or plane (see Fig. 8–6). This basic relation between points of a line and points of a plane is formalized in Postulate 8–3.

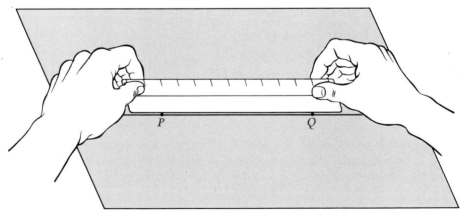

FIGURE 8–6   Using a straightedge to test a plane surface.

FIGURE 8-7   Examples of planes.

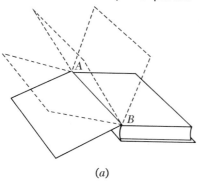

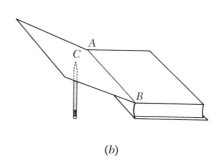

(a)   (b)

Postulate 8-3   If a straight line contains two points of a plane, then the line lies entirely within the plane.

Any drawing used to represent a plane, as in Fig. 8-6, must be recognized as just that. A plane extends indefinitely as a flat surface. Just as a line segment is used frequently to represent a line, so a three- or four-sided figure usually is drawn to represent a plane. The test previously described may be used to identify a surface as a plane; it does not distinguish one plane from another. This fact may be illustrated by using the cover of a book to represent a plane. It can be brought to rest in any one of many different positions, as indicated in Fig. 8-7a. The edge of the cover, lettered AB in the figure, represents the line $\overleftrightarrow{AB}$ which lies wholly within any one of the planes pictured. Figure 8-7b illustrates that the line $\overleftrightarrow{AB}$ and a point not on the line are sufficient to identify a particular plane.

Postulate 8-4   For any given line and a point not on the line there is one and only one plane that contains both the point and the line.

Plane uniquely determined

As an immediate consequence of this postulate we have this theorem.

Theorem 8-2   Any three noncollinear points lie in one and only one plane.

Hypothesis   Given three points A, B, and C not all lying on the same line.

Conclusion   There exists one and only one plane containing the three points A, B, and C.

What conditions are sufficient to determine a plane? Is there any way the given three noncollinear points can be used to get the needed conditions? These questions bring to mind Postulates 8–4 and 8–1, respectively.

Proof

Statements	*Reasons*
The three points A, B, C do not lie on the same line.	Hypothesis
Any two of the points, say A and B, lie on one and only one line.	Postulate 8–1
There is one and only one plane which contains the line $\overleftrightarrow{AB}$ (hence points A and B) and the point C.	Postulate 8–4

Corollary   Two intersecting lines lie in one and only one plane.

Definition 8-8   Lines or points which lie in the same plane are said to be *coplanar*. Otherwise they are said to be *nonplanar*.

If two lines have no points in common, that is, if their intersection is the empty set, they are either *parallel lines* or *skew lines*. In Fig. 8–8 the rails of the railroad track may be used to represent parallel lines r_1 and r_2. An edge of the bridge, such as the one emphasized and lettered AB in the figure, then can represent a line skew both to r_1 and to r_2.

Parallel lines   *Definition 8-9   Parallel lines* are coplanar lines which do not intersect.

Skew lines   *Definition 8-10   Skew lines* are lines which are not coplanar; they are nonplanar.

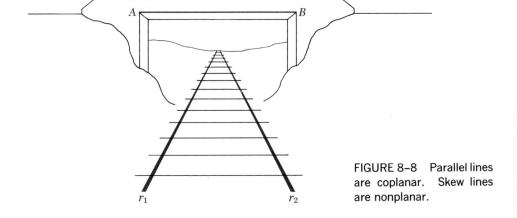

FIGURE 8–8   Parallel lines are coplanar.   Skew lines are nonplanar.

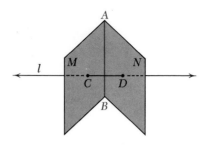

FIGURE 8-9   Two intersecting planes.

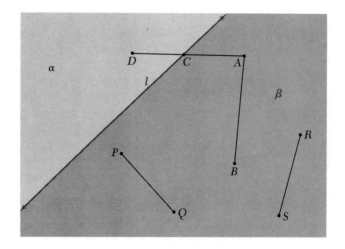

FIGURE 8-10   Half planes.

Definition 8-11   Parallel planes are planes which do not intersect.   Parallel planes

Postulate 8-5   Given a line *l* and a point *P* not contained in *l*. In the   Postulate of
plane determined by *l* and *P* there exists one and only one line through   parallelism
P and parallel to *l*.

Postulate 8-6   If two planes intersect, their intersection is a straight   Intersection of
line.   two planes

 Figure 8-9 shows planes *M* and *N* intersecting in the line $\overleftrightarrow{AB}$, and
the line *l*, which is not parallel to either plane, intersecting the plane
M in the point *C* and the plane *N* in the point *D*.
 Just as a point on a line is the boundary of each of the two half lines
into which the point divides the line, so a line *l* in a given plane will
divide the plane into two *half planes*. The line *l* is in neither half plane,   Half plane
but is the *edge* of each. The two half planes do not intersect: that is,
they have no points in common. In Fig. 8-10, the line *l* divides the

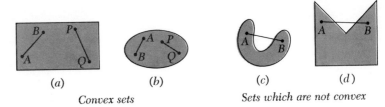

FIGURE 8–11   *Convex sets*   *Sets which are not convex*

plane into the two half planes α (alpha) and β (beta). Two points (A and D) are said to be in different half planes if there is a point of l between A and D. Such a point is the point C. Two points (A and B) are said to be in the same half plane if there is no point of l between A and B. Sometimes a point which is in a particular half plane is used to designate it. For example, the half plane β of Fig. 8–10 might be designated either as the A side or as the B side of l.

In a similar manner, a plane π (pi) may be considered as dividing

Half space   space into two *half spaces* which do not intersect. The plane π is not in either half space, but is called the *face* of each.

It is to be noted that a line is an edge of an infinite number of half planes, but a plane is the face of only two half spaces. Why is this so?

A half plane is an illustration of another very important type of point set, namely, a *convex set*.

Convex set   **Definition 8-12**   A set of points is said to be a *convex set* if it is such that for any two points A and B selected anywhere in the set it is true that the segment $\overline{AB}$ lies entirely within the set.

In Fig. 8–10 the points A and B of the half plane β are such that $\overline{AB}$ lies entirely within the half plane. It should be evident that this would be true for any two points selected anywhere in the half plane, such as P and Q or R and S. The same illustration can be extended to α or any other half plane. The condition of the definition is met, so each half plane is a convex set. Two other illustrations of convex sets are given in Fig. 8–11a and b, and two illustrations of sets of points which are not convex sets are given in Fig. 8–11c and d. In Fig. 8–11c and d, while two points may be chosen such that the line segment joining them lies entirely in the set, it is clear from the picture that this is not true for *any two* points selected anywhere in the set.

Exercises

1   Find different illustrations of point, line, and plane.
2   Which of these statements are true?

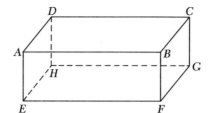

Exercise 3

The dotted lines of the figure indicate lines which cannot be seen. They are behind planes.

(a) A line is a subset of space.
(b) Space is the universal set of points.
(c) A plane is a subset of a line.
(d) A point is a subset of space.
(e) A line is a subset of a plane.
(f) A point is a subset of a line.

3   Use the picture of the box to give illustrations of each of the following: (a) Intersecting lines; (b) parallel lines; (c) skew lines; (d) parallel planes; (e) intersecting planes; (f) line intersecting a plane.

4   Given that points P, Q, and R are in plane M and also in plane N; what can you say about planes M and N?

5   Given that points P, Q, and R are in plane M and points P, Q, and S are in plane N; what can you say about planes M and N?

6   Draw a line and label four points A, B, C, and D on it in alphabetical order from left to right.   Carry out these instructions:

(a) Give as many illustrations as you can of the concept of "betweenness" by using subsets of the given four points.
(b) Name two line segments whose union is a line segment.
(c) Name two line segments whose intersection is a point.
(d) Name two line segments whose intersection is empty.
(e) Name two rays whose intersection is C.
(f) Name two pairs of opposite rays.
(g) Name two rays whose union is the line.

7   Use a stiff piece of cardboard and three sharp pencils to illustrate that one and only one plane contains three points which are not collinear.

8   Use the equipment of Exercise 7 to show that two points are not sufficient to determine a plane.   What does this say about one line?

9   Prove the corollary to Theorem 8–2.

10 Given four nonplanar points, how many distinct lines and planes do they determine?   Identify each line and plane by naming the points which determine it.

11 Repeat Exercise 10 for five nonplanar points, no three of which are collinear.   There are two distinct cases.

12 Draw pictures to illustrate the four relative positions of three distinct coplanar lines.

$$
\begin{array}{cccccccccccccccc}
N & M & L & K & J & I & H & 0 & & A & B & C & D\ E & F & G \\
-3 & -2\tfrac{1}{2} & -2 & -\sqrt{3} & -1\tfrac{1}{3} & -1 & -\tfrac{1}{2} & 0 & & \tfrac{2}{3} & 1 & 1\tfrac{1}{2} & 2\ \sqrt{5} & 2\tfrac{2}{3} & 3
\end{array}
$$

Exercise 16

13   Use sheets of paper to illustrate the relative positions of three distinct planes in space.

14   Describe the union of two half lines; of two half planes; of two half spaces.

15   Give an illustration of a plane which separates space into two half spaces.

16   Use the figure as an aid in solving these exercises.

(a)   What is the length of each of the segments $\overline{OG}$, $\overline{OJ}$, $\overline{MA}$, $\overline{CF}$, $\overline{LC}$?

(b)   Show that H is the midpoint of the segment $\overline{MC}$.

(c)   What is the midpoint of each of the segments $\overline{OG}$, $\overline{LD}$, $\overline{LB}$, $\overline{JF}$?

(d)   What is the length of each of the segments $\overline{OE}$, $\overline{OK}$, $\overline{KE}$, $\overline{BE}$, $\overline{MK}$?

17   Use a sheet of paper as the representation of a plane π.   Draw a line l in this plane.   Now place three points P, Q, and R in the plane π in such a manner that the point P will be on the Q side of l but not on the R side of l.

8–4   THE CONCEPT OF ANGLE

Angle

The union of two distinct rays with a common end point is called an *angle*.   Such a union might take the form of any one of the four typical angles of Fig. 8–12.   The two rays are the *sides* of the angle and the common end point is its *vertex*.   The symbol $\angle$ is used to indicate an angle; the plural form is $\&$.   Each of the angles of the figure would be indicated by the symbol $\angle ABC$, read "angle A, B, C," or $\angle CBA$, read "angle C, B, A."   At times when there is no ambiguity as to what rays are its sides an angle may be designated by reading merely the letter at

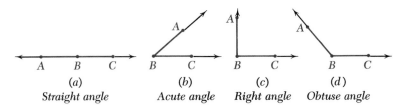

(a)   (b)   (c)   (d)

Straight angle   Acute angle   Right angle   Obtuse angle   FIGURE 8–12

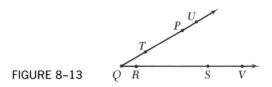

FIGURE 8–13

its vertex. For example, each angle of the figure might be designated as ∠B and read "angle B." The positions of the points marked on each side, as an aid in labeling an angle, are immaterial. The angle of Fig. 8–13 is the same whether read as ∠PQR, ∠PQV, ∠TQS, or ∠Q. Name other ways of reading the same angle.

In Fig. 8–12a the sides of ∠ABC are opposite rays. In such a case the angle is called a *straight angle*. In a sense this is an exceptional angle and will not enter into our discussions a great deal. There are a few cases, however, where the concept makes a very pertinent contribution.

For every line segment there exists a positive real number which is the measure of the length of the segment. Its meaning becomes significant once the unit is determined. Similarly, for every angle there exists a positive real number called *the measure of the angle*. While there are several different units of angular measure, the one most commonly used is the *degree*, with subunits of minutes and seconds such that 60 seconds = 1 minute (60″ = 1′), and 60 minutes = 1 degree (60′ = 1°). A familiar instrument for measuring angles is the protractor, which has a scale from 0 to 180 marked as in Fig. 8–14. Each number on the scale indicates the measure of the angle in degrees. In the figure the center of the protractor is placed at the vertex B of the angle ABC, and the diameter (the 0 to 180 line) is placed along $\overrightarrow{BC}$, arbitrarily selected as the *initial side* of the angle. The measure of the angle is then given by the number which corresponds to $\overrightarrow{BA}$, the *terminal side* of the angle. The symbol m∠ABC is used to represent "the measure of the angle ABC." In the figure, m∠ABC = 35, or the angle ABC is a 35-degree angle, or the angle ABC is a 35° angle.

Postulate 8–7   The measure of a straight angle is 180. (m∠DBC = 180.)

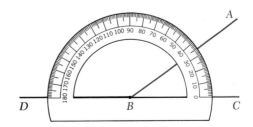

FIGURE 8–14   Protractor measures angle.

Measure of an angle

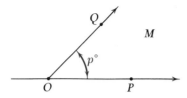

FIGURE 8–15

Conversely, if the ray $\overrightarrow{OP}$ is contained in the edge of a half plane M, then for every positive real number p between 0 and 180 there exists one and only one ray $\overrightarrow{OQ}$ in M such that the measure of $\angle POQ$ is p (Fig. 8–15).

Congruent angles

Definition 8–13   Angles with the same measure are called *congruent angles.*

If $\measuredangle ABC$ and PQR are congruent angles, we may indicate this fact in either of two equivalent forms: $m\angle ABC = m\angle PQR$ (measure of $\angle ABC$ = measure of $\angle PQR$), or $\angle ABC \cong \angle PQR$ (angle ABC is *congruent to* angle PQR).

Interior and exterior of an angle

With the exception of the straight angle, any angle separates a plane into three disjoint sets of points: the points of the angle, those *interior* to the angle, and those *exterior* to the angle.   In Fig. 8–16, points P and Q are in the interior of $\angle ABC$ since they are each on the A side of ray $\overrightarrow{BC}$ *and also* on the C side of ray $\overrightarrow{BA}$.   The points R, S, and T are in the exterior of the angle for the respective reasons listed here:

R is on the A side of ray $\overrightarrow{BC}$ *but not also* on the C side of ray $\overrightarrow{BA}$.

T is on the C side of ray $\overrightarrow{BA}$ *but not also* on the A side of ray $\overrightarrow{BC}$.

S is neither on the A side of ray $\overrightarrow{BC}$ nor on the C side of ray $\overrightarrow{BA}$.

The dotted line of Fig. 8–16 represents a ray which joins the vertex B of $\angle ABC$ to the point P in the interior of the angle.   Thus the two angles ABP and CBP have a common vertex and a common side, formed by the ray $\overrightarrow{BP}$ which is entirely within the interior of $\angle ABC$, and are such that $m\angle ABP + m\angle CBP = m\angle ABC$.   Two such angles are called *adjacent angles.*

Adjacent angles

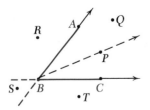

FIGURE 8–16   Interior and exterior of $\angle ABC$.

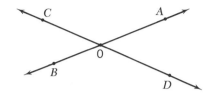

FIGURE 8–17   Vertical angles.

The point of intersection of two intersecting lines may be considered as the common end point of four rays which are oppositely directed in pairs. In Fig. 8–17 the rays $\overrightarrow{OA}$ and $\overrightarrow{OB}$ are opposite rays, as are the rays $\overrightarrow{OC}$ and $\overrightarrow{OD}$. Thus there are formed the two straight angles AOB and COD. Other pairs of significant angles are also formed. Angles AOD and BOC have a common vertex and their sides are respective opposite rays: $\overrightarrow{OD}$ of one angle is opposite to $\overrightarrow{OC}$ of the other, and $\overrightarrow{OA}$ of the first angle is opposite to $\overrightarrow{OB}$ of the second. Such angles are called *vertical angles.* Name another pair of vertical angles to be found in the figure. The angle AOC and the angle BOC have the ray $\overrightarrow{OC}$ as a common side, while the other two sides are the opposite rays $\overrightarrow{OA}$ and $\overrightarrow{OB}$. They are related in such a manner that $m\angle AOC + m\angle BOC = m\angle AOB$ and thus are adjacent angles. When the sum of the measures of two angles, whether they are adjacent or not, is equal to the measure of a straight angle, the angles are said to be *supplementary angles.* $\measuredangle AOC$ and BOC are supplementary angles. Each angle is said to be the *supplement* of the other.

Vertical angles (margin note)

Supplementary angles (margin note)

Theorem 8-3   Angles which are supplements of the same angle are congruent angles.

Hypothesis $\measuredangle AOD$ and BOC each a supplement of $\angle AOC$ (Fig. 8–17).

Conclusion $\angle AOD \cong \angle BOC$.

From the hypothesis we have that $\measuredangle AOD$ and AOC are supplementary and also that $\measuredangle BOC$ and AOC are supplementary. This means that the sum of the measures of each supplementary pair of angles is 180. Definition 4–1 implies that the measure of each angle of a supplementary pair of angles can be expressed in terms of 180 and the measure of the other angle.

The conclusion we wish to draw is that $\angle AOD$ is congruent to $\angle BOC$. From Definition 8–13 we know that this conclusion can be drawn if we can establish that $m\angle AOD = m\angle BOC$. How can we use the hypothesis and what we know about angle measure to establish this relation of equality between the measures of these two angles?

Proof

Statements	*Reasons*
$m \angle AOD + m \angle AOC = 180$	Supplementary $\angle\!\!s$
$m \angle AOD = 180 - m \angle AOC$	Definition 4–1
$m \angle BOC + m \angle AOC = 180$	Supplementary $\angle\!\!s$
$m \angle BOC = 180 - m \angle AOC$	Definition 4–1
$\angle AOD \cong \angle BOC$	Definition 8–13

Corollary 1 Angles which are the supplements of congruent angles are congruent.

Corollary 2 Vertical angles are congruent.

Right angle

If two supplementary angles are congruent, each angle is called a *right angle.* As a result of this definition and Postulate 8–7 we have Theorem 8–4 and its corollary, the proofs of which are left to the reader.

Theorem 8-4 The measure of a right angle is 90.

Corollary All right angles are congruent.

Acute and obtuse angles

Definition 8-14 An *acute angle* is an angle whose measure is less than 90. An *obtuse angle* is an angle whose measure is greater than 90 but less than 180. (See Fig. 8–12.)

The statement of Theorem 8–4 is sometimes used as the definition of a right angle. It is equivalent to the one used here. Theorem 8–5, which states an important property of two intersecting lines, follows as an immediate consequence of Theorem 8–4. Two angles the sum of

Complementary angles

whose measures is 90 are *complementary angles.* Each angle is the *complement* of the other.

Theorem 8-5 If one of the angles formed by two intersecting lines is a right angle, then all the angles formed are right angles.

The proof of this theorem is also left to the reader.

Definition 8-15 Two lines which intersect at right angles are called *perpendicular lines.*

Perpendicularity

Definition 8-16 If a line l intersects a plane π in a point P in such a manner that it is perpendicular to every line lying in the plane π and passing through P, then and only then is the line l said to be perpendicular to the plane π.

Postulate 8-8   Given a line *l* and a point *P* not of *l*. In the plane determined by *P* and *l* one and only one line can be drawn through *P* perpendicular to *l*. Whether *P* is or is not a point of *l*, one and only one plane can be passed through *P* perpendicular to *l*. (See Figs. 8–18 and 8–19.)

Up to this point in the discussion of angles, the only ones in which we have been interested are those formed by the union of two rays with a common end point. Such angles are frequently referred to as *plane angles*, since two intersecting rays are always sufficient to fix or determine a plane. There are angles of interest which might by contrast be called *space angles*, since they are not formed by lines in planes but by planes in space. Of these the *dihedral angle* is important here.

Dihedral angle

Definition 8-17   A *dihedral angle* is the union of two nonplanar half planes and their common edge. This common edge is called the *edge*, and its union with each half plane is called a *face*, or *side*, of the angle.

In Fig. 8–20 a letter has been placed in each face of the dihedral angle to facilitate the reading of the angle. The dihedral angle *C-AB-D* of the figure has the line $\overleftrightarrow{AB}$ as its edge and the planes *CAB* and *DAB* as its two faces. A point *P* in space is interior to ∠*C-AB-D* if it is on the *D* side of the half plane *C* and also on the *C* side of the half

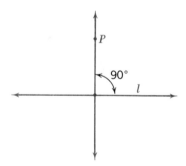

FIGURE 8–18   Mutually perpendicular lines.

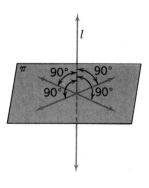

FIGURE 8–19   Line *l* perpendicular to plane *π*.

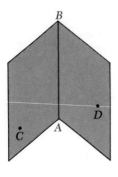

FIGURE 8-20   Dihedral angle *C-AB-D*.

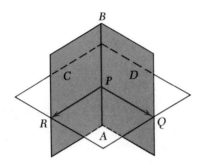

FIGURE 8-21   Plane $\angle RPQ$ of dihedral $\angle C$-*AB-D*.

plane *D*. Under what conditions would a point be said to be exterior to $\angle C$-*AB-D*?

In Fig. 8–21 a point *P* has been marked on the edge $\overleftrightarrow{AB}$ of the dihedral angle. By Postulate 8–8 one and only one plane can be passed through *P* perpendicular to the line $\overleftrightarrow{AB}$. Furthermore, this plane will intersect the planes forming the dihedral angle in lines of which rays $\overrightarrow{PR}$ and $\overrightarrow{PQ}$ will be subsets. These rays with the common end point *P* form the plane angle *RPQ*. By Definition 8–16 the rays $\overrightarrow{PR}$ and $\overrightarrow{PQ}$ are each perpendicular to the edge $\overleftrightarrow{AB}$ of the dihedral angle. The angle *RPQ* is called the *plane angle* of the dihedral angle *C-AB-D*.

Postulate 8-9   All plane angles of a given dihedral angle are congruent.

As a consequence of Postulate 8–9 the measure of a dihedral angle is the same as the measure of any one of its plane angles. There are two very important properties of dihedral angles which are derived immediately from this fact:

1   Two dihedral angles are said to be *congruent* if and only if their plane angles are congruent.

2   A dihedral angle is said to be a *right dihedral angle* if and only if its plane angle is a right angle.

Just as two lines intersect in a point to form pairs of vertical plane angles, so two planes intersect in a line to form pairs of *vertical dihedral angles*. An immediate consequence of the previously stated properties of dihedral angles is this theorem.

Theorem 8–6   **Vertical dihedral angles are congruent.**

The proof of this theorem is left as an exercise for the reader.

Exercises

1 Locate and label three noncollinear points as A, B, and C. Draw the lines which these points determine. Are $\angle ABC$ and $\angle CBA$ the same angle or different angles? Why? Are $\angle ABC$ and $\angle BCA$ the same angle or different angles? Why?

2 How many different angles can you identify in the figure determined by the three lines of Exercise 1?

3 Use the accompanying picture of two parallel lines l and m to describe (*a*) the intersection of the half plane on the P side of l with the half plane on the P side of m; (*b*) the intersection of the half plane on the Q side of l with the half plane on the Q side of m; (*c*) the intersection of the half plane on the P side of m with the half plane on the Q side of l.

4 Use a clean sheet of paper to represent a plane. In this plane draw two perpendicular lines and locate a point P as in the accompanying figure. Now shade the portion of the figure which represents the intersection of the half plane on the P side of $\overleftrightarrow{X'X}$ with the half plane on the P side of $\overleftrightarrow{Y'Y}$. Identity this portion of the figure by using the letters of the figure other than P.

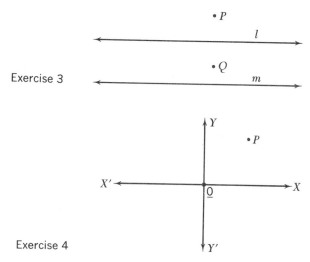

Exercise 3

Exercise 4

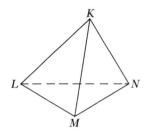

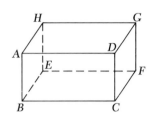

Exercise 6

5   Use the pages of a book or two sheets of paper as an aid in describing the interior and exterior of a dihedral angle.

6   For each three-dimensional configuration of the accompanying figure, carry out these instructions:

(a) Count the points, lines, and planes represented.

(b) Count and name the plane angles.

(c) Count and name the dihedral angles.

(d) If the line $\overleftrightarrow{AD}$ is perpendicular to the plane represented by the figure *HABE*, is there a significant relation between the plane angle *BAH* and the dihedral angle *G-AD-C*?

(e) If, in addition to the relation of (d), the lines $\overleftrightarrow{AH}$ and $\overleftrightarrow{AB}$ are also perpendicular to each other, what can be said about the dihedral angle *G-AD-C*?

(f) If the line $\overleftrightarrow{KM}$ is not perpendicular either to the line $\overleftrightarrow{ML}$ or to the line $\overleftrightarrow{MN}$, is the plane angle *LMN* the plane angle of the dihedral angle *L-KM-N*?   Why?

(g) How many planes are represented as passing through each line of each figure?

(h) Select one line from each figure.   Explain why there exist planes other than those represented which might be passed through the selected line.

(i) What is the minimum number of planes necessary to determine a line in space?   Why?

(j) How many planes are represented as passing through each point of each figure?

(k) Select one point from each figure.   Explain why there exist planes other than those represented which might be passed through the selected point.

(l) What is the minimum number of planes necessary to determine a point in space?   Why?

7   Prove the two corollaries of Theorem 8–3.

8   Prove Theorem 8–4.   Also prove its corollary.

9   Prove Theorem 8–5.

10 What are the measures of the complement and supplement of each of these plane angles?

(a) 10°   (b) 45°   (c) 60°   (d) $(90 - A)°$

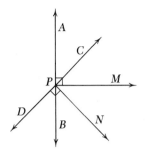

Exercise 12

11   The measure of one of the angles formed by two intersecting lines is 35. What is the measure of each of the remaining angles?

12   In the figure the lines $\overleftrightarrow{AB}$ and $\overleftrightarrow{CD}$ intersect at P. From P the rays $\overrightarrow{PM}$ and $\overrightarrow{PN}$ are drawn in the plane determined by $\overleftrightarrow{AB}$ and $\overleftrightarrow{CD}$. $m\angle APM = 90$ and $m\angle DPN = 90$.

   (a) Are there any other right angles in the figure?
   (b) Name pairs of complementary angles.
   (c) Name pairs of supplementary angles.
   (d) Name pairs of congruent angles.

13   Given four plane angles A, B, C, and D so related that A and B are supplementary, B and D are complementary, and $m\angle C - m\angle D = 45$. How do the measures of angles A and C compare?

14   Prove Theorem 8-6.

15   *Prove Theorem 8-7:* Plane angles which are the complements of the same angle, or of congruent angles, are congruent angles.

16   *Prove Theorem 8-8:* If two plane angles are complementary, then each angle is an acute angle.

17   *Prove Theorem 8-9:* If two unequal plane angles are supplementary, then one and only one is an acute angle.

18   *Prove Theorem 8-10:* In a plane, one and only one line can be drawn perpendicular to a given line at a fixed point of the line.

8-5 THE CARTESIAN CONCEPT OF POSITION

Take a look at the corner of your room where the floor meets two of the walls. You see a picture such as that of Fig. 8-22 in which the ray $\overrightarrow{OZ}$ represents the intersection of the two walls, and each of the rays $\overrightarrow{OX}$ and $\overrightarrow{OY}$ represents the intersection of a wall and the floor. Properly constructed walls and floors are flat surfaces and thus represent planes. Let your imagination help you to visualize the extension of both walls and the floor in all directions, each retaining its characteristics of a flat

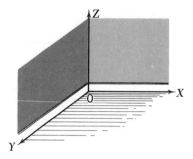

FIGURE 8–22   Room corner.

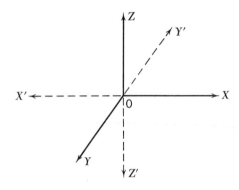

FIGURE 8–23   Cartesian frame of reference.

surface. The picture visualized should then be of the form of Fig. 8–23, where the line $\overleftrightarrow{Z'Z}$ now represents the intersection of the planes of the two walls, and each of the lines $\overleftrightarrow{X'X}$ and $\overleftrightarrow{Y'Y}$ represents the intersection of the plane of the floor with that of a wall. In such a configuration the lines are said to be *mutually perpendicular* (each line is perpendicular to the other two), and also the planes are mutually perpendicular.

If now a convenient unit is chosen and used, as in Sec. 6–3, to construct a number line on each of the three lines $\overleftrightarrow{X'X}$, $\overleftrightarrow{Y'Y}$, and $\overleftrightarrow{Z'Z}$, we have three mutually perpendicular number lines with a common point as the zero point, or *origin*. Such a configuration is called a *cartesian*

Frame of
reference

frame of reference.† In such a frame of reference the line $\overleftrightarrow{X'X}$ is called the *x axis;* the line $\overleftrightarrow{Y'Y}$, the *y axis;* and the line $\overleftrightarrow{Z'Z}$, the *z axis.* In Fig. 8–23 the colored portion of each line represents the positive real numbers, while the dotted portion represents the negative real numbers. With such a frame of reference any set of three real numbers will locate a unique point in space, our universal set of points. Thus, if x is used to represent the number of units to be measured along the x axis, y the number along the y axis, and z the number along the z axis, then the *ordered triple* of real numbers (x,y,z) locates a specific point in space.

† Named after the Frenchman, René Descartes, who first suggested such an idea in one of three appendices to a book published in 1637.

This is called an ordered triple since the order of listing the numbers is always x-axis number, y-axis number, z-axis number. Each number serves as a coordinate on its respective axis. The entire set of three axes constitutes a *cartesian coordinate system*. Since the lines and planes are respectively mutually perpendicular, the system is also called a *rectangular coordinate system*. In such a frame of reference the symbol $P(x,y,z)$ is to be read "the point P whose coordinates are x, y, and z." In Fig. 8–24 the locations of two points $P(3,1,4)$ and $Q(-5,-4,2)$ have been indicated. A frame of reference with axes identified and lettered as in Figs. 8–23 and 8–24 is called a *left-handed system*. This name is due to the fact that if you use the index finger of your left hand to point in the direction of the positive x axis, the middle finger can then point along the positive y axis, and the thumb along the positive z axis. If the x and y axes were interchanged, you would then have a *right-handed system*.

Rectangular
coordinate
system

Our principal use of a cartesian frame of reference will be in the plane. In this case there are two perpendicular number lines with a common zero point. The two coordinate axes will be the x axis $(\overleftrightarrow{X'X})$ and the y axis $(\overleftrightarrow{Y'Y})$, drawn as shown in Fig. 8–25. Each axis is frequently called by two other names: the x axis is also called the *horizontal axis* or the axis of *abscissas*, and the y axis is at times called either the *vertical axis* or the axis of *ordinates*. In the plane a point is located by an *ordered pair* of real numbers in the form (x,y), with the x coordinate written first. In the figure the locations of the two points $P(4,3)$ and $Q(-3,-2)$ are indicated. Note that the positive x values are always to the right of the origin and the negative values to the left. On the y axis the positive values are always above the origin and the negative values below. In such a frame of reference any point in the plane

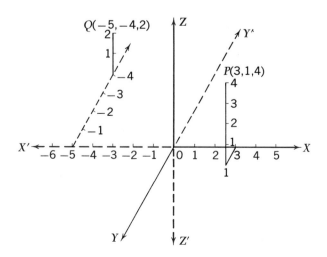

FIGURE 8–24   Cartesian coordinates in space.

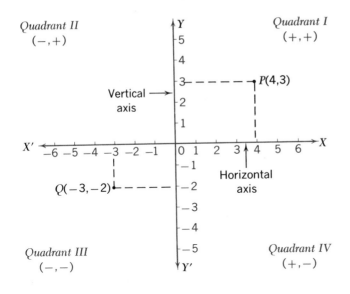

Quadrant II (−,+)

Quadrant I (+,+)

Vertical axis

$P(4,3)$

X' −6 −5 −4 −3 −2 −1   0 1 2 3 4 5 6 X

Horizontal axis

$Q(-3,-2)$

Quadrant III (−,−)

Quadrant IV (+,−)

FIGURE 8–25
Cartesian coordinates in a plane.

is uniquely located. The two axes divide the plane into four sections called *quadrants*. They are identified as the first, second, third, and fourth quadrants and are labeled with the respective Roman numerals I, II, III, IV. The method used to identify each quadrant is to label it with the signs of the coordinates which will locate points in that quadrant. As indicated in Fig. 8–25, the signs for each quadrant are I(+,+), II(−,+), III(−,−), and IV(+,−).

Quadrants of the plane

8–6 POSITION ON THE EARTH'S SURFACE

Angular measure affords a very significant adaptation of the cartesian method to the location of points on the surface of the earth. For this purpose the earth is assumed to be a true sphere. Any circle on the surface of a sphere whose center coincides with the center of the sphere is called a *great circle*. All other circles on the sphere are called *small circles*. Geometry tells us that three points, not all on the same straight line, will fix the position of a specific circle and that no other distinct circle will pass through these same three points. Since this is true there is one and only one great circle which will pass through both the North Pole and the South Pole and through any other one point on the surface of the earth. The equator is the great circle which lies in the plane perpendicular at the center of the sphere to the diameter joining the North Pole to the South Pole (see Fig. 8–26).

Frame of reference on the earth's surface

The frame of reference for locating points on the earth's surface consists of the equator and the great circle which passes through Green-

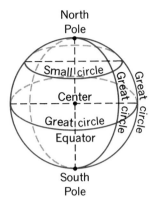

FIGURE 8–26   Great and small circles on earth's surface.

wich, England, and through the two poles.   This great circle is called
the *prime meridian,* or sometimes the *Greenwich meridian.*   All other
great circles on the earth's surface that pass through the two poles are
called *meridians.*   *Longitude* is measured by the number of degrees,
minutes, and seconds in the central angles† of the equator, and is either
east (E) or west (W), depending on which direction it is measured from
the prime meridian.   The number of degrees, minutes, and seconds in
the central angle of a meridian is called *latitude.*   It is either north (N)
or south (S), depending on whether it is measured from the equator in
the direction of the North Pole or the South Pole.   In Fig. 8–27 a west
longitude and a north latitude are indicated.

The origin of this frame of reference is the point *O,* where the prime

† A central angle of a circle is an angle whose vertex is at the center of the circle
(see Fig. 8–31).

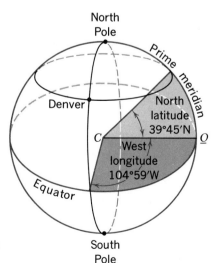

FIGURE 8–27   Longitude and latitude on earth's
surface.

meridian and the equator intersect. Figure 8–28 lists the longitudes and latitudes, correct to the nearest minute, of several different localities. For example, Denver, Colorado, is located at 104°59′ west longitude and 39°45′ north latitude. This means that its location on the earth's surface is 104°59′ west of the prime meridian and 39°45′ north of the equator. Such information is extremely important in air and sea travel and world communication. Natal and Sydney are in the *Southern Hemisphere* (half sphere), while all other cities of the table are in the *Northern Hemisphere.* Rome, Sydney, and Yokohama are in the *Eastern Hemisphere,* and the others are in the *Western Hemisphere.*

An added fact of great significance is that the key for uniformity of patterns of time throughout the world is the basic relationship that 15° of longitude is equivalent to 1 hour of time. This is based on the fact that there are 360° of longitude around the world and 24 hours in one

Time zones   day (360° ÷ 24 = 15°). Time zones are established in terms of this relationship; of course there are many adjustments in the basic pattern to adapt to intrinsic characteristics of local situations. Each zone is approximately 15° "wide," and its time is fixed in accordance with that meridian passing through it which is an exact multiple of 15°. There are seven such time zones in the United States: *Eastern,* which determines its time from the 75th west meridian; *Central,* the 90th west meridian; *Mountain,* the 105th west meridian; *Pacific,* the 120th west meridian; *Yukon,* the 135th west meridian; *Alaskan,* the 150th west meridian; and *Bering,* the 165th west meridian. Camden (Eastern), St. Louis (Central), Denver (Mountain), Fresno (Pacific), Honolulu (Alaskan), and Dutch Harbor (Bering) are cities of the United States, each situated very near the time-standard meridian of its respective zone. Notice that the difference in longitude between any two of these cities approximates very closely an exact multiple of 15°. To find the time difference between any two cities one can find the difference between the two exact multiples of 15° which most nearly correspond to the respective longitudes of the cities. The difference in time in

FIGURE 8–28   Longitude and latitude of selected cities.

CITY	LONGITUDE	LATITUDE
Camden, New Jersey	75° 7′ W	39° 57′ N
Denver, Colorado	104° 59′ W	39° 45′ N
Dutch Harbor, Alaska	166° 33′ W	53° 33′ N
Fresno, California	119° 47′ W	36° 44′ N
Honolulu, Hawaii	157° 52′ W	21° 18′ N
Natal, Brazil	35° 13′ W	5° 47′ S
Rome, Italy	12° 30′ E	41° 54′ N
St. Louis, Missouri	90° 12′ W	38° 38′ N
Sydney, Australia	151° 12′ E	33° 52′ S
Yokohama, Japan	139° 40′ E	35° 27′ N

hours will then be the same as the obtained multiple of 15°. Although the Yukon time zone crosses a portion of the United States, the section is a very small and thinly populated area of Alaska. For this reason it is not too significant as a time zone of the United States.

The *international date line* is halfway around the world from the prime meridian. Thus it is the 180° meridian, whether measured westward or eastward from the prime meridian. This is where the new day starts. For a person crossing the international date line from the Western Hemisphere to the Eastern Hemisphere, the day of the week advances one day: for example, 8 A.M. Sunday becomes 8 A.M. Monday. Analogously, Monday becomes Sunday if the direction is reversed.

Example When it is Sunday in Honolulu, Hawaii, what day is it in Sydney, Australia?

Since Honolulu is near the 157° west meridian and Sydney is near the 151° east meridian, the international date line is between them. So when it is Sunday in Honolulu it is Monday in Sydney.

Example What is the difference in time between (1) Fresno, California, and Camden, New Jersey; (2) Dutch Harbor, Alaska, and Denver, Colorado; (3) Honolulu, Hawaii, and Yokohama, Japan; (4) St. Louis, Missouri, and Rome, Italy?

1 Fresno is near the 120° west meridian and Camden is near the 75° west meridian. There is a difference of 45° of longitude in the time-standardizing meridians of these two cities. Therefore, there is a difference of 3 hours in time.

2 Dutch Harbor is near the 165° west meridian and Denver is near the 105° west meridian. The difference of 60° of longitude corresponds to a difference of 4 hours of time.

3 Honolulu is near the 150° *west* meridian and Yokohama is near the 135° *east* meridian. The difference in longitude, in a case such as this where one city is in a west longitude zone and the other in an east longitude zone, is found by *adding* the two longitude measures. The difference in longitude between Honolulu and Yokohama is 150° + 135° = 285°. This difference in longitude corresponds to a difference of 19 hours in time.

4 St. Louis is near the 90° west meridian and Rome is near the 15° east meridian. The difference in longitude is 105°, so there is a difference of 7 hours of time.

Exercises

1 Use two pages of an open book and the top of a table or desk to represent a cartesian frame of reference in space with x, y, and z axes, as indicated in Fig. 8–23.

2 Use the frame of reference of Exercise 1 to describe the position of each of these points: (0,0,0); (2,0,0); (0,−3,0); (0,0,1); (0,0,−4); (−5,0,0); (0,6,0).

3 Use the frame of reference of Exercise 1 to describe the position of each of these points: (3,1,0); (4,−2,0); (−3,5,0); (−4,−6,0); (4,0,2); (3,0,−3); (−5,0,4); (−1,0,−1); (0,1,3); (0,−1,2); (0,4,−3); (0,−5,−6).

4 Use the frame of reference of Exercise 1 to describe the position of each of these points: (2,1,4); (5,−2,3); (−8,4,1); (−3,−7,−5); (1,−3,−4); (−2,−5,4); (3,2,−4); (−8,6,−4).

5 Exercise 4 has exhibited points located in each of eight distinct regions into which space is separated by three coordinate planes. These regions are called *octants*. In a left-handed cartesian frame of reference the coordinate signs which will locate a point in an octant identify it by number in the following manner: Octant I(+,+,+); II(+,−,+); III(−,−,+); IV(−,+,+); V(+,+,−); VI(+,−,−); VII(−,−,−); VIII(−,+,−). Select a set of coordinates that will locate a point in each of the eight octants described.

6 Write four ordered pairs of numbers which are such that used as coordinates of points in a plane they will locate points, one in each of the four quadrants. Use a sheet of graph paper to draw a cartesian frame of reference and then plot each of the four points whose coordinates you selected.

7 Plot the three points (1,6), (−2,0), and (0,4). These are three collinear points. How can you test to see whether they seem to be collinear?

8 Plot the points (2,5), (−4,−3), and (6,−1). These points are not collinear. How many distinct lines can you draw containing distinct pairs of these points? Draw them.

9 How many distinct lines can you draw containing distinct pairs of the points you plotted in Exercise 6? Draw them.

10 Select ordered pairs to give you five distinct points in a plane, no three of which are collinear. Draw the lines which are determined by distinct pairs of these points.

11 Which city of the United States, included in Fig. 8–28, is situated most nearly on the same circle of latitude with Yokohama, Japan?

12 Are Sydney, Australia, and Honolulu, Hawaii, on approximately the same meridian (circle of longitude)? Why?

13 How many hours' difference in time exist between each pair of cities: St. Louis and Denver; Dutch Harbor and Camden; Honolulu and Fresno; Honolulu and Denver?

14 Which city is farther east: Natal, Brazil, or Camden, New Jersey? Why?

FIGURE 8–29
Simple closed
curves in a
plane.

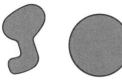

8–7   THE CONCEPT OF SHAPE

One of the basic concepts of the geometry of a plane is that of a simple   Simple closed
curve
closed curve which lies entirely in the plane.   Rather than give a
rigorous definition of such a curve it will suffice for this discussion to
present a few typical illustrations.   This is done in Fig. 8–29, in which
each picture also illustrates the fact that a simple closed curve which lies
entirely in a plane separates the plane into three disjoint sets of points:
the set of points in the *interior* of the curve; the set of points of the curve;
and the set points in the *exterior* of the curve.   The points A and B of
Fig. 8–30 are situated so that one of them (A) is in the interior and the
other (B) is in the exterior, since every line segment, whether straight or
not, joining A and B has at least one point in common with the curve.
The points C and D, both of which are in the interior, are joined by a line
segment which has no points in common with the curve.   The same is
true for points E and F, both of which are in the exterior.   The figure
also illustrates that a simple closed curve does not intersect itself.
    There are basically two types of simple closed curves in a plane with
which we are to be concerned, namely, *circles* and *polygons*.

Definition 8–18   A *circle* is a simple closed curve in a plane all points   Circle
of which are at a fixed distance from a fixed point.   The fixed distance
is called the *radius* and the fixed point the *center* of the circle.
(See Fig. 8–31.)

    A *chord* of a circle is a line segment whose end points are points of
the circle.   A *diameter* of the circle is a chord which contains the center
of the circle, and its length is always twice the length of the radius.   A

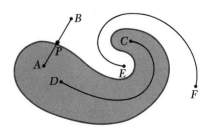

FIGURE 8–30   Exterior, interior, and points of a
simple closed curve.

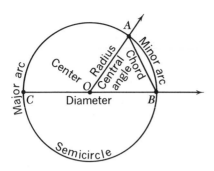

FIGURE 8–31   Elements of a circle.

central angle is an angle whose vertex is the center of the circle.   If the sides of the central angle intersect the circle in points *A* and *B*, then these two points and all points of the circle interior to the angle form a *minor arc* $\overset{\frown}{AB}$, while the two points and all points of the circle exterior to the angle form a *major arc* $\overset{\frown}{ACB}$.   Similarly, the chord $\overline{AB}$ can be said to separate the circle into a minor arc and a major arc.   If the chord is a diameter of the circle, then the two arcs are congruent and each is called a *semicircle*.   Two or more circles with the same center are said to be *concentric circles*.

Postulate 8–10   **It is always possible to draw a circle with a given point as center and a fixed length as radius.**

Polygon   *Definition 8–19*   **A *polygon* is a simple closed curve in a plane which is the union of a finite number of line segments so situated that no two segments have a point of intersection other than a common end point and no two line segments with such a common end point are collinear. Each line segment is a *side* of the polygon, and each point common to two line segments is a *vertex*.   The angle formed at each vertex is an *angle of the polygon.***

Some of the more familiar polygons are illustrated in Fig. 8–32.   A *triangle* has three vertices and three sides; a *quadrilateral,* four vertices and four sides; a *pentagon,* five vertices and five sides; and a *hexagon,* six vertices and six sides.   In general, an *n-gon* is a polygon with *n* vertices and *n* sides.   The triangle and the quadrilateral are the most generally useful of the four polygons shown.   Two other polygons which are used fairly frequently are the *octagon* (8-gon) and the *deca-*

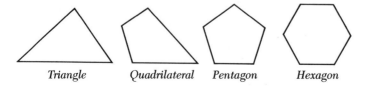

| Triangle | Quadrilateral | Pentagon | Hexagon |

FIGURE 8–32
Kinds of polygons.

gon (10-gon).   If the set of interior points of a polygon is a convex set, the polygon is a *convex polygon*.   Each of the polygons of Fig. 8–32 is a convex polygon.   The polygon of Fig. 8–11d is a polygon that is not convex.

There are several basic classifications of triangles which are of signifi-cance.   They may be classified according to characteristics of angles or according to characteristics of sides, as shown in Fig. 8–33.   While it is not too difficult to prove, we shall accept without proof the proposi-tion that *the sum of the measures of the angles of any triangle is 180.* This, of course, implies that no triangle can have more than one of its angles either a right angle or an obtuse angle.   Thus a triangle may have all its angles acute angles (*an acute-angle triangle*); or it may have one right angle (*a right triangle*); or it may have one obtuse angle (*an obtuse-*

Classification of triangles

FIGURE 8–33   Classification of triangles.

KIND OF TRIANGLE	CHARACTERISTICS		TYPICAL FIGURE
	ANGLES	SIDES	
Scalene	No two congruent.	No two congruent.	
Isosceles	Only two congruent.	Only two congruent.	
Equilateral or equiangular	All three congruent.	All three congruent.	
Acute Angle	All acute angles. No two, only two, or all three may be congruent.	No two, only two, or all three may be congruent.	No 2 ≅ Only 2 ≅ All 3 ≅
Right	One angle is a right angle. The other two angles are acute and may or may not be congruent.	Two sides including the right angle may or may not be congruent. Hypotenuse is the longest side.	No sides ≅ 2 sides ≅ No angles ≅ 2 angles ≅
Obtuse Angle	One angle is an obtuse angle. The other two angles may or may not be congruent.	Two sides including the obtuse angle may or may not be congruent.	No angles ≅ No sides ≅ 2 sides ≅ 2 angles ≅

angle triangle). In an acute-angle triangle there are three possibilities: No two angles are congruent (*scalene triangle*); only two angles are congruent (*isosceles triangle*); or all three angles are congruent (*equiangular triangle*). In either a right triangle or an obtuse-angle triangle, there always are two acute angles, which may or may not be congruent.

The three sides of any triangle have three possible distinguishing relationships: no two sides are congruent (*scalene triangle*); only two sides are congruent (*isosceles triangle*); or all three sides are congruent (*equilateral triangle*). From the above discussion a scalene triangle is seen to be one that has no two angles and no two sides congruent; an isosceles triangle has only two angles and only two sides congruent; and an equilateral triangle, which is also equiangular, has all three sides and all three angles congruent. In an isosceles triangle the side which is not one of the two congruent sides is called the *base* of the triangle.

In a right triangle the side opposite the right angle is always the longest side and is called the *hypotenuse.* The other two sides are called *legs.* One of the most famous and significant theorems in mathematics relates the hypotenuse and legs of any right triangle. Although its proof is beyond the scope of this book, the theorem will be listed here because of its interest and general usefulness.

Pythagorean theorem

Theorem 8–11   The Pythagorean Theorem   **The square of the length of the hypotenuse of a right triangle is equal to the sum of the squares of the lengths of the two legs.**

In the right triangle ABC of Fig. 8–34 the angle at C is the right angle, c is the length of the hypotenuse, and the lengths of the two legs are a and b, respectively. The pythagorean theorem then states that

$$c^2 = a^2 + b^2$$

The theorem gets its name from the fact that the discovery and first proof of it was by the outstanding Greek mathematician Pythagoras (ca. 540 B.C.). One book has been published† in which the author has compiled 370 proofs of this one theorem. It was through the application of this theorem to an isosceles right triangle that Pythagoras and his followers discovered the irrational number $\sqrt{2}$. For example, if the

† E. S. Loomis, "The Pythagorean Theorem," 2d ed., Edwards Brothers, Inc., Ann Arbor, Michigan, 1940.

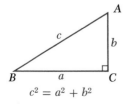

$$c^2 = a^2 + b^2$$

FIGURE 8–34   The pythagorean theorem.

FIGURE 8–35   Typical plane quadrilaterals.

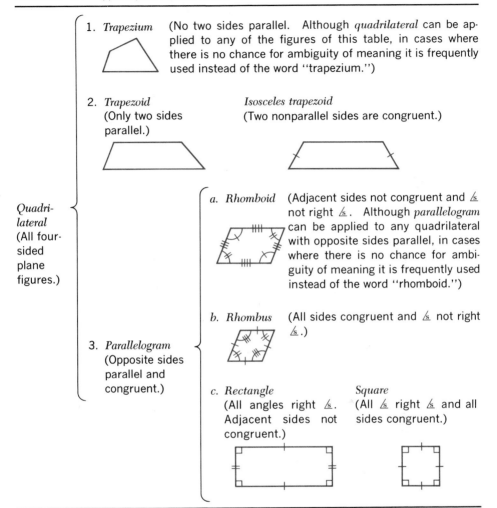

1. *Trapezium*   (No two sides parallel. Although *quadrilateral* can be applied to any of the figures of this table, in cases where there is no chance for ambiguity of meaning it is frequently used instead of the word "trapezium.")

2. *Trapezoid*   *Isosceles trapezoid*
(Only two sides   (Two nonparallel sides are congruent.)
parallel.)

*Quadri-
lateral*
(All four-
sided
plane
figures.)

3. *Parallelogram*
(Opposite sides
parallel and
congruent.)

a. *Rhomboid*   (Adjacent sides not congruent and ∠ not right ∠. Although *parallelogram* can be applied to any quadrilateral with opposite sides parallel, in cases where there is no chance for ambiguity of meaning it is frequently used instead of the word "rhomboid.")

b. *Rhombus*   (All sides congruent and ∠ not right ∠.)

c. *Rectangle*   *Square*
(All angles right ∠.   (All ∠ right ∠ and all
Adjacent sides not   sides congruent.)
congruent.)

length of each leg is 1 unit, then $c^2 = (1)^2 + (1)^2 = 2$, and the length of the hypotenuse is $\sqrt{2}$ units.

Regardless of the type of triangle being discussed, an accepted, and frequently used, symbol for "triangle" is △. The plural form of the symbol is △.

Just as all triangles fall into distinct classifications according to fundamental characteristics, so do all plane quadrilaterals. These classifications with their distinguishing characteristics are shown in Fig. 8–35.

The only distinction made in classifications of polygons of more than four sides which is of significance to this discussion has to do with whether or not they are regular polygons.

Classification
of plane quad-
rilaterals

Regular
polygon **Definition 8-20** **A regular polygon is a polygon all of whose sides and all of whose angles are congruent.**

Thus, there are pentagons and regular pentagons, hexagons and regular hexagons, octagons and regular octagons, decagons and regular decagons. Which of the three-sided and four-sided polygons are regular?

In space we are interested in solids and their surfaces. One convenient pattern to follow in the classification of solid figures is to put the *sphere* in a set by itself.

Sphere **Definition 8-21** **A *sphere* is the set of all points in space at a given distance from a given point. The given distance is the *radius* of the sphere and the given point is the *center*. Two or more spheres with the same center are called *concentric spheres*. A *chord* of the sphere is a line segment whose end points are on the sphere. A *diameter* of the sphere is a chord which contains the center of the sphere and has length twice the length of the radius.** (See Fig. 8–36.)

Theorem 8–12 is an immediate consequence of the definitions of circle and sphere. The proof of the theorem is left to the reader.

Theorem 8-12 **The intersection of a sphere and a plane through its center is a circle.**

The *interior of a sphere* is the set of points which contains the center and all those points of space whose distance from the center is less than the length of the radius of the sphere, and the *exterior of a sphere* is the set of all points of space whose distance from the center of the sphere is greater than the length of the radius. A sphere is a surface that is curved instead of being flat like a plane.

Classification
of solid figures
With the sphere classified in one set, a second set of solids would then contain all various types of prisms and the *circular cylinder*. Four types of *prisms* are shown in Fig. 8–37. The polygons of the boundary surfaces of the prisms are called *faces*. The lines in which the faces intersect are called *edges*. Two of the faces of each prism are in parallel planes and are called the *bases* of the prism. In the figure the bases are outlined in color. The faces between the parallel planes are called

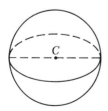

FIGURE 8-36   Sphere.

FIGURE 8–37   Familiar solids of two bases.

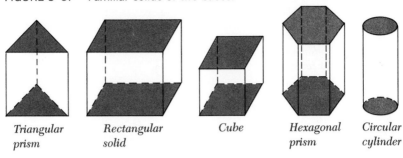

Triangular prism	*Rectangular solid*	*Cube*	*Hexagonal prism*	*Circular cylinder*

FIGURE 8–38   Familiar solids of one base.

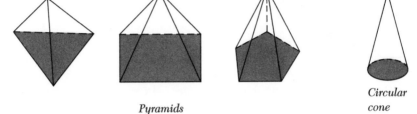

Pyramids

Circular cone

lateral faces and together make up the *lateral surface* of the prism. While the bases may be of any polygonal pattern, the lateral faces are parallelograms. In the *rectangular prism,* or *rectangular solid,* as it is frequently called, all faces are rectangles. The *cube* is a rectangular solid all of whose faces are squares or, equivalently, all of whose edges are equal. In common with prisms, the cylinder has two bases. For the cylinder, however, the bases are not polygons. They may be any type of curve, and the lateral surface is a corresponding curved surface. The only type of cylinder that will concern us here is the *circular cylinder,* i.e., one whose bases are circles.

A third set of the familiar solids would contain *pyramids* and *circular cones* (Fig. 8–38). This group has the common characteristic of having only one base, shown in color. The base of a circular cone is a circle, and its lateral surface is curved. While the base of a pyramid may be any type of polygon, its lateral faces are triangles. The common vertex of these triangles is called the *vertex* of the pyramid. If the base is a regular polygon, the pyramid is called a *regular pyramid.*

Because of their basic composition, prisms and pyramids belong to another important classification of solids known as *polyhedrons* (solids of many faces). Of great importance in this group of solids are the five regular polyhedrons. They are so called because their faces are all regular polygons (Fig. 8–39).

Regular polyhedrons

Tetrahedron
(4 faces)

Cube
(hexahedron;
6 faces)

Octahedron
(8 faces)

Dodecahedron
(12 faces)

Icosahedron
(20 faces)

FIGURE 8–39
Regular polyhedrons.

8–8   THE CONCEPT OF SIMILARITY

Fundamentally, two geometric figures are similar if they have the same shape.   As illustrations of similar plane figures (Fig. 8–40) we may cite any two line segments, any two circles, and any two regular polygons of the same number of sides.   In space, similar figures would be any two spheres and any two regular polyhedrons with the same number of faces (Fig. 8–41).

Similarity of polygons and polyhedrons is not necessarily restricted to those which are regular.   The more general concept of similarity in the plane is in accordance with this definition.

Similar
polygons

Definition 8-22   **Two polygons, for which a one-to-one correspondence between vertices has been established, are said to be similar if and only if their corresponding angles are congruent and there exists a constant ratio between corresponding sides.**

FIGURE 8–40   Similar plane figures.

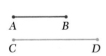

Two spheres
of different size

Two cubes
of different size

Two regular
tetrahedrons of
different size

FIGURE 8–41
Similar solid figures.

The symbol $\sim$ is used to indicate that two figures are similar to each other. In other words, if polygon P is similar to polygon Q we might indicate this fact by writing "polygon $P \sim$ polygon Q."

It should be obvious that regular polygons of the same number of sides meet the criteria of the definition. It can be established that two triangles which satisfy either criterion will necessarily satisfy the other. In other words, two triangles whose corresponding angles are congruent are similar; also two triangles whose corresponding sides are proportional are similar. That this is not true for polygons in general is illustrated by an examination of the rectangle, square, and rhombus of Fig. 8–42. The angles of the rectangle and square are all congruent, but the ratios of corresponding sides are not constant $\left(\dfrac{12}{3} \neq \dfrac{4}{3}\right)$. The ratios of corresponding sides of the square and rhombus are constant $\left(\dfrac{8}{3} = \dfrac{8}{3}\right)$, but the corresponding angles are not congruent. (All angles of the square are right angles, while two angles of the rhombus are acute angles and two are obtuse angles.)

As a consequence of the special nature of triangles, there are two other significant conditions of similarity. One of these will be stated as a theorem whose proof is left to the reader. Although the second can be proved as a theorem, its proof is beyond the scope of this treatment and it will be stated as a postulate.

Theorem 8–13   Two triangles are similar if two angles of one are congruent to two angles of the other.   Similarity of triangles

Postulate 8–11   Two triangles are similar if two pairs of corresponding sides are proportional and the included angles are congruent.

Although there exist criteria for determining similarity of nonregular polyhedrons, they are not of concern to this treatment.

Example

1   Given the triangles ABC and DEF such that $m \angle A = 24$, $m \angle B = 126$, and $m \angle C = 30$; $m \angle D = 30$, $m \angle F = 126$, and $m \angle E = 24$. The angles of the two triangles can be made to correspond in such a manner that the corresponding angles are congruent. This correspondence is $\angle A \leftrightarrow \angle E$, $\angle B \leftrightarrow \angle F$, and $\angle C \leftrightarrow \angle D$. Thus the similar triangles are ABC and EFD.

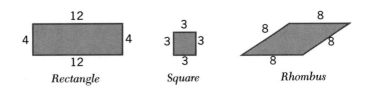

FIGURE 8–42
Dissimilar polygons.   *Rectangle*   *Square*   *Rhombus*

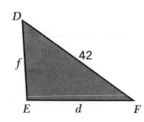

FIGURE 8–43   Similar triangles.

2   Given the triangles ABC and DEF such that $AB = 3$, $BC = 4$, and $CA = 5$; $DE = 12$, $EF = 16$, and $FD = 20$. If the vertices of the two triangles be made to correspond so that $A \leftrightarrow D$, $B \leftrightarrow E$, and $C \leftrightarrow F$, then the ratios of corresponding sides remain constant $\left(\dfrac{3}{12} = \dfrac{4}{16} = \dfrac{5}{20} = \dfrac{1}{4} \right)$. Therefore ABC and DEF are similar triangles.

3   Given triangles ABC and DEF such that $m \angle A = 75$ and $m \angle B = 42$; $m \angle F = 75$ and $m \angle D = 42$. If $\angle A \leftrightarrow \angle F$ and $\angle B \leftrightarrow \angle D$, then $\triangle ABC$ and FDE are similar.

4   Given the triangles ABC and DEF such that $m \angle A = 52$, $m \angle D = 52$, and $\dfrac{AB}{DF} = \dfrac{AC}{DE} = 2$. Here $\angle A \cong \angle D$ and the including sides are proportional. The ratios of the sides show that vertex B corresponds to vertex F, and C to E. It then follows that the similar triangles are ABC and DFE. Furthermore, the constant ratio of 2 states that the length of each side of $\triangle ABC$ is twice the length of its corresponding side in $\triangle DFE$.

The authority for the first two illustrations is the definiton of similarity and the fact that, in the case of triangles, either set of criteria implies the other. For the third illustration the authority is Theorem 8–13, and for the fourth illustration it is Postulate 8–11.

Example   In $\triangle ABC$, $AB = 15$, $BC = 25$, $CA = 30$. In the similar $\triangle DEF$, $FD = 42$; find the lengths of DE and EF.

In Fig. 8–43, f represents the side $\overline{DE}$ and d represents $\overline{EF}$. The correspondence of vertices as given is $A \leftrightarrow D$, $B \leftrightarrow E$, and $C \leftrightarrow F$. The ratios of the sides are $\dfrac{f}{15} = \dfrac{d}{25} = \dfrac{42}{30} = \dfrac{7}{5}$. Since $25 = 5 \times 5$, $d = 5 \times 7 = 35$; $15 = 3 \times 5$, so $f = 3 \times 7 = 21$.

Exercises

1   Draw figures, similar to that of Fig. 8–30, to illustrate interior and exterior points for the following simple closed curves: (*a*) circle; (*b*) triangle; (*c*) rectangle; (*d*) hexagon.

2   Can a straight line segment joining an interior point of a simple

closed curve to an exterior point have more than one point in common with the curve? Illustrate your answer.

3 A simple description of a simple closed curve in a plane is that it may be represented by a curve which can be drawn with a pencil on a sheet of paper without lifting the pencil and such that the starting point and end point coincide but the curve has no other points which coincide. Draw illustrations of simple closed curves in a plane using only curved lines; using only straight line segments; using combinations of the two.

4 Draw illustrations of closed curves in a plane which are not simple closed curves. Use curved lines only; use straight line segments only; use combinations of the two.

5 A famous German mathematician, Leonhard Euler (pronounced oil'er) (1707–1783), discovered a formula which expresses the relation existing between the number of faces (F), number of vertices (V), and number of edges (E) of any polyhedron. The formula is $F + V - E = 2$. Verify this formula for the polyhedrons of Figs. 8–37 to 8–39.

6 Prove Theorem 8–12.

7 Prove Theorem 8–13.

8 Which of the following conditions are sufficient to make the two given triangles similar? Name the similar triangles, when they exist, by ordering the vertices to indicate correspondence.

(a) $m \angle A = 35$, $m \angle B = 105$, $m \angle C = 40$; $m \angle D = 40$,
    $m \angle E = 35$, $m \angle F = 105$
(b) $m \angle A = 50$, $m \angle B = 90$; $m \angle D = 50$, $m \angle E = 90$
(c) $m \angle A = 47$, $m \angle B = 95$, $m \angle C = 38$; $m \angle D = 47$,
    $m \angle E = 113$, $m \angle F = 20$
(d) $m \angle B = 50$, $BA = 15$, $BC = 12$; $m \angle D = 50$, $DE = 24$,
    $DF = 30$
(e) $AB = 40$, $BC = 10$, $CA = 35$; $EF = 20$, $FD = 5$, $DE = 25$
(f) $m \angle A = 45$, $m \angle B = 65$; $m \angle D = 65$, $m \angle E = 70$
(g) $AB = 24$, $BC = 32$, $CA = 40$; $EF = 25$, $FD = 20$, $DE = 15$
(h) $m \angle A = 72$, $AB = 75$, $AC = 48$; $m \angle D = 72$, $DE = 25$,
    $DF = 24$
(i) $AB = 18$, $BC = 12$, $CA = 20$; $DE = 9$, $EF = 6$, $FD = 10$

9 Are these quadrilaterals similar?

(a) Rectangle $ABCD$ with $AB = DC = 12$, $AD = BC = 3$
    Rectangle $EFGH$ with $EF = HG = 20$, $EH = FG = 5$
(b) Parallelogram $ABCD$ with $AB = DC = 75$, $AD = BC = 15$;
    $m \angle A = m \angle C = 135$, $m \angle B = m \angle D = 45$
    Parallelogram $EFGH$ with $EF = HG = 100$, $EH = FG = 20$;
    $m \angle E = m \angle G = 135$, $m \angle F = m \angle H = 45$
(c) Rectangle $ABCD$ with $AB = DC = 84$, $AD = BC = 63$
    Rectangle $EFGH$ with $EF = HG = 125$, $EA = FD = 50$

10   The length of the sides of $\triangle ABC$ are as follows: $AB = 35$, $BC = 20$, and $CA = 40$. In the similar $\triangle DEF$, $DE = 42$. What are the lengths of DF and EF if the vertices correspond in this manner: $A \leftrightarrow D$, $B \leftrightarrow E$, $C \leftrightarrow F$.

8–9   THE CONCEPT OF SIZE

We have seen how any simple closed curve in a plane separates the plane into three disjoint sets of points: the set of points interior to the curve, the set of points of the curve, and the set exterior to the curve. The union of the set of interior points and the set of points of the curve is called a

Closed region — *closed region*, and the curve is the *boundary* of the region. If the simple closed curve is a circle, the region is called a *circular region;* if it is a polygon, the region is called a *polygonal region*. In particular, a closed region is called a *triangular region* or *a rectangular region* according to whether its boundary is a triangle or a rectangle (Fig. 8–44).

There is a positive real number associated with each line segment which tells the number of units of linear measure in the length of the line segment. This number is called the distance between the two end points of the segment. Similarly, the measure of an angle is a positive real number which tells the size of the angle in units of angular measure. Likewise, for every circular region or polygonal region there exists a positive real number, called the *area of the region,* which describes its size in units of area (square) measure. In a somewhat analogous fashion, spherical and polyhedral regions in space are defined. For each such region there exists a positive real number, the *volume of the region,* which describes its size in terms of units of volume (cubic) measure.

8–10   THE CONCEPTS OF CONGRUENCE AND SYMMETRY

Previously we have seen that two line segments are congruent when they have the same length. Also two angles, whether plane angles or dihedral angles, are congruent if they have the same measure. Since

Circular region   *Triangular region*   *Rectangular region*   FIGURE 8–44   Closed regions.

two line segments, two plane angles, or two dihedral angles are always figures of the same shape, the condition that they be congruent is equivalent to stating that they must be figures of the same shape and size. This is in fact the basic condition for congruence.

Definition 8-23 Two geometric figures are said to be *congruent* if they are the same in shape and size.

This definition is equivalent to saying that two geometric figures are congruent if they are so related that they would fit exactly if one were moved, without changing its shape or size, and placed on the other. For example, two circles whose radii are congruent are said to be *congruent circles*. Any polygonal region can be divided into a finite number of triangular regions such that any two of them either do not intersect or do intersect in a line segment or a point. Since this is the case, the congruency of polygons fundamentally can be based on the congruency of triangles. There are three basic conditions which are both necessary and sufficient for the congruency of triangles. These conditions are stated here as postulates.

Postulate 8-12 If two triangles correspond to each other in such a way that two sides and the included angle of one triangle are congruent to the corresponding sides and included angle of the other, the two triangles are congruent.

Postulate 8-13 If two triangles correspond to each other in such a way that two angles and the included side of one triangle are congruent to the corresponding two angles and included side of the other, then the triangles are congruent.

Postulate 8-14 If two triangles correspond to each other in such a way that the three sides of one triangle are congruent to the corresponding three sides of the other triangle, then the triangles are congruent.

It should not be too difficult a conclusion to draw that corresponding parts of any two congruent figures are also congruent.

A plane region is *symmetric with respect to a point* if this point bisects every line segment through it with end points in the boundary of the region. The point is called the *center of symmetry*. The region is *symmetric with respect to a line* if the line forms with the boundary of the region two congruent figures such that if one were folded over on the line, it would coincide with the other. The line is called an *axis of symmetry*. The regular hexagon (Fig. 8–45a) has each of the diagonals shown as axes of symmetry and their point of intersection as a center of symmetry. The hexagon has three other axes of symmetry. Can you

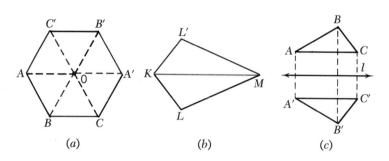

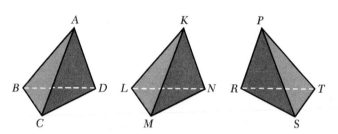

FIGURE 8–45
Symmetric plane
regions.

(a)   (b)   (c)

FIGURE 8–46   Congruent
or symmetric solids.

describe them?   The kite-shaped quadrilateral *KLMN* of Fig. 8–45*b*
has *KM* as an axis of symmetry but has no center of symmetry.   In this
figure the triangles *KLM* and *KL'M* can be shown to be congruent.
Two plane regions are said to be symmetric with respect to an axis of
symmetry if their boundaries are congruent figures and the correspondence is such that if one were folded over on the axis it would coincide
with the other.   The triangles *ABC* and *A'B'C'* of Fig. 8–45*c* are symmetric with respect to the line *l*.

In space two polyhedrons are said to be congruent if their corresponding parts are congruent and arranged in the same order.   If the
corresponding parts are arranged in the reverse order, the two polyhedrons are said to be symmetric.   In Fig. 8–46 the polyhedrons *A-BCD*
and *K-LMN* are congruent.   They are each symmetric to *P-RST*.   Two
symmetric solids are somewhat like two gloves or two shoes of the same
pair.   They are sized alike but shaped in reverse order to each other.

Exercises

1   Given the following information about ⧍ *ABC* and *DEF*, illustrated on page 235: △*ABC* ≅ △*DEF*; *A* ↔ *D*, *B* ↔ *E*, and *C* ↔ *F*.
What can you say about the corresponding angles and sides of the
two triangles?   Give reasons to support your answer.

2   In the quadrilateral *ABCD* shown, $\overline{AB} \cong \overline{AD}$ and $\overline{BC} \cong \overline{DC}$.   (Note
that the congruences are indicated by writing the same symbol on

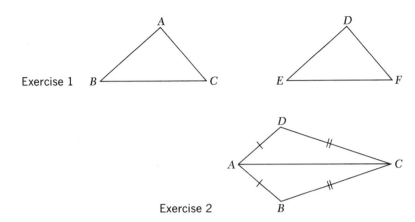

Exercise 1

Exercise 2

each segment of a congruent pair.   This practice is followed generally for line segments and angles.)   Is it a correct statement to
say that the line segment $\overline{AC}$ bisects $\angle DAB$ and $\angle DCB$?   Why
or why not?   (*Hint:* An angle is bisected by a line if the line divides
it into two congruent angles.)

3   Referring to the figure below, prove $\triangle KLM \cong \triangle PLO$.

4   In the parallelogram $PQRS$ shown below, prove $\triangle PQR \cong \triangle RSP$.
What angle is congruent to $\angle SRP$?   To $\angle SPR$?   Is the parallelogram symmetric with respect to the diagonal $\overline{PR}$?   Why?

Prove the theorems in Exercises 5 to 8.

5   *Theorem 8–14.*   Two triangles are congruent if two angles and a
side of one are respectively congruent to two angles and a side of
the other.

6   *Theorem 8–15.*   Two right triangles are congruent if the two legs
of one are congruent to the two legs of the other.

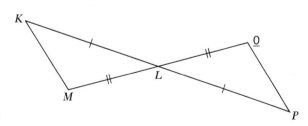

Exercise 3

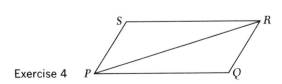

Exercise 4

7   *Theorem 8–16.* In an isosceles triangle the angles opposite the congruent sides are congruent. (*Hint:* From the common point of the two congruent sides draw a line to the midpoint of the opposite side.)

8   *Theorem 8–17.* An equilateral triangle is also equiangular.

9   Describe three axes of symmetry of a regular hexagon other than those pictured in Fig. 8–45a.

10   For each of the given figures determine whether or not there exist one or more axes of symmetry and also a center of symmetry: (*a*) circle; (*b*) sphere; (*c*) isosceles triangle; (*d*) scalene triangle; (*e*) equilateral triangle; (*f*) quadrilateral with no two sides equal; (*g*) square; (*h*) rectangle; (*i*) parallelogram; (*j*) rhombus; (*k*) cube.

8–11   CONSTRUCTIONS WITH STRAIGHTEDGE AND COMPASS

Postulates 8–1 and 8–3 make it possible to draw a straight line connecting any two points in space, and assure us that this line will always lie in a plane. Postulate 8–10 makes it always possible to draw in a plane a circle with a given point as center and a given line segment as radius. The instruments used for these constructions are the *straightedge,* or *unmarked ruler,* for drawing a line segment to represent the straight line, and the *compass* for drawing a circle. Since these postulates are in essence included among the original postulates of Euclid, constructions with the straightedge and compass are frequently referred to as "euclidean constructions." Among such constructions there are a few that are considered the basic ones. These are the ones of interest in this discussion. As the different constructions are studied, it will become quite apparent that they depend upon the intersection properties of two lines, a line and a circle, and two circles. The intersection of two lines has been taken care of by Theorem 8–1, Postulate 8–5, and the discussion of page 200. The corresponding properties of the line and circle and of two circles will be taken care of here by Postulates 8–15 and 8–16, each of which is a provable theorem, but with proof beyond the scope of this treatment.

Postulate 8–15   Given a line and a circle in the same plane:

1   They have two points in common if the distance d from the center of the circle to the line is less than the radius r: $d < r$. (See Fig. 8–47a.)

2   They have one point in common if $d = r$. (See Fig. 8–47b.)

3   They have no points in common if $d > r$. (See Fig. 8–47c.)

When $d < r$, the portion of the line containing the two points of the line between P and Q form a chord of the circle. When $d = r$, the line

Margin notes:

Euclidean constructions

Intersection of line and circle

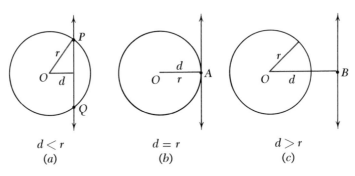

FIGURE 8–47   Inter-
section of a line and a
circle.

$d < r$
(a)

$d = r$
(b)

$d > r$
(c)

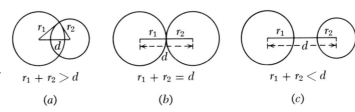

FIGURE 8–48   Inter-
section of two
circles.

$r_1 + r_2 > d$
(a)

$r_1 + r_2 = d$
(b)

$r_1 + r_2 < d$
(c)

which has one point A in common with the circle is called a *tangent* to
the circle, the point A is called the *point of tangency*, and it can be
shown that the radius $\overline{OA}$ forms a right angle with the tangent at the
point of tangency.

Postulate 8–16   Given two circles, with radii r_1 and r_2, in the same
plane with distance d between their centers.

· Intersection of
two circles

  1 They have two points of intersection if the sum of each two of
r_1, r_2, and d is greater than the third.   The two points will be on opposite sides of the line joining the centers.   (See Fig. 8–48*a*.)
  2 They have one point of intersection if the sum of any two is equal
to the third.   (See Fig. 8–48*b*.)
  3 They have no points in common if the sum of any two is less than
the third.   (See Fig. 8–48*c*.)

Only one of the three possible relations is illustrated in each diagram
of Fig. 8–48.   The reader should draw figures to represent the other
cases.

Construction 8–1   At a point on a given line, construct an angle congruent to a given angle.

Basic
geometric
constructions

We are given the line l and $\angle ABC$ (Fig. 8–49).
  Mark a point P on the line l.   Select one of the half lines of which P
is the boundary as the set of points which with P is to be one side of the
desired angle.   This is the ray $\overrightarrow{PT}$ of the figure.   With the vertex B of

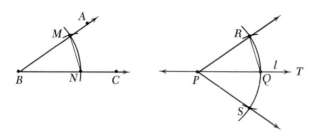

FIGURE 8–49   Construction of an angle congruent to a given angle.

$\angle ABC$ as a center and any convenient radius, draw the arc of a circle cutting the sides of the angle in the points M and N.   With this same radius and P as a center, draw the arc of a circle cutting $\overrightarrow{PT}$ in Q.   With Q as a center and $\overline{MN}$ as a radius, draw the arc of a circle.   The two circles will intersect in the two points R and S.   The rays $\overrightarrow{PR}$ and $\overrightarrow{PS}$ form with $\overrightarrow{PQ}$ the angles QPR and QPS, each of which is congruent to $\angle ABC$.

Proof

Statements	*Reasons*
Draw the line segment $\overline{RQ}$	Postulate 8–1
In $\triangle$ QPR and NBM, $\overline{PQ} \cong \overline{BN}$, $\overline{PR} \cong \overline{BM}$, $\overline{RQ} \cong \overline{MN}$	They were so constructed
$\triangle QPR \cong \triangle NBM$	Postulate 8–14
$\angle QPR \cong \angle NBM$	Definition 8–23

A similar argument will prove $\angle QPS \cong \angle NBM$.

Construction 8-2   Construct a triangle whose sides are congruent to three given line segments.

Given the three line segments a, b, c (Fig. 8–50).
Draw any line l and on it mark the point A.   With A as a center and c as a radius, draw the arc of a circle cutting l in B.   Also with A as a center and b as a radius, draw the arc $\widehat{PQ}$.   With B as a center and a as a radius, draw arc $\widehat{RS}$.   These two arcs will intersect in two points C

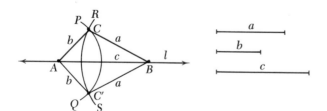

FIGURE 8–50   Construction of a triangle with sides congruent to three given line segments.

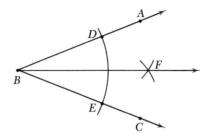

FIGURE 8-51   Bisection of a given angle.

and C'.   Draw $\overline{AC}$ and $\overline{BC}$, also $\overline{AC'}$ and $\overline{BC'}$.   Either $\triangle ABC$ or $\triangle ABC'$ is the required triangle.   Prove this statement.

What would happen in this construction if the sum of any two sides were not greater than the third?

Why could this construction be used to reproduce a given triangle?

Construction 8-3   Bisect a given angle.

Given the angle ABC (Fig. 8–51).

With B as a center and any convenient radius, draw the arc of a circle cutting rays $\overrightarrow{BA}$ and $\overrightarrow{BC}$ in points D and E, respectively.   With D as a center and a radius greater than one-half DE, draw a circle.   With E as a center and the *same radius*, draw another circle.   By Postulate 8–16 these two circles will intersect in two points, one of which will be on the opposite side of the line $\overleftrightarrow{DE}$ from B.   Call this point F.   Draw the ray $\overrightarrow{BF}$ which will bisect $\angle ABC$.

The proof of this construction is left to the reader.

Construction 8-4   Bisect a given line segment.

Given the line segment $\overline{PQ}$ (Fig. 8–52).

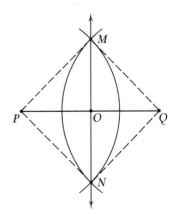

FIGURE 8-52   Bisection of a line segment.

With P as a center and any radius which is greater than one-half PQ, draw a circle. With Q as a center and the *same radius,* draw another circle. By Postulate 8–16 these two circles will intersect in two points M and N, which are on opposite sides of $\overline{PQ}$. By Postulate 8–1 there exists a line joining these two points. Since the two points are on opposite sides of $\overline{PQ}$, the line $\overleftrightarrow{MN}$ will have a point in common with $\overline{PQ}$, call it O. This point O is the midpoint of $\overline{PQ}$.

Proof

Statements	Reasons
Draw line segments $\overline{PM}$, $\overline{PN}$, $\overline{QM}$, and $\overline{QN}$	Postulate 8–1
$\overline{PM} \cong \overline{QM}$, $\overline{PN} \cong \overline{QN}$	Why?
$\triangle PMN \cong \triangle QMN$	Postulate 8–14
$\angle PMO \cong \angle QMO$	Definition 8–23
$\triangle PMO \cong \triangle QMO$	Postulate 8–12
$\overline{PO} \cong \overline{OQ}$	Definition 8–23
Therefore O is the midpoint of $\overline{PQ}$	Definition 8–7

Corollary   The line $\overleftrightarrow{MN}$ forms right angles with $\overline{PQ}$.

Definition 8-24   The *perpendicular bisector* of a line segment is the line which passes through the midpoint of the segment and forms right angles with the segment. Any point on this perpendicular bisector is the same distance from each of the end points of the segment.

The line $\overleftrightarrow{MN}$ of Fig. 8–52 is the perpendicular bisector of the segment $\overline{PQ}$.

Construction 8-5   Draw a line through a given point so that it is perpendicular to a given line.

The construction is the same whether P is on the line (Fig. 8–53a) or is not on the line (Fig. 8–53b).

With P as a center and a convenient radius, draw a circle that will cut the line l in two points A and B. With any radius that is greater than PA or PB, use A and B each as a center to draw an arc of a circle. These two arcs will intersect in a point C. Draw $\overleftrightarrow{PC}$.

Why is $\overleftrightarrow{PC}$ the perpendicular bisector of $\overline{AB}$?

Since $\overleftrightarrow{PC}$ is the perpendicular bisector of $\overline{AB}$, it follows that it is perpendicular to the line l of which the segment $\overline{AB}$ is a subset.

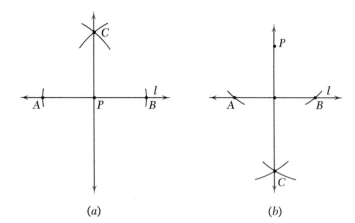

FIGURE 8–53   Construction of a line perpendicular to a given line.

(a)   (b)

Exercises

1   *Construction 8–6.*   Referring to the figure below, construct a triangle which will have line segments *a* and *b* as sides and ∠*C* as the included angle.

2   *Construction 8–7.*   Referring to the figure below, construct a triangle with angles *B* and *C* as two of its angles and line segment *a* as the included side.

3   Construct a triangle which will have as sides line segments whose lengths are 3, 4, and 6 inches, respectively.

4   Draw three line segments and then use them as sides to construct a triangle.   What precaution do you have to take in selecting the line segments?

5   Draw two angles and a line segment.   Construct a triangle which will have the two given angles as two of its angles and the given segment as a side opposite one of these angles.   What precaution must you remember in determining the sizes of the two given angles?   Discuss the different possibilities of this construction.

6   Prove that Construction 8–2 is a valid construction.

7   Prove that Construction 8–3 is a valid construction.

8   Prove the corollary to Construction 8–4.

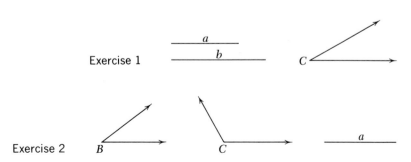

Exercise 1

Exercise 2

9   (a) Construct an isosceles triangle.
    (b) Construct the perpendicular bisector of the base of the isosceles triangle.
    (c) Why should this perpendicular bisector pass through the point common to the two equal sides?

10 (a) Construct an equilateral triangle.
    (b) Construct the perpendicular bisector of each side.
    (c) Why should the perpendicular bisector of each side pass through the point of intersection of the other two sides?
    (d) If you have made a careful construction, the three perpendicular bisectors will seem to have a point in common. Why should they have a point in common, and therefore intersect?

11 Use a line segment of 1-inch length as a radius to draw a circle. If you mark any point on this circle and use it as a center with the same 1-inch radius to mark another point on the circle and then repeat this until you have gone around the entire circle, you should have returned to the same point from which you started and have six points marked. Join these six points. The figure you have constructed is a regular hexagon. Construct the six axes of symmetry of this regular hexagon.

12 Construct a regular hexagon. Do not erase the circle used in drawing the hexagon. By selective shading you can get a simple architectural design.

13 Construct a regular hexagon. Draw the line segments joining alternate vertices. You should now have an equilateral triangle. Shading will again produce an architectural design.

14 Draw a circle with any convenient radius. Now draw one of its diameters and then construct the perpendicular bisector of this diameter. Mark the points where this perpendicular bisector cuts the circle. Join these points to the end points of the given diameter. You should have a square.

15 Draw a circle with any convenient radius. Draw two diameters so that they form an angle of 30°. Use Exercise 14 to construct two squares each with one of these diameters as a diagonal. By shading you can get an architectural design. (*Hint:* Use a protractor as an aid in getting an angle of 30°.)

8-12 THE STRUCTURE OF A GEOMETRY

From the historian T. L. Heath† we learn that Euclid, when he compiled the 13 books of his *Elements*, listed as first principles 23 definitions,

† T. L. Heath, "The Thirteen Books of Euclid," 2d ed., vol. I, pp. 153–155, Dover Publications, Inc., New York, 1956.

5 postulates, and 5 common notions.   The common notions were statements accepted as true assertions related to all areas of quantitative subject matter rather than to geometry in particular.   The postulates were specifically related to geometry.   We are concerned here with the 5 postulates.

1   A straight line can be drawn from any point to any other point.   Euclidean
2   A finite straight line can be produced continuously in a straight   postulates
line.
3   A circle may be described with any center and distance.
4   All right angles are equal to one another.
5   If a straight line falling on two straight lines makes the interior angles on the same side together less than two right angles, the two straight lines, if produced indefinitely, meet on that side on which the angles are together less than two right angles.

This fifth postulate is the famous *parallel postulate*, which has been referred to by some writers as one of the greatest single statements in the history of science.   It has been stated in this chapter as Postulate 8–5 in the equivalent, but more readily comprehensible, form known as Playfair's postulate.   The other four postulates also have been stated in the same or equivalent form to that used by Euclid.   For these reasons the geometry of this chapter represents a portion of what is familiarly known as *euclidean geometry*.   This is in contrast to the non-euclidean geometries of Bolyai (1802–1860), Lobachevski (1793–1856), and Riemann (1826–1866).   Each of these geometries was arrived at through a distinct contradiction of the parallel postulate.

In the Bolyai-Lobachevski geometry, the first four euclidean postulates remain intact, while the parallel postulate is replaced by:

Given a line *l* and a point *P* not contained in *l*.   In the plane determined   Replacements
by *l* and *P* there exist more than one line through *P* and parallel to *l*.   of the parallel
postulate

In the riemannian geometry the parallel postulate is replaced by:

Given a line *l* and a point *P* not contained in *l*.   In the plane determined by *l* and *P* there exists no line through *P* and parallel to *l*.

In this geometry there is also a basic difference in the statement of the second postulate.

As might be expected, there are differences in the theorems of euclidean geometry and those of either noneuclidean geometry.   These   Noneuclidean
will occur, however, only in those cases where the contradictory postu-   geometries
lates are appealed to as support for the argument needed to establish a particular theorem.   For example, the congruency theorems, stated here as Postulates 8–12 to 8–14, are provable in euclidean geometry

without any appeal to the parallel postulate. They are equally valid in both noneuclidean geometries. On the other hand, appeal to this postulate is necessary to prove the euclidean theorem:

The sum of the angles of a triangle is equal to two right angles.

The corresponding noneuclidean theorems are:

Bolyai-Lobachevski: The sum of the angles of a triangle is less than two right angles.

Riemann: The sum of the angles of a triangle is greater than two right angles.

   The question thus arises as to which theorem is to be accepted. The answer to this question is that the decision is determined not by examining the theorems but by examining the postulates. Each theorem is a valid theorem in its respective context. Also, mathematicians have been able to establish that each noneuclidean geometry is as consistent as is euclidean geometry. No internal inconsistencies have been discovered throughout the centuries of study of euclidean geometry. While this is not proof of the fact, it does lend strong support to the feeling that no internal inconsistencies ever will be discovered. Thus, in geometry as in the study of number, a change in the basic postulates produces a change in the subject matter of the derivable system. The choice of postulates will be controlled primarily by the context of study. Euclidean geometry will continue to furnish the geometrical model for the solution of the more general problems of engineering, science, and environmental experience. On the other hand, the two-dimensional noneuclidean geometry of Riemann can be represented on the surface of a sphere and thus can serve as a model for the solution of certain types of navigational problems. Furthermore, Riemann created a large set of noneuclidean geometries, one of which (and distinct from the one suggested here) Einstein used as the model for his general theory of relativity. Also, it has been suggested that probably the best model for the study of binocular vision is to be found in the geometry of Bolyai and Lobachevski.†
   The procedure followed in the development of this chapter has been to use patterns of deductive reasoning to derive from first principles (postulates and definitions) specific properties (theorems) of the system. Such a technique is known as *synthetic* in contrast to the *analytic* technique which, through recourse to cartesian coordinates, employs equations as an aid in making the interpretations and derivations from first principles. The analytic technique, which was introduced in Secs.

† Howard Eves and Carroll V. Newsom, "An Introduction to the Foundations and Fundamental Concepts of Mathematics," p. 72, Holt, Rinehart and Winston, New York, 1960.

8–5 and 8–6, will be pursued in somewhat more detail in Chap. 10. A geometry may be either synthetic or analytic, depending upon the technique of investigation used.

Another important characteristic of a geometry is the space in which it is oriented. The development of this chapter has been restricted to spaces of one, two, and three dimensions. In the discussion of points on a line the orientation was in one dimension; in the study of points and lines in a plane it was in two dimensions; and in the study of points, lines, and planes in space it was in three dimensions. In a cartesian frame of reference one coordinate is required to locate a point in one dimension; two coordinates to locate a point in two dimensions; and three coordinates to locate a point in three dimensions. One of the great advantages of the use of cartesian coordinates and the analytic technique is the facility afforded for the extension of geometric concepts to many dimensions. For example, the geometry of the relativity theory is four-dimensional in that *time* is one of the coordinates. A point is oriented in this space by the ordered quadruple (x,y,z,t) where x, y, and z are the ordinary cartesian coordinates of a three-dimensional space, and t is the time coordinate.

In our brief study of geometry we have employed such techniques as "moving along a line" or "turning through an angle." In more elegant language these acts are known, respectively, as *transformations* of *translation* and *rotation*. If you move this book along a table or turn it over you will not affect the size of the book; its measurements will remain unchanged, or *invariant*. Measurements of length, angle size, area, and volume are among the more important invariants under the transformations of translation and rotation. Along with all other invariable quantities and relations, these invariants become the topics of study in the geometry which employs these transformations. *(margin: Translation and rotation)*

Another familiar type of transformation is *projection*. Any visit to a movie theater will furnish many illustrations of the use of this transformation. It is not difficult to comprehend that measurements, such as those mentioned previously, are no longer invariants under this transformation. As an illustration, one has but to reflect upon the relation of the image on the screen to the image on the movie film. The relative positions of point of light, film image, and screen can change length, angle size, area, and volume almost at will. There are other types of invariants which become the subject matter for study in the geometry of projection. A few examples are the relations of points on a line, of lines passing through a point, and certain types of ratios. It is of significance to note that these are also invariants under translation and rotation. *(margin: Projection)*

There are still other types of transformations which lead to other forms of geometric study.

In conclusion we might summarize the steps necessary to structure an area of geometric study in the following manner. (The order of listing is not necessarily the only sequence of selection.) *(margin: Steps for structuring an area of geometric study)*

1   Select the space in which the study is to be oriented.

2   List the fundamental postulates, undefined elements, and defined terms upon which the study is to be based.

3   Determine whether the synthetic method, the analytic method, or some combination of the two is to be used.

4   Build the configurations to be studied.

5   Select the transformations to be used.

6   Identify the invariants to be studied.

INVITATIONS TO EXTENDED STUDY

1   Describe the relative positions of three distinct lines in space.

2   Use the concept of half planes to define the interior and exterior of an angle.

3   *Prove this theorem:* If a plane intersects two parallel planes, then it intersects them in parallel lines.

4   Polar coordinates are used to establish a coordinate system in the plane which is distinct from a rectangular system.   Investigation of such a system can be both challenging and interesting.

5   Describe the four quadrants of a cartesian frame of reference in the plane as the intersections of half planes.

6   Describe the eight octants of a left-handed cartesian frame of reference in space as the intersection of half spaces.

7   Discuss the application of the concept and principles of similarity in the enlargement of photographs.

8   Use Postulate 8–12 as an accepted truth and then prove as theorems Postulates 8–13 and 8–14.

9   Use the pythagorean theorem to prove that the distance d between the two points $P_1(x_1,y_1)$ and $P_2(x_2,y_2)$ is given by the formula

$$d = \sqrt{(x_2 - x_1)^2 + (y_2 - y_1)^2}$$

Prove these theorems.

10   The three bisectors of the angles of a triangle intersect in a common point.

11   The point of intersection of the bisectors of the angles of a triangle is the center of the circle inscribed in the triangle.   (*Hint:* A circle is *inscribed* in a triangle if it is tangent to each side of the triangle.   A line is *tangent* to a circle if it is perpendicular to a radius of the circle at a point of the circle.)

12   The three perpendicular bisectors of the sides of a triangle intersect in a common point.

13   The point of intersection of the perpendicular bisectors of the sides of a triangle is the center of a circle circumscribed about the triangle. (*Hint:* A *circle* is *circumscribed* about a triangle if the three vertices of the triangle are points of the circle.)

14 The three medians of an equilateral triangle are also altitudes of the triangle. (*Hint:* A *median* of a triangle is a line drawn from a vertex to the midpoint of the opposite side. An *altitude* of a triangle is a line drawn from a vertex perpendicular to the opposite side.)

15 The sum of the measures of the interior angles of a quadrilateral is twice the measure of a straight angle.

Perform these two constructions.

16 Draw a triangle and inscribe a circle in it.

17 Draw a triangle and circumscribe a circle about it.

18 Find illustrations in nature, in art, and in architecture of the use of the concept and principles of symmetry.

19 Use the basic constructions given in Chap. 8 to create and construct architectural designs.

the concept of
measurement

GUIDELINES FOR CAREFUL STUDY

In Chap. 6 the concept of the real number line was introduced. By
selecting one point on a line, which was designated as the reference
point, and then a second point to establish the distance between the two
points as a "unit distance" it was possible to set up a one-to-one correspondence between the points of the line and the set of all real numbers.

In Chap. 8 this unit distance was identified as a measurable line segment in terms of which the length of any line segment, or the distance
between two points, could be determined. The existence of a positive
real number as the measure of any straight line segment was postulated,
and the technique for finding the distance between any two points on
the number line was defined. Similarly, the existence of positive real
numbers as measures for angles, areas, and volumes, respectively, was
postulated. The investigation and discussion of techniques for finding
and using such measures, in the main, was reserved until later. It is
the purpose of this chapter to pursue this study further and to examine
the difficulties that are present along with the precautions necessary

in making and using the more familiar measurements essential to every-day living.

The following questions will serve as helpful guidelines to careful study of Chap. 9.

1 What is the real number line?

2 What is meant by the measure of a line segment? An angle? An area? A volume?

3 What is the technique for finding the distance between two points?

4 When are two line segments said to be congruent? Two angles? Two triangles?

5 When are two triangles said to be similar?

6 What is meant by the ratio of the lengths of two line segments?

7 What is meant by a measurement?

8 What is meant by the process of measuring?

9 Why are all measurements obtained through the use of a measuring scale necessarily approximate?

10 What is the basic distinction between exact and approximate numbers?

11 What is the basic distinction between direct and indirect measurement?

12 What are some of the reasons for the existence of standard units of measure?

13 What is the metric system of measurements and what are its basic units? How are other units of the various scales of this system formed and named?

14 What is meant by a denominate number? How are denominate numbers used in computation?

15 What is the basic distinction between precision and accuracy in measurement? How do they affect computation with measurement numbers?

16 What is the basic distinction between apparent error, permissible error, tolerance, and relative error?

17 What is scientific (standard) notation and how may it be used?

18 What is meant by the sine, cosine, and tangent of an angle? How may they be used in making measurements?

19 What is meant by a statistical measure?

20 What are some of the distinctions between the three measures of central tendency of a distribution?

21 What are some of the implications and precautions to be realized in the use of each measure of central tendency of a distribution?

22 What is the distinction between the variance and the standard deviation of a distribution? For what purposes are these measures used?

INTRODUCTION

The word "measurement" carries with it a certain ambiguity of meaning. In one sense it is synonymous with "mensuration," which is the subject matter of that branch of geometry which deals with the finding of lengths, areas, volumes, and other forms of quantifying size. In a second sense it means the result of any such quantification of size. It is in the first sense that the word is used in the title of this chapter. Within the chapter it will be used in the connotation of the second meaning, as set forth in Definition 9–1. In either context we are confronted with a further extension of the concept of number which we now have the responsibility to investigate.

This new extension is somewhat different from those of previous chapters. There is no need here for the invention of new numbers but rather for a more flexible concept of the quantifying characteristics of real numbers to provide for a contrast between exact and approximate quantification. Also there is no necessity for defining new operational procedures and remodeling definitions of recognized well-defined operations. Rather, the demand now is for an adaptation of the familiar techniques of addition, subtraction, multiplication, and division used in operating with numbers resulting from exact quantification to patterns for computing with numbers resulting from approximate quantification. Also, there is need for the establishment of guidelines for the use and interpretation of the results obtained from such computation.

9–1   COUNTING, ESTIMATING, MEASURING

In Chap. 1 *counting* was identified as the process of determing the cardinal number of a set. The numbers which result from such a process can be verified because of the discrete and unitary character of the elements being enumerated. Furthermore, the counting process, in essence, establishes a one-to-one correspondence between the elements of some chosen set of elements and a subset of the set of natural numbers. The numbers which result from counting are thus records of exact results, as they establish a *measurement* which answers the question: How many?

Definition 9–1 **A *measurement* is the quantitative characteristic of a set, object, or entity of any description which is subject to correlation with the set of real numbers.**

Example   How many chairs are needed to accommodate the members of the Glee Club?

By actual count of the members of the Glee Club the measurement of the "size" of the group would be determined.   The count could be verified and established as an exact result which would answer the question which posed the problem, namely: How many?

A second significant technique used in determining measurements is that of *estimating*.   For example, scientists have established 93,000,000 miles as the approximate measurement of the distance from the earth to the sun.   Such an estimate is not a wild guess, but is based on established scientific procedures which produce results that are accepted with a high degree of confidence.   Similar techniques produce such measurements as "the mass of the earth is approximately 6,000,000,000,000,000,000,000,000,000 (six octillion) grams" and "a molecule of water is about 0.00000000000000000000000296 (296 ten-septillionths) gram."   Less scientific, yet significant, measurements are estimates such as "2,000,000 people witnessed the Rose Parade." Such an estimate as this last one is, in kind, a count, but one based on such procedures as use of past experience, knowledge of the capacity of the witnessing area, and traffic conditions, rather than on a procedure of establishing a one-to-one correspondence with the natural numbers. An interesting measurement which results from a rather carefully planned pattern of counting, yet is an estimate, is the census figure. The Bureau of the Census announced that "according to the final count of the returns of the Census of 1960, the population of the United States is 179,323,175."   Although this number, which is the official measurement of the "size" of the population of the United States, has the appearance of an exact number and was derived from very refined techniques for counting large collections of objects, it is necessarily an approximation to the true population figure.   This is due, of course, to the fact that change in the population figure, caused by birth, death, immigration, and emigration, was taking place even during the time the count was in process.

In the above discussion a measurement has been exhibited as a number, obtained as the result of some pattern of counting or estimating to serve as a quantifier of size.   There is still a third means of arriving at a measurement of a quantity, and that is the process of *measuring*. Quantities such as length, width, area, volume, and capacity are characterized by continuity, rather than discreteness, of composition.   Any effort to determine the measurement of such quantities must, of necessity, resort to a combination of counting and estimating.   It is accomplished through the use of accepted scales on which countable units have been marked.   Thus, in *measuring* the length of a table top, one would use a yardstick or tape and count the number of units (feet or inches) and estimate the fractional part of the chosen unit. A combination of the results of these two processes would give the measurement for the length of the table. Such measurements, once obtained, are not capable of verification in the same sense as a measurement resulting from the count of the size of a small gathering of people, for example. The qualities of discreteness and unitariness are absent. Although the inch may have been used, and a number of inches counted, in the process of arriving at the measurement, the unit is divisible and one cannot be assured that separate divisions will agree. Furthermore, the second application of the measuring instrument, although it may be the same instrument applied by the same individual, is subject to variation. Any measurement resulting from an act of measuring is, by the very nature of the act, an approximation.

Results from measuring are approximate

9-2   EXACT AND APPROXIMATE NUMBERS†

Exact numbers have been the primary concern in the development of this text up to this point. From a study of the natural numbers and their properties we proceeded to a consideration of the integers, the rational numbers, and the real numbers as they evolved as desirable extensions of the natural number system. At each point of the development the need for extension grew out of a desire to maintain the property of closure with respect not only to the established operations but also to the new operations that were defined to meet computational needs.

In contrast, approximate numbers are obtained as the result of estimating and measuring. They are also obtained as the result of rounding numbers or giving decimal expression, for computational purposes, to certain types of rational numbers.

If a square of any dimension is constructed, the length of its diagonal will be $\sqrt{2}$ times the length of a side. Here $\sqrt{2}$ is used as an exact number. It is obtained as the result of the extraction of the positive square root of the exact number 2. Any rational approximation to this numerical value would be an approximate number. The quotient of

---

† Attention should be called to the fact that the phrases "exact numbers" and "approximate numbers" are used here with explicitly defined connotations. There are writers who feel that the adjectives "exact" and "approximate" should not be used to qualify the numbers, but rather the ideas they are attempting to express. Thus, 12 would carry an exact connotation, whether it be "a number expressing an exact count," as when used to enumerate the number of inches in 1 foot, or "a number expressing an approximation," as when used to record the result from an act of measuring or estimating. While it is agreed that the essence of number is exactness, it seems that the effort to avoid the phrases "exact numbers" and "approximate numbers" introduces a great deal of undesirable circumlocution into discussions where needed distinctions are made between "counting results" and "measuring results." For the benefits of simplicity of expression and reference, the two terms will be used in this chapter within the context described in this section.

$5 \div 3$ gives the rational number $\dfrac{5}{3}$. This quotient may also be expressed in decimal form as $1.\overline{6}$. In either the common fraction or the repeating decimal fraction form, this number is an exact number. If, however, it were used in a computational situation which required decimal expression, an approximation such as 1.7, 1.67, or 1.667 would have to be used. If a person visits a grocery store and makes a purchase of one can of peas, priced at three cans for 64 cents, he pays the approximate price of 22 cents and not the exact price of $21\frac{1}{3}$ cents. Furthermore, even the context of use will at times determine whether a number is exact or approximate. This is the case when a person speaks of 2 pounds of apples. If he is enumerating the number of pounds, then 2 is exact, but if he is telling how much the apples actually weigh, then 2 is approximate. Also, if "4 quarts" is used to express a measure of capacity, then 4 is used as an approximate number, while in the tabular definition of 1 gallon (4 quarts = 1 gallon), it is used as an exact number.

Exercises

1 Distinguish between exact and approximate numbers.

State whether you think each number used in these exercises is exact or approximate and give reasons to support your answer.

2 Light travels with a speed of 186,000 miles per second.

3 There are 5,280 feet in 1 mile.

4 The auditorium will seat 1,200 people.

5 The school library has 14,400 books.

6 Forty-three boys reported for football practice.

7 $\sqrt{10} = 3.162$; $\sqrt[3]{125} = 5$.

8 We drove 485 miles yesterday.

9 The fastest time for the 100-yard dash is 9.3 seconds.

10 There are 86,400 seconds in 24 hours.

11 The speed record for automobiles is 536.71 miles per hour.

12 The score of the baseball game was 5 to 0.

13 The 1960 population figure for the city of Los Angeles was 2,479,015.

14 Harry is 5 feet 11 inches tall and weighs 168 pounds.

15 Mrs. Byrd bought 2 chickens. They weighed 4 pounds 8 ounces and she paid $2.29 for them.

16 The Declaration of Independence was signed on July 4, 1776.

17 The postal rate for first-class mail is "5 cents per ounce or any fraction thereof." The cost for sending a 6-ounce letter will be 30 cents.

9-3   THE APPROXIMATE NATURE OF MEASUREMENT

It should be quite evident that a measurement resulting from an estimation is intrinsically approximate.   It is not always so immediately evident that a measurement which results from the application of a measuring scale is just as essentially approximate, regardless of how refined the scale graduation might be.   The approximate nature of such a measurement is illustrated in Fig. 9-1.   Here a ruler, which has been graduated to tenths of an inch, is being used to measure the length of the line segment $\overline{AB}$.   The point A is at the zero point of the scale of the ruler.   The point B lies between the 4- and 5-inch marks, so it is determined by counting that the total number of complete inches in the length is 4.   The number of tenths of an inch beyond the 4-inch mark can also be counted and discovered to be 3.   In other words, the number of complete tenths of an inch that B is removed from A is 43, or, as we should write it, 4.3 inches.   Close examination justifies the estimate that B is a little more than halfway between the 4.3-inch mark and the 4.4-inch mark.   Thus, we use both counting and estimating to arrive at the measurement of 4.36 inches for the line segment $\overline{AB}$.   The 6 appearing in the measurement is, of course, questionable.   It has resulted from an estimate, and the care of making the estimate is a very significant factor in determining just what number should be used.

Sources of error in measuring

Carelessness is not the only source of error in making this reading.   Two people looking at the picture in the figure can see B at slightly different positions on the ruler because of the difference in the way in which they look at the picture.   If another person were to take the same or another ruler and use it, there could be a difference in the way he would fit the zero point at A.   Also, the rulers themselves might not be perfectly made.   Changes in temperature or other weather conditions, carelessness, poor eyesight, inexperience, and many other error sources combine to make it impossible for us to obtain anything but an approximate measurement.   This would be the case even if the end point B *appeared* to be exactly at the 4-inch mark of the ruler.   Thus the two readings, in this latter case, of "$\overline{AB}$ is 4 inches long" and "$\overline{AB}$ is 4.0 inches long" are significantly different statements.   Because of the approximate nature of measurement, the first measure can only mean that the measurer is implying that the length of $\overline{AB}$ lies somewhere between 3.5 and 4.5 inches.   The second statement denotes that the length of $\overline{AB}$ lies somewhere between 3.95 and 4.05 inches.

FIGURE 9-1   Ruler graduated to tenths of an inch.

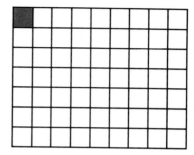

FIGURE 9-2   Determining the area of a rectangle.

9-4   DIRECT AND INDIRECT MEASUREMENT

The illustration in the preceding section is that of a *direct measurement*. It is an illustration of a situation in which a graduated scale, a measuring instrument, was applied directly to the object whose measurement was to be determined.   Not all measurements can be obtained from such direct procedures.   The rectangle of Fig. 9–2 is 7 units wide by 9 units long.   What is the area of this rectangle?   We have seen how, in order to determine the length or width of such a rectangle, we can apply a measuring instrument and read the appropriate measurement.   We have no such device to apply in order to determine the area, so we have to resort to indirect methods.   Any measurement obtained by such methods is called an *indirect measurement*.   By observation, we realize that each small square in the diagram represents a unit of square measure (unit of area) of the type corresponding to the linear unit used in measuring the length and width.   Therefore, it is only necessary to contrive a scheme for counting these small squares.   Geometry provides us with a method that is intuitively acceptable.   We can observe that in each horizontal row there are 9 such small squares and that there are 7 such rows.   It is evident then that there must be $7 \times 9 = 63$ square units in the area of the rectangle.   Of course, similar reasoning, or the commutative property of multiplication, tells us that 9×7 gives the correct number of square units also.   Another form of indirect measure is provided by the use of the pythagorean theorem (8–11) to find the length of the hypotenuse of a right triangle when the lengths of the two legs are known, or the length of the diagonal of a square when we know the length of a side.

Types of indirect measurement

There are many important methods of making indirect measurements.   When a person steps on a scale he reads from a graduation a number which he uses to complete the sentence: My weight is ____ pounds.   Weight is, by definition, the force with which a body is attracted toward the earth.   In popular usage, however, it signifies the quantity of mass of a given body because the masses of different bodies may be compared accurately.   This is due to the fact that the gravitational pull of the earth will be equally large on each of the bodies

FIGURE 9-3   Scale compares man's weight with standard unit of one pound.

being compared. Thus the scale used for determining the "weight" of an individual compares the mass of the body of the person being weighed with that of the standard unit of weight, the pound.† The result of this comparison is translated, usually by means of a system of sensitive multiplying levers, into a number which the person reads as "so many pounds." This simply means that gravitational pull on his body is the indicated multiple of what it would be on the standard pound.

† The "Battle of the Pounds" raged for several centuries in England. The struggle was an effort to establish "one weight through the King's dominions." Finally in 1878 the avoirdupois pound, the official United States unit, was legalized by Parliament as the official pound and defined as equivalent to 7,000 grains. Originally, the "grain" was the average weight of grains taken from the middle of the ears of wheat. It is now defined more scientifically in relation to the weight of a cubic inch of distilled water at 62° Fahrenheit and 30 inches of barometric pressure; under these conditions a cubic inch of water weighs 252.458 grains.

FIGURE 9-4   A Fahrenheit thermometer.

Temperature is another important indirect measurement. The measuring instrument, a thermometer, consists essentially of some confined substance which has at least one measurable property that changes with change in temperature. The ordinary household thermometer (Fig. 9–4) consists of mercury confined in a glass tube with hairlike bore, which has a numerical scale in degrees either etched on it or imprinted alongside it. This tube, from which all air has been exhausted, has a bulb on one end and is sealed at the other. The scale is a Fahrenheit scale, invented by G. D. Fahrenheit in 1714. On this scale the boiling point of water is 212° and the freezing point is 32° above 0°. The 0° point marks the temperature resulting from a mixture of equal quantities, by weight, of snow and common salt. The scale and mercury give a number to the temperature by measuring the expansion differences between the mercury and the glass container.

The thermometer used most frequently in scientific laboratories has the centigrade scale, invented by the Swedish astronomer Anders Celsius in 1742. On this scale the boiling point of water is 100° and the freezing point is 0°.

These are the most familiar of the many different types of thermometers, designed for many different purposes, but all using a somewhat similar pattern to give reliable measurements of temperature.

Other significant forms of indirect measurement will be discussed later in the chapter.

Exercises

1 Explain how measurements of weight are determined by means of counting and estimating.

2 Why are measurements of length, area, volume, and capacity only approximations?

3 In the definition "one foot is 12 inches," is the number 12 used as an exact number or as an approximate number?

4 The following statement is made: There are 750 seats in the school auditorium.

    (*a*) Explain how this number might be an approximate number.
    (*b*) Explain how it might be an exact number.

Which of the measurements in Exercises 5 to 18 are direct and which are indirect? Give reasons to support your answer.

5 The size of an angle, by means of a protractor
6 Time, by means of a watch or clock
7 Distance, by means of the odometer in an automobile
8 Speed, by means of the speedometer in an automobile

9   The height of an airplane, by means of an altimeter

10   The height of a boy, by means of a tape measure

11   Atmospheric pressure, by means of a barometer

12   Amount of gas or electricity used, by means of a meter

13   The velocity of the wind, by means of an anemometer

14   The revolutions of an airplane engine, by means of a tachometer

15   The amount of dress goods purchased, by means of a yardstick

16   The contents of a measuring cup, by means of graduations etched on its side

17   The area of a triangle, by means of the formula $A = \frac{1}{2}bh$ where b represents the linear units in the base and h the linear units in the altitude

18   The contents of a grain bin, by means of a bushel measure

9-5   THE NEED FOR MEASUREMENT UNITS

We have seen how the natural numbers came into existence in man's efforts to give quantitative characterization to a set of objects. They provide man with a means of measuring the quantitative content of discrete sets of objects, i.e., of answering the question: How many? When a person states that a room contains 65 chairs, he has, in a very true sense of the word, measured a certain type of content of the room. The unit used in making the measurement is "chair." Indeed, if he has counted each chair in the room, he has secured an exact measure of this particular room content, one that is unchanging and verifiable. As has been pointed out previously, such exactness of measurement is always possible when the content to be measured is composed entirely of discrete elements. This is not the case, however, when the content is of fluid, or continuous, composition. For example, a statement that a pitcher contains 4 pints of water can be exact *only* if the individual means that he filled a pint container four times and emptied it each time into the pitcher. If the "4 pints" is used in the sense of a measure of capacity, then it must be considered as approximate because of the various elements of error present, such as judgment as to fullness of the container each time, calibration of the container, and care in pouring. Thus, there would be an exact answer to the question: How many? Only an approximate answer would be possible to the question: How much? The length of a distance and the weight of a mass are also measurements of "objects" of fluid, or continuous, content. The numbers used to express such measurements are called *denominate numbers* to distinguish them from the exact numbers used to give the measurement in situations of discrete content.

Denominate numbers

Sets of discrete elements provide natural units, such as the "chair" of the preceding paragraph, for measuring the content of the set. When there are no such identifiable discrete elements, man has to invent ways and means of providing a suitable unit of measure which can be counted in order to obtain an appropriate measurement. The "pint" of the preceding paragraph, which is a subunit of the official gallon; the yard with its subunits foot and inch; and the bushel with its subunits peck, quart, and pint are such inventions which man has created in his effort to systematize and standardize measurement in those situations characterized by continuity of structure.

Primitive man, in his effort to provide suitable units, took recourse in convenience. His principal concern was to have a unit that would enable him to establish a measure that would be personally satisfying. He was not confronted with concern for his neighbor, either far or near, nor was he involved in problems of commerce, industry, or travel. It was quite natural that he used units which were personally convenient (see Fig. 9–5). The digit (width of a finger), palm (width of hand palm), span (distance between tips of thumb and little finger in outstretched hand), cubit (distance from elbow to tip of outstretched hand), furlong (length of furrow man could plow before resting oxen), pace (distance between heel of one foot and heel of the same foot when next in contact with ground—a double step), and others were in frequent use. Similar convenient designations of units were practiced in other forms of making measurements.

It is of course evident that there would be wide differences in measurements resulting from the use of such personally oriented units.

Primitive units

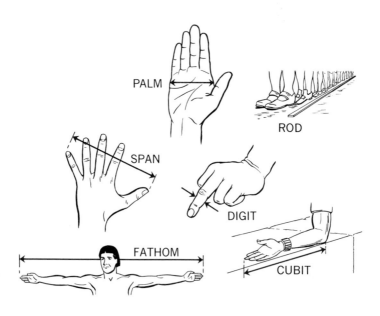

FIGURE 9–5   Early units of measure.

Thus, the demands of commerce and industry led naturally and persistently to the desirability and necessity for standard units of measure—units not only of national but also of international identity.

9-6   STANDARD UNITS OF MEASURE

Historically, it is quite natural that the basic standard units of weights and measures used in the United States would be the same as those used in England.   There are, however, a few slight differences.   For example, an automobile gasoline tank, which has a capacity of 18 United States gallons, will hold only 15 imperial gallons (the standard gallon of Canada and all other countries of the United Kingdom).   Because of slight differences in official definition the imperial gallon is approximately equivalent to 1.2 United States gallons.   Although such discrepancies are sources of inconvenience in international trade, they are relatively minor in nature and do not affect materially the uniformity of standards between the two countries.

The Constitution of the United States vested in Congress the right to fix all standards of weights and measures.   From 1789 to 1893 constant study and thoughtful effort were directed toward the fixing of such standards.   In 1789 President George Washington, in his first message to Congress, emphasized the need for such standards.   In 1893 the *international meter* and *kilogram* were accepted as the basic standards for measuring length and mass in the United States, such action having been legalized by Congress in 1866.   Under such prescriptions the *yard* was defined to be $\frac{3,600}{3,937}$ meter, or 36.00 units (inches), of which there are 39.37 in a meter.   The official *avoirdupois pound* was defined to be 7,000 grains, which makes it approximately equivalent to 0.454 kilogram.   In accordance with an agreement between their Directors of Standard Laboratories, the United States, the United Kingdom, Canada, New Zealand, South Africa, and Australia now use the following equivalences: the international yard is equal to 0.9144 meter, and the international pound is equal to 0.45359237 kilogram.   This agreement has been in effect since July 1, 1959.[†]

Toward the latter part of the eighteenth century a group of French scientists, under the leadership of Delambre and Méchain, undertook a geodetic survey for the purpose of determining the length of the standard meter.   As a result of this survey the meter was standardized at one ten-millionth part of the meridional distance from the equator to the pole.   This was eventually replaced, in 1889, by the International

Standard international units

† *Science*, **129** (Jan. 30, 1959):260.

Protopype Meter, which is defined to be the length between two marks on a platinum-iridium bar when this bar is at 0° centigrade or 32° Fahrenheit. Originally, the kilogram was designed to be based upon the meter, but it was discovered that masses could be compared with greater accuracy without any reference to measures of volume, which were in turn related to linear measures. As a result, it was found desirable to define an independent unit of mass, so the International Prototype Kilogram—the mass of a platinum-iridium cylinder—was arbitrarily defined to be 15,432.356 grains. The unit of capacity, the *liter*, was then defined as the volume of a kilogram of water under a pressure of 76 centimeters of mercury at 4° centigrade. It is a volume of approximately 1 cubic decimeter.

The International Prototype Meter and Kilogram are kept in a subterranean vault at the International Bureau of Weights and Measures at Sèvres, France, near Paris. Copies are on file with the National Bureau of Standards in Washington, D.C. These are checked periodically with the originals at the International Bureau. Although there has been fairly general approval and acceptance of these standard units, scientists have been interested in seeking more satisfactory definitions— ones which would be more inherently invariant. As a consequence, upon the recommendation of the Advisory Committee for the Definition of the Metre and the International Committee on Weights and Measures, the International Conference on Weights and Measures adopted in 1960 a new definition of the international meter. It is now defined to be 1,650,763.73 wavelengths of the orange-red radiation in vacuum of krypton 86.

The metric system of weights and measures is entirely decimal in nature. The basic units are meter, gram, and liter. In each table prefixes are then used to indicate both higher and lower units on each scale. Greek derivatives are used as prefixes to indicate higher points on the scale, while Latin derivatives are used to indicate points of lower division. The table of linear measure is given in Fig. 9–6. The tables for weight and capacity may be constructed in exactly the same manner, using *gram* as the basic unit for weight and *liter* for capacity. **The metric system**

The English system of weights and measures is nondecimal in structure. Furthermore, there is no simple pattern, as in the metric **The English system**

FIGURE 9–6   Metric linear measure.

10 millimeters (mm)	= 1 centimeter (cm)
10 centimeters	= 1 decimeter (dm)
10 decimeters	= 1 meter (m)
10 meters	= 1 dekameter (dkm)
10 dekameters	= 1 hectometer (hm)
10 hectometers	= 1 kilometer (km)
10 kilometers	= 1 myriameter (M)

system, that may be followed in building the several tables of linear, area, volume, capacity, and weight measure. For proper use each such table must be learned as a separate entity. There are, of course, tables of equivalents which relate each basic English unit to its corresponding international standard. This confusion in table structure, as compared with the simplicity of structure of the metric system, is one of the arguments used by those who have proposed that the metric system of weights and measures be made the universally accepted system. The basic decimal structure of the metric system is another of the supporting arguments used by such groups.

9–7   DENOMINATE NUMBERS

Despite the recognized fact that all measurement of continuous content is by nature approximate, man has made a constant effort to provide better instruments and more appropriate units for the purpose of obtaining the closest possible agreement between the observed measurement of a quantity and its true measurement. This has led to the prescription and definition of units and subunits, with their concomitant interrelationships, all of which are summarized for our ready use in familiar tables of weights and measures.

In these modern days of jet propulsion, satellite projection, and atomic fission we have seen both macroscopic expansion and microscopic division of these units. For example, the Mach numbers have been defined for better measurement of supersonic speeds and the light-year for astronomic distances. A plane traveling at Mach 2 would be traveling at a speed twice the speed of sound in the surrounding atmosphere or, under certain conditions, at approximately 1,500 miles per hour. The announced speed of one of the early man-made satellites was Mach 24. This meant that it traveled at a speed of approximately 18,000 miles per hour.

The astronomical unit of 1 light-year is defined to be the distance light will travel in 1 year's time, or a distance of 5,870,000,000,000 miles. One of the purposes of this unit is to express the distances of different stars and planets from the earth. The North Star, for example, is a distance of 47 light-years from the earth. This means that, when you look at this star, the light you see was emitted from the star 47 years ago. Alpha Centauri is the closest star to the earth, at a distance of 4.3 light-years. To appreciate something of the significance and convenience of the light-year as a unit for measuring astronomical distances, you might express in miles each of the two mentioned distances, 47 light-years and 4.3 light-years. In contrast, the *atomic mass unit* is used in discussions involving atomic weights. It is defined to be

Mach numbers

The light-year

The atomic mass unit

0.00000000000000000000000001660 gram, or 1,660 octillionths gram. This is equivalent to 0.0000000000000000000000000000366 pound, or 366 hundred-octillionths pound. Atomic nuclei are made up of two kinds of primary particles: *protons* and *neutrons*. The proton has a mass of 1.00758 atomic mass units and carries a single unit of positive electric charge. The neutron has a mass of 1.00897 atomic mass units and carries no electric charge. This nucleus is surrounded by negatively charged particles called *electrons*. The mass of an electron is 0.00055 atomic mass unit.

The above illustrations are given simply to emphasize the tremendous flexibility and sensitivity of both the English and the metric systems of measurement. The numbers used to enable us to describe the results of such measurements, no matter how large or how small they may be, are recognized as belonging to the denominate numbers introduced earlier.

The introduction of denominate numbers is not an extension of the real number system and does not create a demand for definition of operational processes in order that we might use them. Rather, it presents a new context in which previously defined operations with the real numbers may be used, thus calling for pertinent adaptations and interpretations. Consider the two following examples.

Example Jack walked a distance of 300 yards from his house to the store. He then walked from the store to school, a distance of 400 yards. (1) What was the total distance he walked? (2) What is the distance d from Jack's home to the school? Note carefully the two questions.

The answer to the first question is simple. Jack walked a total distance of 700 yards. Three illustrations are given in Fig. 9–7 to indicate that the answer to the second question is impossible until more is known about the relative locations of home, store, and school. Only three of the many possible relative positions of home, store, and school are

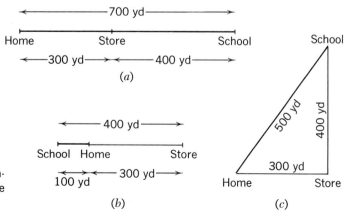

FIGURE 9–7   Three interpretations of distance data.

shown. In each case the actual distance from Jack's home to the school is shown in color. With the orientation as indicated in each respective illustration of Fig. 9–7, a different computation (indicated below) is necessary to find the answer to the question.

1   *Addition* $d = 300 \text{ yd} + 400 \text{ yd} = 700 \text{ yd}$
2   *Subtraction* $d = 400 \text{ yd} - 300 \text{ yd} = 100 \text{ yd}$
3   *Pythagorean theorem* $d = \sqrt{(400)^2 + (300)^2} = 500 \text{ yd}$

This example has illustrated the necessity of thorough recognition and careful consideration of all the physical characteristics of a problem situation before being able to determine the nature of the operational procedure needed to solve the problem.

Example Consider the two following methods of finding the length of a line segment $\overline{AC}$.

1   A yardstick is used to find that one part $\overline{AB}$ of the line segment is 2 feet long, and the remaining portion $\overline{BC}$ is 4 inches long. There would be no difficulty presented in determining that the length of $\overline{AC}$ is the sum of the determined lengths, that is, $AC = 2 \text{ ft} + 4 \text{ in.}$, or, better, 2 ft 4 in.

2   A yardstick is used to find that $\overline{AB}$ is 2 feet long and a meterstick to find that $\overline{BC}$ is 4 decimeters long. Although the basic technique is the same as in the previous case, there would be no inclination to find the sum 2 ft + 4 dm and give the length of $\overline{AC}$ as 2 ft 4 dm. It would be recognized that before any combination could be made, it would be necessary either to express both the measurements in the English system or to express both in the metric system.

This second example has illustrated the fact that two measurements of like character and in the same system may be combined into one measurement by addition, but that the numerical coefficients are not added unless the units are like units. When the units are not like units, the addition is indicated by juxtaposition. The result is a mixed measurement number. In fact, the measurement 2 ft 4 in. could have been written $2\frac{1}{3}$ ft; the use of the unit "inch" provides a means of avoiding fractions.

Computation with denominate numbers   In addition, subtraction, and multiplication of denominate numbers not only does one have the ordinary conversion problems incident to place value in the structure of the numbers used, but also there are problems of conversion from one denomination to the other. These are made, of course, in terms of the pertinent tables of weight or measure.

Example Find the sum of the following measurements: 5 yd 2 ft 8 in.; 8 yd 2 ft 11 in.; 5 yd 1 ft 9 in.; 6 yd 5 in. Notice (Fig. 9–8) that the columns align measurements expressed in the same units. It then follows

FIGURE 9–8

5 yd	2 ft	8 in.
8 yd	2 ft	11 in.
5 yd	1 ft	9 in.
6 yd	0 ft	5 in.
24 yd	5 ft	33 in.
26 yd	1 ft	9 in.

FIGURE 9–9

	6 hr	36 min	30 sec
			5 sec
	30 hr	180 min	150 sec
	33 hr	2 min	30 sec
1 day	9 hr	2 min	30 sec

that the numerical coefficients in each column can be added. The first sum is 24 yd 5 ft 33 in., but it is the accepted practice that the simplification of this result calls for the modification of any given denominate number to a form such that no denomination of a lower order contains any integral multiples of units of higher order. Thus 33 in. = 2 ft 9 in., so the 9 in. is recorded in this denomination while the 2 ft is combined with the 5 ft already obtained in the sum to give 7 ft, which converts to 2 yd 1 ft. Hence the accepted answer for this sum is 26 yd 1 ft 9 in.

Example What is the product of 5 × 6 hr 36 min 30 sec? The first product (Fig. 9–9) is the usual multiplication.

150 sec = 2 min 30 sec
180 min + 2 min = 182 min
= 3 hr 2 min
30 hr + 3 hr = 33 hr = 1 day 9 hr

A result of this kind might be left in either of the last two forms indicated, depending upon the emphasis in a particular problem situation.

Example Subtract 5 gal 3 qt 2 pt from 8 gal 1 qt 1 pt. In this exercise there is the problem of converting higher denominations to equivalent lower denominations in order that the subtraction will be possible. The exercise is rewritten (Fig. 9–10) to exhibit what takes place. This, of course, is not necessary in the working of the problem, but it can be helpful.

1 qt = 2 pt   1 pt + 2 pt = 3 pt   3 pt − 2 pt = 1 pt
1 gal = 4 qt   4 qt + 0 qt = 4 qt   4 qt − 3 qt = 1 qt
7 gal − 5 gal = 2 gal

FIGURE 9–10

8 gal	1 qt	1 pt
5 gal	3 qt	2 pt

7 gal	4 qt	3 pt
5 gal	3 qt	2 pt
2 gal	1 qt	1 pt

There are two types of problems that arise in division, depending on whether the emphasis is on partition or on measurement.

Example

1 What is $\frac{1}{3}$ of 11 lb 3 oz? This is a partition division. $11\,\text{lb} \div 3 =$ 3 lb with 2 lb as a remainder (Fig. 9–11a).

2 lb = 32 oz

32 oz + 3 oz = 35 oz

35 oz ÷ 3 = $11\frac{2}{3}$ oz

$\frac{1}{3}$ of 11 lb 3 oz = 3 lb $11\frac{2}{3}$ oz

2 What is the ratio of 1 bu 2 pk 2 qt to 3 pk 6 qt? This is a measurement division. Before the division can be accomplished the two meas-

FIGURE 9–11

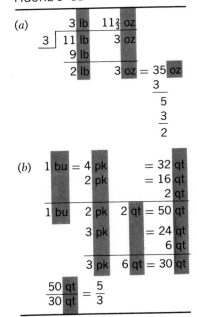

ures must be converted to the same denomination.   This is usually accomplished best by changing to lower denominations (Fig. 9–11*b*). The ratio of 1 bu 2 pk 2 qt to 3 pk 6 qt is the same as the ratio of 50 qt to 30 qt or 5 to 3.

Exercises

1 Construct the tables for weight and capacity in the metric system.
2 Under the equivalence established by the definition of 1 yard, express 1 inch in terms of 1 meter.   Make your computation correct to four decimal places.
3 Use the result of Exercise 2 to express 1 inch in terms of centimeters.
4 The new official definition of 1 meter is 1,650,763.73 wavelengths of the orange-red light of krypton 86.   How many such wavelengths in 1 inch?
5 If 1 avoirdupois ounce = 437.5 grains, express 1 grain in terms of the avoirdupois ounce.   Make your computation correct to five decimal places.

Using the data given on pages 262 and 263, determine the answers to the questions in Exercises 6 to 10.

6 What is the distance to the North Star in miles?
7 What is the distance to the star Alpha Centauri in miles?
8 What is the weight in grams of one proton?
9 What is the weight in grams of one electron?
10 What is the weight in grams of one neutron?

In Exercises 11 to 13, find the sums.

11	4 yd 2 ft 6 in.	12	6 hr 17 min 26 sec	13	1 bu 2 pk 3 qt
	5 yd 5 in.		8 hr 45 min		2 bu 3 pk 5 qt
	2 yd 1 ft 8 in.		9 hr 20 min 56 sec		4 bu 7 qt
	3 yd 2 ft		10 hr 6 min 8 sec		2 bu 1 pk 6 qt

In Exercises 14 to 17, find the differences.

14	6 sq yd 3 sq ft 32 sq in.	15	year	month	day
	1 sq yd 8 sq ft 84 sq in.		1963	5	9
			1928	8	25

16	5 m 9 cm 6 mm	17	3 g 2 dg 5 cg 2 mg
	2 m 2 dm 8 cm 4 mm		1 g 8 cg 9 mg

18   Use only decimal fractions to solve Exercises 16 and 17.
19   Find this sum in two different ways: (a) without the use of decimal fractions; (b) using only decimal fractions.

2 l 5 dl 4 cl 1 ml;   8 dl 5 ml;   4 l 7 cl

In Exercises 20 to 23, find the products.

20   6 ft 7 in.   21   4 bu 1 pk 5 qt 1 pt
      ×8   ×7

22   5 gal 3 qt 1 pt   23   3 days 16 hr 35 min 45 sec
              ×3   ×6

In Exercises 24 to 27, find the quotients.   What is the remainder in each case?

24   6⟌8 sq yd 2 sq ft 100 sq in.   25   5⟌12 gal 1 pt

26   8⟌12 m 8 cm   27   3⟌4 g 9 dg 5 cg

In Exercises 28 to 31, find the ratios.

28   3 yd 8 ft to 4 ft 3 in.   29   1 bu 2 pk 4 qt to 3 bu 1 pk
30   4 m 7 dm 3 cm 2 mm to 23 m 6 dm 6 cm
31   5 mg to 1 kg
32–35   Work Exercises 26, 27, 30, and 31 using only decimal fractions.

9–8   PRECISION AND ACCURACY

As has been pointed out previously, the fact that all measurement is by nature approximate does not prevent man from creating units and constructing instruments to enable him to secure observed values that most nearly represent true values of any desired measurements.   In the manufacturing industry, for example, the Johansson gauge blocks are used to make the refined measures necessary in such engineering problems as cylinder grinding and piston fitting.   These blocks are so highly polished and possess such adhesive properties that when fitted together they may be used as a standard for making measurements with an error of less than one hundred-thousandth of an inch (0.00001 in.).   Such quality of refinement in a measuring instrument is called *precision*. Thus, the more precise of two carefully made measurements is the one that has been made with the scale showing the greater degree of refinement in unit subdivision.

Precision

FIGURE 9–12   Precision
in measurement.

The picture in Fig. 9–12 shows a 6-in. ruler graduated to sixteenths of an inch. It is being used to measure the length of the line segment $\overline{AB}$. The point A is flush with the zero mark of the ruler, and the identification of the position of the point B will give the desired length of $\overline{AB}$. How long is $\overline{AB}$? There are six possible answers, depending on how precisely we wish to make the measurement.

1   *To the nearest inch*, $\overline{AB}$ is 4 in. long.   This means that B lies nearer to the 4-in. mark than to any other inch mark on the scale.   In other words, it lies somewhere between $3\frac{1}{2}$ and $4\frac{1}{2}$ in.   Thus, in this case there is a maximum possible error of $\frac{1}{2}$ in.   Another way of giving the length is 4 in. $\pm \frac{1}{2}$ in.

2   *To the nearest half-inch*, $\overline{AB}$ is also 4 in. long.   This means that B lies nearer to the 4-in. mark (or the mark which indicates eight half-inches from A) than to any other half-inch mark on the scale.   In other words, it lies somewhere between $3\frac{3}{4}$ and $4\frac{1}{4}$ in.   This time the maximum possible error is $\frac{1}{4}$ in.   Another way of giving the length is 4 in. $\pm \frac{1}{4}$ in.

3   *To the nearest quarter-inch*, $\overline{AB}$ is $4\frac{1}{4}$ in. long.   This means that B lies nearer to the $4\frac{1}{4}$-in. mark (or the 17-quarter-inch mark from A) than to any other quarter-inch mark on the scale.   In other words, it lies somewhere between $4\frac{1}{8}$ and $4\frac{3}{8}$ in.   Another way of giving the length is $4\frac{1}{4}$ in. $\pm \frac{1}{8}$ in.

4   *To the nearest eighth-inch*, $\overline{AB}$ is $4\frac{2}{8}$ in., or $4\frac{1}{4}$ in., long.   Explain what this means.   Remember that, in this case, $4\frac{1}{4}$ in. is simply a way we have of writing 18 eighth-inches.   Why can this measure be written as $4\frac{1}{4}$ in. $\pm \frac{1}{16}$ in.?   If this measure should be given merely by stating the mixed number, why does $4\frac{1}{4}$ in. not give the true picture?

5   *To the nearest sixteenth-inch*, what is the length of $\overline{AB}$?   What is the maximum possible error?   What would be used to fill the blanks in the statement $\overline{AB}$ is ____ in. $\pm$ ____ in.?

6   One could even make an estimate of the length of $\overline{AB}$ correct *to the nearest thirty-second of an inch*.   What estimate would you make? What is the maximum possible error of the most justifiable reading you can give the measurement?

For the line segment $\overline{AB}$ of Fig. 9–12 there exists an exact measurement.   The measurements resulting from the six illustrated techniques are all approximations to this unobtainable true measurement. Connected with each approximation, therefore, there is an error which is, of course, unobtainable. As has been pointed out, in each reading of the measurement there is a maximum possible error which is $\frac{1}{2}$ of the smallest unit of measure used. This maximum possible error is called the

apparent, or *absolute*, error. Thus, it follows that *the more precise of two measures is that one which has the smaller apparent error*. For example, in the above illustration the measurement $4\frac{1}{4}$ in. $\pm \frac{1}{16}$ in. is more precise than $4\frac{1}{4}$ in. $\pm \frac{1}{8}$ in. The apparent error of the first measurement $\left(\frac{1}{16} \text{ in.}\right)$ is smaller than the apparent error of the second measurement $\left(\frac{1}{8} \text{ in.}\right)$. It should be evident that twice the apparent error of a measurement gives the interval about the observed measurement within which the actual measurement (which is unobtainable) must lie. Similarly, where measurements are recorded in decimal fractions the degree of precision is indicated by the number of decimal places involved. A measure recorded as 6.3 in. would be less precise than one recorded as 6.30 in. In the first case, the measurement is made to the nearest tenth of an inch; the apparent error is 0.05 in.; the measurement lies between 6.25 and 6.35 in. In the second case, the measurement is made to the nearest hundredth of an inch; the apparent error is 0.005 in.; the measurement lies between 6.295 and 6.305 in.

This last illustration emphasizes the falsity of a statement that is sometimes heard, namely, to annex a zero to the right of a decimal fraction does not affect the fraction. This is manifestly incorrect. As illustrated above, the significance of the measure 6.3 in. was changed materially by annexing the zero, since 6.30 in. means something entirely different. The true and usable statement is: To annex a zero to the right of the decimal does not change *the value* of the decimal. The two decimals 6.3 and 6.30 have the same material value for computational purposes. The results derived from the computation, however, are subject to significantly different interpretations depending upon which measure was used. Similarly, it should be quite obvious that, in measurement numbers, $7\frac{9}{8}$ in. is quite different from 7 in. The first measurement, $7\frac{9}{8}$ in., means that the unit of precision is $\frac{1}{8}$ in. and the measurement is 7 in. $\pm \frac{1}{16}$ in., while 7 in. can mean only that the unit of precision is 1 in. and the measurement is 7 in. $\pm \frac{1}{2}$ in. or, possibly, 7 in. ± 0.5 in.

Another important type of error that figures very significantly in

industry is the *permissible error,* better known as *tolerance.* It is simply Tolerance
a value defining the amount of the maximum allowable error or departure from true value or performance. For example, the specified tolerance of ± 0.004 in. on a shaft whose dimension is specified as
2.000 in. $\pm$ 0.004 in. means that all shafts measuring anywhere between
1.996 and 2.004 in. will be considered as satisfactory.

Precision in language usage is thus seen to be essential for specifica-
tion of precision in measurement. If, for example, the length of the
line segment $\overline{AB}$ on page 269 is stated to be 4 in., what are you, the
reader, to think is meant? No prescription has been made as to the
unit of precision. All that you can do is to assume that the smallest unit
specified indicates the desired precision. Therefore, all you can interpret the statement to mean is that the length is given to the nearest inch;
i.e., the length of $\overline{AB}$ is 4 in. $\pm \frac{1}{2}$ in., or merely somewhere between $3\frac{1}{2}$
and $4\frac{1}{2}$ in. If the person making the statement wants you to know that,
to the nearest half-inch, the line segment is 4 in. long, or 4 in. $\pm \frac{1}{4}$ in.,
it is his responsibility so to state. What would the statement have to be
to carry the meaning that the length of a given line segment is 4 in.
correct to the nearest sixteenth of an inch?

In dealing with the errors of measurement we have concern not only
for their size but also for their significance. For example, an error of
$\frac{1}{2}$ in. in a measurement of 6 ft 4 in. (76 in.) is far less serious than is an
error of $\frac{1}{2}$ in. in 4 in. This significance is measured by the ratio of the
error to the measurement, which is known as *relative error.* Relative error

The more accurate of two measurements is that one which has the Accuracy
smaller relative error.

The relative error of a given measure may also be expressed as a *per cent* Per cent of error
of error by converting the ratio into a decimal fraction and multiplying
by 100. As will be seen later, there is no point in carrying such a division out to more than the first nonzero digit.

While the criterion of the relative error is a very valuable one in the
determination of the usefulness of any given measure, it should be kept
in mind that the intended use of the measure also enters into the determination of the seriousness of the accompanying error. An error of
$\frac{1}{2}$ in. in the wrong direction when a person is walking along a 6 ft 4 in.
ledge of a high mountain cliff could be far more serious than an error of
$\frac{1}{2}$ in. in the wrong direction when he is rolling a marble down a 4-inch
track.

Example   Consider these two measurements: (1) The distance from the earth to the moon is 239,000 miles.   (2) The estimated diameter of the average atom is 0.0000000079 in. (79 ten-billionths of an inch).

1   What is the apparent error of each measurement?
2   What is the relative error of each measurement?
3   What is the per cent of error of each measurement?
4   Which measure is the more precise?
5   Which measure is the more accurate?

1   The apparent error in 239,000 miles is 500 miles; in 0.0000000079 in. it is 0.00000000005 in.

2   The relative error in 239,000 miles is $\dfrac{500}{239,000} = \dfrac{5}{2,390} = \dfrac{1}{478} = 0.002$; in 0.0000000079 in. the relative error is $\dfrac{0.00000000005}{0.0000000079} = \dfrac{5}{790} = \dfrac{1}{158} = 0.006$.

3   The per cent of error in 239,000 is 0.2%; in 0.0000000079 it is 0.6%.

4   The measurement 0.0000000079 in. is the more precise of the two.

5   The measurement 239,000 miles is the more accurate of the two.

The comparisons of this example emphasize the importance of attention to *significant digits*, or *significant figures*, in a number expressing a measurement or an approximation of any kind.   The significant digits in any number may be determined in accordance with the following criteria:

1   **Any nonzero digit is significant.**
2   **Zeros used merely for the purpose of placing the decimal point are not significant.**
3   **All other zeros are significant.**

Each of the numbers 632, 25.0, 0.250, 304, and 0.000123 has three significant figures.   There should be no question about 632.   In 25.0 the zero is not needed for the placing of the decimal point; therefore, since it is used, it is significant.   In 0.000123, all zeros are merely for placing the decimal point, so they are not significant.

In the example the distance to the moon is given to three significant figures, while the estimated diameter of the average atom is given to two significant figures.   Thus the more accurate measurement was that one given to the greater number of significant figures.   This is in general true.   For example, a measurement of 3,256 miles is far less precise

Significant
digits

but much more accurate than 7.6 in.; 0.5 mile is much larger than 0.05 in., but $\dfrac{0.5}{3,256} = \dfrac{5}{32,560}$ is much smaller than $\dfrac{0.05}{7.6} = \dfrac{5}{760}$. The more accurate of two numbers having the same number of significant digits would be that one which has the larger digit in the extreme left significant-digit position of the number. The measurement 0.00934 in. is both more precise and more accurate than 39.4 in. Why?

Example How many significant digits are there in each of these measurements: (1) 16 ft 2 in.; (2) 6 lb $5\frac{1}{2}$ oz; (3) 6 gal 2 qt 1 pt; and (4) 6°32′14″?

1 The smallest unit of measure in 16 ft 2 in. is 1 inch. The 16 ft 2 in. is merely an accepted form for recording the measurement of 194 in. There are three significant digits.

2 The unit of precision in 6 lb $5\frac{1}{2}$ oz is $\frac{1}{2}$ ounce. The measurement is 203 half-ounces, and there are three significant digits.

3 The unit of precision is 1 pint in 6 gal 2 qt 1 pt. The measurement is 53 pints, and there are two significant digits.

4 The unit of precision is 1 second. The measurement is 23,534 seconds, and there are five significant digits.

9-9   SCIENTIFIC NOTATION

A bit of reflection should make it rather obvious that the nonsignificant zeros, necessary for positional evaluation in very large or very small numbers, can contribute no significant figures to the result of any computation. They must be taken into consideration only in order to ensure that the significant figures of the result are assigned their proper positional values. In other words, nonsignificant figures can serve only as aids in the proper placing of the decimal point in a given or computed approximate number.

Since scientists constantly have to work with very large numbers or very small numbers, they have contrived a special notation that simplifies very materially computation with such numbers. It is known as *scientific notation*, sometimes referred to as *standard notation*, and is an exponential notation which is based on three fundamental principles:

1 Only significant figures can produce significant figures in the results of a computation.

2 Our number system is a decimal system.

3 Multiplying a number by 10 multiplies the place value of each digit of the number by 10, and dividing the number by 10 divides the place value of each digit by 10.

The approximate distance from the earth to the sun has been given as 93,000,000 miles. Written in scientific notation this distance is given as 9.3×10^7. Observe how this is accomplished:

Converting to scientific notation

1 The significant digits of the number are recorded in their positions relative to each other (in this number they are 9 and 3).

2 These digits are then written so that there is only one digit to the left of the decimal point (9.3).

3 This number is then multiplied by the power of 10 necessary to restore its digits to their proper positional value in the original number. (The 9 is in the ones place in 9.3 and in the ten-millions place in 93,000,000. The ten-millions place is seven positional places to the left of the ones place. The necessary multiplier is, therefore, 10^7. Of course, this same multiplier will also restore 3 to its proper positional value.)

The value of the atomic mass unit has been given as 0.000000000000000000000001660 gram; this number written in scientific notation is 1.660×10^{-24} gram. Notice that the negative exponent means that the decimal point must be moved to the left in translating from scientific notation to positional notation. Notice also how scientific notation removes all questions as to significance or nonsignificance of zeros. This fact is emphasized a bit more clearly by considering the established figure for the velocity of light, 3.00×10^{10} centimeters per second. There is no question here concerning the significance of the two zeros, and it is readily recognized that this figure is correct to three significant figures. This same number written in positional notation would be 30,000,000,000 centimeters per second, and a means for indicating the significance of the two zeros must be invented. Here the second zero from the left has been underscored to indicate that it is significant, thus automatically giving significance to the zero between it and the 3. Other devices are used to indicate significant zeros in such numbers. There is no generally accepted practice. Scientific notation removes the necessity for the standardization of any such symbol.

Explain the scientific notation form in each of these examples:

Positional Notation	*Scientific Notation*
239,000	2.39×10^5
0.00118	1.18×10^{-3}
34.00	3.400×10^1
150,000,000	1.5000×10^8
0.0000000079	7.9×10^{-9}

FIGURE 9-13   Computation of errors.

$M + E$	$M + E$
$+\ m + e$	$-(m + e)$
$(M + m) + (E + e)$	$(M - m) + (E - e)$

9-10   ADDITION AND SUBTRACTION

If two measurements are combined by the process of addition, it should be evident that the error in the computed measurement will be the algebraic sum of the errors in the given measurements (see Fig. 9–13). Similarly, if one measurement is subtracted from another, the error in the computed measurement will be the algebraic difference between the errors in the given measurements.   Thus, if all measurements used in addition or subtraction were given with their respective errors, it would be a simple matter to arrive at a resultant measurement and its pertinent error.   In actuality, however, measurements are given most frequently with no specified error, so that the only error known in each case is the maximum possible error.   It is safe to assume, however, that these errors will tend to balance against each other in that some will be negative and some positive.   It should be evident that, if the measurements are given to different degrees of precision, the error in the least precise measure will always be larger than all other errors.   For this reason, in any addition or subtraction, the result cannot be any more precise than the least precise measurement used in the computation.

Example   Assume that each of four teams, composed of two individuals each, has been given a tape measure graduated so that measurements to the nearest thousandth of a foot can be made.   Each team is asked to measure the length of one side of a four-sided plot of ground, and no specifications are made as to how the measurements are to be made.   It is conceivable that the four measurements shown in Fig. 9–14

FIGURE 9-14   Finding the perimeter of a polygon.

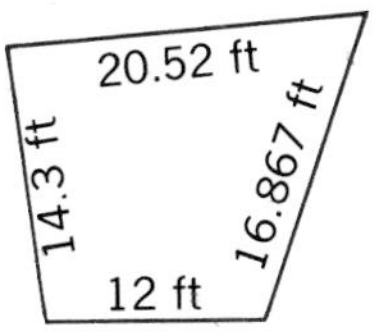

	MINIMUM SUM	MAXIMUM SUM	COMPUTED SUM
	11.5	12.5	12
	14.25	14.35	14.3
	20.515	20.525	20.5
	16.8665	16.8675	16.9
	63.1315	64.2425	63.7
	The most justified result is 64.		
	(a)	(b)	(c)

Figure labels: 20.52 ft, 14.3 ft, 16.867 ft, 12 ft

might be the result. What is the most justified measurement for the perimeter of the figure? The *perimeter* of a polygon is the distance around it. In this case it is the sum of the four measurements that can be obtained from the obtained data.

Consider each of the three sums given here. The sum in column (a) gives the minimum possible value for the sum, and the one in column (b) gives its maximum possible value. So the true value lies somewhere between these extremes. In column (c) each measurement was rounded to within one position of the same degree of precision as that of the least precise, namely, 12 ft. The sum was then rounded to the lowest degree of precision. It will be observed that the value so obtained is well within the limits found in columns (a) and (b).

For these reasons the standard rule for the addition or subtraction of approximate numbers is:

Addition and subtraction with approximate numbers

In addition and subtraction of approximate numbers, when expressed decimally, first round all numbers to within one position of the same degree of precision as the least precise number, then compute. The result should then be rounded to the lowest degree of precision.

The above illustration consists of measurements which are expressed in decimal-fraction fashion. The procedure for addition and subtraction of measures expressed in terms of common fractions is illustrated in the next example.

Example   What is the sum of the measurements of a four-sided figure whose sides have the following measurements: $14\frac{1}{2}$ in.; $21\frac{1}{4}$ in.; $9\frac{3}{8}$ in.; $18\frac{5}{16}$ in.?

The $14\frac{1}{2}$ in. is the least precise of the four measurements. It thus controls the precision of the final answer. In order to accomplish the addition, equivalent fractions with false precision must be introduced (see Fig. 9–15). The correction for this has to be taken care of by the form in which the answer is given. This answer must be qualified because it is not correct to sixteenths of an inch but only to one half-inch. Therefore, the perimeter is $63\frac{7}{16}$ in. correct to the nearest half-inch,

FIGURE 9–15   Precision in English units.

$14\frac{1}{2}$ = $14\frac{8}{16}$ (an incorrect degree of precision)
$21\frac{1}{4}$ = $21\frac{4}{16}$ (an incorrect degree of precision)
$9\frac{3}{8}$ = $9\frac{6}{16}$ (an incorrect degree of precision)
$18\frac{5}{16}$ = $18\frac{5}{16}$ (correct precision)

$63\frac{7}{16}$ (an incorrect degree of precision)

The correct answer is $63\frac{7}{16}$ in. $\pm \frac{1}{4}$ in.

or $63\frac{7}{16}$ in. $\pm \frac{1}{4}$ in.   This means that the limits of the computed perim-

eter are $63\frac{3}{16}$ in. and $63\frac{11}{16}$ in. rather than $63\frac{13}{32}$ in. and $63\frac{15}{32}$ in., or $63\frac{7}{16}$ in.

$\pm \frac{1}{32}$ in.

9-11   MULTIPLICATION AND DIVISION

Just as precision is the guide to satisfactory computation in the addition and subtraction of approximate numbers, so accuracy serves as the guide in multiplication and division.   The detail of analysis is quite a bit more technical than in addition and will be dispensed with here. However, an example involving limits can again serve as an indication of the procedure to use.

Example   How many square feet are there in the area of a rectangle whose dimensions are 14.82 by 26.3 ft?

The minimum dimensions that could be represented by the given measurements are 14.815 by 26.25 ft, thus giving a minimum area of 388.89375 sq ft.   Similarly, the maximum dimensions are 14.825 by 26.35 ft, giving a maximum area of 390.63875 sq ft.

When the more accurate number 14.82 is rounded to the same number of significant digits as 26.3 and the product obtained, we have $14.8 \times 26.3 = 389.24$.   This is seen to be well within the limits of the extreme values for the product.   Since the computation could not be expected to yield a result more accurate than the accuracy of the least accurate number used, the product of the measurement would be given as 389 sq ft, a measurement still well within the computed limits.

Example   The product of two measurements is 389 sq ft.   If one measurement is 14.82 ft, what is the other?

The limiting values can be obtained here by dividing the minimum possible value of the product by the maximum possible value of the given measurement, and the maximum possible value of the product by the minimum possible value of the measurement.   These results are shown in columns (*a*) and (*b*), respectively, of Fig. 9–16.   Also, in column (*c*) is shown the computed value obtained by rounding the more accurate number to the fewer number of significant figures.   The quotient is within the extreme limits, but the justified result obtained when rounding this quotient to three significant figures is 26.3 ft.   The fact that this is outside the extremes is not disturbing since the figure in the extreme right position of any approximate number is always in question.

FIGURE 9–16   Significant digits in division.

MINIMUM VALUE		MAXIMUM VALUE		COMPUTED VALUE	
	26.20 . . . ft		26.29 . . . ft		26.28 ft
14.825	388.50000	14.815	389.50000	14.8	3890
	296 50		296 30		296
	92 000		93 200		930
	88 950		88 890		888
	3 0500		4 3100		420
	2 9650		2 9630		296
	8500		1 34700		1240
			1 33335		1184
			1365		56
	(*a*)		(*b*)		(*c*)

These two examples suffice to illustrate the rule commonly given for the multiplication and division of approximate numbers:

Multiplication and division with approximate numbers

In the multiplication and division of two approximate numbers, express both numbers to the same degree of accuracy (same number of significant figures) as the one of lesser accuracy. The result will have this same degree of accuracy.

In a series of such computations this same rule applies, but it usually is safer and productive of better results to carry one extra digit along until the final result is obtained. Thus, for example, when an approximate number is raised to an integral power, the final result can be given to the same number of significant figures as contained in the original number.

Example   A cube, each of whose sides is 1.81 in. will have a volume = $(1.81 \text{ in.})^3 = 5.93$ cu in.

Any time an exact number enters any such computation with approximate numbers, it has no effect at all on the degree of approximativeness. An exact number may be thought of as having as many significant digits as one desires.

Example   The circumference of a circle whose radius is 4.16 in. is $2\pi(4.16 \text{ in.})$. In this formula 2 is an exact number and π has been computed to many significant figures, so 4.16 is the number that controls the accuracy of the result. The answer can be given to three significant figures. It is 26.1 in.

Finally, the process of extracting square roots enters into a sufficient number of the computations of elementary mathematics to justify mentioning the rule governing the results of extracting square roots of approximate numbers.

The square root of an approximate number can be computed correct to the same number of significant digits as the given number.   Square root

Example   What is the radius of a circle whose area is 7.64 sq in.?
    The formula is: $A = \pi r^2 = 3.14 r^2$ where the value of π is taken correct to three significant digits.
    Therefore we have

$$7.64 = 3.14 r^2$$

$$r^2 = \frac{7.64}{3.14} = 2.43$$

$$r = \sqrt{2.43} = 1.56 \text{ in.}$$

Exercises

1   In any given approximate number, what digits are considered to be significant digits?
2   Explain the difference between these three measurements: 8 ft; 8.0 ft; 8.00 ft.   Give the limits in each case.
3   Explain the difference between each pair of measurements: 4 in. and $4\frac{9}{8}$ in.; 15 ft 4 in. and $15\frac{1}{3}$ ft.   Give the limits in each case.
4   Scientists tell us that a speed of approximately Mach 33.4 is required to hurl an object out of the earth's atmosphere.   Use 750 miles per hour as the approximate equivalent of Mach 1 to express this required speed in miles per hour.
5   What is the unit of precision in each of these measures?

(a) 8 ft 3 in.   (b) 5 bu 3 pk   (c) 10 lb 5 oz
(d) 58 min 15 sec   (e) 6 pk   (f) 1 gal 2 qt
(g) 0.00020 in.   (h) 117.000 miles   (i) 2 min 15.2 sec
(j) 221,000 miles   (k) 10,000 dollars (l) 5 yd 1 ft 10.0 in.

6   What are the maximum apparent error, the relative error, and the per cent of error in each measure of Exercise 5?
7   Which is the more precise and which the more accurate in each of the following pairs of measurements?

(a) 123.6 in. or 24.3 ft   (b) 36 min or 360 sec
(c) 30 ft or 3 yd   (d) 58 ft or 572 miles
(e) 195 lb or 80 oz   (f) 5 gal 3 qt or 3 qt 1 pt

8   Find the perimeter of each of these polygons.

(a) Sides: 8 ft 3 in.; 6 ft 9 in.; 4 ft 6 in.
(b) Sides: 10 ft 8 in.; 12 ft 9 in.; 18 ft 7 in.

(c) An equilateral triangle each of whose sides is 16.00 in.
(d) A square each of whose sides is 5 yd 2 ft 8 in.
(e) A rectangle with sides 6 ft 10 in. and 4 ft 8 in.
(f) Sides: 216.3 ft; 400.0 ft; 320.26 ft; 315.780 ft; 293.504 ft
(g) Sides: 16 in.; 20.00 in.; 17.3 in.; 8 in.; 11.2 in.; 7.001 in.
(h) A regular pentagon each of whose sides is 40.0 in.
(i) A regular hexagon each of whose sides is 32.06 in.
(j) A regular octagon each of whose sides is 2.5 in.

9 Write formulas for finding the perimeter of each of these polygons:
(a) triangle; (b) equilateral triangle; (c) rectangle; (d) square;
(e) regular pentagon; (f) regular hexagon.

10 Find the area and perimeter of a rectangular field which is 46.00 by 3.64 ft. Why should the area be given only to the nearest square foot while the perimeter should be given to the nearest one-hundredth of a foot? (*Hint:* The formula for the area is $A = lw$ where l and w represent the two dimensions.)

11 Find the area and perimeter of a square each of whose sides is 56.4 in. Why can the perimeter be given correct to the nearest tenth of an inch and the area only to the nearest 10 square inches? (*Hint:* The formula for the area is $A = s^2$ where s represents the length of a side.)

12 Find the side of a square with each of the given areas:

(a) 2.25 sq in.   (b) 144 sq in.   (c) 323 sq in.

13 Find the circumference and area of a circle whose radius is as given:

(a) $r = 2.5$ in.   (b) $r = 0.134$ ft

(*Hint:* Use $\pi = 3.14$.)

14 Find the circumference of a circle whose area is 445 sq in.

15 Find the area of a circle whose circumference is 7.62 in.

16 Write in scientific notation each of the numbers in the following statements:

(a) The diameter of the smallest visible particle is approximately 0.005 centimeter.
(b) There are approximately 800,000,000,000,000,000,000,000 molecules in 1 pound of cane sugar.
(c) The diameter of an average red blood corpuscle is 0.0000316 in.
(d) The wavelength of visible light varies from 0.000072 to 0.000040 cm.
(e) The speed of sound through a steel rod is 16,410.0 ft per sec.
(f) The average distance of the planet Jupiter from the earth is 483,900,000 miles.

17 Write in positional notation each of the numbers in the following
statements:

(a) The average length of time a movie image remains on the
screen is 6.4×10^{-2} sec.
(b) The mass of the earth is approximately 6.0×10^{27} grams.
(c) The nearest known star is approximately 2.5×10^{13} miles
from the earth.
(d) The mass of one molecule of water is approximately
3×10^{-23} gram.
(e) The speed of light is approximately 1.86×10^{5} miles per sec.

Use scientific notation to work Exercises 18 to 21.

18 Compute the distance in miles from the earth to the North Star; to
Alpha Centauri. (See page 262 for distances in light-years. Compare answers and technique with Exercises 6 and 7 of Sec. 9–7.)
19 Compute the mass in grams of a proton, a neutron, and an electron.
(See page 263 for data. Compare answers and technique with
Exercises 8 to 10 of Sec. 9–7.)
20 The star Arcturus is 223,700,000,000,000 miles from the earth.
How many years does it take light from Arcturus to reach the
earth?
21 The approximate velocity of sound in water is 4,720 feet per sec.
How deep is a lake at a point where it takes sound 0.030 sec to
travel from the surface to the bottom of the lake and back?

9–12 THE TANGENT AND COTANGENT RATIOS

History has it that the Greek mathematician Thales (ca. 600 B.C.) used
a familiar property of similar triangles to find the heights of pyramids.
One version is that he noted the length of the shadow of the pyramid
at a time when the length of his shadow was the same as his height, thus
making the height of the pyramid the same as the length of its shadow.
Another version of the story is that he equated the ratio between the
height of a stake and the length of its shadow to the ratio between the
unknown height of a pyramid and the length of its shadow. From this
proportion he was able to determine the height of the pyramid. These
ratios are at times referred to as "shadow ratios." There seems to be
no record of just what technique he used to measure the distance from
the tip of the shadow to a point directly below the apex of the pyramid.

The shadow
ratio

Example Assume that the distance from the point of the shadow of a
pyramid to the center of its base is 160 feet at the same time the shadow

of a stake, 16 feet high, is 8 feet long (see Fig. 9–17).   What is the height of the pyramid?

The line segments $\overline{PS}$ and $\overline{AB}$, which represent sun rays, are parallel. From this fact it can be established that the angles of triangles PRS and ACB are congruent.   It then follows from Theorem 8–13 and the implications of Definition 8–22 to triangles (pages 228 and 229) that the two triangles are similar and that ratios of corresponding sides are equal. Therefore we have

$$\frac{h}{160} = \frac{16}{8}$$

from which $h = 320$ feet.

This use of the equality of ratios of corresponding sides of similar triangles provides a very effective technique for making indirect measurements not only of inaccessible heights but also of other types of length.

Example   To measure the distance across a stream, surveyor's instruments were used to set up the diagram of Fig. 9–18.   The angles BCA and AED are right angles.   The points C, A, and E are collinear as are the points B, A, and D. $CA = 30$ yd, $AE = 10$ yd, and $DE = 25$ yd. Find CB.

Why are $\measuredangle$ CAB and DAE congruent?

Why are $\triangle$ CAB and DAE similar?

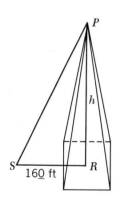

FIGURE 9–17   Using similar triangles to find heights.

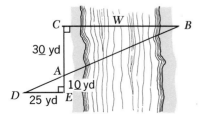

FIGURE 9–18   Using similar triangles to find distances.

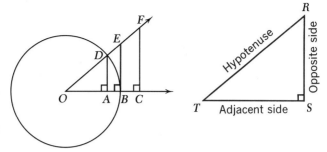

FIGURE 9–19   The tangent ratio.

Why is $\dfrac{w}{30} = \dfrac{25}{10} = \dfrac{5}{2}$?

From this proportion it follows that $w = 75$ yd.

The two preceding examples illustrate two simple applications of the similarity relationship to right triangles.   Further significance of this relationship may be discovered through an investigation of the similar right triangles of Fig. 9–19.   The central angle of the circle with center at O is the common angle of the right triangles DAO, EBO, and FCO.   The angles DAO, EBO, and FCO are congruent angles since each is a right angle.   It thus follows (Theorem 8–13) that the three triangles are similar.   Also the angles ODA, OEB, and OFC are congruent angles, each of which is a complement of the angle O.   From these similar triangles there is a set of equal ratios which correspond to the "shadow ratio" used previously.   They are

$$\frac{DA}{OA} = \frac{EB}{OB} = \frac{FC}{OC}$$

It should be evident from the property of similar triangles that, if a point P were taken anywhere along the ray $\overrightarrow{OF}$ and a line segment $\overline{PM}$ were drawn perpendicular to the ray $\overrightarrow{OC}$, the triangle PMO would be similar to each of the triangles of the figure.   Then

$$\frac{PM}{OM} = \frac{DA}{OA} = \frac{EB}{OB} = \frac{FC}{OC}$$

Furthermore, if $\angle STR$ in the right triangle RST is congruent to $\angle O$, then $\triangle RST$ is similar to each of the triangles DAC, EBO, and FCO. From these similar triangles we have

$$\frac{RS}{TS} = \frac{DA}{OA} = \frac{EB}{OB} = \frac{FC}{OC}$$

Each of the illustrations has been selected to make the point that, for any given angle, the ratio

Measure of the length of the side opposite the angle
───────────────────────────────────────
Measure of the length of the side adjacent to the angle

or, more briefly, the ratio

$$\frac{\text{Opposite side}}{\text{Adjacent side}}$$

is a fixed ratio. In other words, there is a specific value of this ratio associated with each acute angle; and, conversely, with each value of the ratio there is associated a specific acute angle. For this reason we say that the ratio is a *function* of the angle, and we give it the name *tangent ratio*. Symbolically, we write tangent $\angle O$ or tan $\angle O$. In other words,

The tangent ratio

$$\tan \angle O = \frac{\text{opposite side}}{\text{adjacent side}} = \frac{DA}{OA} = \frac{EB}{OB} = \frac{FC}{OC}$$

The reason this ratio is given the name tangent may be discovered from a further study of $\triangle EBO$ of Fig. 9–19. If the circle is considered as a unit circle, that is, a circle whose radius is one unit, then $OB = 1$, and $\tan O = \dfrac{EB}{OB} = \dfrac{EB}{1} = EB$. An examination of the figure exhibits $\overline{EB}$ as a line segment of the line tangent to the circle with B as the point of tangency.

In $\triangle RST$ of Fig. 9–19, angle TRS is the complement of angle STR. The side opposite $\angle TRS$ is $\overline{TS}$, and the adjacent side is $\overline{RS}$; therefore $\tan \angle TRS = \dfrac{TS}{RS}$. This ratio may be written in terms of $\angle STR$ as follows:

$$\text{Tangent of complementary angle of } \angle STR = \frac{\text{adjacent side}}{\text{opposite side}}$$

The cotangent ratio

The symbol cot $\angle STR$, abbreviation for "*cotangent* of angle STR," is used to represent this ratio:

$$\cot \angle STR = \frac{\text{adjacent side}}{\text{opposite side}}$$

If A is used to represent any angle, we have

$$\tan A = \frac{\text{opposite side}}{\text{adjacent side}} \tag{9–1}$$

$$\cot A = \frac{\text{adjacent side}}{\text{opposite side}} \tag{9–2}$$

A comparison of formulas (9–1) and (9–2) brings to light a very important relation which exists between the tangent and cotangent of any angle, namely,

$$\cot A = \frac{1}{\tan A} \tag{9–3}$$

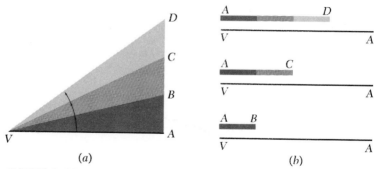

FIGURE 9–20   (*a*) The tangent ratio increases as the angle increases. (*b*) Ratios compared.

or, in equivalent form,

$$\tan A \cot A = 1 \tag{9-4}$$

We have seen that as long as $\angle A$ remains fixed in size the tangent ratio remains constant in value. What happens as $\angle A$ changes in size? The three angles AVB, AVC, and AVD of Fig. 9–20 have the same vertex V and the same initial side $\overline{VA}$. The tangent ratios are

$$\tan \angle AVB = \frac{AB}{VA} \qquad \tan \angle AVC = \frac{AC}{VA} \qquad \tan \angle AVD = \frac{AD}{VA}$$

In the ratios the length of the adjacent side $\overline{VA}$ remains fixed. A comparison of the change in the angle with the corresponding change in the length of the opposite side reveals that the value of the ratio increases as the angle increases and decreases as the angle decreases.

From formula (9–3) we have that the tangent and cotangent are reciprocal functions. This means that, as the value of the tangent function increases, the value of the cotangent function decreases and, as the value of the tangent function decreases, the value of the cotangent function increases. Furthermore, from Fig. 9–20, it should be evident that, for an angle of $0°$, the length of the opposite side is 0. From this fact we have $\tan 0° = 0$. It therefore follows from the reciprocal relation (9–3) that *cot* $0°$ *is undefined*, since division by zero is an undefined operation. Similarly, as we shall be able to establish more clearly in the next section, $\cot 90° = 0$ and *tan* $90°$ *is undefined*.

9–13   THE SINE AND COSINE RATIOS

Another set of equal ratios between corresponding sides of the similar triangles of Fig. 9–19 is

$$\frac{DA}{OD} = \frac{EB}{OE} = \frac{FC}{OF} = \frac{RS}{TR} = \frac{\text{opposite side}}{\text{hypotenuse}}$$

This ratio, which also remains constant for any fixed angle, is called the *sine* ratio, abbreviated to *sin*. Thus, if A represents any given angle, we have

The sine ratio

$$\sin A = \frac{\text{opposite side}}{\text{hypotenuse}} \qquad (9\text{--}5)$$

Still another set of equal ratios from Fig. 9–19 is $\dfrac{OA}{OD} = \dfrac{OB}{OE} = \dfrac{OC}{OF}$.

Closer examination of each right triangle involved in these ratios will reveal that each ratio is the sine of the angle which is the complement of the central angle O. Each of these ratios is in turn equal to $\dfrac{TS}{TR}$ of triangle RST, which is the sine of the complement of $\angle STR$. If the symbol A is used to represent the angle at O and its equal angle STR, we have

The cosine ratio

$$\text{Sine of the complement of } A = \frac{TS}{TR} = \frac{\text{adjacent side}}{\text{hypotenuse}}$$

Following the pattern of Sec. 9–12, we define "sine of the complement of A" as the *cosine A*, which is abbreviated to read *cos A*. Thus

$$\cos A = \frac{\text{adjacent side}}{\text{hypotenuse}} \qquad (9\text{--}6)$$

From a study of Fig. 9–21 we can obtain background for the labels sine and cosine attached to these functions and also an idea as to how the value of the ratio changes with change in the size of the angle. The etymology of the word "sine" has it derived from an Arabic word meaning "half chord." If, in Fig. 9–21, we consider the circle as a unit circle, we have

$$\sin \angle BOP = PB \qquad \sin \angle NOC = NC \qquad \sin \angle MOD = MD$$

In each case the function is indeed a half chord. Also it is to be observed that as the size of the angle increases the sine of the angle increases in value.

Similarly, $\cos \angle POB = OP$; $\cos \angle NOC = ON$; and $\cos \angle MOD =$

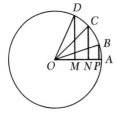

FIGURE 9–21   The sine function and the cosine function.

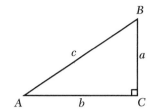

FIGURE 9–22

OM, from which it is clear that, as the size of the angle increases, the value of the cosine decreases.

When the angle is a 0° angle, the terminal side of the angle coincides with the initial side. This means, in Fig. 9–21, that the point *B*, for example, would coincide with point *A*. Thus, for a 0° angle the measure of the length of the opposite side is 0, while the measure of the length of the adjacent side is the same as that of the hypotenuse. From these facts it follows that sin 0° = 0 and cos 0° = 1. Similarly, when the angle is a 90° angle, the measure of the length of the adjacent side is 0 while the measure of the length of the opposite side is the same as the measure of the hypotenuse. From these facts we have sin 90° = 1 and cos 90° = 0.

From the preceding discussion it should be rather evident that there exists a definite relationship between sin *A* and cos *A*. However, it is not a reciprocal relationship such as that existing between tan *A* and cot *A* (see formula 9–10).

Frequently it is helpful and convenient to use a right triangle such as *ACB* of Fig. 9–22, with right angle at *C* and its sides lettered to correspond to the angles opposite, as a triangle of reference. With this reference we have

$$\sin A = \frac{\text{opposite side}}{\text{hypotenuse}} = \frac{a}{c}$$

$$\cos A = \frac{\text{adjacent side}}{\text{hypotenuse}} = \frac{b}{c}$$

(9–7)

$$\tan A = \frac{\text{opposite side}}{\text{adjacent side}} = \frac{a}{b}$$

$$\cot A = \frac{\text{adjacent side}}{\text{opposite side}} = \frac{b}{a}$$

These functions are called *trigonometric functions*. The word "trigonometry" literally means "triangle measure," and it is from the use of these functions in measurement problems associated with triangles that they have derived their name. Actually, they have many significant interpretations and uses other than those associated with triangles. It is beyond the scope of this book to pursue their study beyond their association with the right triangle.

Trigonometric functions

An examination of formulas (9–7) brings to light certain fundamental relations that exist between the four functions. For example,

$$\frac{\sin A}{\cos A} = (\sin A) \div (\cos A) = \frac{a}{c} \div \frac{b}{c}$$

$$= \frac{a}{c} \times \frac{c}{b} = \frac{a}{b}$$

$$= \tan A$$

Hence we have

$$\tan A = \frac{\sin A}{\cos A} \tag{9–8}$$

Similarly,

$$\cot A = \frac{\cos A}{\sin A} \tag{9–9}$$

Formulas (9–8) and (9–9) may be used to get a clearer picture of why tan 90° and cot 0° are undefined. Since cos 90° = 0, it follows from (9–8) that tan 90° is undefined. Also, since sin 0° = 0, it follows from (9–9) that cot 0° is undefined.

A fundamental relation existing between sin A and cos A is an immediate consequence of the pythagorean theorem (8–11). An application of this theorem to $\triangle ACB$ of Fig. 9–22 gives

$$c^2 = a^2 + b^2$$

If both sides of this equality are multiplied by $\frac{1}{c^2}$, we get

$$\frac{1}{c^2} \times c^2 = \frac{1}{c^2} \times (a^2 + b^2)$$

which by the property of the multiplicative inverse and the distributive property gives

$$1 = \frac{a^2}{c^2} + \frac{b^2}{c^2}$$

Comparison with formulas (9–7) now yields

$$\sin^2 A + \cos^2 A = 1 \tag{9–10}$$

9–14   TRIGONOMETRIC IDENTITIES

Formulas (9–8) to (9–10) express relationships between the respective functions which are true equalities for all values of the angle for which the functions are defined. Such equalities are called *identities*.

Definition 9-2   A *trigonometric identity* is a stated equality between expressions composed of trigonometric functions which is true for all values of the angle for which the functions are defined.

The fact that this definition is restricted to trigonometric functions of angles and not stated as generally as it might be is not of concern here. This discussion is limited to the acute angles of a right triangle, with the exception that angles of $0°$ and $90°$ have been included.   It must be remembered that cot A is undefined when $m \angle A = 0°$ and tan A is undefined when $m \angle A = 90°$.

Formulas (9–8) to (9–10) and also (9–3) and (9–4) may now be stated in the form of the identities which they are.   The symbol $\equiv$ is used to indicate such an identity and is read "is identically equal to."†

$$\tan A \equiv \frac{\sin A}{\cos A} \tag{9-11}$$

Fundamental identities

$$\cot A \equiv \frac{\cos A}{\sin A} \tag{9-12}$$

$$\tan A \equiv \frac{1}{\cot A} \tag{9-13}$$

$$\tan A \cot A \equiv 1 \tag{9-14}$$

$$\sin^2 A + \cos^2 A \equiv 1 \tag{9-15}$$

Identity (9–11) holds for all values of A except $90°$ since tan $90°$ is not defined; identity (9–12) holds for all values of A except $0°$ since cot $0°$ is not defined.   Identities (9–13) and (9–14) hold for all values of A except $0°$ and $90°$, and identity (9–15) holds for all values of A.

Identities between expressions composed of trigonometric functions may be established in any of three ways.

1   Start from a known identity and derive the desired relation.

2   Transform the expression on either side of the stated equality into the expression of the other side, or into an expression which is identically equal to it.

3   Transform each of the expressions of the stated equality into the same expression or into two expressions which are known to be identically equal.   When this technique is used one must be sure that the steps can be reversed on either side of the equality (significant only when dealing with identities more intricate than those of interest here).

Example

1   Derive formula (9–14) from formula (9–13).

Formula (9–13) is an identity as a consequence of the definitions of

---

† Attention is called to the fact that the symbol $\equiv$ was used in Chap. 7 with an entirely different connotation.   Since the contexts of the two uses are always clearly distinct from each other, there is no confusion in this seeming ambiguity.

tan A and cot A. Multiply both sides of this known identity by cot A to get tan A cot $A \equiv 1$.

2   Prove $\cos A \equiv \sqrt{1 - \sin^2 A}$ for $0° \leq A \leq 90°$.

Formula (9–15) is a known identity, whence

$$\sin^2 A + \cos^2 A \equiv 1 \qquad \text{or} \qquad \cos^2 A \equiv 1 - \sin^2 A$$

Extracting the square root, we get

$$\cos A \equiv \pm \sqrt{1 - \sin^2 A}$$

By definition $\cos A \geq 0$, whence

$$\cos A \equiv \sqrt{1 - \sin^2 A}$$

Example   Prove that $\cos^4 A - \sin^4 A \equiv \cos^2 A - \sin^2 A$.

We shall attempt to convert the expression on the left side of this equality into the one on the right.

$\cos^4 A - \sin^4 A$ may be written as the difference of two squares in the form

$$\cos^4 A - \sin^4 \equiv (\cos^2 A)^2 - (\sin^2 A)^2$$

Factoring this difference of two squares, we get

$$\cos^4 A - \sin^4 A \equiv (\cos^2 A + \sin^2 A)(\cos^2 A - \sin^2 A)$$

From formula (9–15) we have

$$\cos^2 A + \sin^2 A \equiv 1$$

whence

$$\cos^4 A - \sin^4 A \equiv 1 \cdot (\cos^2 A - \sin^2 A)$$
$$\equiv \cos^2 A - \sin^2 A$$

9–15   TABLE OF NATURAL FUNCTIONS

In the isosceles right triangle KLM of Fig. 9–23 with $ML = LK = s$, we have $MK = s\sqrt{2}$ (Theorem 8–11). From these facts it follows that

$$\sin 45° = \frac{s}{s\sqrt{2}} = \frac{1}{\sqrt{2}} = \frac{1}{2}\sqrt{2} = 0.7071 \qquad \text{correct to four places}$$

$$\cos 45° = \frac{s}{s\sqrt{2}} = \frac{1}{\sqrt{2}} = \frac{1}{2}\sqrt{2} = 0.7071$$

$$\tan 45° = \frac{s}{s} = 1$$

$$\cot 45° = \frac{s}{s} = 1$$

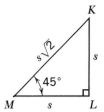

FIGURE 9–23

The triangle PQR of Fig. 9–24 is an equilateral triangle. The line segment $\overline{PS}$ is perpendicular to the base at its midpoint. By the pythagorean theorem we have

$$(PS)^2 + (QS)^2 = (PQ)^2$$

or

$$(PS)^2 + \left(\tfrac{1}{2}s\right)^2 = s^2$$

$$(PS)^2 = \tfrac{3}{4}s^2$$

$$PS = \frac{\sqrt{3}}{2}s$$

Hence

$$\sin 6\underline{0}° = \frac{\dfrac{s\sqrt{3}}{2}}{s} = \tfrac{1}{2}\sqrt{3} = 0.8660 = \cos 3\underline{0}°$$

$$\cos 6\underline{0}° = \frac{\dfrac{1}{2}s}{s} = \tfrac{1}{2} = 0.5000 = \sin 3\underline{0}°$$

$$\tan 6\underline{0}° = \frac{\dfrac{s\sqrt{3}}{2}}{\dfrac{s}{2}} = \sqrt{3} = 1.732 = \cot 3\underline{0}°$$

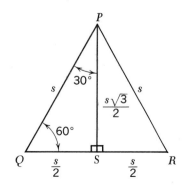

FIGURE 9–24

$$\cot 60° = \frac{\frac{1}{2}s}{\frac{s\sqrt{3}}{2}} = \frac{1}{\sqrt{3}} = \frac{\sqrt{3}}{3} = 0.5774 = \tan 30°$$

Table of natural functions

The values computed for the functions of 0°, 30°, 45°, 60°, and 90° are merely illustrations of what can be done for angles of any size. These values are frequently referred to as *natural functions*. Tables of such values have been constructed for use in making various types of indirect measurements. Figure 9–25 is such a table. This table is very brief and is given primarily for illustration purposes. In steps of 1° the approximate values of the four functions are listed for all angles from 0° to 90°. Notice that there are no values given either for tan 90° or for cot 0°. These function values do not exist since the respective functions are not defined for these angles. Also notice that as the angle values increase so do the values of the sine and tangent functions, but the values of the cosine and cotangent functions decrease.

The next two examples illustrate how the table may be used (1) to find the function value for a given angle and (2) to find the acute angle which corresponds to a given function value.

Example   (1) What are the values of sin 25°, cos 38°, tan 12°, cot 45°? (2) What are the values of sin 48°, cos 87°, tan 62°, cot 75°?

1   The entries in the extreme left column of the table are angle measures, in intervals of 1°, from 0° to 45°. For angle values of the left column the function label is at the top of each respective column. In the column under the label "sin" and opposite 25° the entry 0.4226 is the value of sin 25°. Similarly, cos 38° = 0.7880, tan 12° = 0.2126, and cot 45° = 1.000.

2   In the extreme right column the entries are, in intervals of 1°, angle measures from 45° to 90°. For angle values of the right column the function label is at the bottom of each respective column. In the column over the label "sin" and opposite 48° the entry 0.7431 is the value of sin 48°. Similarly, cos 87° = 0.0523, tan 62° = 1.881, and cot 75° = 0.2679.

The explanation of the organization of the table of natural functions lies in the fact that in such an arrangement of angle values the entry in the left column is the complement of the entry directly opposite it in the right column. This means that the same function value serves for two angles. For example, sin 25° = 0.4226 = cos 65°; cos 38° = 0.7880 = sin 52°; tan 62° = 1.881 = cot 28°; cot 45° = 1.000 = tan 45°.

Example   (1) Given sin A = 0.8746, what is the measure of ∠A?

FIGURE 9-25   Natural functions of acute angles.

DEGREES	sin	cos	tan	cot	DEGREES
0°	.0000	1.000	.0000	. . . . .	90°
1°	.0175	.9998	.0175	57.29	89°
2°	.0349	.9994	.0349	28.64	88°
3°	.0523	.9986	.0524	19.08	87°
4°	.0698	.9976	.0699	14.30	86°
5°	.0872	.9962	.0875	11.43	85°
6°	.1045	.9945	.1051	9.514	84°
7°	.1219	.9925	.1228	8.144	83°
8°	.1392	.9903	.1405	7.115	82°
9°	.1564	.9877	.1584	6.314	81°
10°	.1736	.9848	.1763	5.671	80°
11°	.1908	.9816	.1944	5.145	79°
12°	.2079	.9781	.2126	4.705	78°
13°	.2250	.9744	.2309	4.331	77°
14°	.2419	.9703	.2493	4.011	76°
15°	.2588	.9659	.2679	3.732	75°
16°	.2756	.9613	.2867	3.487	74°
17°	.2924	.9563	.3057	3.271	73°
18°	.3090	.9511	.3249	3.078	72°
19°	.3256	.9455	.3443	2.904	71°
20°	.3420	.9397	.3640	2.747	70°
21°	.3584	.9336	.3839	2.605	69°
22°	.3746	.9272	.4040	2.475	68°
23°	.3907	.9205	.4245	2.356	67°
24°	.4067	.9135	.4452	2.246	66°
25°	.4226	.9063	.4663	2.145	65°
26°	.4384	.8988	.4877	2.050	64°
27°	.4540	.8910	.5095	1.963	63°
28°	.4695	.8829	.5317	1.881	62°
29°	.4848	.8746	.5543	1.804	61°
30°	.5000	.8660	.5774	1.732	60°
31°	.5150	.8572	.6009	1.664	59°
32°	.5299	.8480	.6249	1.600	58°
33°	.5446	.8387	.6494	1.540	57°
34°	.5592	.8290	.6745	1.483	56°
35°	.5736	.8192	.7002	1.428	55°
36°	.5878	.8090	.7265	1.376	54°
37°	.6018	.7986	.7536	1.327	53°
38°	.6157	.7880	.7813	1.280	52°
39°	.6293	.7771	.8098	1.235	51°
40°	.6428	.7660	.8391	1.192	50°
41°	.6561	.7547	.8693	1.150	49°
42°	.6691	.7431	.9004	1.111	48°
43°	.6820	.7314	.9325	1.072	47°
44°	.6947	.7193	.9657	1.036	46°
45°	.7071	.7071	1.000	1.000	45°
DEGREES	cos	sin	cot	tan	DEGREES

(2) For what value of A is $\cos A = 0.8746$?   (3) Given $\tan A = 0.1944$, how many degrees in $\angle A$?   (4) For what value of A is $\cot A = 0.1944$?

  1   For $\sin A = 0.8746$ the table shows 0.8746 over "sin" and opposite 61° *in the right column;* therefore $m \angle A = 61°$.

  2   For $\cos A = 0.8746$, the table shows 0.8746 under "cos" and opposite 29° *in the left column;* therefore $m \angle A = 29°$.

  3   For $\tan A = 0.1944$, the number is in the column under "tan" and opposite 11°; therefore $m \angle A = 11°$.

  4   For $\cot A = 0.1944$, the number is in the column over "cot" and opposite 79°; therefore $m \angle A = 79°$.

If Fig. 9–25 were restricted merely to use for the entries found therein, its value would be extremely limited.   An established principle, followed as a guide in the use of tables such as this one, is:

Use of table **Two significant figures in function values correspond to angle measurement correct to the nearest degree; three significant figures in function values correspond to angle measures correct to the nearest ten minutes; and four significant figures in function values correspond to angle measures correct to the nearest minute.**

Such fractional parts of degrees can be found by a process called *interpolation,* which is illustrated in the next two examples.

Example

  1   In Fig. 9–26, assume the numbers 5, 12, and 13 to be exact numbers.   Use $\sin B = \dfrac{5}{13}$ to find $\angle B$ correct to the nearest minute.

$$\sin B = \frac{5}{13} = 0.3846 \qquad \text{correct to four significant figures}$$

The number 0.3846 is not to be found in the table, so we look for the two numbers nearest to it and then build this auxiliary table by using these values with their corresponding angle measures.

$$1° = 60' \begin{bmatrix} \quad 23° \\ \left[\begin{matrix} \angle B \\ x \\ \quad 22° \end{matrix} \right. \end{bmatrix} \qquad \begin{matrix} 0.3907 \\ 0.3846 \\ \qquad 0.3746 \end{matrix} \; \begin{matrix} \\ 0.0100 \\ \end{matrix} \; \begin{matrix} 0.0161 \\ \\ \end{matrix}$$

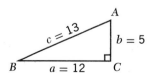

B $a = 12$ C $c = 13$ $b = 5$ A

FIGURE 9–26

This table shows that the measure of $\angle B$ lies between $22°$ and $23°$. Remember that the sine of any angle increases in value as the measure of the angle increases. This means that $m \angle B$ is larger than $22°$ but smaller than $23°$. The auxiliary table shows that a difference of $60'$ in the angle corresponds to a difference of 0.0161 in the sine. Our problem is to find how much difference in the angle will correspond to the difference of 0.0100 in the sine. This can be found from the proportion

$$\frac{x}{60'} = \frac{0.0100}{0.0161} = \frac{100}{161}$$

$$x = \frac{100}{161} \times 60' = 37' \qquad \text{correct to the nearest minute}$$

Since the angle increases with the sine, this is to be added to $22°$ to get the measure of $\angle B$.

$$m \angle B = 22°37'$$

2   Use $\tan B = \dfrac{5}{12}$ to find the measure of $\angle B$.

$$\tan B = \frac{5}{12} = 0.4167$$

The auxiliary table is

$$1° = 60' \begin{bmatrix} \text{---}23° \\ \quad\text{---}\angle B \\ x \\ \text{---}22° \end{bmatrix} \qquad \begin{matrix} 0.4245\text{---} \\ 0.4167\text{---} \\ \quad\quad 0.0127 \\ 0.4040\text{---} \end{matrix} \; 0.0205$$

$$\frac{x}{60'} = \frac{0.0127}{0.0205} = \frac{127}{205}$$

$$x = \frac{127}{205} \times 60'$$

$$x = 37'$$

The tangent function also increases as the angle increases, so we have

$$m \angle B = 22°37'$$

Example   Find the measure of the hypotenuse $\overline{RT}$ of the right triangle RST of Fig. 9–27.

$$\cos 62°15' = \frac{0.8562}{d} \qquad \text{or} \qquad d = \frac{0.8562}{\cos 62°15'}$$

The first problem is that of finding $\cos 62°15'$, and the angle is not listed as an entry in the table. This means that we have to interpolate between values for $62°$ and $63°$. In order to do this we must remember that the function value for the cosine of an angle decreases as the size of

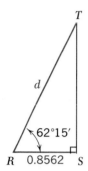

R 0.8562 S FIGURE 9–27

the angle increases. Since this is true, we shall have to *subtract* the interpolated value from that for the cos 62°. The auxiliary table is

$$
60'\left[\begin{array}{c} -63° \\ 15'\left[\begin{array}{c} -62°15' \\ \\ -62° \end{array}\right. \end{array}\right. \qquad \left.\begin{array}{c} 0.4540 \\ \\ 0.4695 \end{array}\right]x\right]0.0155
$$

$$\frac{x}{0.0155} = \frac{15'}{60'} = \frac{1}{4}$$

$$x = \frac{0.0155}{4} = 0.0039$$

$$\cos 62°15' = 0.4695 - 0.0039 = 0.4656$$

Therefore

$$d = \frac{0.8562}{0.4656} = 1.839 \qquad \text{correct to four significant figures}$$

Exercises

1   Given the two similar triangles ACB and RST illustrated on page 297. Find the measure of $\overline{AB}$ and $\overline{RS}$.

2   If the length of the shadow of a flagpole is 65 feet at the same time the length of a man's shadow is the same as his height, what is the height of the flagpole?

3   In order to measure the length of a lake, surveying instruments were used to set up the diagram of the figure on page 297. The angles ADP and BCP are right angles. Using the data of the figure, find the length of the lake.

In Exercises 4 to 15, prove the trigonometric identities for the acute angle A.

4   $\cos A \tan A \equiv \sin A$ 5 $\sin A \cot A \equiv \cos A$

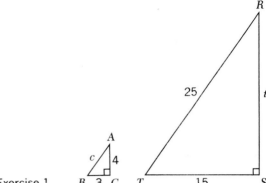

Exercise 1

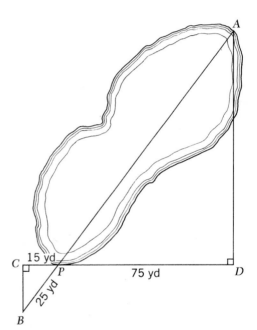

Exercise 3

6 $1 + \cot^2 A \equiv \dfrac{1}{\sin^2 A}$

7 $\tan^2 A + 1 \equiv \dfrac{1}{\cos^2 A}$

8 $\sin (90° - A) \equiv \cos A$
   $\cos (90° - A) \equiv \sin A$
   $\tan (90° - A) \equiv \cot A$
   $\cot (90° - A) \equiv \tan A$

9 $\sin A \equiv \sqrt{1 - \cos^2 A}$

10 $\cos^4 A - \sin^4 A \equiv 1 - 2 \sin^2 A$

11 $\dfrac{1 + \sin A}{\cos A} \equiv \dfrac{\cos A}{1 - \sin A}$

12 $\tan^4 A - 1 \equiv \dfrac{1 - 2 \cos^2 A}{\cos^4 A}$

13 $\dfrac{\sin^2 A}{1 + \cos A} \equiv 1 - \cos A$

14 $(\tan A - \cot A) \sin A \cos A + \cos^2 A \equiv \sin^2 A.$

15 $(\tan A + \cot A) \sin A \cos A - \sin^2 A \equiv \cos^2 A.$

16 Find each of these function values: sin 45°, tan 75°, cos 58°, cot 16°, sin 67°12′, cos 23°50′, tan 24°45′, cot 68°19′.

17 Find the measure of the angle A in each of these cases: sin A = 0.8090; cos A = 0.7771; tan A = 0.4040; cot A = 2.246.

18 Find the measure of the angle x correct to the nearest minute in each of these cases: sin x = 0.5540; cos x = 0.6556; tan x = 1.590; cot x = 0.6480.

19 To reach a bridge which is 35 feet above the level of the road an incline was started at a distance of 525 feet from the bridge. Correct to the nearest 10′, what was the angle at which the approach had to rise?

20 Find the height of a telephone pole if at a point 125 feet from the base of the pole the line of sight to the top of the pole is 21°30′.

21 A guy wire is to be run from a point 25.00 feet up on a pole to a point on the ground at a distance of 18.00 feet from the base of the pole. What angle will this guy wire make with the ground?

22 What will be the length of the guy wire of Exercise 21?

23 What is the measure of the central angle whose chord is 25.0 inches if the radius of the circle is 35.0 inches?

9–16   STATISTICAL MEASURES

Whether in the school, the community, business, or industry, it frequently is not only convenient but necessary to rely on certain established techniques for detecting, analyzing, and interpreting information from large masses of data. For example, it is much more convenient, and frequently gives much more significant information, to speak in terms of the mean test score of a large group of students than to try to think in terms of the scores of all the individual students. Such a set of *Distribution* measures or values of the same, or similar, things is called a *distribution*. The *mean*, as used here, is a *statistical measure of central tendency* of a distribution, or a score which indicates a central point about which all other scores are distributed. There are two other measures of central tendency, the *mode*, and the *median*. The distinctions between these three measures are clarified by the three following definitions and the accompanying example.

Mean   **Definition 9–3   The *mean* of a distribution is that term which results from dividing the sum of all the terms by the total number of terms.**

Definition 9-4   The *mode* of a distribution is that term which occurs   Mode
most frequently.

Definition 9-5   The *median* of a distribution is that term of such size   Median
that, of all the remaining terms, there are just as many greater as there
are smaller.

Example   Compute the mean, median, and mode for the distribution
of test scores given in Fig. 9–28.

1   The total number of scores is 35.   The total sum of all the terms
is 210.   Mean $= \dfrac{210}{35} = 6$.

2   There are 35 different scores.   The mid-score is therefore the
eighteenth one.   Starting with either the highest score, 10, or the lowest
score, 2, the median is 7.

3   There are two scores which occur with much more frequency
than any of the others.   For this reason this distribution is said to be
bimodal.   It has two modes: they are the scores 9 and 7.

A purely descriptive way of thinking about these three measures is:
1. *The mean is a computed measure.*   It is obtained by finding the
arithmetic average of all terms of the distribution.
2. *The median is a counted measure.*   It is obtained by merely arranging the terms in sequence of size and then counting from either
the largest or the smallest term to that one which is the middle term.
When there is an odd number of terms, as in the example, there is no
ambiguity as to which is the middle one.   When there is an even number of terms there exists an ambiguity as to what the middle term is,

FIGURE 9–28   Distribution of test scores.

SCORE	FREQUENCY	SUM OF TERMS
10	1	10
9	7	63
8	1	8
7	9	63
6	4	24
5	2	10
4	3	12
3	4	12
2	4	8
1	0	0
Total	35	210

Mean score $= \dfrac{210}{35} = 6$ Median score $= 7$ Mode $= 9$ and 7 since there are two instead of one.   If, in the example, the total number of scores were increased to 36 by adding 1 to the frequency of any score from 1 through 6, then such an ambiguity would exist.   The two middle terms would be the eighteenth and nineteenth.   Counting from the lowest score upward, the eighteenth score would be 6, and 7 would be the nineteenth.   Counting from the largest score downward, 7 would be the eighteenth and 6 the nineteenth.   In such cases as this an acceptable interpretation is to take the average of the two middle terms as the median.   In this modified example the median score would be 6.5.

If, in the example, the total frequency of 36 were brought about by increasing by 1 the frequency of any of the scores 7 through 10, both the eighteenth and nineteenth terms would be 7, counting from either end.   There would be no ambiguity in this case, and the median score would be 7.

3. *The mode is an observed measure.*   It is obtained by merely observing that it is the term of the distribution which occurs the greatest number of times.   There can be distributions of only one mode or of more than one, such as the bimodal distribution of the example.   While they seldom occur in distributions of any significant size, it is conceivable that there could be situations in which no mode exists.

Generally speaking, the mean is considered the best measure of central tendency to use for purposes of describing a distribution as a whole.   This is due to the fact that it is sensitive to any change whatsoever in the pattern of a distribution while the median and the mode are not.   This sensitivity, however, at times serves as a distinct disadvantage; in particular, this is true if the distribution is characterized by measures concentrated at one of the extremes.   This limitation is caused by the fact that one of the properties of the mean is that there is a balance between the distances of the scores from the mean.   This is illustrated in Fig. 9-29, where the distribution of the example has been repeated.   In this figure the column headed "Deviation" indicates how much each score deviates, or differs, from the mean score 6.   The deviation, or difference, for any given score is found in this manner: If the mean of the distribution is M, then the deviation d for any score S is given by $d = S - M$.   For example, the deviation which corresponds to 4 is -2 since $4 - 6 = -2$, and the deviation which corresponds to 9 is $+3$ since $9 - 6 = 3$.   Thus all scores smaller than 6 have a negative deviation and those larger than 6 have a positive deviation.   The column headed "Total Deviations" shows that the total of the negative deviations exactly balances the total of the positive deviations.   This property is one which is characteristic of the mean and not of either the median or the mode.

Each measure of central tendency performs a significantly intrinsic function.   As we have seen, the mean is sensitive to all characteristics of a distribution and makes a good measure to indicate the size of *all* terms of a set of data.   There are times when the better measure is the

Deviation

FIGURE 9-29   Computation of variance and standard deviation.

SCORE	FREQUENCY	DEVIATIONS (SCORE — MEAN)	TOTAL DEVIATIONS (FREQ. × DEVIATION)	SQUARES OF DEVIATIONS
10	1	+4	+4	16
9	7	+3	+21	441
8	1	+2	+2	4
7	9	+1	+9	81
6	4	0	+36	
5	2	−1	−2	4
4	3	−2	−6	36
3	4	−3	−12	144
2	4	−4	−16	256
1	0	−5	0	0
	35		−36	982

Mean score = 6

Variance = $\dfrac{982}{35}$ = 28.06

Standard deviation = $\sqrt{28.06}$ = 5.30

median, since it is not affected by extremes of the distribution.   For example, it would be a far better indicator of the salary status of a community composed entirely of salaried employees of a given large business or industrial company having only two or three highly salaried executives.   Also, there are times when the mode is the only measure of interest.   This would be the case if a retail merchant or a manufacturer were interested in the most popular model or product.   The mode would show the concentration of frequencies to indicate popularity.

In spite of the effectiveness of the mean for studying relative sizes of distribution of data, it has distinct limitations.   For example, a set of scores on the test of the previous example could be as follows:

{6,6,6,6,6,6,6,6,6,6}

In this case 10 students took the test and each student had a score of 6. The mean, as well as the median and mode, of this distribution is 6.   But the distribution has an element of concentration not possessed by the distribution of the example discussed.   It is quite evident that the *scatter*, or *variability*, of a set of scores carries as great significance in   · Variability characterizing a distribution as does its central tendency.   A much more intelligent comparison of two distinct distributions of scores can be obtained through combining an examination of their respective measures of variability with a study of their respective means.

The problem of determining a measure of the variability of a set of scores involves finding some number, determined from the scores, with these properties: (1) it should be independent of the mean of the distribution; (2) it should not be affected by the signs of the deviations from the mean; (3) it should be small when the scores are clustered closely together and large when they are widely scattered; and (4) it should be more sensitive to the intrinsic nature of the deviations than to their total frequency.

There are two related measures which meet these requirements and which serve, in combination with the mean, to give a rather complete picture of any distribution of scores. They are called *variance* and *standard deviation*.

Variance **Definition 9-6**   The *variance* of a distribution is the quotient of the sum of the squares of the deviations from the mean divided by the total frequency.

Standard deviation **Definition 9-7**   The *standard deviation* of a distribution is the positive square root of the variance.

Either of these two measures can be used to describe the variability of a distribution. No effectiveness is lost or gained in choosing one over the other. It should be evident that when one is small the other is small, and when one is large the other is large. The symbol for the variance is σ^2 (read "sigma squared"), and for the standard deviation it is σ ("sigma"). The standard deviation possesses certain mathematical properties not possessed by the variance, but these are of no concern to this discussion. It is of significance here to see just how these measures meet the four conditions previously specified: (1) they are independent of the mean since their computation uses only the deviations from the mean and in no way involves the mean; (2) they are not affected by the signs of the deviations since each deviation is squared; (3) they are affected by the scatter of the scores since the squares of large deviations will be large and the squares of small deviations will be small; and (4) they are more sensitive to the intrinsic nature of the deviations than to their total frequency since this is a fundamental characteristic of the mean of a set of measures.

The computation and use of these two measures of variability are illustrated in the next example.

Example   Compute the mean, variance, and standard deviation for the data of Figs. 9–29 and 9–30.

Note that the total frequency and the mean of the two distributions are exactly the same. In Fig. 9–30, however, the scores are clustered more closely about the mean than are those of Fig. 9–29. This fact is reflected in the smaller variance and standard deviation of this distribu-

FIGURE 9–30   Computation of variance and standard deviation.

SCORE	FREQUENCY	DEVIATION (SCORE − MEAN)	TOTAL DEVIATIONS (FREQ. × DEVIATION)	SQUARES OF DEVIATIONS
10	0	+4	0	0
9	0	+3	0	0
8	5	+2	+10	100
7	9	+1	+9	81
6	10	0	+19	
5	5	−1	−5	25
4	4	−2	−8	64
3	2	−3	−6	36
2	0	−4	0	0
1	0	−5	0	0
	35		−19	306

Mean score = 6

Variance = $\dfrac{306}{35}$ = 8.74

Standard deviation = $\sqrt{8.74}$ = 2.96

tion as compared with the same measures of the other, as shown in this summary.

	Figure 9–29	*Figure 9–30*
Mean	*6*	*6*
Variance	28.06	8.74
Standard deviation	5.30	2.96

When the mean and variance or standard deviation for a given distribution are known, we have two very effective measures for comparing the distribution with any other similar distributions.

Exercises

Compute the three measures of central tendency for the distributions in Exercises 1 to 3.

1 36, 33, 38, 48, 46, 35, 44, 37, 42, 34, 41, 47, 32, 45, 40, 39, 43
2 3, 4, 5, 5, 5, 9, 8, 7, 7, 4, 5, 5, 6, 7, 7, 7, 8, 3, 6, 5, 5, 7, 6, 8, 7, 5, 5, 7, 6, 5, 9
   Hint: First make a frequency distribution similar to that of Fig. 9–28.

3 *Score*	*Frequency*	*Score*	*Frequency*
110	2	96	17
108	1	94	8
106	4	92	4
104	4	90	5
102	4	88	2
100	6	86	3
98	8		

4   In each of the Exercises 1, 2, and 3, show that the total of all negative deviations from the mean is the same as the total of all positive deviations.

5   Find the variance and standard deviation of each of the distributions of Exercises 1 to 3.

6   The mean of one set of IQ scores is 98 with a standard deviation of 6, and the mean of a second set is 110 with a standard deviation of 15.   How do the two distributions compare?

7   If you are told that the mean of a set of scores is 10 and the variance is 0, what can you say about the scores?

INVITATIONS TO EXTENDED STUDY

1   Make a catalog of those uses of number which give rise to approximate numbers rather than exact numbers.

2   Make a catalog of primitive units of measure along with their limitations.

3   Make a comparative study of the characteristic properties of measurement as practiced in selected leading countries of the world.

4   Make a study of the historical background of the various standard units of measure.

Prove these three trigonometric identities.

5   $\dfrac{\sin^3 A + \cos^3 A}{\sin A + \cos A} \equiv 1 - \sin A \cos A$

6   $\sin A(1 - \tan^2 A)\left(\dfrac{1}{\cos A - \sin A} + \dfrac{1}{\cos A + \sin A}\right) \equiv 2 \tan A$

7   $\dfrac{\sin A \cos A}{\sin^2 A - \cos^2 A} \equiv \dfrac{\tan A}{\tan^2 A - 1}$

8   Show that in any acute-angle triangle ABC

$$\dfrac{a}{\sin A} = \dfrac{b}{\sin B} = \dfrac{c}{\sin C}$$

where a, b, and c are the sides opposite the respective angles A, B, and C.

9   Extend the definitions of the trigonometric functions of angles to those of the second, third, and fourth quadrants.

10   Extend the definitions of the trigonometric functions of angles to negative angles.

11   Look up the use of the *radian*, *mil*, and *grad* as units of angle measure.

12   Investigate the use of *percentiles* and *percentile ranks* to describe the position of a term in a distribution.

13   Investigate the use of *quartiles* and *deciles* to describe the position of a term in a distribution.

14   Investigate the use of the concepts of *range* and *class interval* in the construction of a frequency distribution.

15   Investigate the use of the class interval and the *guessed mean* in computing the mean, variance, and standard deviation of a given distribution.

the concepts of relation and function

GUIDELINES FOR CAREFUL STUDY

In the early chapters of this book we were concerned with the concept of number and with sets of numbers. Operations were defined, and basic postulates became the laws to govern the use of these operations on certain specified sets of elements comprising different number systems. Within each system, in addition to other properties derivable from those postulated, certain fundamental relations were discovered to exist. Such relations as equal, greater than, and less than, each identifiable by certain intrinsic characteristics, were used to establish a correspondence which compared one number or a set of numbers with another number or set of numbers.

Similarly, in Chaps. 8 and 9, points and sets of points, identified as various types of geometric configurations, were compared by means of such relations as concurrency, collinearity, coplanarity, congruency, and similarity as well as longer than, shorter than, larger than, and smaller than. These relations were discovered to be of great significance in the contemplation of position, shape, and size.

Not only is the concept of relation fundamental to the intelligent study of the structure of number systems and geometric configurations; it is indeed a cornerstone of all mathematical endeavor, whether elementary or advanced. It is the purpose of this chapter to examine this concept more closely and under cloak of greater generality. We shall be particularly interested in a specific type of relation that is called *function,* and in its tremendous importance in elementary mathematics.

The following questions will serve as helpful guidelines to careful study of Chap. 10.

1   What are the properties of equality?
2   What is the law of trichotomy?
3   What is meant by the union and intersection of two sets?
4   What is meant by the concepts of concurrency, collinearity, and coplanarity?
5   When are two geometric configurations said to be congruent? Similar?
6   What is a cartesian (rectangular) frame of reference?
7   What is the number line?
8   What is a number field?
9   What is a numeral?
10   What is a constant? A variable? A parameter?
11   What is an ordered pair?
12   What is a relation? A function?
13   What are the domain and range of a relation or function?
14   What is the meaning of the symbol $f(x)$?
15   What is the formula for the linear function, and why is it called the linear function?
16   What is meant by the slope of a straight line?
17   What are the different forms for the equation of a straight line?
18   What is meant by a zero of a function?
19   What is a system of equations? What is its solution set?
20   What is meant by a consistent system of equations?
21   Why is an inequality of the form $y > ax + b$ not a function?
22   What is meant by a strict inequality? A mixed inequality?
23   What is meant by direct variation? Inverse variation? Joint variation?
24   What is a constant of variation?
25   What is a statistical graph?
26   What are the different types of statistical graph and what are some of their distinguishing characteristics?
27   What parts do intuition, induction, and deduction play in an intelligent approach to problem solving?

INTRODUCTION

The relations emphasized in the previous chapters are those which can
be classified as relations of *conjunction, equivalence,* or *order. Union*
and *intersection* relate the elements of two or more sets; *concurrency*
relates lines, planes, or lines and planes which have a point in common; *collinearity* relates points, planes, or points and planes which have
a line in common; and *coplanarity* relates points, lines, or points and
lines which have a plane in common. *Equality, congruence,* and
similarity have in common the three *characteristic properties of
equivalence* (Fig. 10–1). The inequality relations *greater than* ($>$)
and *less than* ($<$) do not satisfy the reflexive and symmetric properties.
They do, however, satisfy the transitive property, and, through this
property, they serve to order the natural numbers and the integers as
well as the numbers of either the field of rational numbers or the field
of real numbers. They order the points on the number line, and, since
positive real numbers serve as measures of size, these two relations also
order geometric configurations when comparisons of size are made.

It now becomes desirable to examine the general concept of relation,
which lends great power and facility to mathematical investigation.
The previously discussed relations will be seen to be special cases of this
more general concept. In actuality our principal concern will be with
the concept of *function*, a particular type of relation, but one that has
sufficient generality to be of great significance in the study of
mathematics.

10–1   VARIABLE AND CONSTANT

The concepts of *variable* and *constant* are fundamental to any discussion of relation and function. In Chap. 3 the letter n was used to represent a natural number, that is, it was used to represent any element of

FIGURE 10–1

PROPERTIES OF EQUIVALENCE	ILLUSTRATION
1 *Reflexive:* $a = a$	1 5 dollars = 5 dollars
2 *Symmetric:* If $a = b$, then $b = a$.	2 If 5 dollars = 10 half-dollars, then 10 half-dollars = 5 dollars.
3 *Transitive:* If $a = b$ and $b = c$, then $a = c$.	3 If 5 dollars = 10 half-dollars and 10 half-dollars = 500 pennies, then 5 dollars = 500 pennies.

the set of natural numbers $N = \{1,2,3,4, \ldots \}$.   In Chap. 4 the letter i was used to represent any element of the set of integers

$$Z = \{0, \pm 1, \pm 2, \pm 3, \ldots \}$$

and in Chap. 5 the letter q was used to represent any number of the form $\frac{a}{b}$ where a and b are integers and $b \neq 0$, that is, any element of the set of all rational numbers.   The letters n, i, and q thus were used as symbols to represent any element of a set of elements.   They were, therefore, used as *variables* in accordance with this definition.

Definition 10-1   **A *variable* is a symbol used to represent any arbitrary element of a given set containing two or more elements.   The set is called the *domain* or *replacement set*, of the variable.** Variable and its domain

If the replacement set for a symbol contains only one element, then the symbol is called a *constant*.   The numeral 2 is a symbol which repre- Constant sents the quantitative characterization of each of the following sets: the eyes of a normal person, the hands of a normal person, the feet of a normal person, the half-dollars in a dollar, the nickels in a dime.   Since the replacement set for this symbol contains only one element, it is a constant.   The Greek letter π (pi) is a symbol used to represent any element of a set of ratios, each that of the circumference of any given circle to its respective diameter.   Since it can be proved that these ratios are all equal, the set contains one and only one element and, therefore, the symbol is a constant.   Attention has been called previously to the fact that this constant ratio is an irrational number and cannot be expressed as the quotient of two integers, or as a finite decimal, or as an infinite repeating decimal.†   For computational purposes the best that can be done is to use rational approximations which conform to the specifications of other data in any given problem situation.

Frequently in working with formulas and, in particular, with equations a variable is called an *unknown*.   This is fairly common in courses in elementary algebra.   There is still another use of symbols in this context which is of importance.   It is, in fact, something of a hybrid of the concepts of constant and variable.   Consider, for example, the familiar formula $d = rt$, which gives the distance traveled in any given amount of time at any specified rate.   In this formula each of the symbols d, r, and t is a variable.   The symbol d represents any element of a set of numbers used as measures of distance; r represents any element from a set of measures of rate or speed of travel; and t represents any element from a set of measures of time.   Let us change the emphasis slightly and set the formula in the context to give the distance traveled at a *constant rate of speed* in a given time.   In this interpretation we have not

† See Sec. 6–2.

changed the character of representation for the symbols d and t—they still are variables with the same domains as specified previously—but we have changed the character of representation for r. It is now used to represent a constant rate of speed. It is a constant representing one fixed value. But what fixed value is it? The formula may be used to find the distance traveled in any given time at 40 miles per hour, 50 miles per hour, 186,000 miles per second, or any arbitrary speed one might choose to use. Such a symbol is called an *arbitrary constant,* or a *parameter.* In other words, a parameter is a symbol which, by its arbitrary selection, characterizes an existing relationship between the variables of a given discussion. Attention will be called in subsequent pages to other specific occurrences of the use of parameters.

Arbitrary constant (parameter)

10–2   RELATION AND FUNCTION

In Sec. 4–3 attention was called to the fact that the definition of "positive integers" is such as to establish a one-to-one correspondence between the set of all positive integers and the set of all natural numbers. The definition thus sets up a relation that exists between these two sets such that to a given natural number there corresponds one and only one positive integer. Later it was established that Theorem 8–13 can be used to set up a relation of similarity between a triangle such as $\triangle ABC$ of Fig. 10–2 and any triangle which has two of its angles respectively congruent to two of the angles of $\triangle ABC$. This is a one-to-many correspondence, since there exist many distinct triangles which meet the conditions of the theorem. Triangles DEF, DLM, and DRS of Fig. 10–2 are three such triangles. Similarly, any one of the three postulates 8–12 to 8–14 can be used to establish a one-to-many correspondence of congruency with $\triangle ABC$.

The three relations described here, though quite distinct in nature, have one very basic characteristic in common, namely, each relation sets up a correspondence between an element of one set and one or more elements of a second set. If, in the first example, we use the symbol p as a variable to represent any element of the set of all positive integers, then the relation may be symbolized by the set of pairs of ele-

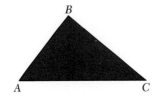
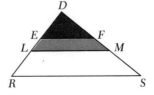

FIGURE 10–2   Similarity of triangles.

n	p
1	$+1$
2	$+2$
3	$+3$
4	$+4$
5	$+5$
6	$+6$
7	$+7$

FIGURE 10–3   Selected values for $p = +n$.

ments $\{(n,p)\,|\,p = +n$ and n is a natural number$\}$. The relation is thus seen to be one of equality. Similarly, if t is used to represent $\triangle ABC$, each of the other two relations also may be represented by a set of pairs of elements. The relation of similarity may be expressed in the form $\{(t,s)\,|\,s \sim t$ and t is a triangle$\}$, and the relation of congruency in the form $\{(t,c)\,|\,c \cong t$ and t is a triangle$\}$. In each set selector the respective relation is described by its appropriate formula.

Whether the relation was established by verbal description, as in the first paragraph of this section, or by formula, as in the second paragraph, it is true in each case that two sets of elements are involved. This is the essential common characteristic that makes it possible to give a clear-cut definition of the concept of relation as used in mathematics. Before attempting the definition, however, it is desirable to clarify the language and symbolism used.

A symbol of the form (x,y) is called an *ordered pair* simply because a pair of symbols x and y is used and one of them, x, is written first and the other, y, is written second. Thus (x,y) is a symbol for a set of ordered pairs in which x is the *first element* and y is the *second element*. For example, the symbol (n,p) of the preceding illustration represents the set of all ordered pairs of which the first element, n, is a natural number and the second element, p, is a positive integer. We shall list a few selected members of this set of ordered pairs:

Ordered pair

$$\{(1,+1),(2,+2),(3,+3),(4,+4), \dots \}$$

In this relation, to each first element there corresponds one and only one second element. This correspondence is also shown very explicitly by the table of values of Fig. 10–3, in which a few selected values are paired.

The relations of similarity and congruence of the previous paragraphs do not lend themselves very well to table representation. A simple illustration, which has their common characteristic of a one-to-many correspondence yet does submit to table representation, is that of the relation "is the square root of." This relation may be expressed as the ordered pair of real numbers (x,y) where x is any positive real number, y represents the elements of the set of all real numbers, and the formula defining the relation between x and y is $y = \pm\sqrt{x}$. A few selected elements from this set of ordered pairs are $(0,0)$, $(1,+1)$, $(1,-1)$, $(2,+\sqrt{2})$, $(2,-\sqrt{2})$, $\left(\frac{64}{9}, +\frac{8}{3}\right)$, $\left(\frac{64}{9}, -\frac{8}{3}\right)$, $(9,+3)$, $(9,-3)$. Here again this correspondence is expressed very clearly in the table of selected values of Fig. 10–4. The symbol $(x, \pm\sqrt{x})$ might be used to represent this same set of ordered pairs.

Whether the correspondence is one-to-one or one-to-many, a relation is clearly and explicitly characterized by a set of ordered pairs.

Relation, its domain and range

Definition 10-2   A *relation* is a set of ordered pairs in which there is associated with each first element at least one second element. The set of all possible first elements is called the *domain* of the relation, and the set of all possible second elements is called the *range.*

In the symbol (x,y) representing a set of ordered pairs, the variable x representing elements from the domain of the relation is called the *independent variable;* the variable y representing elements from the range is called the *dependent variable.* Thus in the relation (x,y) described by the formula $y = \pm\sqrt{x}$, the independent variable x represents any element to be selected from the domain of the relation, the set of all positive real numbers; and the dependent variable y represents any element from the range of the relation, the set of all real numbers. Similarly, in the relation (n,p) described by the formula $p = +n$, the independent variable n selects elements from the domain of the relation, the set of all natural numbers; and the dependent variable p selects elements from the range of the relation, the set of all positive integers.

Dependent and independent variables

Each of the relations represented by the respective symbols (n,p) and (x,y) has been depicted by verbal description, formula, ordered pairs, and a table of values. Another very helpful technique for portraying the distinctive characteristics of any particular relation is the graph. Figure 10–5 presents the graph of each of the relations (n,p) and (x,y) of the present discussion. Each graph is an incomplete graph, since only a few of the related pairs are pictured. Since the domain and range of each relation are both infinite sets of points, it is impossible to

x	y
0	0
1	± 1
2	$\pm\sqrt{2}$
4	± 2
$\dfrac{64}{9}$	$\pm\dfrac{8}{3}$
9	± 3

FIGURE 10-4   Selected values for $y = \pm\sqrt{x}$.

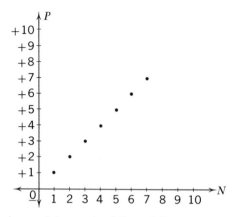

Incomplete graph of the relation $p = +n$ whose domain is the set of all natural numbers and range is the set of all positive integers

(a)

Incomplete graph of the relation $y = \pm\sqrt{x}$ whose domain is the set of all positive real numbers and range is the set of all real numbers

(b)

FIGURE 10-5

draw a complete graph in either case. The graph of $p = +n$ (Fig. 10-5a) consists only of a set of discrete points. This is due to the fact that each variable can be replaced only by integral values. No fractions or irrational numbers can be used. The graph of $y = \pm\sqrt{x}$ (Fig. 10-5b) is a curve with no breaks in it. There are points whose coordinates involve fractions, such as $C\left(\frac{64}{9}, \frac{8}{3}\right)$ and $D\left(\frac{64}{9}, -\frac{8}{3}\right)$, and irrational numbers, such as $A(2, \sqrt{2})$ and $B(2, -\sqrt{2})$, as well as the points whose coordinates are ordered pairs of integers, $(0,0)$, $(1, -1)$, $(4,2)$, $(4, -2)$, $(9,3)$ and $(9, -3)$. It can be proved that, for any arbitrarily selected positive real number, there exists in the field of real numbers two numbers, equal numerically but opposite in sign, each of which when squared will give the arbitrarily selected number. This is illustrated graphically in Fig. 10-5b by the fact that if, at any arbitrarily selected point on the x axis, a line is drawn perpendicular to the x axis, it will cut the graph of the curve $y = \pm\sqrt{x}$ in two points, each of which represents a square root of the real number identified with the point. In Fig. 10-5b, let $P(5,0)$ represent the arbitrary point on the positive x axis; then the two points on the curve determined by the line perpendicular to $\overrightarrow{OX}$ at P are L, which is the point $(5, \sqrt{5})$, and M, which is the point $(5, -\sqrt{5})$. The line segments $\overline{PL}$ and $\overline{PM}$ are congruent segments whose common length is $\sqrt{5}$ units. Since this construction is possible whatever position the point P takes on the positive x axis, the graph of the relation $y = \pm\sqrt{x}$ has no breaks in it and is thus said to be a *continuous curve*. This particular curve is called a *parabola*.

Continuous curve

Before proceeding further it will be well to recall the techniques for location of points in the plane. In Fig. 10–5a the axes of the rectangular frame of reference are lettered O,N and O,P. The use of the letters N and P in place of X and Y is to aid in the association of symbols. The values of the independent variable n in the relation (n,p) will be selected from the N axis, or $\overrightarrow{ON}$, and the values for the dependent variable p will then be found on the P axis, or $\overrightarrow{OP}$. The point $(1, +1)$ is then located by moving one unit from the origin O in the positive direction along $\overrightarrow{ON}$ and then one unit in the positive direction along a line through the point $(1,0)$ and parallel to $\overrightarrow{OP}$. The remaining points of this graph are located in this fashion and, when marked, they constitute the incomplete graph of the relation, as indicated previously. In plotting the incomplete graph of $y = \pm\sqrt{x}$ we keep in mind that each axis is a real number line. This means that for any real number there is a point on the line, and, conversely, to any point marked on the line there corresponds a real number. We thus select a few values at random from the domain of the relation and then determine the corresponding values from the range. The table of Fig. 10–4 presents such a set of pairs of values. These are then used to plot points which are points of the relation. Since the curve is known to have no breaks in it, we then proceed to draw a smooth curve through the selected points. For a curve such as the parabola of Fig. 10–5b the mere plotting of points is a rather crude technique. The best we can hope to get by doing so is a general idea of what the curve looks like. More advanced mathematics provides more refined techniques for getting better pictures of any such curve.

Up to this point of our discussion the similarities of the two relations (n,p), where $p = +n$, and (x,y), where $y = \pm\sqrt{x}$, have been emphasized. They both can be depicted by verbal description, formula, ordered pairs, table of values, and graph. Secondly, both are characterized by a clearly delineated domain and range from which values are selected by an independent variable and a dependent variable, respectively. Thirdly, both can be represented by an ordered pair of variables, one of which, for convenience, may be called the first element and the other the second element. In spite of all these very important characteristics of similarity, the two relations possess one characteristic of dissimilarity which is of great significance. This distinguishing characteristic is most vividly portrayed by the formula, the table of values, or the graph. From the graphs of Fig. 10–5 it should be quite evident that the relation (x,y), where $y = \pm\sqrt{x}$, is such that to each value of the first element, or independent variable, there correspond *more than one* value for the second element, or dependent variable. On the other hand, the relation (n,p), where $p = +n$, is such that to each value of the first element there corresponds *one and only one* value of the second element. This is the important element of dissimilarity between the two relations.   All relations which have in common with (n,p) this important characteristic are called *functions* in accordance with this definition.

Definition 10-3 A *function* is a relation such that to each first element there corresponds one and only one value of the second element. The set of all possible first elements is called the *domain* of the function, and the set of all possible second elements the *range*.

Function, its domain and range

To put it another way and further clarify this definition, we can describe a function as a set of ordered pairs for which the formula or rule defining the relation is such that, when a value is assigned to the first element of the ordered pair, there is absolutely no doubt whatsoever as to what the value is that should be assigned to the second element.

Example   Consider these four sets of ordered pairs.   Which represent functions?

   1 $\{(1,2), (1,3), (1,4), (2,5), (2,6), (3,7)\}$
   2 $\{(3,1), (4,1), (5,2), (6,2)\}$
   3 $\{(1,3), (2,3), (3,3), (4,3), (5,3)\}$
   4 $\{(1,2), (2,5), (3,4), (4,6), (5,7)\}$

Set 1 of ordered pairs represents a relation which is not a function, since to the first element 1 there correspond three values of the second element, namely, 2, 3, and 4.   To the first element 2 there correspond the two values 5 and 6.

Each of the three remaining sets of ordered pairs is a function since to each first element in each set there corresponds one and only one second element.   This means that once a value is selected for a first element, there is absolutely no ambiguity as to what value of the second element is to be associated with it.   It is immaterial that, in illustrations 2 and 3, the same value of the second element is associated with more than one value of the first element.   This is not involved in the criterion which singles out and identifies a relation as being a function.   It bears repeating that the criterion of distinction is that to each value of the first element selected from the domain of the relation, there corresponds one and only one value for the second element, selected from the range.

The complete graph of each of these relations, as shown in Fig. 10–6, supports the statement made about each particular relation in the preceding paragraph.

Because of its tremendous importance in mathematical thought, mathematicians have devised special symbols to represent a function. The fact that there are different symbols is not disturbing, since they connote the same basic idea.   The differences are merely due to a desire to underscore clarification for a particular context being studied or in-

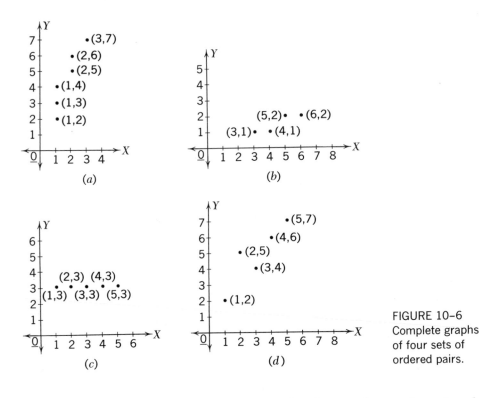

FIGURE 10-6
Complete graphs
of four sets of
ordered pairs.

vestigated.   The simplest and, by far, the most frequently used symbol in elementary mathematics is $f(x)$, which is read "function of x" or "function at x."   The second of these two translations is possibly the more accurate of the two in the meaning it carries.

Example   The relation "increased by one" is a function which may be represented by the symbol $\{[x,f(x)]$ where $f(x) = x + 1\}$.   If the domain is the set of all real numbers, the range is also the set of all real numbers.   The incomplete graph of the function is that shown in Fig. 10-7.   The symbol for the value of $f(x)$ at 0 is $f(0)$, and it is found by replacing x by 0 in the formula $f(x) = x + 1$, whence $f(0) = 1$. Similarly, the value of the function at $x = 3$ is 4, $f(3) = 3 + 1 = 4$; $f(5) = 5 + 1 = 6$; $f(-4) = -4 + 1 = -3$; continuing in this fashion, the value of the function at $x = a$ is $f(a) = a + 1$.

The graph of $f(x) = x + 1$ is known to be a straight line.   It is continuous since there are no breaks in it.   It can be obtained by constructing a table of values such as those of Figs. 10-3 and 10-4, plotting the points determined by the associated values, and then drawing a smooth curve through these points.   However, Postulate 8-1 provides us with a much more refined technique for getting an accurate picture of the graph.   Since "for any two distinct points in space there exists one and only one straight line which contains these two points," it follows that

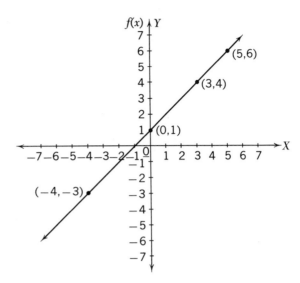

FIGURE 10–7   Incomplete graph
of $f(x) = x + 1$.

if we plot any two points, such as $(0,1)$ and $(3,4)$, which are determined
by the function, the straight line which is the graph of the function may
be drawn by fitting a straightedge to these two points and then drawing
the line along its edge.

Exercises

1   Verify the statement that equality, congruency, and similarity are
equivalence relations.
2   Why are concurrency, collinearity, and coplanarity not equivalence relations?
3   Distinguish between the concepts of constant, variable, and
parameter.
4   Distinguish between the concepts of relation and function.
5   What is meant by the domain and range of a relation or function?
6   Which of the following are equivalence relations?   Give reasons
to support your answer in each case.

(a) "Is less than or equal to" applied to numbers
(b) "Is as tall as" applied to people
(c) "Is shorter than" applied to distances
(d) "Is an ancestor of" applied to people
(e) "Is the square of" applied to numbers
(f) "Has the same area as" applied to geometric figures
(g) "Was born in the same town as" applied to people
(h) "Is a factor of" applied to positive integers

(i) "Is the supplement of" applied to plane angles
(j) "Has the same shape as" applied to geometric figures
(k) "Is perpendicular to" applied to straight lines in a plane
(l) "Is not equal to" applied to natural numbers
(m) "Has the same length as" applied to straight line segments

7   Which of these sets are functions?

(a) $\{(x,2x)\,|\,x$ is a positive integer$\}$
(b) $\{(x, x + 3)\,|\,x$ is a positive integer$\}$
(c) $\{(x,\sqrt{2x^2})\,|\,x$ is a real number$\}$
(d) $\{(x,\pm\sqrt{2x})\,|\,x$ is a positive real number$\}$
(e) $\{(x, 2x + 5)\,|\,x$ is an integer$\}$
(f) $\{(x, 2x \pm 3)\,|\,x$ is a real number$\}$

(g) $\left\{\left(x,\dfrac{1}{x}\right)\,\middle|\,x$ is a negative real number$\right\}$

8   What are the domain and range of each relation of Exercise 7?
9   Complete the expression $f(x) =$ _____ for each function of Exercise 7.
10 For each relation of Exercise 7, list 10 ordered pairs which are members of the set describing the relation.
11 For each relation of Exercise 7, construct a table of values associated with it.
12 Draw an incomplete graph to represent the relations of Exercise 7a to c.
13 Explain how the symbol k in each of these formulas may be considered to be a parameter:

(a) $y = x + k$ (b) $y = kx$ (c) $y = \dfrac{k}{x}$

14 Write a formula representing a function and illustrating the concepts of constant, parameter, dependent variable, and independent variable.
15 Given the set $S = \{0,1,2,3,4,5,6,7,8,9\}$. In each of the exercises select a dependent variable and an independent variable, then write the formula which expresses the relation involving the stated operation on each element of the set S:

(a) Multiplied by 3
(b) Divided by 5
(c) Increased by 4
(d) Decreased by 1
(e) Multiplied by $\dfrac{1}{2}$
(f) Multiplied by 2 and this product decreased by 1

(g) Decreased by 1 and this difference multiplied by 2
(h) Divided by 3 and this quotient increased by 4
(i)   Increased by 4 and this sum divided by 3

16   Write the set of ordered pairs for each relation of Exercise 15.
17   Are any of the relations of Exercise 15 also functions? Why?
18   Construct tables of paired values which represent each relation
of Exercise 15.
19   How can the sets of ordered pairs or the table of values help in
deciding whether a given relation is also a function?
20   Use the tables of values of Exercise 18 to draw the graph of each
relation of Exercise 15.
21   Are the graphs of Exercise 20 complete graphs or incomplete
graphs?
22   How can the graph of a relation help in deciding whether a given
relation is also a function?
23   Which of the graphs on page 320 are graphs of functions?   Explain your decision for each relation.
24   Select a set of ordered pairs which belong to the graph of each
relation of Exercise 23.
25   If each graph of Exercise 23 is considered as a complete graph,
what are the domain and range of each relation?   The presence of
dots at the ends of line segments or curves indicates whether or not
the point is on the graph.
26   Construct a table of values associated with the graph of each relation of Exercise 23.
27   Write a formula which expresses each of these relations:

(a) The distance an automobile will travel in a given time if it
travels at an average speed of 40 miles per hour
(b) The simple interest at 6% for one year on a given principal
(c) A salesman's monthly salary if he is paid $250 a month plus a
5% commission on all sales for the month
(d) The cost of gasoline at 30 cents per gallon
(e) The circumference of a circle is 2π times the radius
(f) The area of a square in terms of its side
(g) The perimeter of a regular hexagon in terms of its side

28   Which, if any, of the relations of Exercise 27 are also functions?
29   Select a set of ordered pairs related to each relation of Exercise 27.
30   Construct a table of values for each relation of Exercise 27.
31   Indicate the dependent and independent variable for each relation
of Exercise 27.
32   Use the table of values of Exercise 30 as an aid in drawing an incomplete graph of each relation of Exercise 27.

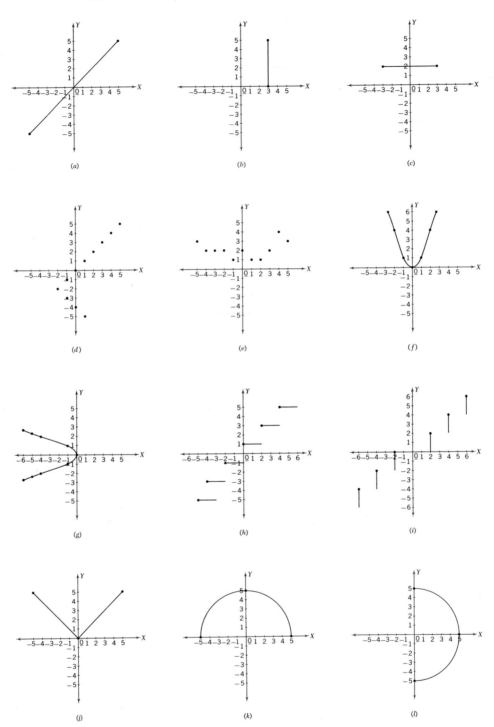

(a)   (b)   (c)

(d)   (e)   (f)

(g)   (h)   (i)

(j)   (k)   (l)

Exercise 23

10-3   THE LINEAR FUNCTION

An important function in elementary mathematics is the *linear func-* The function
tion, which is defined by a formula of the form $y = mx + k$

$$y = mx + k \qquad m \neq 0 \qquad\qquad (10\text{-}1)$$

or, to use the functional notation,

$$f(x) = mx + k \qquad m \neq 0 \qquad\qquad (10\text{-}2)$$

In either of these two forms x is the independent variable and y, from
(10-1), or $f(x)$, from (10-2), is the dependent variable. The symbols
m and k are parameters, or arbitrary constants. It can be proved that
the graph of such a function is always a straight line. We shall accept
this as a true statement and proceed to investigate the role that x and
y, as well as m and k, play in shaping this graph.

First, let us examine the part which x and y play by observing that
for any given linear function the symbol $\{(x,y)\}$ will represent the set
of ordered pairs defining the function. These ordered pairs are coordinates of points of the line which is the graph of the function. In
Fig. 10-8 the ordered pairs $(-3,-6)$, $(-1,-2)$, $(0,0)$, $(2,4)$, and $(4,8)$,
which are selected by the linear function $y = 2x$, are seen to be coordinates of points all of which lie on the line determined by any two of
them. If each of the several different forms of the linear functions
shown as labels of lines in Figs. 10-8, 10-10, and 10-11 are tested in

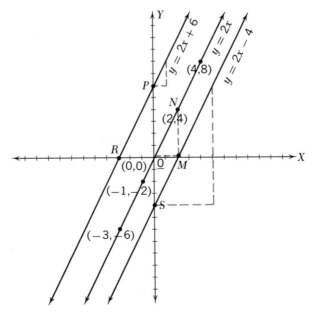

FIGURE 10-8

this same manner, it will be found that each function will select ordered pairs (x,y) as coordinates of points of the line associated with it. This statement should be verified by the reader. Thus we say that, in any linear function, the x and y represent the x coordinate and y coordinate, respectively, of any point of the straight line which is the graph of the particular function. A particular point of interest on the graph of a linear function is the point where it crosses the x axis. Since the y coor-

Zero of the
function
dinate of this point is 0, the x coordinate is called the *zero of the function*, or the x intercept of the graph.

Now, let us take a look at the parts m and k play in the formula. In Fig. 10–8 there are three lines, one representing the line $y = 2x$, another the line $y = 2x + 6$, and the third the line $y = 2x - 4$. Notice that, in each of these functions, the value of m is 2, while there is a different value for k in each equation. These lines are parallel lines. For the line $\overleftrightarrow{ON}$, which is the graph of the function $y = 2x$, count the number of units of length in the segment $\overline{OM}$ ($OM = 2$); now count the number of units of length in $\overline{MN}$ ($MN = 4$). The ratio $\dfrac{MN}{OM} = \dfrac{4}{2} = 2$. Repeat this experiment by starting at the points P and R on the line $\overleftrightarrow{RP}$, the graph of $y = 2x + 6$; then use the points S and M on the line $\overleftrightarrow{SM}$, the graph of $y = 2x - 4$. In each case the ratio which corresponds to $\dfrac{MN}{OM}$ should be 2. This ratio is a very important characteristic used in describing straight lines in the plane. It is called the *slope* of the line. In order to get a clearer picture of just what is meant by the slope of a straight line, we shall examine the line $\overleftrightarrow{ON}$ a bit more closely. This line can be described as the set of all ordered pairs (x,y) such that $y = 2x$ and x is a real number. This states that the domain of the given function is the set of all real numbers of the x axis and the range is the set of all real numbers of the y axis. From this fact it should be clear that, as the formula selects pairs of real numbers as coordinates of points of the line, for each change of one unit in the horizontal, or x coordinate there are two units of change in the vertical, or y coordinate. In other words, the ratio of the change in the y coordinate to the change in the x coordinate is constant and equal to 2. This describes what takes place in selecting coordinates of the points of any one of the three lines of Fig. 10–8 or any line parallel to them, as was verified by the experiment described previously in this paragraph.

It is well to raise at this point the question as to how one can proceed to find the slope of an arbitrary line. Consider the line s of Fig. 10–9, and let the points P_1 (read "P-one") and P_2 be any two arbitrarily selected points of the line. It is convenient to associate with P_1 and P_2, respectively, ordered pairs of coordinates (x_1,y_1) and (x_2,y_2). The line segment $\overline{P_1M}$ is drawn parallel to the x axis, and the line segment $\overline{MP_2}$

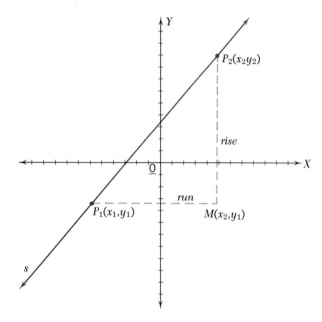

FIGURE 10–9

is parallel to the y axis. It thus follows that the coordinates of M are (x_2,y_1). The change in the x coordinate in going from P_1 to P_2 is represented in the figure by the horizontal line segment $\overline{P_1M}$, which is the *run* of the line segment $\overline{P_1P_2}$ and may be expressed as $x_2 - x_1$. The change in the y coordinate is represented by the vertical line segment $\overline{MP_2}$, called the *rise* of the line segment $\overline{P_1P_2}$. This change in the y coordinate, or the rise, may be expressed as $y_2 - y_1$. The slope of the line is then given by

Slope of a line

$$m = \frac{\text{change in } y \text{ coordinate}}{\text{change in } x \text{ coordinate}} = \frac{\text{rise}}{\text{run}}$$

or

$$m = \frac{y_2 - y_1}{x_2 - x_1} \tag{10–3}$$

Since P_1 and P_2 were any two points of the line s, this formula gives the value of the slope of the line. In selecting two arbitrary points of a line in order to use formula (10–3), it is immaterial which is called P_1 and which is called P_2; the value of m will remain the same. The only thing to remember is this: after a y coordinate is selected for y_2 in the numerator of the formula, the x coordinate associated with it must be the x_2 of the denominator.

Example Use formula (10–3) to determine that 2 is the slope of line $\overleftrightarrow{ON}$ of Fig. 10–8.

The points (4,8) and (2,4) are two points of the line:

$$m = \frac{8 - 4}{4 - 2} = \frac{4}{2} = 2 \qquad \text{or} \qquad m = \frac{4 - 8}{2 - 4} = \frac{-4}{-2} = 2$$

Similarly, the points (4,8) and $(-3,-6)$ are two points of the line:

$$m = \frac{8 - (-6)}{4 - (-3)} = \frac{8 + 6}{4 + 3} = \frac{14}{7} = 2$$

or

$$m = \frac{(-6) - 8}{(-3) - 4} = \frac{(-6) + (-8)}{(-3) + (-4)} = \frac{-14}{-7} = 2$$

The words "run" and "rise" are convenient words to use in discussing the slopes of lines. If we always think of passing from one point to another along a line segment so that the run is positive, then, if the segment rises as in Figs. 10–8 and 10–9, the rise is also positive. If the segment falls, as in Fig. 10–10, then the rise is negative.

Example Use formula (10–3) to find the slope of each line of Fig. 10–10.

1   The points $(-2,8)$ and $(4,-4)$ are two points of the line $y = -2x + 4$.

$$m = \frac{8 - (-4)}{-2 - 4} = \frac{12}{-6} = -2$$

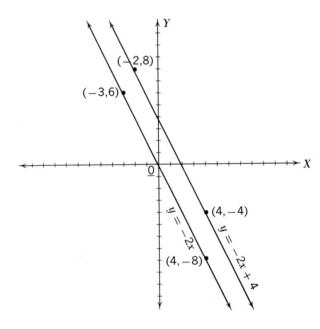

FIGURE 10–10

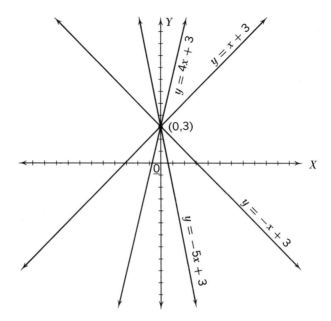

FIGURE 10–11

2   The points $(-3,6)$ and $(4,-8)$ are two points of the line $y = -2x$.

$$m = \frac{-8 - 6}{4 - (-3)} = \frac{-14}{7} = -2$$

If, in the linear function

$$y = mx + 3 \tag{10-4}$$

we assign x the value 0, then $y = 3$. This means that regardless of what value m has in formula (10–4), the graph of the function will be a line passing through the point (0,3). This is indicated in Fig. 10–11, where four lines are shown passing through the point (0,3): one with $m = 4$, one with $m = 1$, one with $m = -1$, and one with $m = -5$. The point (0,3) where these lines all cross the y axis is at a distance of 3 units along the y axis from the origin. The 3 of the formula thus indicates the length of that portion of the y axis *intercepted* between the point (0,3) and the origin. For this reason it is said to be the y *intercept* of the line which is the graph of the function. For example, the line of Fig. 10–11, which is the graph of the function $y = 4x + 3$, is a line whose slope is 4 and whose y intercept is 3 units since it passes through the point (0,3). The parameters m and k of the linear function represent the slope and y intercept, respectively, of the line which is the graph of the function. Indeed, the formula for the linear function is at times called *the slope-intercept form of the equation of a straight line*, since it is an equation whose graph is a straight line with slope m and whose y intercept is k units.

Slope-intercept equation

The lines of Fig. 10–11 also serve to illustrate a very important characteristic of the slope m of a line. When two lines with unequal slopes are compared, the steeper line is the one for which m has the larger numerical value, or absolute value (see Definition 6–1).

Example   In Fig. 10–11 the lines which are the respective graphs of the functions $y = x + 3$, $y = 4x + 3$, and $y = -5x + 3$ are lines which have unequal slopes. The slope of $y = 4x + 3$ is 4 and that of $y = x + 3$ is 1. Since $|4| > |1|$, the first of these two lines is the steeper line. Also since $|-5| > |4|$ and $|-5| > |1|$, it follows that the line which is the graph of $y = -5x + 3$ is the steepest line of the three.

On the other hand, the lines $y = x + 3$ and $y = -x + 3$ have unequal slopes—one being the negative of the other—but are of the same degree of steepness. This is because their slopes have the same numerical value since $|-1| = |1| = 1$. As a result of the fact that their slopes are opposite in sign, the two lines are sloped in different directions.

While the graph of a linear function is always a straight line, it must not be inferred that the equation associated with a straight line is necessarily in the form of a linear function. For example, in Fig. 10–12 the line l through the point (0,4) and parallel to the x axis is such that 4 is the unique value of the second element y to be associated with any arbitrarily chosen value of the first element x in the ordered pair (x,y)

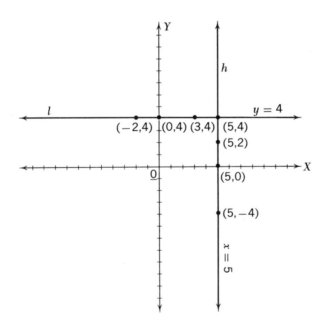

FIGURE 10–12

which represents any one of the ordered pairs serving as coordinates of points of the line. In fact, the symbol for the set of ordered pairs of this line can be written in better form as $\{(x,4)\}$. As indicated in the figure, the ordered pairs $(-2,4)$, $(0,4)$, $(3,4)$, and $(5,4)$ are coordinates of a few selected points of this line. It is obvious that, in changing from one point to another along this line, the vertical rise is always zero. To change from the point $(0,4)$ to the point $(3,4)$, for example, the rise is 0 and the run is 3. The slope of the line is thus given by $m = \dfrac{0}{3} = 0$.

Since y is 4 for any x, we say that the equation of this line is $y = 4$. Also, since for each value of x there is one and only one value of y, we say that the line l of Fig. 10–12 is the graph of the constant function $y = 4$. Similarly, the formula $y = k$, where k is a constant, represents the *constant function* (x,k). Although the graph of any constant function will be a straight line parallel to the x axis, the function cannot be considered as a special case of a linear function since its slope m is 0, while for a linear function $m \neq 0$. The constant function

The straight line h of Fig. 10–12 also demands particular attention. Since this line is parallel to the y axis, the values of x are the same for all points on the line. The formula $x = 5$ and the set of ordered pairs $\{(5,y)\}$ may be used to associate values of y with 5 in such a way as to get points on the line h. As indicated in the figure, the points $(5, -4)$, $(5,0)$, $(5,2)$, and $(5,4)$ are four points of the line. Thus we see that the formula $x = 5$, the set of ordered pairs $\{(5,y)\}$, and the line h are such that with the one value 5 of the first element x there are associated many values of the second element y in the symbol (x,y). It follows then that in this case a relation, and *not* a function, is defined. Furthermore, an examination of the figure should reveal the fact that, in changing from one point to another along this line, the run will always be zero. Since division by zero is undefined, we say that the slope of the graph of the relation $\{(5,y)\}$ is undefined. Similarly, the formula $x = c$, or the set of ordered pairs $\{(c,y)\}$, defines a relation whose graph is a line parallel to the y axis at a distance of c units from it and whose slope is undefined. The relation
$x = c$

10–4   THE LINEAR EQUATION

The equation

$$ax + by + c = 0 \tag{10–5}$$

is the equation of a straight line if both a and b are not zero. If both a and b were zero, the equation would take the form Equation of a straight line

$$0 \cdot x + 0 \cdot y + c = 0$$

from which it would follow that $c = 0$. This would mean that the co-ordinates of any point in the plane would satisfy the equation, and it would lose its significance. There are three cases to consider:

Case I $a \neq 0$ *and* $b = 0$ Under this hypothesis Eq. (10–5) becomes $ax + c = 0$, or $x = -\frac{c}{a}$. This is the equation of a line parallel to the y axis at a distance of $-\frac{c}{a}$ units from it. The set of points of this line is the set of ordered pairs represented by the symbol $\left\{\left(-\frac{c}{a}, y\right)\right\}$. A particular example of this case is represented in Fig. 10–12 by the line h whose equation is $x = 5$. If, in Eq. (10–5), we place $a = 1, b = 0$, and $c = -5$, it becomes the equation $x - 5 = 0$, or $x = 5$, in which $-\frac{c}{a} = 5$.

Case II $a = 0$ *and* $b \neq 0$ Under this hypothesis Eq. (10–5) becomes $by + c = 0$, or $y = -\frac{c}{b}$. This is the equation of a line parallel to the x axis at a distance of $-\frac{c}{b}$ units from it. The set of points of this line is the set of ordered pairs represented by the symbol $\left\{\left(x, -\frac{c}{b}\right)\right\}$, which is the symbol for the constant function. A particular example of this case is represented in Fig. 10–12 by the line l whose equation is $y = 4$. If, in Eq. (10–5), we place $a = 0, b = 1$, and $c = -4$, it becomes the equation $y - 4 = 0$, or $y = 4$, in which $-\frac{c}{b} = 4$.

Case III $a \neq 0$ *and* $b \neq 0$ Under this hypothesis, as in Case II, we may solve the equation for y, this time obtaining

$$y = -\frac{a}{b}x - \frac{c}{b}$$

This is in the form of the linear function where the slope $m = -\frac{a}{b}$ and the y intercept $k = -\frac{c}{b}$. From the discussion of Sec. 10–3 the graph of this function is known to be a straight line which passes through the point $\left(0, -\frac{c}{b}\right)$ and is not parallel to either axis. Particular examples of this case are the lines of Fig. 10–8 to 10–11. For example, for $a = 2$, $b = 1$, and $c = -4$, Eq. (10–5) becomes $2x + y - 4 = 0$ or $y = -2x + 4$, whose graph is shown in Fig. 10–10; for $a = 2, b = -1$, and $c = 0$, Eq. (10–5) becomes $2x - y = 0$ or $y = 2x$. Its graph is shown in Fig. 10–8.

If in formula (10–3) we consider the ordered pair (x_1, y_1) as the coordinates of a fixed point of a line of slope m and use the ordered pair (x, y) to represent any other point of the line, we obtain this form of the formula:

$$m = \frac{y - y_1}{x - x_1}$$

or, in better form,

$$y - y_1 = m(x - x_1) \tag{10–6}$$

This formula represents the equation of a straight line with given slope m and passing through the point (x_1, y_1). It is called *the point-slope form of the equation of a straight line.*

Point-slope equation

From Postulate 8–1 we know that for any two points in space, there exists one and only one line containing both of them. The equation of the line through the two points can be obtained by using formula (10–3) to determine the slope of the line and then using formula (10–6) with either point as the fixed point to determine the equation.

Example   Find the equation of the line: (1) with slope of $-\frac{1}{2}$ and passing through the point $(2, -3)$; (2) passing through the two points $(5, 6)$ and $(8, -1)$.

1   Since $m = -\frac{1}{2}$ and the given point is $(2, -3)$, we have upon substitution in formula (10–6)

$$y - (-3) = -\frac{1}{2}(x - 2)$$

or

$$y + 3 = -\frac{1}{2}x + 1$$

whence

$$x + 2y + 4 = 0$$

2   From formula (10–3),

$$m = \frac{6 - (-1)}{5 - 8} = \frac{6 + 1}{-3} = -\frac{7}{3}$$

From formula (10–6), using $(5, 6)$ as the fixed point and $-\frac{7}{3}$ as the slope, we get

$$y - 6 = -\frac{7}{3}(x - 5)$$

or

$$7x + 3y - 53 = 0$$

From formula (10–6), using $(8, -1)$ as the fixed point, we get

$$y - (-1) = -\frac{7}{3}(x - 8)$$

$$y + 1 = -\frac{7}{3}(x - 8)$$

$$7x + 3y - 53 = 0$$

Example   Given the equation $2x + 3y - 12 = 0$.   (1) What are the slope and the y intercept of the line which is the graph of this equation? (2) What is the x intercept of the line?

1   To find the slope and y intercept, change the equation into the form of the linear function.   This can be done by solving for y to get

$$y = -\frac{2}{3}x + 4$$

This line has a y intercept of 4 units and a slope of $-\frac{2}{3}$.   It goes through the point $(0,4)$.

2   To find the x intercept of a line, it is necessary to find where it crosses the x axis.   This can be accomplished by substituting $y = 0$ in the equation and then solving for x to get $x = 6$.   This line passes through the point $(6,0)$, and its x intercept is 6 units.

Example   The relation that exists between the set of odd integers and the set of all integers is a linear function.   What is the formula for this function if the odd integer 1 corresponds to the integer 0 and the odd integer -9 corresponds to the integer -5?

If we use the symbol o to represent an odd integer and i to represent any integer, we may write the linear function which relates o to i in the form

$$o = mi + k$$

We are given that o is 1 when i is 0.   From the formula we then have

$$1 = m0 + k$$

from which we get $k = 1$.

The relation between o and i may now be written as

$$o = mi + 1$$

Since $o = -9$ when $i = -5$, we have

$$-9 = m(-5) + 1$$
$$-9 = -5m + 1$$
$$5m = 10$$
$$m = 2$$

Therefore the linear function which relates the odd integers to all integers such that 1 corresponds to 0, and -9 to -5, is

$$o = 2n + 1$$

The set of ordered pairs of real numbers (x,y) which represent the coordinates of points of the graph of a linear equation in the two variables x and y is called the *solution set* of the equation.

The technique of finding ordered pairs which belong to the solution set of a given equation makes use of *equivalent equations*, which are equations that have the same solution set. For any given equation the coefficients will be real numbers, and for each variable the domain will be the set of all real numbers. Since this is true, we may use all the properties of real numbers in manipulating equations. This means that, in order to derive an equation equivalent to a given equation, we may:

Solution set of an equation

Equivalent equations

1   Add the same number to both members of an equation or subtract the same number from both members.

2   Multiply both members of an equation by the same nonzero number or divide both members by the same nonzero number.

These procedures have been used previously in this section and will be used throughout the chapter for the purpose of deriving equivalent equations.

Example

1   The equation $5x - 15 = 0$ is equivalent to the equation $x = 3$, since their common solution set is $\{3\}$. The derivation of the second equation from the first follows these steps:

$$5x - 15 = 0$$
$$(5x - 15) + 15 = 0 + 15$$
$$5x + [(-15) + 15] = 15$$
$$5x = 15$$
$$\frac{1}{5}(5x) = \frac{1}{5} \cdot 15$$
$$\left(\frac{1}{5} \cdot 5\right)x = 3$$
$$1 \cdot x = 3$$
$$x = 3$$

The reader should identify which properties from the field of real numbers are used.

2   In a previous example the equation $y = -\frac{2}{3}x + 4$ was used as an equation equivalent to $2x + 3y - 12 = 0$.

$$2x + 3y - 12 = 0$$
$$(2x + 3y - 12) + (-2x + 12) = 0 + (-2x + 12)$$
$$3y + [(2x - 12) + (-2x + 12)] = -2x + 12$$
$$3y = -2x + 12$$
$$\frac{1}{3}(3y) = \frac{1}{3}(-2x + 12)$$
$$y = -\frac{2}{3}x + 4$$

Again the reader should identify which properties from the field of real numbers are used.

Exercises

1   Write the formula for the linear function whose graph is described by each set of data.

(a) Has slope 3 and y intercept of 2

(b) Has slope $-\frac{1}{2}$ and passes through the point $(0,6)$

(c) Has slope $\frac{3}{2}$ and passes through the origin

(d) Has slope -5 and y intercept -3

(e) Has slope 1 and passes through the point $(-1,2)$

(f) Has slope -3 and x intercept of 2

2   Describe a technique other than that used in the example on page 330 for finding the y intercept of a given linear function.

3   Find the zero of each linear function of Exercise 1.

4   Show that the slope-intercept form of the equation of a straight line can be obtained as a special case of the point-slope form of the equation.

5   Find the equation of the straight line whose graph is described by each set of data.

(a) Has slope $-\frac{2}{3}$ and passes through the point $(0,1)$

(b) Has slope 4 and passes through the point $(2,3)$

(c) Has slope $-\frac{5}{4}$ and passes through the point $(-4,-2)$

(*d*) Passes through the two points (1,2) and (4,5)
(*e*) Passes through the two points (−2,4) and (3,−1)
(*f*) Has *x* intercept 5 and *y* intercept 2
(*g*) Has slope 4 and *x* intercept 4
(*h*) Has zero slope and passes through the point (1,−3)
(*i*) Has slope $-\dfrac{5}{3}$ and passes through the origin

6 Show that the equation of a straight line whose *x* intercept is *h* and *y* intercept is *k*, with $hk \neq 0$, may be written in the form $\dfrac{x}{h} + \dfrac{y}{k} = 1.$

7 Write the formula for the linear function which relates the odd integers to all the integers under the conditions specified.

(*a*) −1 corresponds to 0 and 5 to 3.
(*b*) 3 corresponds to 0 and 9 to 3.

8 Write the formula for the linear function which relates the even integers to all the integers under the conditions specified.

(*a*) 0 corresponds to 0 and 10 to 5.
(*b*) 2 corresponds to 0 and −12 to −7.
(*c*) 4 corresponds to 0 and 12 to 4.

9 The relation between Fahrenheit temperature *F* and centigrade temperature *C* is a linear function. What is the formula for this function if $F = 32$ when $C = 0$ and $F = 212$ when $C = 100$?

10 Draw the graph of the function of Exercise 9.

11 The relation between the circumference *C* of a circle and its radius *r* is a linear function. What is the formula for this function if $C = 0$ when $r = 0$, and $C = 6\pi$ when $r = 3$?

12 The relation between the total distance *d* traveled and the time *t* spent in traveling at a uniform speed is a linear function. What is the formula for this function if $d = 0$ when $t = 0$ and $d = 120$ when $t = 2$?

13 What is the equation of the *x* axis? Of the *y* axis?

10–5 SYSTEMS OF LINEAR EQUATIONS

When attention is directed to the set of ordered pairs which is the solution set of two or more equations, the set of equations is called a *system of equations*. The solution set of such a system is the intersection of the two solution sets of the respective equations, in other words, the set of ordered pairs which are common solutions of the two equations.

System of equations

The discussion of Secs. 10–3 and 10–4 has established the fact that the graph of each equation of the system

$$a_1x + b_1y = c_1 \qquad (10\text{–}7)$$
$$a_2x + b_2y = c_2 \qquad (10\text{–}8)$$

(A)

is a straight line. If $b_1 = 0$, Eq. (10–7) reduces to the equivalent equation $x = \dfrac{c_1}{a_1}$, whose graph is a line with undefined slope parallel to the y axis. Similarly, if $b_2 = 0$, Eq. (10–8) reduces to $x = \dfrac{c_2}{a_2}$, whose

Parallel lines   graph is parallel to the y axis. If also $\dfrac{c_1}{a_1} \neq \dfrac{c_2}{a_2}$, the two lines are parallel and have no points in common. This means that there exists no set of ordered pairs as the solution set of the system. Therefore if $b_1 = b_2 = 0$, the condition for the two equations to have a common solution set is $\dfrac{c_1}{a_1} = \dfrac{c_2}{a_2}$. If we let k represent this common ratio, the solution set of the system becomes the set of ordered pairs $\{(k,y)\}$ where $k = \dfrac{c_1}{a_1} = \dfrac{c_2}{a_2}$ and y can be any real number. In other words, the two equations reduce to the common equivalent equation $x = k$, whose graph has points with coordinates (k,y). It is of significance to note that the condition $\dfrac{c_1}{a_1} = \dfrac{c_2}{a_2}$ may be written in the equivalent forms $\dfrac{a_2}{a_1} = \dfrac{c_2}{c_1}$, or $a_2c_1 - a_1c_2 = 0$, which states that the ratios between these corresponding coefficients in the two equations are constant. Another way of saying this same thing is to say that these coefficients are proportional.

If $b_1 \neq 0$, the slope of the line of Eq. (10–7) is $-\dfrac{a_1}{b_1}$ and its y intercept is $\dfrac{c_1}{b_1}$. If $b_2 \neq 0$, the slope of the line of Eq. (10–8) is $-\dfrac{a_2}{b_2}$ and its y intercept is $\dfrac{c_2}{b_2}$. The solution set of these two equations will be the set of ordered pairs representing the coordinates of points common to the two lines which are the graphs of the equations. Thus it becomes evident that the existence of such a common solution set depends on the relationship between the slopes and y intercepts of the lines which are the graphs of the respective equations. If the slopes are the same and the y intercepts are different, the lines will be parallel and there exists no common point and hence no solution set for the system (see Figs. 10–8 and 10–10).

If the slopes are the same and the y intercepts are also the same, the
Coincident lines   two lines will be the same line. This means that the two equations will reduce to the same equivalent equation and thus have a common solution set. The two lines are said to be *coincident*.

If the slopes are different and the y intercepts have the same value k, then the two lines have the unique point $(0,k)$ in common and its coordinates become the unique solution of the system (see Fig. 10–11). The essential fact here is that, if the slopes are different, the two lines will have one point in common whose coordinates will be the unique solution set of the system. This point may or may not be a common y intercept.

This discussion may be summarized very conveniently in the following manner:

The system **B** of equations is equivalent to system **A**.

$$(a_1b_2 - a_2b_1)x = b_2c_1 - b_1c_2 \qquad (10\text{–}9)$$
$$(a_1b_2 - a_2b_1)y = a_1c_2 - a_2c_1 \qquad (10\text{–}10)$$ **(B)**

Equation (10–9) results from multiplying Eq. (10–7) by b_2 and Eq. (10–8) by $-b_1$ and then adding the two equations. Equation (10–10) results from multiplying Eq. (10–7) by $-a_2$ and Eq. (10–8) by a_1 and then adding. In the resulting system the variables x and y have the common coefficient $a_1b_2 - a_2b_1$, which may be different from zero or equal to zero.

Case I $a_1b_2 - a_2b_1 \neq 0$ In this case we may divide both sides of each equation by $a_1b_2 - a_2b_1$ to obtain

$$x = \frac{b_2c_1 - b_1c_2}{a_1b_2 - a_2b_1} \qquad (10\text{–}11)$$

(C)

$$y = \frac{a_1c_2 - a_2c_1}{a_1b_2 - a_2b_1} \qquad (10\text{–}12)$$

This system of equations is equivalent both to system **B** and to system **A**. Hence the pair of values of x and y which is the solution set of system **C** is also the solution set for system **A**. This fact can be verified by substitution in the two equations of **A**. The graph of the given system would be two lines intersecting in the point whose coordinates are given by Eqs. (10–11) and (10–12).

In this case the system of equations **A** has a *unique* solution. The equations are said to be *consistent*. Their graphs have one and only one point in common.

Definition 10-4 A system of equations is said to be *consistent* if the equations have at least one solution in common. If the equations have no solutions in common, the system is said to be *inconsistent*.

Example Find the solution set of the system

$$2x + 3y = 1 \qquad (1)$$
$$7x + 5y = 9 \qquad (2)$$

Intersecting lines

Unique solution

Consistent and inconsistent systems

To get Eq. (3) of the equivalent system, multiply (1) by 5 and (2) by -3 and then add. To get equation (4), multiply (1) by -7 and (2) by 2 and then add.

$$-11x = -22 \tag{3}$$
$$-11y = 11 \tag{4}$$

Since the common coefficient of x and y is not zero, we can divide to get

$$x = 2 \quad \text{and} \quad y = -1$$

The substitution of these values in the original system of equations will verify that the ordered pair $(2, -1)$ is the unique solution of the original system. Figure 10–13 shows that the lines which are the graphs of the two equations intersect in the point $(2, -1)$.

Case II $a_1b_2 - a_2b_1 = 0$ It is evident that, when this condition exists, system **C** cannot be obtained. Also the equations in **B** would become

$$0 \cdot x = b_2c_1 - b_1c_2$$
$$0 \cdot y = a_1c_2 - a_2c_1 \tag{D}$$

Since the product of 0 by any real number is 0, there are no values of x and y which will satisfy these equations unless *both* $b_2c_1 - b_1c_2 = 0$ and $a_1c_2 - a_2c_1 = 0$. Thus we have two separate conditions to investigate.

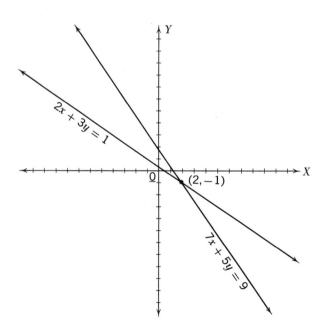

FIGURE 10–13

$1 \quad a_1b_2 - a_2b_1 = 0, \ b_2c_1 - b_1c_2 = 0, \ a_1c_2 - a_2c_1 = 0.$

If $a_1b_2 - a_2b_1 = 0$, then $a_1b_2 = a_2b_1$, from which it follows that

$$\frac{a_1}{a_2} = \frac{b_1}{b_2}.$$

Similarly, if $b_2c_1 - b_1c_2 = 0$ and $a_1c_2 - a_2c_1 = 0$, then $\dfrac{b_1}{b_2} = \dfrac{c_1}{c_2}$

and $\dfrac{a_1}{a_2} = \dfrac{c_1}{c_2}.$

From these equalities it follows that the ratio of corresponding coefficients of the two equations is constant. Symbolically,

$$\frac{a_1}{a_2} = \frac{b_1}{b_2} = \frac{c_1}{c_2} = k, \text{ or } a_1 = ka_2, \ b_1 = kb_2, \text{ and } c_1 = kc_2.$$

In other words, each equation may be obtained from the other by multiplying it by a nonzero constant. The equations are consistent, and the solution set of the system is the same as the solution set of either equation. The graph of the two equations would be two coincident lines; that is, they would be the same line.

Example Find the solution set of the system

$3x - 4y = 12$
$6x - 8y = 24$

An examination of these two equations reveals the fact that a constant ratio exists between corresponding coefficients.

$$\frac{3}{6} = \frac{-4}{-8} = \frac{12}{24} = \frac{1}{2}$$

This means that the second equation may be obtained from the first one by multiplying it by 2. The solution set of either equation is also the solution set of the other and, consequently, is the solution set of the system. From Fig. 10–14 it can be seen that the same line may be considered as the graph of either equation.

$2 \quad a_1b_2 - a_2b_1 = 0$, and either $b_2c_1 - b_1c_2 \neq 0$ or $a_1c_2 - a_2c_1 \neq 0$, or both are different from zero.

In this case the equations of system **D** express inconsistent situations, since in one or both of the equations we would have an inconsistency of the form $0 = k$ where $k \neq 0$. There would be no values of x and y which would satisfy both equations. The solution set would be empty, and the graphs of the two equations would be parallel lines.

Example Find the solution set of the system

$3x - 4y = 12$
$6x - 8y = 48$

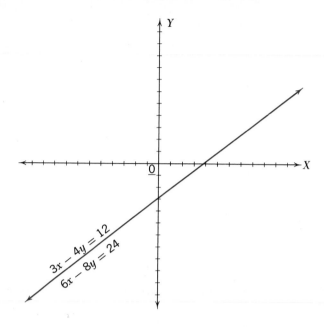

FIGURE 10–14

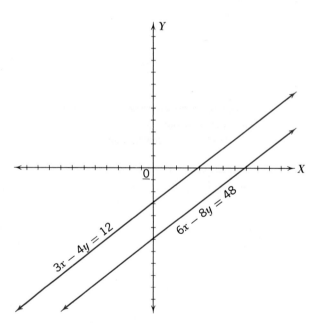

FIGURE 10–15

In this system

$$a_1b_2 - a_2b_1 = 3(-8) - (6)(-4) = -24 + 24 = 0$$
$$b_2c_1 - b_1c_2 = (-8)(12) - (-4)(48) = -96 + 192 = 96$$
$$a_1c_2 - a_2c_1 = (3)(48) - (6)(12) = 144 - 72 = 72$$

The equivalent system thus is

$0 \cdot x = 96$
$0 \cdot y = 72$

It should be evident that no values of x and y can satisfy these two equations. The system is inconsistent and there exists no solution set.

If each of the two equations is expressed in the form of a linear function, we have the equivalent system

$$y = \frac{3}{4}x - 3$$

$$y = \frac{3}{4}x - 6$$

The graphs of these two functions are parallel lines, since they have the same slope but different y intercepts. The graphs are shown in Fig. 10–15.

Exercises

Determine whether each system of equations is or is not consistent. For each consistent system, determine the solution set. Draw the graph of each system.

1 $3x + 4y = -1$
   $2x - y = 3$

2 $4x - y = 8$
   $8x - 2y = 16$

3 $4x - y = 8$
   $12x - 3y = 16$

4 $\frac{1}{2}x + \frac{1}{3}y = 4$
   $x - y = -2$

5 $\frac{2}{3}x - \frac{3}{2}y = -5$
   $\frac{1}{2}x + \frac{1}{3}y = 5$

6 $x - y = -3$
   $-\frac{1}{3}x + \frac{1}{3}y = 1$

7 $0.05x + 0.2y = 0.25$
   $0.1x + 0.4y = 0.5$

8 $ax + by = c$
   $3ax + 3by = 4c$

9 $lx + my = h$
   $klx + kmy = hk$

10 $1.2x - 4.8y = 9.6$
   $3.6x - 14.4y = 28.8$

11 $0.3x + 0.4y = 11$
   $x - y = -10$

12 $4x - 8y = 14$
   $x + 5y = -7$

13 $8x - y = 16$
   $4x - \frac{1}{2}y = 7$

14 $7x - 3y = -12$
   $-\frac{7}{3}x + y = 4$

15    $3x + 5y = 7$
      $2x + 3y = 8$

16    $\frac{2}{3}x - \frac{4}{5}y = \frac{5}{6}$

      $\frac{1}{2}x - \frac{3}{5}y = \frac{5}{3}$

17    $\frac{2}{3}x - \frac{2}{9}y = \frac{2}{3}$

      $\frac{4}{5}x + \frac{4}{15}y = 0$

18    $0.5x - 0.4y = 1$
      $2.5x - 2y = 5$

19    $0.25x + 0.20y = 0.90$
      $0.4x + 0.3y = 1.39$

20    $0.25x + 0.20y = 0.90$
      $x + 0.80y = 4$

10–6   THE RELATION OF INEQUALITY

Law of trichotomy — Attention has been called previously to the fact that for any two real numbers a and b, the law of trichotomy always holds. In other words, whether a and b are integral, rational, or irrational, it is always true that one of three relations holds: $a = b$, a is greater than $b(a > b)$, or a is less than $b(a < b)$. Furthermore, if $a > b$, then it is true that $a = b + c$ for some positive real number c; and if $a < b$, then $a + d = b$ for some positive real number d.

The relations $<$ and $>$ are neither reflexive nor symmetric, but they are transitive. (See Theorem 3–5. Although this theorem is stated for natural numbers, it holds true for any real numbers.) These relations

Inequalities — are called *strict inequalities* in contrast to $\leq$ (*is less than or equal to*) and $\geq$ (*is greater than or equal to*), which are called *mixed inequalities*.

In Chap. 3 certain other theorems concerning inequalities were either proved or stated as exercises. These same theorems can be proved for real numbers. They will be stated here, without proof, for real numbers.

Theorem 10-1   If a, b, c are real numbers such that $a < b$ and $b < c$, then $a < c$.

Theorem 10-2   If a, b, c are real numbers such that $a < b$, then $a + c < b + c$.

Theorem 10-3   If a, b, c, d are real numbers such that $a < b$ and $c < d$, then $a + c < b + d$.

Theorem 10-4   If a and b are real numbers such that $a < b$ and c is a positive real number, then $ac < bc$.

Theorem 10-5 If *a* and *b* are real numbers such that $a < b$ and *c* is a negative real number, then $ac > bc$.

Another true theorem can be derived from each of these theorems by replacing $<$ by $>$. The proof of each theorem is left as an exercise for the reader. The theorems also hold if each strict inequality is replaced by its corresponding mixed inequality.

Example Replace these inequalities with equivalent inequalities of the form $-a < x < a$: (1) $|x| < 3$; (2) $|x - 5| < 4$.

1   $|x| < 3$ means that x must be a number which is larger than -3 but smaller than $+3$. Any such number has an absolute value (numerical value) which is less than 3. The domain of values for x is thus the portion of the number line between -3 and $+3$, as shown by the colored portion of line *l* of Fig. 10–16. In other words, $-3 < x < 3$.
2   $|x - 5| < 4$ means that x must be such that $-4 < x - 5 < 4$. By theorem 10–2, $-4 + 5 < (x - 5) + 5 < 4 + 5$ or $1 < x < 9$.

The interval of the number line which is the domain of x is the colored portion of line *m* of Fig. 10–16.

In each case of this example the domain of x does not include the end points of the interval. For this reason it is called an *open interval*. Strict inequalities always imply open intervals. If the inequalities had been mixed, as in $|x| \leq 3$ and $|x - 5| \leq 4$, then the domain of x in each case would have included the end points of the interval, in which case the interval would have been called a *closed interval*.

Intervals

Example Express each of these closed intervals in an equivalent form using the absolute-value sign: (1) $-1 \leq x \leq 1$; (2) $-2 \leq x \leq 6$.

1   $-1 \leq x \leq 1$ states that x must be numerically less than or equal to 1, and this condition may be written $|x| \leq 1$.
2   $-2 \leq x \leq 6$. In order to use the absolute-value sign it is necessary to have the two limits equal but opposite in sign. This may be accomplished in this case by adding -2 to each member of the in-

FIGURE 10–16

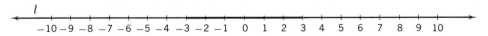

Complete graph of $|x| < 3$

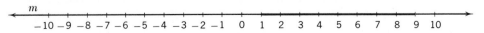

Complete graph of $|x - 5| < 4$

equality. Theorem 10–2 states that the inequality is not disturbed. Thus, $(-2) + (-2) \leq x + (-2) \leq 6 + (-2)$ or $-4 \leq x - 2 \leq 4$, which may be written as $|x - 2| \leq 4$.

Inequality in two variables

An inequality in two variables is of the form

$$ax + by > c \qquad \text{or} \qquad ax + by < c$$

where a, b, and c are real numbers. If $b > 0$, we may use Theorems 10–2 and 10–4 to get

$$y > -\frac{a}{b}x + \frac{c}{b} \qquad \text{or} \qquad y < -\frac{a}{b}x + \frac{c}{b}$$

If $b < 0$, we use Theorems 10–2 and 10–5 to get

$$y < -\frac{a}{b}x + \frac{c}{b} \qquad \text{or} \qquad y > -\frac{a}{b}x + \frac{c}{b}$$

Thus in either case we have formulas which give many values of y for each value of x. We have in each case, therefore, a formula that expresses a relation which is not a function. The graph of such a relation can be obtained by first plotting the line which is the graph of $ax + by = c$. For the strict inequality $y > -\frac{a}{b}x + \frac{c}{b}$, the graph will be that half plane which contains those points such that, for a given x, the y coordinate is greater than the corresponding y coordinate of the point of the line. For the strict inequality $y < -\frac{a}{b}x + \frac{c}{b}$, the y coordinate of each point of the half plane will be less than the corresponding y coordinate of the point on the line. For any mixed inequality the graph will also include the line.

Graph of an inequality

Example Plot the graph of the strict inequality $2x + 3y > 6$.

Using Theorems 10–2 and 10–4, we may write this inequality as

$$y > -\frac{2}{3}x + 2.$$

To plot the graph of the equation $2x + 3y = 6$ we write it in the form $y = -\frac{2}{3}x + 2$. The graph is therefore a line with slope $-\frac{2}{3}$ and passing through the point $(0,2)$. An incomplete graph of the inequality is then the colored half plane of Fig. 10–17. Note that the line which is the graph of $2x + 3y = 6$ is not colored. Since this is a strict inequality, the points of the line are not part of the graph. To check the graph, select points in the colored half plane and test their coordinates in the inequality. For example, the point $(5,2)$ gives $2(5) + 3(2) = 16$, and $16 > 6$.

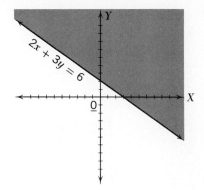

FIGURE 10-17   Incomplete graph of $2x + 3y > 6$.

Example   Plot the graph of the mixed inequality $10x - 2y \geq 7$.

Using Theorems 10-2 and 10-5, we may write this inequality in the form $y \leq 5x - \dfrac{7}{2}$. Notice that, when both sides of the inequality are multiplied by $-\dfrac{1}{2}$, the inequality changes its sense. It changes from $\geq$ to $\leq$, which is in accordance with Theorem 10-5.

To plot the graph of the equation $10x - 2y = 7$ we may write it in the form $y = 5x - \dfrac{7}{2}$. The graph is a line with a slope of 5 and a y intercept of $-\dfrac{7}{2}$. An incomplete graph of the inequality is then the colored half plane of Fig. 10-18, *including* the line which is the graph of the equation $10x - 2y = 7$. To check the graph, use points $(2,2)$ and $(3,-5)$. We find for $(2,2)$: $10(2) - 2(2) = 20 - 4 = 16$, and $16 > 7$; for $(3,-5)$: $10(3) - 2(-5) = 30 + 10 = 40$, and $40 > 7$.

The solution set for two inequalities in two unknowns can be found by graphing the solution set of each inequality and then taking the intersection of the two sets.

System of inequalities

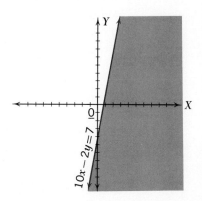

FIGURE 10-18   Incomplete graph of $10x - 2y \geq 7$.

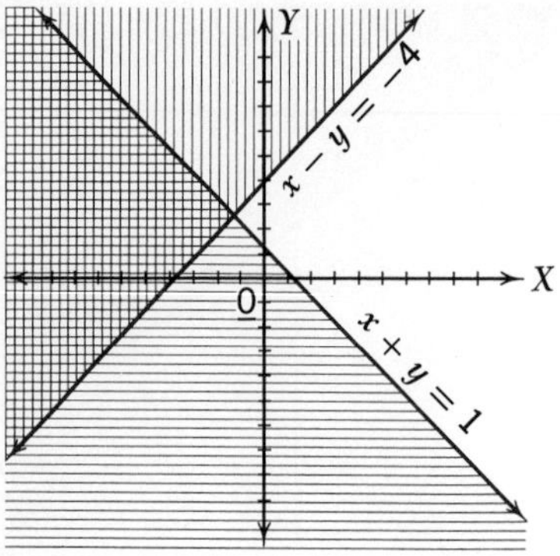

FIGURE 10-19   Incomplete graphs of $x + y \le 1$ and $x - y \le -4$.

Example Find the solution set of the system of inequalities

$$x + y \le 1$$
$$x - y \le -4$$

The portion of Fig. 10-19 which is shaded with horizontal lines is an incomplete graph of $x + y \le 1$. The portion shaded with vertical lines is an incomplete graph of $x - y \le -4$. The cross-hatched portion of the graph then represents the intersection of the two sets. The coordinates of any point lying within this area will satisfy both inequalities. It should be noted that, since both inequalities are mixed, both lines are to be included in the graph of the solution set.

Exercises

Express each of the following in the equivalent form using absolute values.

1	$-2 < x < 2$	2	$-5 \le x \le 5$
3	$-1 \le x \le 5$	4	$-1 < x - 1 < 2$
5	$0 \le x + 2 \le 4$	6	$2 \le x - 3 \le 8$
7	$4 < x - 5 < 8$	8	$-3 \le x + 1 \le 2$
9	$-5 \le x + 2 \le 6$		

Express each of the following in the equivalent interval form $(a \le x \le b$ or $a < x < b)$.

10	$|x| \le 1$	11	$|x| \le 8$	12	$|x - 1| \le 2$
13	$|x + 3| < 4$	14	$|x + 5| < 2$	15	$|x - 2| < 2$

For what values of x are these inequalities true?

16 $2x + 1 < 0$ 17 $3x - 5 < 0$

18 $2x + 1 < x + 2$ 19 $-4x + 2 \geq x - 8$

20 $2x - \dfrac{1}{3} \leq x + \dfrac{2}{3}$ 21 $x + 2 \geq 3x + 4$

Draw the graph of each inequality.

22 $x \geq 2$ 23 $x \leq -3$ 24 $y > 1$

25 $-2x > 1$ 26 $2x + y > 4$ 27 $x - y < 6$

28 $2x - y \leq 6$ 29 $3x + 2y \geq -12$ 30 $x - 4y \leq -12$

Draw the graph of the solution set of each system of inequalities.

31 $x + 2y > 2$ 32 $y \leq x$ 33 $y \leq x - 3$

    $2x - y > 2$ $x + y \leq 1$ $x + y \leq 2$

34 $x + y \geq -6$ 35 $x - y > -3$ 36 $3y - x < 6$

    $y \leq 0$ $x + y < 3$ $x + 2y > 8$

37 Prove Theorem 10–1.

38 Prove Theorem 10–2.

39 Prove Theorem 10–3.

40 Prove Theorem 10–4.

41 Prove Theorem 10–5.

10–7   VARIATION

Whether in business, industry, or ordinary environmental occurrence, one of the most common ways of describing relationships that exist is in terms of *variation*. We shall be concerned with three distinct types of variation: *direct variation, inverse variation,* and *joint variation.*   Direct
  In *direct variation* two variables are so related that the ratio between   variation
them remains constant. As one variable increases the other increases, and as one decreases the other decreases. In other words, if y varies directly as x, the relationship can be expressed in either of two ways: $\dfrac{y}{x} = k$ or $y = kx$, where k is a constant. The constant k is called the *constant of proportionality* or *constant of variation.*

Example   The circumference C of a circle varies directly as its diameter d. Find the value of C when $d = 6$, if $C = 12.56$ when $d = 4$.
  The formula is $C = kd$.

Since $C = 12.56$ when $d = 4$, we have

$$12.56 = k(4) \qquad \text{or} \qquad k = 3.14$$

The formula now may be written

$$C = 3.14d$$

so when $d = 6$, we have

$$C = 3.14(6) = 18.84$$

Inverse variation   In *inverse variation* two variables are so related that their product remains constant. If y varies inversely as x, then $xy = k$, where k is the constant of proportionality. This same relation may be written in the form $y = \dfrac{k}{x}$, which states that y varies directly as the reciprocal of x. As one variable increases the other decreases, or as one decreases the other increases.

Example   The time it takes a person to travel a fixed distance varies inversely with the average speed at which he travels. How long will it take a person to drive a given distance at an average speed of 45 miles per hour, if it would take him 9 hours traveling at an average speed of 40 miles per hour?

If s represents average speed and t the time traveled, the formula is

$$k = st \qquad \text{or} \qquad t = \frac{k}{s}$$

When $t = 9$, $s = 40$, so $k = 360$ and

$$360 = 45t \qquad \text{or} \qquad t = \frac{360}{45}$$

$$t = 8$$

Joint variation   In *joint variation* three variables are so related that one varies directly as the product of the other two. If z varies jointly as x and y, then $z = kxy$, where k is the constant of proportionality.

Example   The area A of a triangle varies jointly as its base b and its altitude h. What is the area of a triangle whose base is 15 feet and whose altitude is 8 feet if 84 square feet is the area of a triangle whose base is 24 feet and whose altitude is 7 feet?

The formula is $A = kbh$.

$$84 = k(24)(7)$$

$$84 = 168k$$

$$k = \frac{1}{2}$$

Therefore the formula is $A = \frac{1}{2}bh$. When $b = 15$ and $h = 8$,

$A = \frac{1}{2}(15)(8)$

$A = 60$ sq ft

Exercises

1 The perimeter of a certain type of regular polygon varies directly as the length of one of its equal sides. What is the perimeter of such a polygon whose sides are 8 inches if the perimeter of a similar polygon is 72 inches when its side is 12 inches?

2 The volume V of a sphere varies directly as the cube of its radius r. When $r = \frac{5}{2}$, $V = \frac{125\pi}{6}$. What is the value of V for $r = 6$?

3 For a gas of constant volume, its pressure varies directly as its absolute temperature. If the pressure is 30 pounds per square inch when the absolute temperature is 600°F, what will be the pressure if the temperature falls to 500°F?

4 The current I in amperes in an electric circuit varies inversely as the resistance R in ohms when the electromotive force is constant. If, in a given circuit, I is 24 amperes when R is 1.5 ohms, what is I when R is 0.5 ohm? What is R when I is 75 amperes?

5 The weight of an object above the surface of the earth varies inversely as the square of its distance from the center of the earth. If a man weighs 147 pounds on the earth's surface, what will be his weight at distance of 160 miles above the earth? Take the radius of earth to be 3,960 miles and compute the answer correct to the nearest pound.

6 At a constant rate of simple interest the return on an investment varies jointly as the principal invested and the time. If the return on $1,200 for 1 year is $54, what would be the return on $2,500 for 3 years? On $850 for 9 months?

7 The force f of the wind, blowing against a flat surface at right angles to the direction of the wind, varies jointly as the area A of the surface and the square of the speed v of the wind. The force with which a 15 miles per hour wind strikes a surface of 20 square feet is 20 pounds. What is the force against an area of 15 feet square if the wind's speed is 25 miles per hour?

8 The variable y varies directly as x and inversely as z. When $x = 2$ and $z = 10$, $y = 10$. What is the value of y when $x = 3$ and $z = 15$?

9 The intensity I of light received from a source varies directly as the candlepower c and inversely as the square of the distance d from the

source.   How far from a 200-candlepower light would a screen
have to be to receive the same amount of light as a screen placed
25 feet from a 50-candlepower light?

10–8   STATISTICAL GRAPHS

In Sec. 10–2 five methods were presented for describing a relation that
exists between variables.   These methods are verbal description, formula, set of ordered pairs, table of values, and graph.   In contradistinc-
tion to the types of relations discussed so far, there are those sets of data
related to each other in patterns not subject to formula representation.
The graphs used to depict such relationships are often referred to as
statistical graphs and are usually grouped in four distinct classifications:
the *broken-line graph,* the *bar graph,* the *circle graph,* and the
pictograph.

Broken-line
graph
The *broken-line graph* is used primarily to show trends.   Comparisons also can be read from it rather easily.   Figure 10–20 shows temperature readings at 2-hour intervals for a 24-hour period.   A casual glance
will tell at what times the temperature was rising or falling.   More careful inspection will answer such questions as: At what hours was the
temperature the same?   At what hour was the temperature the lowest?
The highest?   Between what hours did the most rapid rise occur?   The
most rapid fall?   There are many other questions that can be answered.
There are also some questions which cannot be answered.   For example, although the graph tells what the temperature was at every even

FIGURE 10–20   Two-hour periods.

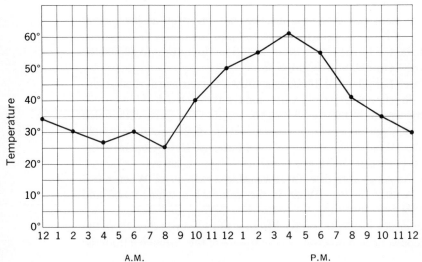

FIGURE 10–21   Population growth in the United States.

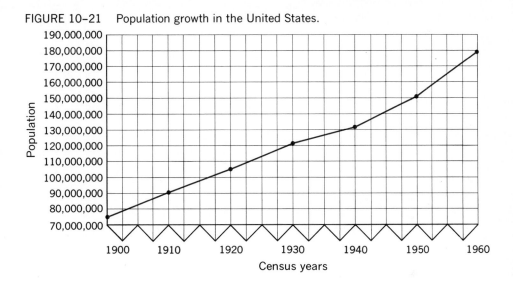

hour during the 24-hour period, it does not tell what it was at any odd-hour period. The line segment which joins the dots that indicate the temperatures at 8 A.M. and 10 A.M. simply indicates that, in general, the temperature was rising during this 2-hour interval. It does not say anything about what the temperature was at any specific time within this interval.

Another precaution is necessary in interpreting broken-line graphs. The graph of Fig. 10–21 tells the story of the growth in population in the United States during the first six decades of the twentieth century. It is a very simple matter to observe from the graph that the general characteristic has been an increasing population. Furthermore, it is evident that the increase has been rather uniform over each 10-year period. But when the comparison between the population figure for one year with that for another is read just from the graph, there can be serious distortion in interpretations. For example, the population for 1960 might seem to be more than twice that for 1930 and more than three times that for 1920. A look at the actual population figures for these years reveals the fact that these ratios are far from correct. This false impression is due to the fact that the population figures are large, all in excess of 75,000,000, and yet, in order to get any significant picture at all, a scale with a unit no larger than 10,000,000 had to be used. As a result, in order to get the picture in the space available it became necessary to use 70,000,000 as a *false zero line*. This is indicated by the wavy line rather than the usual straight line and by the legend on the vertical scale. Careless attention to such details of graph structure frequently leads to grossly erroneous interpretations of the message of the graph. Another form used in drawing graphs representing data involving this type of difficulty is shown in Fig. 10–22. In this graph, showing the same information as that of Fig. 10–21, the true zero line

FIGURE 10–22   Population growth in the United States.

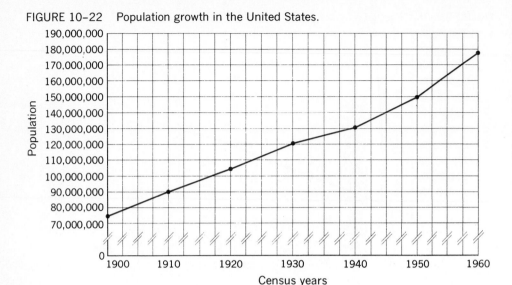

is shown, but a break is made in the vertical axis to provide for the deletion of those population figures which bear no pertinence to the graph. It is evident that the same dangers of misinterpretation are present as in the graph with the false zero line.

Bar graph   The *bar graph* is used essentially for making comparisons. There are three types to be considered: the *vertical bar*, the *horizontal bar*, and the *composite bar* or *100% bar*. The vertical bar graph derives its name from the fact that the bars are drawn in a vertical position. From such a graph, when appropriate, trends can also be read by noting the characteristic behavior of the lengths of the bars. For example, a vertical-bar graph might be used to portray the facts about wheat production in the United States for a given period of time. In Fig. 10–23 a comparison of the heights of the bars will answer pertinent questions concerning relative yearly crop production. Also by noting the tendency in the heights of the bars one can get an answer to the question as to the trend in wheat production over the period of time pictured. On the other hand, a similar graph might be used to compare wheat production in each of a selected number of different states during the period of 1 year. In this case there would be no pertinent interpretation related to trends.

If the bars of a graph are in the horizontal position, then the graph is called a *horizontal bar graph*. Such a graph can be used effectively for comparisons but not very well for picturing trends. In Fig. 10–24 a horizontal bar graph is used to present the rainfall picture for a certain city over a period of 30 years. The average number of inches in each 3-year period is indicated by the appropriate length of a bar.

In most cases the decision as to whether a vertical or a horizontal bar

FIGURE 10–23 Wheat production in the United States (correct to nearest 100,000,000 bushels). [SOURCE: World Almanac, 1962]

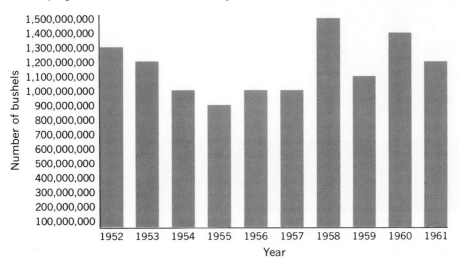

FIGURE 10–24 Average rainfall for a certain city for three-year periods.

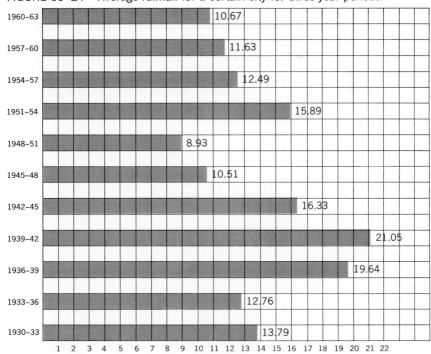

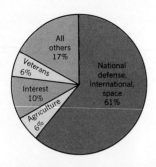

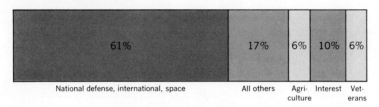

61%	17%	6%	10%	6%
National defense, international, space	All others	Agri-culture	Interest	Vet-erans

FIGURE 10–25
Estimated national
budget.

graph is to be used is quite arbitrary.   There are times when the nature
of the data might make one type quite appropriate and the other just
as decidedly inappropriate.   Just as in the case of the broken-line graph,
in order to protect against distorted and unwarranted interpretations
from either type of bar graph, it is very important to pay careful attention to the position of the zero line.

Circle graph   The *composite bar graph* and the *circle graph* are used for the same
basic purpose, namely, to compare parts with a whole or parts with
parts.   The only distinction between the two is illustrated in Fig. 10–25,
in which the two types of graph are used to picture an estimated
national expenditure budget.   In the bar graph a bar of arbitrary size is
used to represent 100%, while in the circle graph a circle of arbitrary
radius is used.

FIGURE 10–26   Homes of United States with radios.

YEAR	NUMBER OF HOMES		
1930	12,000,000		
1935	23,000,000		
1940	29,000,000		
1945	34,000,000		
1950	45,000,000		
1955	52,000,000		
1960	55,000,000		

Scale: 1 picture for each 5,000,000 homes
Source: 1962 World Almanac

The *pictograph* is merely a bar graph in which small pictures instead   Pictograph
of solid bars are used to emphasize the comparisons. Each small figure
represents a selected number of units of data. The pictograph of
Fig. 10–26 shows in 5-year intervals over a 30-year period the total
number of houses with radios in the United States. Each figure represents 5,000,000 homes.

Exercises

1 What are the relative advantages and disadvantages of the table of
values, the formula, and the graph as a means for the presentation
of quantitative data?
2 What are the distinguishing characteristics of the bar graph, the
broken-line graph, and the circle graph?
3 What are some of the basic similarities and dissimilarities between
the circle graph and the composite, or 100%, bar graph?
4 Draw a broken-line graph of the data below showing the normal
monthly temperatures of a certain southern city.
5 Answer these questions about the graph of Exercise 4.

(*a*) During what months was the temperature rising?
(*b*) During what months was the temperature falling?
(*c*) When was the most abrupt rise in temperature?
(*d*) When was the most abrupt fall in temperature?
(*e*) For what two months was the normal temperature the same?

6 Draw a bar graph of the data below showing the number of tons of
walnuts produced in the United States yearly for a period of
10 years.

Exercise 4

MONTH	TEMPERATURE	MONTH	TEMPERATURE	MONTH	TEMPERATURE
Jan.	40	May	72	Sept.	73
Feb.	42	June	77	Oct.	62
March	50	July	80	Nov.	49
April	60	August	79	Dec.	42

Exercise 6

YEAR	TONS	YEAR	TONS
1951	77,400	1956	71,800
1952	83,800	1957	66,600
1953	59,200	1958	88,700
1954	75,400	1959	62,500
1955	77,400	1960	72,100

Exercise 7

Savings	10%	Health	9%
Food	26%	Church	10%
Rent	18%	Household expenses	12%
Clothing	15%		

7 Draw both a circle graph and a composite bar graph of the family budget plan shown above.
8 Select data from reliable sources suitable for presentation by (*a*) horizontal bar graph; (*b*) vertical bar graph; (*c*) broken-line graph; (*d*) circle graph.
9 Draw the graph to represent each set of data selected in Exercise 8.
10 Draw a composite bar graph to represent the data used for the circle graph of Exercise 8.

10-9   THE NATURE OF PROBLEM SOLVING

One of the primary concerns in solving problems is the seeking of relationships which exist in the problem situation between known data and unknown elements.   Once these are discovered and formalized, the course for finding the solution is usually fairly easy to chart.   Whether a problem is simple or complex, it is distinctly characterized by three

Significant attributes of a problem

significant attributes, namely, the data, the unknown, and the particular conditions which relate the data to the unknown.   Any successful approach to obtaining a solution for a given problem, therefore, necessarily calls for a careful analysis of the problem situation in order to discover what the essential data are, what the unknown elements are, what fundamental relations tie the data and the unknown together, and what operations are pertinent.   Furthermore, it is imperative that the validity and significance of any obtained solution be checked carefully in the context of the given specifications.

Example   The air distance between two large airports is 2,268 miles. The scheduled time for the eastbound flight of a jet airliner between the two airports is 45 minutes shorter than that for the scheduled westbound flight.   What are the scheduled time and the average speed for each flight?

The *known* elements are:
  The distance between the two airports is 2,268 miles.
  The time differential in the schedule for the two flights is 45 minutes.
  The formula relating distance d, speed s, and time t is $d = st$.

The unknown elements are:

The scheduled time for each of the two flights, which we shall represent by t_1 and t_2.

The average speed for each of the two flights, which we shall represent by s_1 and s_2.

The formula $d = st$ requires that s and t be expressed in the same time units. For this reason we shall specify the unknowns more carefully.

$t_1 = $ time in hours for eastbound flight
$t_2 = $ time in hours for eastbound flight
$s_1 = $ average speed in miles per hour for eastbound flight
$s_2 = $ average speed in miles per hour for westbound flight

The relations which exist between known and unknown may now be expressed in these equations:

$$s_1 t_1 = 2{,}268 \text{ miles} \tag{1}$$

$$s_2 t_2 = 2{,}268 \text{ miles} \tag{2}$$

$$t_2 - t_1 = \frac{3}{4} \text{ hour} \tag{3}$$

As we attempt to find a unique solution for this system of equations, we may drop the units. This is due to the fact that the proper association of units will be taken care of by any valid solution process. Efforts to find a unique solution of the system soon bring to light a hidden difficulty. One procedure could be to substitute from Eq. (3) into either Eq. (1) or Eq. (2). From (3) we obtain $t_1 = t_2 - \frac{3}{4}$, which may be combined with (1) to give $s_1\left(t_2 - \frac{3}{4}\right) = 2{,}268$, or

$$s_1 t_2 - \frac{3}{4} s_1 = 2{,}268 \tag{4}$$

Similarly, from Eqs. (2) and (3) we may derive

$$s_2 t_1 + \frac{3}{4} s_2 = 2{,}268 \tag{5}$$

Either Eq. (4) or Eq. (5) reveals the fact that we have *one* equation with *two* unknowns, and we cannot determine a unique solution for either equation. In either case additional information is needed in order to fix a unique solution of the system. For example, if we are given that $t_2 = 5\frac{1}{4}$ hours, we have from Eq. (4) that $5\frac{1}{4} s_1 - \frac{3}{4} s_1 = 2{,}268$, or $s_1 = 504$ miles per hour. From Eq. (2), $s_2 = 432$ miles per hour, and from Eq. (3), $t_1 = 4\frac{1}{2}$ hours. Similar results can be obtained for a specified value for any one of the four unknowns.

This is an example of a problem situation in which the data are insufficient to determine a unique solution of the system. Note that a unique solution could not be determined as long as the number of equations was less than the number of unknowns.

If $5\frac{1}{4}$ is accepted as the value of t_1, the values determined for s_1, s_2, and t_2 will satisfy the conditions expressed in Eqs. (1) to (3). This fact should be verified by substitution in these equations.

The solving of problems can in no sense be regarded as a trial-and-error process of haphazard guessing or unsystematic reasoning. While haphazard guessing can be of no material benefit in problem solving, "educated guesses" have great potential for being very effective aids. An "educated guess" is a judgment which has more than mere chance or the law of averages as its justification; it is based on a background of pertinent information, related past experiences, intuitive exploration, and inductive reasoning. Following one's intuition is largely a process of attempting to capitalize on significant hunches. Such guesses, however, have some form of authoritative justification; they are not merely chance occurrences. They arise from an implicit perception of the total problem situation and a careful perusal of all its essential pertinencies. While intuitive reasoning, through its appeal to analogy and specialization, can be very helpful in the discovery of effective leads to be followed in the search for the solution of a given problem, it is by no means a conclusive process. It can lead through analogy to the recognition of special cases which can vary from those with the same problem structure but simpler data to analogous problem situations with simpler structure. Such analogous situations may take the form of diagrams illustrating the basic relations between the data and the unknown, concrete examples similar to the more abstract problem situation, or simpler special cases which are significant components of the more difficult general problem.

Induction is fundamentally a process of reasoning that carries one from the particular to the general. Such a pattern of thinking can lead one to examine the intuitively recognized special cases in the quest for a characteristic thread of similarity, regularity, or coherence which might suggest techniques for dealing with the more general situation. Just as is the case with intuition, the most significant techniques of induction are analogy, specialization, and generalization. Through the analogies of special cases, generalizations are sought in order that they might be checked against other specializations. Such generalizations lead to the formalization of formulas or rules which summarize and characterize recognized basic relations that exist between data, and between data and unknown. Great care must be exercised, however, in drawing conclusions from any inductive process. Such conclusions should never be stated as actualities, but only as probabilities, possibly worthy of further investigation.

Intuitive reasoning

Induction

Example An illustration of the danger of making intuitive generalizations based upon the mere evidence of an abundance of specific verifications is to be found in the three following formulas:

1 $p = n^2 - n + 11$ will yield a prime for p for all values of n from 1 through 10. However, for $n = 11$, $p = 11^2$, which is not a prime.

2 $p = n^2 - n + 41$ will yield a prime for all values of n from 1 through 40. For $n = 41$, $p = 41^2$, which is not a prime.

3 $p = n^2 - 79n + 1,601$ will yield a prime for all values of n from 1 through 79. For $n = 80$,

$$p = 80 \cdot 80 - 79 \cdot 80 + 1,601 = (80 - 79)80 + 1,601 = 1,681 = 41^2$$

which is not a prime.

It should be observed that in each of the above cases, the generalization "if p is a prime for some value of n, say $n = k$, then p is a prime for $n = k + 1$" is *not* a true statement. In case 1, p is a prime for $n = 10$ but *not* for $n = 11$. In case 2, p is a prime for $n = 40$ but *not* for $n = 41$. In case 3, p is a prime for $n = 79$ but *not* for $n = 80$. It is for this reason that no one of these three formulas can be used as a formula to give a prime for positive integral values of n.

Example From the annals of history comes the story that the great mathematician Karl Friedrich Gauss (1777–1855), in his tenth year, greatly astonished his arithmetic teacher by giving him the sum of a long list of integers almost by the time the stating of the exercise was completed. The integers were of such a nature that the differences between pairs of consecutive integers were all the same.

The simplest case of such a problem would be to find the sum of consecutive integers from 1 to some specified number. Let us examine such a problem by requesting the sum S of the first 50 positive integers.

If $S = 1 + 2 + 3 + 4 + 5 + \cdots + 50$, what is S?

Rather than attempt to write the 50 integers down and add them, it will be more interesting and challenging to see whether a rule or formula can be detected which will yield the sum. With this in mind we shall change the problem to read What is the sum of the first n positive integers? Let us investigate special cases to see whether we can detect a pattern of similarity or regularity.

If $n = 1$	$S = 1$	$= 1 \times 1$
If $n = 2$	$S = 1 + 2 = 3$	$= 1 \times 3$
If $n = 3$	$S = 1 + 2 + 3 = 6$	$= 2 \times 3$
If $n = 4$	$S = 1 + 2 + 3 + 4 = 10$	$= 2 \times 5$
If $n = 5$	$S = 1 + 2 + 3 + 4 + 5 = 15$	$= 3 \times 5$
If $n = 6$	$S = 1 + 2 + 3 + 4 + 5 + 6 = 21$	$= 3 \times 7$
If $n = 7$	$S = 1 + 2 + 3 + 4 + 5 + 6 + 7 = 28$	$= 4 \times 7$

Here are seven values of n, and for $n > 1$, the sum can be written as the product of two factors, one of which is prime. The primes are the consecutive primes $3, 5, 7$. The other factors are the integers $1, 2, 3, 4$, with each one, except 4, appearing twice. These facts might lead one to guess that for $n = 8$ the sum would be 4×11 since 11 is the next prime after 7 and 4 has appeared only once as a factor. This thought is soon exploded since, if $n = 8$,

$$S = 1 + 2 + 3 + 4 + 5 + 6 + 7 + 8 = 36 = 4 \times 9$$

and 9 is not a prime.

There is another pattern characteristic of these first seven sums. When n is even, one of the factors in the product which expresses the sum is 1 more than n; we may write it as $n + 1$. The other factor is one-half of n, which we may write as $\dfrac{n}{2}$. In other words, in each case when n is even, the sum S may be expressed in the form $\dfrac{n}{2} \times (n + 1)$, or $\dfrac{n(n + 1)}{2}$. On the other hand, when n is odd, we note that one of the two factors is n, and the other one is $\dfrac{n + 1}{2}$. In other words, in these cases also, $S = \dfrac{n(n + 1)}{2}$.

If this formula is checked against a few more special cases, it will be found to yield the sum for each value of n used. For example,

For $n = 8$ $S = \dfrac{8 \times 9}{2} = 36$

For $n = 9$ $S = \dfrac{9 \times 10}{2} = 45$

For $n = 10$ $S = \dfrac{10 \times 11}{2} = 55$

The reader should first check these sums by actual addition and then check in a few more individually selected cases. These checks merely serve to lend support to the intuitive guess that maybe this formula will work in all cases. The fact is that this proves to be a good hunch to follow for further investigation.

In addition to the fact that the formula gives the sum for the first 10 positive integers, we can also prove that, if it gives the sum for any positive integer k, it will also give the sum for the positive integer $k + 1$. This is the property that was missing for each formula of the example on page 357. The theorem to be proved may be stated in this form:

Theorem 10-6 If the formula $S = \dfrac{n(n + 1)}{2}$ gives the sum of the first n positive integers when n is any positive integer k, then it will also give the sum for $n = k + 1$.

Hypothesis $1 + 2 + 3 + \cdots + k = \dfrac{k(k+1)}{2}$, where k is a positive integer.

Conclusion $1 + 2 + 3 + \cdots + k + (k+1) = \dfrac{(k+1)[(k+1)+1]}{2}$.

Proof

Statements	*Reasons*
1 $1 + 2 + 3 + \cdots + k = \dfrac{k(k+1)}{2}$	Hypothesis
2 $1 + 2 + 3 + \cdots + k + (k+1)$ $= \dfrac{k(k+1)}{2} + (k+1)$	E–4
3 $\dfrac{k(k+1)}{2} + (k+1)$ $= \dfrac{k(k+1) + 2(k+1)}{2}$	Definition 5–5
4 $\dfrac{k(k+1) + 2(k+1)}{2}$ $= \dfrac{(k+2)(k+1)}{2}$	Distributive property
5 $\dfrac{(k+2)(k+1)}{2}$ $= \dfrac{(k+1)[(k+1)+1]}{2}$	Commutative and associative properties
6 $1 + 2 + 3 + \cdots + k + (k+1)$ $= \dfrac{(k+1)[(k+1)+1]}{2}$	Steps 2 to 5; E–3

In order to complete the argument that the formula $S = \dfrac{n(n+1)}{2}$ will give the sum of the first n positive integers, it is necessary to recall two facts from earlier chapters.

1 In Chap. 4 a one-to-one correspondence was established between the set of positive integers and the set of natural numbers such that finding sums and products of elements of one set was equivalent to finding the sums and products of the corresponding elements of the other set. Such a correspondence is called an *isomorphism* [from the two Greek words *iso* (the same) and *morphous* (form)]. The set of positive integers $\{p\}$ and the set of natural numbers $\{n\}$ are *isomorphic* under the correspondence $p = +n$ which preserves addition and multiplication.

Isomorphism

2   In Chap. 3 the *principle of finite induction* was stated as postulate N–8 of the natural number system.   Because of its significance to the present argument, it will be restated here.

N–8   Finite Induction   If $P \subseteq N$ such that (1) $1 \in P$ and (2) $(k + 1) \in P$ whenever $k \in P$, then $P = N$.

In our present argument, let the set P be the set of all positive integers (natural numbers) for which $S = \dfrac{n(n + 1)}{2}$ for $n \in P$.   For this set P we have these properties:

1 $1 \in P$.   (In fact, the 10 specific examples exhibit the fact that not only is $1 \in P$ but also 2, 3, 4, 5, 6, 7, 8, 9, 10 $\in P$.)
2   If $k \in P$, then $(k + 1) \in P$.   (This is the theorem just proved.)

From these two facts it then follows by the principle of finite induction that the set P is the set of all natural numbers (positive integers). In other words, the formula $S = \dfrac{n(n + 1)}{2}$ gives the sum of the first n positive integers for all positive integral values of n.

The pattern of deductive argument used in this example is called *proof by mathematical induction.*

Proof by mathematical induction

Although intuition and induction can make very significant contributions to the correct analysis of any problem situation, it is indeed the pattern of deduction which directs the thought process through the chain of implications which lead from the known data to the final solution of the problem.   In order to discover an effective sequence of implications, answers need to be sought to such questions as: (1) What facts and relationships are implied by the data? (2) What basic formulas are suggested?   (3) How are the unknown elements related to the known? At times it is quite helpful to ask the question: What information would be sufficient to justify drawing the desired conclusion?   Successive repetition of this question concerning each new conclusion reached can lead to the point of recognition of a significant plan of attack for discovering the solution to the problem.

Whatever procedure is followed, problem solving is always characterized by difficulties of at least four distinct types: *comprehension, structure, operation,* and *judgment.*   Before a person can make any sort of intelligent attack on a given problem situation, he must have a clear understanding of the entire problem and its contextual orientation.   He must be able to direct his thinking toward recognizing basic formulas and laws which relate the data, distinguishing essential data from that which is nonessential, discerning the need for additional data, detecting hidden implications, determining the appropriate operational procedures, and finally evaluating the significance and pertinence of

Types of difficulties in problem solving

the results obtained. Even though an individual may have a clear comprehension of just what the problem is, can structure the solving process in an intelligent manner, and is able to carry out the pertinent operations accurately and with facility, problem solving still may be a rather meaningless miscellany of manipulative procedures unless he can interpret the significance of the solution obtained as well as appraise its validity and accuracy.

Exercises

Find the solution set of each exercise.

1 At simple interest what is the interest on $1,200 at 4.8% for 3 months?

2 Two trains depart from the same station at the same time. One train travels east at 60 miles per hour and the other travels west at 50 miles per hour. How long before they will be 495 miles apart?

3 The sum of a number, its half, and its third is 77. What is the number?

4 An airconditioner was installed at a total cost of $395.20. This included a sales tax of 4%. What was the amount of the tax?

5 The sum of two consecutive integers is 83. What are the two integers?

6 The sum of two consecutive even integers is 758. What are the two integers?

7 The sum of two consecutive odd integers is 1,000. What are the two integers?

8 The sum of two integers is 24. Twice the smaller number less the larger number is 3. What are the two integers?

9 The difference between two numbers is 75. If the larger number is divided by the smaller number there is obtained a quotient of 6 and a remainder of 5. What are the two numbers?

10 A refrigerator was purchased on a 3-month term basis for $339.95. The cash price was $325. What rate of interest was paid?

11 A department store bought 25 television sets. Each set cost $185.25. At what price must these sets sell if the cost is to be 65% of the selling price?

12 Use the formula for the linear function to find the equation of the line through the points $(2, -3)$ and $(-5, 4)$.

13 Find the point of intersection of the line of Exercise 12 and the line which has a y intercept of 2 and an x intercept of 4.

14 The length of a rectangle is 30 yards longer than its width. The perimeter is 200 yards. What are the dimensions of the rectangle?

15 The tens digit of a given number is 5 more than the ones digit. If

the digits are reversed, the new number is 9 less than one-half the given number. What is the given number?

16   In the graduating class of City High School there are 180 students. The ratio of boys to girls is 5 to 4. How many of each sex are in the graduating class?

17   A square and an equilateral triangle are to be constructed so that they have the same perimeter. The side of the triangle is to be 2 feet longer than the side of the square. What will be the length of a side of each figure?

18   An investment of $12,000 brings a total yearly return of $515. Part of the investment bears 4% interest and the rest $4\frac{1}{2}$%. How much is invested at each rate?

19   Sidewalks are being constructed along the streets of a residential subdivision. The dimensions of the two street sides of an irregular corner lot are 56 feet and 126 feet. The lengths of the other two sides are 70 feet and 84 feet. How many square feet of cement will be required to build a concrete sidewalk 3 feet wide along the street border of the lot?

20   A firm mailed 300 letters, some of which went by airmail and required 8 cents' postage. The balance of the letters required 5 cents' postage. The total amount of postage was $17.16. How many letters of each kind were mailed?

21   The total of the basic charge and tax on two long-distance telephone calls was $12.43. The tax rate was 10% of the basic charge. The basic charge on one call was $2.90 less than that of the other. What were the basic charge and the amount of the tax on each charge?

22   The average of the four highest speeds attained in the qualifying trials for a recent Indianapolis Speedway Race was slightly more than 150 miles per hour, the speed necessary to make one lap of the track in 1 minute. The average of the four highest speeds of the race was slightly more than 142 miles per hour. Correct to the nearest second, how long did it take a car to make one lap of the track when traveling at this speed?

23   The total receipts for the 1963 baseball World Series were $1,995,189.09, an all-time high for a four-game series. Fifty-one per cent of this amount was the players' pool, of which 30% was divided among the second, third, and fourth teams of the two leagues. The balance was divided so that the Dodgers, the winning team, received 60%. After assigning smaller portions totaling $11,565, the Dodgers voted to divide the balance of their pool into $32\frac{1}{2}$ full shares. The Yankees, after assigning $3,406 in smaller portions, voted to divide the balance of their pool into $35\frac{3}{4}$ full shares. To the nearest dollar, what was the value of one full share to the recipient on each team?

24   Use the techniques of modular arithmetic to prove this theorem

for a number system in base **twelve:** The excess of **e**'s in a product is equal to the excess in the product of the excesses of the two factors.

25 A salesman, having made a call in city A, needs to drive a distance of 108 miles in 2 hours' time to meet an appointment in city B. There are three areas of traffic congestion through which he must pass: the first is 1 mile in length; the second is 2 miles in length; and the third is 5 miles in length. He estimates that the average speeds he will be able to maintain in each of the congested areas are: 1-mile area, 15 miles per hour; 2-mile area, 30 miles per hour; and 5-mile area, 25 miles per hour.   What average speed must he maintain on the open road (outside the congested areas) in order to be on time for his appointment?

INVITATIONS TO EXTENDED STUDY

1 Write the equation of the line through the two points $P_1(x_1,y_1)$ and $P_2(x_2,y_2)$.

2 A linear equation in two variables is said to represent a *family of lines* if it contains one parameter. Describe the family of lines represented by each equation.

(a) $4x + 2y + k = 0$ (b) $kx + 3y - 6 = 0$
(c) $5x - ky + 10 = 0$ (d) $x - ky + k = 0$
(e) $kx + y - k = 0$ (f) $kx + ky + 1 = 0$

3 Name at least two techniques for finding the solution set of three equations in three variables.

4 Discuss the geometric interpretations of systems of three linear equations in three variables.

5 Discuss matrix techniques for dealing with systems of three linear equations in three variables.

6 Prepare a paper on the elementary properties of determinants and matrices.

7 Discuss matrix techniques for dealing with systems of m linear equations in n variables.   There are three cases: $m < n; m = n; m > n$.

8 Present to the class an analysis of the quadratic function and its graph.

9 Develop and illustrate the use of at least four techniques for finding the zeros of the quadratic function of one variable.

10 Prepare a paper on techniques for finding the solution set of a system of two equations in two variables involving (a) one quadratic and one linear equation; (b) two quadratic equations.

11   Solve these inequalities:

(a) $\dfrac{2x - 2}{x + 4} \leq 1$ (b) $\dfrac{x + 4}{x - 1} \geq 0$

(c) $\dfrac{2x - 3}{x - 5} > 2$ (d) $\dfrac{3x + 8}{2x - 1} < 1$

12   Plot these inequalities:

(a) $f(x) \geq |x|$ for $-5 \leq x \leq 5$
(b) $f(x) \leq |x - 2|$ for $-4 < x < 8$

13   Plot these systems of inequalities:

(a) $|x| \leq 4$ (b) $|x - 3| \leq 2$
$\ |x| \geq 2$ $\ |x + 4| \geq 1$

(c) $x \geq 0$ (d) $x \geq 2$
$\ y \geq 0$ $\ y \geq 1$
$\ x + y \leq 2$ $\ x + 2y \leq 12$
$\ y \leq x$

14   Prepare a discussion of inequalities in two variables involving quadratic expressions.

Use mathematical induction to prove each of the propositions in items 15 to 24 for all positive integral values of n.

15   $2 + 4 + 6 + 8 + \cdots + 2n = n(n + 1)$ (the sum of the first n even integers).

16   $1 + 3 + 5 + 7 + \cdots + (2n - 1) = n^2$ (the sum of the first n odd integers).

17   $1^2 + 2^2 + 3^2 + 4^2 + \cdots + n^2 = \dfrac{n(n + 1)(2n + 1)}{6}$

18   $1^2 + 3^2 + 5^2 + 7^2 + \cdots + (2n - 1)^2 = \dfrac{4n^3 - n}{3}$

19   $\dfrac{1}{1 \cdot 2} + \dfrac{1}{2 \cdot 3} + \dfrac{1}{3 \cdot 4} + \cdots + \dfrac{1}{n(n + 1)} = \dfrac{n}{n + 1}$

20   $\dfrac{1}{2} + \dfrac{1}{2^2} + \dfrac{1}{2^3} + \cdots + \dfrac{1}{2^n} = 1 - \dfrac{1}{2^n}$

21   $7^n - 5^n$ is divisible by 2.
22   $x^n - y^n$ is divisible by $x - y$.
23   $x^n + y^n$ is divisible by $x + y$.
24   $x^{2n} - y^{2n}$ is divisible by $x + y$.
25   What subset of the field of rational numbers is isomorphic to the set I of integers?   Substantiate your answer.

BIBLIOGRAPHY

ADAMS, L. J.: "Arithmetic for College Students," Holt, Rinehart and Winston, Inc., New York, 1961.

ADLER, IRVING: "Magic House of Numbers," The John Day Company, Inc., New York, 1960.

————: "Mathematics: The Story of Numbers, Symbols, and Space," Golden Press, New York, 1958.

————: "The New Mathematics," The John Day Company, Inc., New York, 1958.

———— and RUTH ADLER: "Numbers, Old and New," The John Day Company, Inc., New York, 1960.

AIKEN, D. J., and C. A. BESEMAN: "Modern Mathematics: Topics and Problems," McGraw-Hill Book Company, New York, 1959.

ALLEN, HAROLD DON: Understanding through Number Systems, *The Math. Teacher,* **55:**184–188 (1962).

AMERICAN COUNCIL ON EDUCATION, "The Story of Weights and Measures," number 3 (1932); "The Story of Our Calendar," number 4 (1933); "Telling Time throughout the Centuries," number 5 (1933); *Achievements of Civilization.*

ANDREWS, F. EMERSON: "New Numbers," 2d ed., Essential Books, New York, 1944.

BAKST, AARON: Approximate Computation, *Twelfth Yearbook of the National Council of Teachers of Mathematics,* Washington, 1937.

————: "Arithmetic for the Modern Age," D. Van Nostrand Company, Inc., Princeton, N.J., 1960.

BANKS, J. HOUSTON: "Elements of Mathematics," 2d ed., Allyn and Bacon, Inc., Boston, 1961.

————: "Learning and Teaching Arithmetic," 2d ed., Allyn and Bacon, Inc., Boston, 1964.

BEARD, RALPH H.: The Twelve Base, *The Math. Teacher,* **48:**332–333 (1955).

BELL, CLIFFORD, CLELA D. HAMMOND, and ROBERT B. HERRERA: "Fundamentals of Arithmetic for Teachers," John Wiley & Sons, Inc., New York, 1962.

BELL, E. T.: "The Development of Mathematics," 2d ed., McGraw-Hill Book Company, New York, 1945.

BELLMAN, RICHARD: On the Concepts of a Problem and Problem Solving, *The Am. Math. Monthly,* **67:**119–134 (1960).

BENDICK, JEANNE: "How Much and How Many: The Story of Weights and Measures," McGraw-Hill Book Company, New York, 1947.

BERGAMINI, DAVID: Mathematics, *Life Sci. Library*, Time Incorporated, New York, 1963.

BLUMENTHAL, L. M.: "A Modern View of Geometry," W. H. Freeman and Company, San Francisco, 1961.

BOTTS, TRUMAN: Numbers, Sets, and Counting, *The Arithmetic Teacher*, 8:281–286 (1961).

———: Linear Measurement and Imagination, *The Arithmetic Teacher*, 9:376–382 (1962).

BOWMAN, M. E.: "Romance in Arithmetic: Currency, Weights, and Measures," London University Press, London, 1950.

BOYER, CARL B.: Viète's Use of Decimal Fractions, *The Math. Teacher*, 55:123–127 (1962).

BOYER, LEE EMERSON: Elementary Approximate Computation, *The Math. Teacher*, 32:249–258 (1939).

BREUER, JOSEPH: "Introduction to the Theory of Sets," translated by Howard F. Fehr, Prentice-Hall, Inc., Englewood Cliffs, N.J., 1958.

BROTHER U. ALFRED, F.D.C.: Prevalence of the Set Concept, *School Sci. Math.*, 62:473–479 (1962).

BRUMFIEL, CHARLES F., ROBERT E. EICHOLZ, and MERRILL E. SHANKS: "Fundamental Concepts of Elementary Mathematics," Addison-Wesley Publishing Company, Inc., Reading, Mass., 1962.

BRUNE, IRWIN: Geometry in the Grades, *The Arithmetic Teacher*, 8:210–219 (1961).

BUCKINGHAM, B. R.: "Elementary Arithmetic: Its Meaning and Practice," Ginn and Company, Boston, 1947.

CAJORI, FLORIAN: "A History of Mathematical Notations," vol. I, The Open Court Publishing Company, La Salle, Ill., 1928.

———: "History of Elementary Mathematics," The Macmillan Company, New York, 1929.

CARNAHAN, WALTER: The Unit Fractions of Ancient Egypt, *School Sci. Math.*, 60:5–9 (1960).

CHACE, A. B., L. S. BULL, H. P. MANNING, and R. C. ARCHIBALD: "The Rhind Mathematical Papyrus," vols. I and II, Mathematical Association of America, Inc., Buffalo, N.Y., 1927 and 1929.

COMMITTEE ON THE UNDERGRADUATE PROGRAM IN MATHEMATICS (CUPM): "Elementary Mathematics of Sets with Applications," chaps. I, II, VII, Mathematical Association of America, Inc., Buffalo, N.Y., 1958.

DANTZIG, TOBIAS: "Number, the Language of Science," 3d ed., The Macmillan Company, New York, 1945.

DAVIS, PHILIP J.: "The Lore of Large Numbers," Random House, Inc., New York, 1961.

DEAN, RICHARD A.: Defining Basic Concepts of Mathematics, *The Arithmetic Teacher*, 7:122–127 (1960).

DELURY, D. B.: Computations with Approximate Numbers, *The Math. Teacher*, 51:521–530 (1958).

DIENES, Z. P.: "The Power of Mathematics," Hutchinson & Co. (Publishers), Ltd., London, 1963.

DUBISCH, ROY: "The Nature of Number," The Ronald Press Company, New York, 1952.

ENCYCLOPAEDIA BRITANNICA: Abacus, Arithmetic, Numbers, Numerals, Weights and Measures (1961).

EVENSON, A. B.: "Modern Mathematics," Scott, Foresman and Company, Chicago, 1962.

EVES, HOWARD: "An Introduction to the History of Mathematics," Holt, Rinehart, and Winston, Inc., New York, 1959.

FÉLIX, LUCIENNE: Modern Mathematics Begins in the Elementary School, translated by Hyman and Phyllis Flyer Kavet, *The Arithmetic Teacher*, 9:32–36 (1962).

FRÈGE, G.: "The Foundations of Arithmetic," 2d ed., Basil Blackwell & Mott, Ltd., Oxford, 1953.

FREITAG, HERTA T., and ARTHUR H. FREITAG: "The Number Story," National Council of Teachers of Mathematics, Washington, 1960.

FRIEND, J. N.: "Numbers," Charles Scribner's Sons, New York, 1954.

FUJII, JOHN N.: "An Introduction to the Elements of Mathematics," John Wiley & Sons, Inc., New York, 1961.

FULKERSON, ELBERT: Writing a Number in Different Bases, *The Math. Teacher*, 53:364–366 (1960).

GALFO, ARMAND J.: When Does $2 + 2 = 10$? *School Sci. Math.*, 63:653–657 (1963).

GIFFEL, WILLIAM J.: Primes and Things, *School Sci. Math.*, 62:684–687 (1962).

GRAY, JAMES F.: "Sets, Relations, and Functions," Holt, Rinehart and Winston, Inc., New York, 1962.

GREENLEAF, NEWCOMB, and ROBERT J. WISNER: The Unique Factorization Theorem, *The Math. Teacher*, 52:600–603 (1959).

HAINES, MARGARET: Modular Arithmetic, *The Arithmetic Teacher*, 9:127–129 (1962).

HAMILTON, E. W.: Number Systems: Fad or Foundation, *The Arithmetic Teacher*, 8:242–245 (1961).

HAMILTON, NORMAN T., and JOSEPH LANDIN: "Set Theory: The Structure of Arithmetic," Allyn and Bacon, Inc., Boston, 1961.

HANNON, HERBERT: A Time to Appraise the New and Re-evaluate the Old in Upper Grades and Junior High School Mathematics, *School Sci. Math.*, 58:171–177 (1963).

HENKIN, LEON, W. NORMAN SMITH, VERNE J. VARINEAU, and MICHAEL J. WALSH: "Retracing Elementary Mathematics," The Macmillan Company, New York, 1962.

HOHN, FRANZ E.: Automatic Addition, *The Arithmetic Teacher*, 10:127–132 (1963).

INGHAM, CAROLYN, and JOSEPH M. PAYNE: An Eighth-grade Unit on Number Systems, *The Math. Teacher*, 51:392–395 (1958).

JERBERT, A. R.: Division by Zero, *School Sci. Math.*, 49:484–488 (1949).

JOHNSON, DONOVAN A.: A Unit on Our Number System, *School Sci. Math.*, 52:556–561 (1952).

——— and WILLIAM H. GLENN: "Exploring Mathematics on Your Own," series of eighteen pamphlets, McGraw-Hill Book Company, New York, 1961.

JONES, BURTON W.: Miniature Number Systems, *The Math. Teacher*, 51:226–231 (1958).

———: "Elementary Concepts of Mathematics," The Macmillan Company, New York, 1963.

JONES, EMILY: Historical Conflict: Decimal versus Vulgar Fractions, *The Arithmetic Teacher*, 7:184–188 (1960).

JONES, PHILLIP S.: "Numbers: Their History and Use," Ulrich's Bookstore, Ann Arbor, Michigan, 1954.

KEEDY, MARVIN L.: "A Modern Introduction to Basic Mathematics," Addison-Wesley Publishing Company, Inc., Reading, Mass., 1963.

LARSEN, HAROLD D., and H. GLENN LUDLOW: "Arithmetic for Colleges," 3d ed., The Macmillan Company, New York, 1963.

LAY, L. CLARK: "Arithmetic: An Introduction to Mathematics," The Macmillan Company, New York, 1961.

LAYTON, W. I.: "College Arithmetic," John Wiley & Sons, Inc., New York, 1959.

LEONARD, JOHN L.: A New Method for Finding Square Root, *School Sci. Math.*, **50**:40–48 (1950).

MARER, FRED, SAMUEL SKOLNIK, and ORDA E. LEWIS: "Arithmetic," Little, Brown and Company, Boston, 1960.

MARKS, JOHN L., JAMES R. SMART, and C. RICHARD PURDY: "Other Bases in Arithmetic," Ginn and Company, Boston, 1963.

MOORE, TABBIE MAE: More about Casting Out Nines, *The Arithmetic Teacher*, **3**:204–206 (1956).

MORTON, R. L.: Decimal and Duodecimal Reciprocals, *The Math. Teacher*, **56**:333–339 (1963).

MOSTELLER, F., R. E. K. ROURKE, and G. B. THOMAS, JR.: "Probability and Statistics," Addison-Wesley Publishing Company, Inc., Reading, Mass., 1962.

MUELLER, FRANCIS J.: "Arithmetic: Its Structure and Concepts," Prentice-Hall, Inc., Englewood Cliffs, N.J., 1956.

————: On the Fraction as a Numeral, *The Arithmetic Teacher*, **8**:234–238 (1961).

NATIONAL COUNCIL OF TEACHERS OF MATHEMATICS: The Metric System of Weights and Measures, *Twentieth Yearbook*, 1948; Emerging Practices in Mathematics Education, *Twenty-second Yearbook*, 1954; Growth of Mathematical Ideas, Grades K-12, *Twenty-fourth Yearbook*, 1959; Enrichment Mathematics for the Grades, *Twenty-seventh Yearbook*, 1963; Enrichment Mathematics for the High School, *Twenty-eighth Yearbook*, 1963; Topics in Mathematics for Elementary School Teachers, *Twenty-ninth Yearbook*, 1964; Washington.

NEWMAN, JAMES R.: "The World of Mathematics," Simon and Schuster, Inc., New York, 1956.

NIVEN, IVAN: "Numbers, Rational and Irrational," Random House, Inc., New York, 1961.

OHMER, MERLIN M., CLAYTON V. AUCOIN, and MARION J. CORTEZ: "Elementary Contemporary Mathematics," Blaisdell Publishing Company, New York, 1964.

OSBORN, ROGER M., VERE DEVAULT, CLAUDE D. BOYD, and W. ROBERT HOUSTON: "Extending Mathematics Understanding," Charles E. Merrill Books, Inc., Columbus, Ohio, 1963.

PAIGE, DONALD D.: Primes and Factoring, *The Arithmetic Teacher*, **9**:449–452 (1962).

PARSONS, KENNETH B., and STANLEY P. FRANKLIN: Divisibility by Two, *The Math. Teacher*, **55**:639 (1960).

PETERSON, JOHN A., and JOSEPH HASHISAKI: "Theory of Arithmetic," John Wiley & Sons, Inc., New York, 1963.

PIAGET, JEAN: "The Child's Conception of Number," Butler and Tanner, Ltd., London, 1952.

————, BARBEL INHELDER, and ALINA SZEMKNSKA: "The Child's Conception of Geometry," Basic Books, Inc., Publishers, New York, 1960.

PÓLYA, G.: "How to Solve It," 2d ed., Anchor Books, Doubleday & Company, Inc., Garden City, N.Y., 1957.

——: "Mathematical Discovery," vol. I, John Wiley & Sons, New York, 1962.

RAPPAPORT, DAVID: Percentage: Noun or Adjective? *Arithmetic Teacher,* **8:**25–26 (1961).

——: The Meanings of Fractions, *School Sci. Math.,* **62:**241–244 (1962).

RASSWEILER, MERRILL, and HARRIS J. MERLE: "Mathematics and Measurements," Harper & Row, Publishers, Incorporated, New York, 1955.

READ, CECIL B.: Arguments against Universal Adoption of the Metric System, *School Sci. Math.,* **50:**297–306 (1950).

——: Comments on Computation with Approximate Numbers, *The Math. Teacher,* **46:**479–483 (1953).

RECKZEH, JOHN K., and ERNEST R. DUNCAN: *E Pluribus Unum:* A Brief Discussion of the "Law of One," *The Arithmetic Teacher,* **8:**413–415 (1961).

RINGENBERG, LAWRENCE A.: "A Portrait of 2," National Council of Teachers of Mathematics, Washington, 1960.

——: Infinite Decimals, *The Math. Teacher,* **55:**10–19 (1962).

RUTLAND, LEON, and MAX HOSIER: Some Basic Geometric Ideas for the Elementary Teacher, *The Arithmetic Teacher,* **8:**357–362 (1961).

SANDERS, PAUL: "Elementary Mathematics: A Logical Approach," International Textbook Company, Scranton, Pa., 1963.

SCHAAF, WILLIAM L.: "Basic Concepts of Elementary Mathematics," John Wiley & Sons, Inc., New York, 1960.

SCHEID, FRANCIS: Clock Arithmetic and Nuclear Energy, *The Math. Teacher,* **52:**604–607 (1959).

SCHIFF, HERBERT J.: Let Them Measure, *School Sci. Math.,* **57:**291–292 (1957).

SCHOOL MATHEMATICS STUDY GROUP (SMSG): "Some Basic Mathematical Concepts," "Euclidean Geometry Based on Ruler and Protractor Axioms," "Structure of Elementary Algebra," "Geometry," "Concepts of Informal Geometry," "Number Systems," "Intuitive Geometry," "Concepts of Algebra," *Studies in Mathematics,* Yale University Press, New Haven, Conn., 1961.

SCOTT, LLOYD: Numeration, Notation, and System: Considerations of Nomenclature, *School Sci. Math.,* **62:**551–555 (1962).

SEEGAR, RAYMOND J.: Fingerprints, *The Arithmetic Teacher,* **8:**339–344 (1961).

SELBY, SAMUEL M., and LEONARD SWEET: "Sets—Relations—Functions: An Introduction," McGraw-Hill Book Company, New York, 1963.

SEYMOUR, KENNETH A.: A General Test for Divisibility, *The Math. Teacher,* **56:**151–154 (1963).

SHUSTER, CARL N.: The Advantages of Decimal Notation, *The Math. Teacher,* **55:**649–650 (1962).

——: Teaching Computation with Approximate Data, *The Math. Teacher,* **42:**123–132 (1949).

——: Approximate Square Roots, *The Math. Teacher,* **45:**17–18 (1952).

SISTER M. BARBARA STASTNY, O.S.F.: A Test for Divisibility, *The Math. Teacher,* **53:**627–631 (1960).

SMART, JAMES R.: "New Understanding in Arithmetic," Allyn and Bacon, Inc., Boston, 1963.

SMITH, DAVID EUGENE: "History of Mathematics," vols. I and II, Ginn and Company, Boston, 1953. Also available through Dover Publications, Inc., New York.

———— and JEKUTHIEL GINSBURG: "Numbers and Numerals," National Council of Teachers of Mathematics, Washington, 1961.

SMITH, ROLLAND R.: Per Cents in the Seventh and Eighth Grades, *J. Educ.*, **136:**34–35 (1953).

STAHL, SHELBY D.: A Discussion of Powers of Whole Numbers, *The Math. Teacher*, **55:**535–537 (1962).

STEIN, EDWIN I.: "Fundamentals of Mathematics," Allyn and Bacon, Inc., Boston, 1961.

STEIN, SHERMAN K.: "Mathematics: The Man-made Universe," W. H. Freeman and Company, San Francisco, 1963.

SUPPES, PATRICK: "Sets and Numbers, Books 1 and 2," Stanford University Press, Stanford, Calif., 1960.

————: Mathematical Logic in the Schools, *The Arithmetic Teacher*, **9:**396–399 (1962).

———— and BLAIR A. MCKNIGHT: Sets and Numbers in Grade One, *The Arithmetic Teacher*, **8:**287–290 (1961).

SWAIN, ROBERT L.: "Understanding Arithmetic," Holt, Rinehart and Winston, Inc., New York, 1957.

TWADDLE, RICHARD D.: A Look at the Base Negative Ten, *The Math. Teacher*, **56:**88–90 (1963).

VAN ENGEN, HENRY: Rate Pairs, Fractions, and Rational Numbers, *The Arithmetic Teacher*, **7:**389–399 (1960).

————: The Reform Movement in Arithmetic and the Verbal Problem, *The Arithmetic Teacher*, **10:**3–6 (1963).

VOLPEL, MARVIN D.: Solving Percentage Problems by the Equation Method, *The Math. Teacher*, **47:**425–427 (1954).

WARD, MORGAN, and CLARENCE ETHEL HARDGROVE: "Modern Elementary Mathematics," Addison-Wesley Publishing Company, Inc., Reading, Mass., 1964.

WEAVER, J. FRED: Misconceptions about Rationalization in Arithmetic, *The Math. Teacher*, **44:**369–376 (1951).

WEINBERG, GEORGE H., and JOHN A. SCHUMAKER: "Statistics: An Intuitive Approach," Wadsworth Publishing Company, Inc., Belmont, Calif., 1962.

WELLS, CHAUNCEY H., JR.: Using a Negative Base for Number Notation, *The Math. Teacher*, **56:**91–93 (1963).

WENDT, ARNOLD: Per Cent without Cases, *The Arithmetic Teacher*, **6:**209–214 (1959).

WIEBE, ARTHUR, J.: "Foundations of Mathematics," Holt, Rinehart and Winston, Inc., New York, 1962.

WILLERDING, MARGARET F.: A Teaching Unit in Modular Arithmetic, *School Sci. Math.*, **60:**511–518 (1960).

————: Other Number Systems: Aids to Understanding, *The Arithmetic Teacher*, **8:**350–356 (1961).

————: A Critical Look at the New Mathematics for the Seventh Grade, *School Sci. Math.*, **62:**215–220 (1962).

WILLIAMS, WENDELL N.: A Complete Set of Elementary Rules for Testing Divisibility, *The Math. Teacher*, **56:**437–442 (1963).

YOUNG, JOHN W.: Symmetry, *Fifth Yearbook of the National Council of Teachers of Mathematics*, pp. 145–146, 1930. Washington.

YOUSE, BEVAN K.: "Arithmetic: A Modern Approach," Prentice-Hall, Inc., Englewood Cliffs, N.J., 1963.

GLOSSARY OF SYMBOLS

Symbol	Interpretation	Page
$a_1, a_2, a_3, \ldots, a_n$	The elements a-one, a-two, a-three, and on to include a-sub n	5
$S = \{s_1, s_2, s_3, \ldots, s_n\}$	S is a finite set whose elements are s_1, s_2, s_3, and so on to s_n	5
$S = \{s \mid s$ is one of the elements $s_1, s_2, \ldots, s_n\}$	S is the set of all s such that s is one of the elements $s_1, s_2, \ldots, s_n$	5
$S = \{s_1, s_2, s_3 \ldots\}$	S is an infinite set whose elements are s_1, s_2, s_3, and so on to s_n	5
$x \in S$	x is an element of the set S	4
$x \notin S$	x is not an element of the set S	5
U	The universal set	3
$\sim S$	The complement of S	7
$P - Q$	The relative complement of set Q in set P	7
$P \subseteq Q$	P is a subset of Q	3
$P \subset Q$	P is a proper subset of Q	4
$P \nsubseteq Q$	P is not a subset of Q	6
$P \not\subset Q$	P is not a proper subset of Q	6
$P \supseteq Q$ or $P \supset Q$	Set P contains set Q	15
$P = Q$	Sets P and Q have the same elements	4
$P \cup Q$	The union of sets P and Q (P cup Q)	8
$P \cap Q$	The intersection of sets P and Q (P cap Q)	8
$\emptyset$	The empty, or null, set	8
$P \cap Q = \emptyset$	P and Q are disjoint sets	9
$n(P)$	The cardinal number of set P	13
–base	The numeral immediately preceding the dash is written in the base indicated (e.g., **234—five** is in base **five**)	36
(x, y)	The ordered pair of elements x and y	59
		215

Symbol	*Interpretation*	*Page*
(x,y,z)	The ordered triple of elements x, y, and z	214
$P \times Q$	The cartesian product of the sets P and Q	60
$a < b$	a is less than b	70 340
$a \leq b$	a is less than or equal to b	80 340
$a \leq b \leq c$	a is less than or equal to b, which is less than or equal to c	168 341
$a > b$	a is greater than b	70 340
$a \geq b$	a is greater than or equal to b	80 340
$a \geq b \geq c$	a is greater than or equal to b, which is greater than or equal to c	168
$p \rightarrow q$	Proposition p implies proposition q	71
0	The additive identity; also the cardinal number of the empty set	13 81
1	The multiplicative identity; also the cardinal number of any set whose elements can be placed in one-to-one correspondence with the elements of the set $\{a\}$	13 65
$-a$	The additive inverse of a	82
a^{-1} or $\dfrac{1}{a}$	The multiplicative inverse of a $(a \neq 0)$	112
$\pm a$	Plus or minus a	82
$a + b$	The sum of a and b	46
$a - b$	The difference between a and b	80
$a \times b$ or $a \cdot b$ or ab	The product of a and b	61
$\dfrac{a}{b}$ or $a \div b$	The quotient of a divided by b $(b \neq 0)$	107
$\dfrac{a}{b}$	A rational number or a fraction if a and b are integers $(b \neq 0)$	108 129
$\dfrac{a}{b}$ or $a{:}b$	The ratio of the two numbers a and b $(b \neq 0)$	132
$a \neq b$	a is not equal to b	83
g.c.f.	Greatest common factor of two or more numbers	98
g.c.d.	Greatest common divisor of two or more numbers	120
a^n	The number of times a is used as a factor if and only if n is a natural number or a positive integer	30

Symbol	Interpretation	Page
$a^{-m} = \dfrac{1}{a^m}$ for $a \neq 0$	By definition	30
$a^0 = 1$ for $a \neq 0$	By definition	30
$a \approx b$	a is approximately equal to b	141
$\sqrt{a}$	The positive square root of a	157
$\sqrt[3]{a}$	A cube root of a	157
0.75	A finite (terminating) decimal	139
$0.\overline{142857}$	An infinite (nonterminating) repeating decimal	139
$3.14159 \cdots = \pi$	An infinite nonrepeating decimal	160
$r\%$	The ratio of r to 100, or the rate per cent	148
$p = rb$	Percentage is the product of the rate per cent and the base	150
$|a|$	The absolute, or numerical, value of a	166
i	The imaginary unit such that $i^2 = -1$	168
$a + bi$	A complex number if a and b are real numbers and $i^2 = -1$	168
$a \equiv b \pmod{m}$	a is congruent to b modulo m	180
$a \equiv b$	a is identically equal to b	289
$\overleftrightarrow{AB}$	The line of indefinite extent on which A and B are two distinct points	193
$\overline{AB}$	The line segment joining points A and B	195
AB	The length of the line segment $\overline{AB}$	196
$\overrightarrow{AB}$	The ray which extends indefinitely in one direction from its end point A	195
$\overparen{AB}$	The arc of a circle	222
$\overline{AB} \cong \overline{CD}$	Line segment $\overline{AB}$ is congruent to line segment $\overline{CD}$	198
$\sim$	Is similar to	229
$\angle ABC$	The angle of which B is the vertex and $\overrightarrow{BA}$ and $\overrightarrow{BC}$ are the rays which form the angle	204
$m \angle ABC$	The measure of $\angle ABC$	205
$\angle ABC \cong \angle PQR$	$\angle ABC$ is congruent to $\angle PQR$	206
$1°$ (one degree)	Unit of angle measure	205
$\overleftrightarrow{X'X}$, or x axis	The horizontal axis, or axis of abscissas, in a two-dimensional cartesian frame of reference	214

Symbol	*Interpretation*	*Page*
$\overleftrightarrow{Y'Y}$, or y axis	The vertical axis, or axis of ordinates, in a two-dimensional cartesian frame of reference	214
$\overleftrightarrow{Z'Z}$, or z axis	The third axis, with $\overleftrightarrow{X'X}$ and $\overleftrightarrow{Y'Y}$, in a three-dimensional cartesian frame of reference	214
$\triangle ABC$	Triangle ABC	225
$\triangle ABC \cong \triangle DEF$	Triangle ABC is congruent to triangle DEF	233
$\leftrightarrow$	Corresponds to	229
$f(x)$	Function of x, or function at x	316
$f(x) = mx + k$	The linear function of x where $m \neq 0$	321
$P(x,y)$	The point P whose two-dimensional rectangular coordinates are x and y	215
$P(x,y,z)$	The point P whose three-dimensional coordinates are x, y, and z	214
$m = \dfrac{y_2 - y_1}{x_2 - x_1}$	The slope of the straight line passing through the two points $P_1(x_1,y_1)$ and $P_2(x_2,y_2)$	323
$ax + by + c = 0$	The linear equation in x and y	327
$y = mx + k$	The slope-intercept form of the equation of a straight line	325
$y - y_1 = m(x - x_1)$	The point-slope form of the equation of a straight line	329
σ^2	Variance of a distribution	302
σ	Standard duration of a distribution	302
$\{(x,k)\}$	The constant function $y = k$	327
$ax + by < c$, or $ax + by > c$	Inequality relation in the two variables x and y	342
$\dfrac{y}{x} = k$, or $y = kx$	y varies directly as x	345
$y = \dfrac{k}{x}$, or $xy = k$	y varies inversely as x	346
$y = kxz$	y varies jointly as x and z	346

ANSWERS TO
ODD-NUMBERED EXERCISES

Sec. 1-1, page 10

1 (*a*) $I = \{1,2,3,4, \ldots\}$
   (*b*) $S = \{6,7,8,9, \ldots, 19\}$
   (*c*) $G = \{$Florida, Alabama, Mississippi, Louisiana, Texas$\}$
   (*d*) $L = \{$Superior, Michigan, Huron, Ontario, Erie$\}$
   (*e*) $E = \{2,4,6,8,10, \ldots\}$
   (*f*) $M = \{$Texas, Arizona, California, New Mexico$\}$
3 No. $M \cap N = \{0\}$, so it is not the empty set
5 (*a*) False; (*b*) false; (*c*) false; (*d*) true; (*e*) false; (*f*) true
7 (*a*) False; (*b*) false; (*c*) true; (*d*) false; (*e*) false; (*f*) false; (*g*) true
9 $A; \emptyset$
11 The diagrams shown are not necessarily the only correct diagrams.

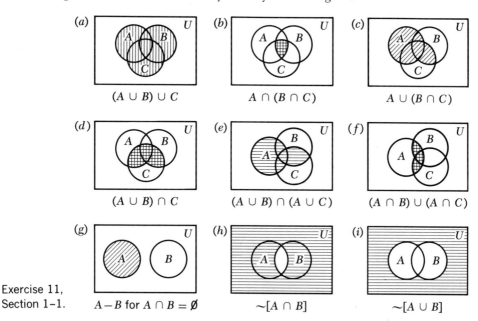

(*a*) $(A \cup B) \cup C$ (*b*) $A \cap (B \cap C)$ (*c*) $A \cup (B \cap C)$

(*d*) $(A \cup B) \cap C$ (*e*) $(A \cup B) \cap (A \cup C)$ (*f*) $(A \cap B) \cup (A \cap C)$

(*g*) $A - B$ for $A \cap B = \emptyset$ (*h*) $\sim[A \cap B]$ (*i*) $\sim[A \cup B]$

Exercise 11,
Section 1-1.

375

13   (a) False: $C - M = \{t\}$; $M - C = \{e,m\}$
     (b) False: There are elements in each which are not in the other.
     (c) True: $C - M = \{t\}$; t is an element of C.
     (d) False: $M \cap (C - M) = \emptyset$ and not M
15   It is a true statement since $\emptyset = \emptyset$.

Sec. 1–4, page 18

 1   When to each element of set P there corresponds one and only one element
     of set Q and to each element of Q there corresponds one and only one
     element of P.
 3   When a one-to-one correspondence exists between pupils and chairs.
 5   It is the property the set has in common with every set with which it can be
     put into one-to-one correspondence.
11   (a) 0; (b) 1; (c) 0; (d) 7; (e) 60
13   {Linda}; {Linda, Sharon}; {Linda, Sharon, Diana}; {Linda, Sharon, Diana,
     Marly}; {Linda, Sharon, Diana, Marly, Cathy}; {Linda, Sharon, Diana,
     Marly, Cathy, Carol}
15   (a) $\perp | \triangle$; (b) $\square \triangle 0 |$; (c) $\perp 0 \perp \perp$
17   (a) True; (b) true

Sec. 2–3, page 27

 1   (a) 56; (b) 301; (c) 499; (d) 20,094
 3   (a) 247; (b) 1,001; (c) 1,962; (d) 1,492; (e) 1,002,004
 5   (See figure on page 377.)

Sec. 2–6, page 33

 1   History reveals that it first originated with the Hindus but was brought to
     Western Europe by the Arabs.
 3   $1,056.013 = 1(10)^3 + 0(10)^2 + 5(10) + 6 + 0(10)^{-1} + 1(10)^{-2} + 3(10)^{-3}$
 5   (a) *Mayan:* simpler notation; (b) *Babylonian:* place value and simpler nota-
     tion; (c) *Egyptian:* place value and simpler notation; (d) *Roman:* place value
     and simpler notation
 7   Its place value is divided by 10.
 9   1 dime = 10 pennies; 1 dollar = 10 dimes = 100 pennies

Sec. 2–10, page 39

 1   (a) **101**; (b) **42**; (c) **35**; (d) **32**; (e) **11010**
 3   Base **five**: (a) **100**; (b) **140** (self-consistent is one word); (c) **114**; (d) **111**;
     (e) **133**
     Base **twelve**: (a) **21**; (b) **39**; (c) **2t**; (d) **27**; (e) **37**
     Base **eight**: (a) **31**; (b) **55**; (c) **42**; (d) **37**; (e) **53**
     Base **two**: (a) **11001**; (b) **101101**; (c) **100010**; (d) **11111**; (e) **101011**
 5   (a) **23** in.; (b) **8t** in.; (c) **40** in.; (d) **ee** in.
 7   (a) **20**; (b) **40**
 9   (a) **3t** (where t is the symbol for ten); (b) $\underset{\underline{\underline{\quad}}}{\cdots}$
11   **b** symbols will be needed (0 and **b** − 1 nonzero symbols).

Exercise 5, Section 2–3.

EGYPTIAN	GREEK	ROMAN	MAYAN
(a)	$\nu\xi\zeta$	CDLXVII	
(b)	$\beta'\phi\eta$	MMDVIII	
(c)	$\delta M\psi\kappa$	$\overline{\text{XL}}$DCCXX	
(d)	$\alpha'\nu\varphi\beta$	MCDXCII	
(e)	$\gamma'\delta$	MMMIV	
(f)	$\mu M\phi$	$\overline{\text{CDD}}$	
(g)	$\rho\xi\alpha M\nu\lambda$	$\overline{\text{MDCXCDXXX}}$	
(h)	$\nu\kappa M\alpha'\omega\varphi\zeta$	$\overline{\text{MMMMCCIDCCCXCVII}}$	

Sec. 3–7, page 55

3   Since we use a decimal system, "carrying" consists in regrouping in terms of powers of ten.

7   The table is symmetric, with the diagonal from the upper left corner to the lower right corner.

9   Associative

11   (See figures on page 378.)

15   (a) 130; (b) 1555; (c) 17304; (d) 14505; (e) 17615; (f) 7156

17   (a) 2030; (b) 14510; (c) 102240; (d) 114403

19   (See figures on pages 378 and 379.)

21   (a) 1078; (b) 23280; (c) 14831; (d) 18490

Sec. 3–13, page 68

1   There is no ambiguity about the product.

3   Numbers are grouped according to powers of ten.

Five

+	0	1	2	3	4
0	0	1	2	3	4
1	1	2	3	4	10
2	2	3	4	10	11
3	3	4	10	11	12
4	4	10	11	12	13

(a)

Exercise 11, Section 3-7.

Eight

+	0	1	2	3	4	5	6	7
0	0	1	2	3	4	5	6	7
1	1	2	3	4	5	6	7	10
2	2	3	4	5	6	7	10	11
3	3	4	5	6	7	10	11	12
4	4	5	6	7	10	11	12	13
5	5	6	7	10	11	12	13	14
6	6	7	10	11	12	13	14	15
7	7	10	11	12	13	14	15	16

(b)

Seven

+	0	1	2	3	4	5	6
0	0	1	2	3	4	5	6
1	1	2	3	4	5	6	10
2	2	3	4	5	6	10	11
3	3	4	5	6	10	11	12
4	4	5	6	10	11	12	13
5	5	6	10	11	12	13	14
6	6	10	11	12	13	14	15

(a)

Exercise 19, Section 3-7.

Eleven

+	0	1	2	3	4	5	6	7	8	9	t
0	0	1	2	3	4	5	6	7	8	9	t
1	1	2	3	4	5	6	7	8	9	t	10
2	2	3	4	5	6	7	8	9	t	10	11
3	3	4	5	6	7	8	9	t	10	11	12
4	4	5	6	7	8	9	t	10	11	12	13
5	5	6	7	8	9	t	10	11	12	13	14
6	6	7	8	9	t	10	11	12	13	14	15
7	7	8	9	t	10	11	12	13	14	15	16
8	8	9	t	10	11	12	13	14	15	16	17
9	9	t	10	11	12	13	14	15	16	17	18
t	t	10	11	12	13	14	15	16	17	18	19

(b)

Twelve

+	0	1	2	3	4	5	6	7	8	9	t	e
0	0	1	2	3	4	5	6	7	8	9	t	e
1	1	2	3	4	5	6	7	8	9	t	e	10
2	2	3	4	5	6	7	8	9	t	e	10	11
3	3	4	5	6	7	8	9	t	e	10	11	12
4	4	5	6	7	8	9	t	e	10	11	12	13
5	5	6	7	8	9	t	e	10	11	12	13	14
6	6	7	8	9	t	e	10	11	12	13	14	15
7	7	8	9	t	e	10	11	12	13	14	15	16
8	8	9	t	e	10	11	12	13	14	15	16	17
9	9	t	e	10	11	12	13	14	15	16	17	18
t	t	e	10	11	12	13	14	15	16	17	18	19
e	e	10	11	12	13	14	15	16	17	18	19	1t

Exercise 19,
Section 3–7.

(c)

7 Each system is closed under multiplication, and multiplication is commutative.
9 (a) l0⊥l; (b) ⊥△⊥△0△; (c) l□00⊥⊥□△
11 4,275
13 (a) $63 \times 36 = 63 \times (4 \times 9) = (63 \times 4) \times 9 = 2,268$
   (b) $85 \times 28 = 85 \times (4 \times 7) = (85 \times 4) \times 7 = 2,380$
   (c) $272 \times 54 = 272 \times (6 \times 9) = (272 \times 6) \times 9 = 14,688$
15 (a) **2210**; (b) **210712**; (c) **1767524**
17 (a) $236 \times 74 = 236 \times (70 + 4) = (236 \times 70) + (236 \times 4) = 17,464$
   (b) $3,024 \times 507 = 3,024 \times (500 + 7) = (3,024 \times 500) + (3,024 \times 7) = 1,533,168$
   (c) $2,526 \times 370 = 2,526 \times (300 + 70) = (2,526 \times 300) + (2,526 \times 70) = 934,620$
19 2,758—ten; 5306—eight; 171t—twelve; 20434—six.
21 20,590—ten; 50156—eight; ll⊥□△△0—verto; 235154—six

Sec. 3–16, page 75

1 Reflexive and symmetric

Sec. 4–5, page 93

1 Each operation annuls (cancels) the effect of the other. $(a + b) - b = a$; $(a - b) + b = a$.
3 To compare two numbers; to find the difference between two numbers; to find how many are left after some are removed
5 (a) No: $a + a = 2a$, which is not in the set.
   (b) No: $a - (-a) = a + a = 2a$, which is not in the set.
   (c) No: $a \times (-a) = -a^2$, which is not in the set.

Numeral	Base					
	two	**three**	**five**	**seven**	**ten**	**twelve**
1	*o*	*o*	*o*	*o*	*o*	*o*
2	*n*	*e*	*e*	*e*	*e*	*e*
10	*e*	*o*	*o*	*o*	*e*	*e*
11	*o*	*e*	*e*	*e*	*o*	*o*
31	*n*	*n*	*e*	*e*	*o*	*o*
43	*n*	*n*	*o*	*o*	*o*	*o*
44	*n*	*n*	*e*	*e*	*e*	*e*
555	*n*	*n*	*n*	*o*	*o*	*o*

Exercise 25, Section 4–6.

7   The sum of the excess of nines in the difference and the excess in the subtrahend must be the same as the excess in the minuend.
9   (a) 1,423; (b) 1,978; (c) 3,086
11   (a) 4443; (b) 4306; (c) 26t6; (d) 1e1e; (e) 899; (f) 5018
13   (a) 375; (b) 612; (c) 667; (d) 2505; (e) 56; (f) 13
15   (a) 2236; (b) 209te; (c) ⊥ △ □ ⊥
17   (a) 653; (b) 857; (c) 2386

Sec. 4–6, page 101

1   For set O: (a) No; (b) no; (c) yes
For set E: (a) Yes; (b) no; (c) yes
3   Yes
5   All other even numbers have 2 as a factor.
7   1. A prime number has only itself and 1 as factors.
9   $192 = 2^6 \times 3$; $108 = 2^2 \times 3^3$; $234 = 2 \times 3^2 \times 13$
Greatest common factor $= 2 \times 3 = 6$
11   $78 = 2 \times 3 \times 13$; $105 = 3 \times 5 \times 7$; $110 = 2 \times 5 \times 11$
No common factor other than 1
25   (See figure above.)

Sec. 5–5, page 124

1   To find the quotient; to compare two numbers; to find how many small sets
of objects there are contained in a larger set; to find how many objects will
be in each set when a larger set is separated into several smaller sets with the
same cardinal number
3   They are inverse relations.
7   First, find the excess of nines in the quotient and in the divisor. Second, find
the excess in the product of these two excesses. Third, find the excess of
nines in the remainder. The excess in the sum of the excesses found in the
second and third steps should then be the same as the excess in the
dividend.

9   If the divisor is subtracted from the dividend the number of times indicated
    by the quotient, the final remainder should be the same as the remainder
    obtained in the division.

11 (a) 52; (b) 105; (c) 83

13 (a) $6{,}798 = 206 \cdot 33 + 0$
    (b) $9{,}672 = 537 \cdot 18 + 6$
    (c) $41{,}935 = 130 \cdot 321 + 205$

15 (a) 35; (b) 231; (c) 537; (d) 102

17 If the greatest common divisor (the last divisor of the algorithm) is 1, the num-
    bers are relatively prime.

19 (a) I△ RI□; (b) ⊥⊥ R△; (c) ⊥□ RIII

21 (a) **1917**; (b) 8,810; (c) **240220**; (d) **1642**; (e) II⊥0□△; (f) **2526**

23 I△0□□⊥   25 **152**

Sec. 5–11, page 135

5   The remainder is 2, and $2 \neq \dfrac{2}{7}$.

7   At the time fractions were introduced into the number system, equality and
    the four operations were defined only for integers.

9   Addition, multiplication, and division with nonzero divisors

11 Definition: $\dfrac{a}{b} + \dfrac{c}{d} = \dfrac{ad + bc}{bd}$

    Common denominator: $\dfrac{a}{b} + \dfrac{c}{d} = \dfrac{ad}{bd} + \dfrac{bc}{bd} = \dfrac{ad + bc}{bd}$

    The two results are identical.

13 $\dfrac{3}{4} - \dfrac{7}{8} = \dfrac{3 \cdot 8 - 4 \cdot 7}{4 \cdot 8} = \dfrac{24 - 28}{32} = \dfrac{-4}{32} = -\dfrac{1}{8}$

    $\dfrac{7}{8} - \dfrac{3}{4} = \dfrac{7 \cdot 4 - 8 \cdot 3}{8 \cdot 4} = \dfrac{28 - 24}{32} = \dfrac{4}{32} = \dfrac{1}{8}$

    The two results are not the same. One counterexample is sufficient to dis-
    prove a general statement.

15 No

17 It unnecessarily would increase the size of the numbers with which one
    would have to work.

19 $\dfrac{5}{6} \div \dfrac{2}{3} = \dfrac{5}{6} \times \dfrac{3}{2} = \dfrac{5}{4}$; $\dfrac{2}{3} \div \dfrac{5}{6} = \dfrac{2}{3} \times \dfrac{6}{5} = \dfrac{4}{5}$

    $\left(\dfrac{5}{6} \div \dfrac{2}{3}\right) \div \dfrac{3}{4} = \left(\dfrac{5}{6} \times \dfrac{3}{2}\right) \div \dfrac{3}{4} = \dfrac{5}{4} \div \dfrac{3}{4} = \dfrac{5}{4} \times \dfrac{4}{3} = \dfrac{5}{3}$

    $\dfrac{5}{6} \div \left(\dfrac{2}{3} \div \dfrac{3}{4}\right) = \dfrac{5}{6} \div \left(\dfrac{2}{3} \times \dfrac{4}{3}\right) = \dfrac{5}{6} \div \dfrac{8}{9} = \dfrac{5}{6} \times \dfrac{9}{8} = \dfrac{15}{16}$

    In each case the two results are not the same. One counterexample is suffi-
    cient to disprove a general statement.
    The statement holds true both for integers and for natural numbers.

21 Cancellation is merely a technique which can be used in situations such as
    this to show the results of a common division. It is permissible since multi-
    plication and division are inverse processes.

    (a) $\dfrac{3}{4}$; (b) $\dfrac{1}{3}$; (c) $\dfrac{13}{7}$; (d) $\dfrac{2}{3}$

23   First the new numerator or denominator must be found by either addition or subtraction, as the case may be.   The common factors may then be canceled.   In some cases it is possible first to use the distributive law and then cancel common factors.   For example, $6 - 4 = 2(3 - 2)$; $9 + 12 = 3(3 + 4)$.

(a) $\dfrac{1}{4}$; (b) $\dfrac{7}{1}$; (c) $\dfrac{1}{3}$; (d) $\dfrac{1}{3}$

25   In such a system it is not necessary that there exist for each nonzero element a multiplicative inverse.

Sec. 5–19, page 152

3   To assist in aligning all digits according to their positional values

5   (a) 3, 0.625; (b) 3, 0.056; (c) 4, 0.0036; (d) 4, 0.1875; (e) 1, 0.2; (f) 3, 0.125; (g) 2, 0.24; (h) 4, 0.0875

7   (a) $\dfrac{9}{200}$; (b) $\dfrac{41}{900}$; (c) $\dfrac{1}{22}$; (d) $\dfrac{5}{111}$

9   0.3%; $\dfrac{1}{2}$%; 0.032; 0.285; $\dfrac{2}{7}$; 0.3; 0.302; 31%; $\dfrac{2}{5}$; 0.403; $\dfrac{3}{7}$; 0.430; $\dfrac{3}{5}$; $0.\bar{6}$; $\dfrac{3}{4}$

11   (a) If n represents the number: $\dfrac{13}{n} = \dfrac{15}{100}$

(b)   If r represents per cent: $\dfrac{13}{15} = \dfrac{r}{100}$

(c)   If n represents the number: $\dfrac{n}{15} = \dfrac{13}{100}$

Sec. 6–6, page 171

3   Rational number; it can be expressed as the quotient of two integers in the form $\dfrac{0}{a}$ where $a \neq 0$.

5
$$(1)^2 = 1 < 3 < 4 = (2)^2$$
$$(1.7)^2 = 2.89 < 3 < 3.24 = (1.8)^2$$
$$(1.73)^2 = 2.9929 < 3 < 3.0276 = (1.74)^2$$
$$(1.732)^2 = 2.999824 < 3 < 3.003289 = (1.733)^2$$
$$(1.7320)^2 = 2.99982400 < 3 < 3.00017041 = (1.7321)^2$$

7   (a) $0.\overline{714285}$; (b) $0.875 = 0.874\bar{9} = 0.875\bar{0}$; (c) $0.\bar{6}$; (d) $7.5 = 7.4\bar{9} = 7.5\bar{0}$

13   (a) $-3 < x < 3$; (b) $-\dfrac{1}{2} \le x \le \dfrac{1}{2}$; (c) $-6 \le x \le 2$; (d) $-2 \le x \le 4$

15   (a) $5 + 3i$, $4 + 7i$; (b) 2, 2; (c) $2 + 5i$, $-4 + 2i$; (d) $7 - 2i$, $11 - 7i$;

(e) $-i$, 12; (f) $6 + 3i$; $8 + 12i$; (g) $2\sqrt{2}$; 5; (h) $1 + \sqrt{3}i$; $-\dfrac{1}{2} + \dfrac{\sqrt{3}}{2}i$;

(i) 1, 1; (j) $\left(2 + \dfrac{\sqrt{3}}{2}\right) - \dfrac{1}{2}i$, $\left(\sqrt{3} + \dfrac{1}{2}\right) + \left(1 - \dfrac{\sqrt{3}}{2}\right)i$

17   (a) $-1 - i$, $\dfrac{1}{2} - \dfrac{1}{2}i$; (b) $-3 - 4i$, $\dfrac{3}{25} - \dfrac{4}{25}i$;

(c) $-5 + 12i$, $\dfrac{5}{169} + \dfrac{12}{169}i$; (d) $\sqrt{2} - \sqrt{3}i$, $-\dfrac{\sqrt{2}}{5} - \dfrac{\sqrt{3}}{5}i$;

(e) $1 + i$, $-\dfrac{1}{2} + \dfrac{1}{2}i$; (f) $2 + \sqrt{3}i$, $-\dfrac{2}{7} + \dfrac{\sqrt{3}}{7}i$

19 Natural number, rational number, irrational number, rational number, negative integer, irrational number, positive integer, pure imaginary, mixed imaginary.

Sec. 7–4, page 187

1 Yes	*3* No	*5* No	*7* No	*9* Yes
11 No	*13* Yes	*15* No	*17* No	

21 In each case the smaller number is the remainder left when the larger number is divided by 7.

27 (*a*) The number formed by the last four digits is a number divisible by 16.
    (*b*) If T = thousands digit, h = hundreds digit, t = tens digit, and u = ones digit, then the test is that $8T + 4h + 10t + u$ be divisible by 16.

29 The number formed by the last two digits is divisible by 25.

31 The number formed by the last four digits is divisible by 625.

33 $10 \equiv 10$ (mod 25), so both tests for divisibility by 25 become the same test; $10 \equiv 10$ (mod 125) and $100 \equiv 100$ (mod 125), so both tests for 125 become the same test.

35 Divisible by 2, 3, 4, 5, 6, 12, 15

37 Divisible by 2, 3, 4, 6, 9, 11, 12, 18, 22

39 Divisible by 2, 11, 22

41 Divisible by 2, 3, 4, 5, 6, 8, 11, 12, 15, 22, 24

43 **2:** Sum of the digits divisible by **2**; **4:** same as for **2**

45 **2:** Sum of the digits divisible by **2**
    3: Digit in ones place divisible by **3**
    4: Same as for **2**
    6: Combination of tests for **2** and **3**
    8: Same as for **2**

Sec. 8–3, page 202

5 Planes M and N have at least line $\overleftrightarrow{PQ}$ in common.

11 No four points coplanar: 10 lines and 10 planes
    Four points coplanar: 10 lines 7 planes

Sec. 8–4, page 211

1 $\angle ABC$ and $\angle CBA$ are the same angle since they have the same vertex and are formed by the same rays; $\angle ABC$ and $\angle BCA$ are not the same angle since they have different vertices and are formed by different rays.

3 (*a*) The intersection is the half plane on the P side of l.
    (*b*) The intersection is the portion of the plane between the two lines l and m.
    (*c*) The intersection is the portion of the plane between the two lines l and m.

11 35, 145, and 145   *13* $m \angle A - m \angle C = 45$

Sec. 8–6, page 219

7 Use a straightedge to see whether it can be made to contact each of the points when placed on the plane.

9 Six lines can be drawn; only four if three points are collinear.

11 Fresno, California

13 St. Louis and Denver, 1 hour; Dutch Harbor and Camden, 6 hours; Honolulu and Fresno, 2 hours; Honolulu and Denver, 3 hours

Sec. 8–8, page 230

9   (a) Yes; (b) yes; (c) no

Sec. 8–10, page 234

1   $\angle A \cong \angle D$; $\angle B \cong \angle E$; $\angle C \cong \angle F$; $\overline{AB} \cong \overline{DE}$; $\overline{BC} \cong \overline{EF}$; $\overline{CA} \cong \overline{FD}$.
Definition 8–23.
9   The lines which join midpoints of opposite sides of the hexagon

Sec. 9–2, page 253

1   Approximate numbers are numbers such as those which express the results obtained from estimating, measuring, or rounding.   Exact numbers are numbers such as those which express the results of counting or of operating on exact numbers.   For example, $\frac{2}{3}$ is an exact number, but the decimal 0.667 is an approximation to $\frac{2}{3}$.

3   Exact.   The number is used in the definition which gives meaning to the concept of 1 mile.

5   This number could be either, depending upon whether it is the result of an actual count of the number of volumes in the library or not.

7   3.162 is an approximate value of the positive square root of the exact number 10, while 5 is an exact value of the real cube root of the exact number 125.

9   Both numbers are approximate.   100 yards is a measure of distance, and 9.3 seconds is a measure of time.

11   Approximate, since it is the result of a measurement

13   1960 is exact since it is a counting number; 2,479,015 is approximate; although it is a form of counting number, it must represent an estimate.

15   The 2 and $2.29 are exact numbers since they express the result of counting. The 4 pounds 8 ounces, as a weight, is approximate; however, the 4 pounds must be considered as an exact count of the number of pounds in the weight. The unit is the ounce and the weight is 72 ounces, which is approximate. From one point of view $2.29 must be considered an approximate number, since it expresses the result of an operation involving an exact number, the price per pound, and an approximate number, the weight of the chickens.

17   The 5 cents and 30 cents are exact numbers.   The 6 ounces expresses a weight, so the 6 is an approximate number.

Sec. 9–4, page 257

1   Whole units are counted on the scale; fractional parts are estimated.
3   Exact   5   Direct   7   Indirect   9   Indirect
11   Indirect   13   Indirect   15   Direct   17   Indirect

Sec. 9–7, page 266

3   1 in. = 2.540 cm   5   1 grain = 0.00229 ounce
7   25,000,000,000,000 miles
9   0.00000000000000000000000000091   gram
11   16 yd 7 in.   13   11 bu 5 qt   15   34 years 8 months 14 days
17   2 g 1 dg 6 cg 3 mg
19   (a) 7 l 4 dl 1 cl 6 ml; (b) 7.416 l
21   30 bu 3 pk 6 qt 1 pt   23   22 days 3 hr 34 min 30 sec

25 2 gal 1 qt $1\frac{2}{5}$ pt   27 1 g 6 dg 5 cg   29 1 to 2

31 1 to 200,000   33 1.65 g   35 0.000005 to 1

Sec. 9–11, page 279

1 All digits except zero when it is used merely for placing the decimal point

3 4 in. means correct to the nearest inch, or 4 in. $\pm\frac{1}{2}$ in.; $4\frac{8}{8}$ in. means correct

to the nearest $\frac{1}{8}$ in., or 4 in. $\pm\frac{1}{16}$ in.

15 ft 4 in. means correct to the nearest inch, or 15 ft 4 in. $\pm\frac{1}{2}$ in.; $15\frac{1}{3}$ ft means

correct to the nearest $\frac{1}{3}$ ft, or $15\frac{1}{3}$ ft $\pm\frac{1}{6}$ ft.

5 (a) 1 in.; (b) 1 pk; (c) 1 oz; (d) 1 sec; (e) 1 pk; (f) 1 qt; (g) 0.00001 in.;
   (h) 0.001 mile; (i) 0.1 sec; (j) 1,000 miles; (k)1 dollar; (l) 0.1 in.

7 (a) 123.6 in. is both more precise and more accurate.
   (b) 360 sec is more precise; they are of the same degree of accuracy.
   (c) 3 yd is more precise; they are of the same degree of accuracy.
   (d) 58 ft is more precise; 572 miles is more accurate.
   (e) 80 oz is more precise; 195 lb is more accurate.
   (f) 3 qt 1 pt is more precise; 5 gal 3 qt is more accurate.

9 (a) $a + b + c$ where a, b, and c each represent the length of one side
   (b) $3s$ where s represents the common length of the three sides
   (c) $2l + 2w$ where l represents the length and w the width of the rectangle
   (d) $4s$ where s represents the common length of the four sides
   (e) $5s$ where s represents the common length of the five sides
   (f) $6s$ where s represents the common length of the six sides

11 Perimeter, 225.6 in.; area, 3,180 sq in.

13 Circumference: (a) 16 in.; (b) 0.842 ft
    Area: (a) 20 sq in.; (b) 0.0564 sq ft

15 4.58 sq in.

17 (a) 0.064 sec
    (b) 6,000,000,000,000,000,000,000,000 grams
    (c) 25,000,000,000,000 miles
    (d) 0.00000000000000000000003 gram
    (e) 186,000 miles per sec

19 Proton: $1.00758 \times 1.660 \times 10^{-24} = 1.673 \times 10^{-24}$ gram
    Neutron: $1.00897 \times 1.660 \times 10^{-24} = 1.675 \times 10^{-24}$ gram
    Electron: $(5.5 \times 10^{-4}) \times (1.660 \times 10^{-24}) = 9.1 \times 10^{-28}$ gram

21 71 ft

Sec. 9–15, page 296

1 $AB = 5$, $RS = 20$

3 Length of the lake is 125 yd.

17 54°; 39°; 22°; 24°

19 3°50′   21 54°15′   23 41°50′

Sec. 9–16, page 303

1 Mean, 40; median, 40; no mode

3 Mean, 97, median, 96; mode, 96

5

	Ex 1	Ex 2	Ex 3
Variance	24	9.29	111.3
Standard deviation	4.9	3.05	10.6

7 The scores are all 10.

Sec. 10–2, page 317

3 A constant is a symbol for which there exists only one value in its replacement set.

A variable is a symbol for which there exist at least two distinct values in its
replacement set.

A parameter is a constant which is subject to arbitrary choice for any given
discussion.

5 The domain of a function is the replacement set of the first element, or independent variable, and the range is the replacement set for the second element, or dependent variable.

7 a, b, c, e, g

9 (a) $f(x) = 2x$; (b) $f(x) = x + 3$; (c) $f(x) = \sqrt{2x^2}$; (e) $f(x) = 2x + 5$;
(g) $f(x) = \dfrac{1}{x}$

13 An arbitrary value may be assigned to it and then it will retain this value as
x selects values from the domain of the function and y selects values from the
range.

15 (a) $y = 3s$; (b) $y = \dfrac{s}{5}$; (c) $y = s + 4$; (d) $y = s - 1$; (e) $y = \dfrac{1}{2}s$;

(f) $y = 2s - 1$; (g) $y = 2(s - 1)$; (h) $y = \dfrac{s}{3} + 4$; (i) $y = \dfrac{s + 4}{3}$

17 They are all functions, since to each value of the first element there corresponds one and only one value of the second element.

19 They can be checked easily to see whether to each value of the first element
there corresponds one and only one value of the second element.

21 They are complete graphs since the domain of each relation is restricted to
the 10 finite elements of set S. This in turn restricts the range of each relation to 10 finite values.

23 a, c, e, f, h, j, k

25 Relation	Domain	Range
a	$-5 \leq x \leq 5$	$-5 \leq y \leq 5$
b	$\{3\}$	$0 \leq y \leq 5$
c	$-3 \leq x \leq 3$	$\{2\}$
d	$\{-2,-1,0,1,2,3,4,5\}$	$\{0,\pm1,\pm2,\pm3,\pm4,\pm5\}$
e	$\{0,\pm1,\pm2,\pm3,\pm4,\pm5\}$	$\{1,2,3,4\}$
f	$-3 < x < 3$	$0 \leq y \leq 6$
g	$-6 \leq x \leq 0$	$-3 < y < 3$
h	$-5 \leq x < 6$	$\{\pm1,\pm3,\pm5\}$
i	$\{\pm6,\pm4,\pm2\}$	$-6 < y \leq 6$
j	$-5 \leq x \leq 5$	$0 \leq y \leq 5$
k	$-5 \leq x \leq 5$	$0 \leq y \leq 5$
l	$0 \leq x \leq 5$	$-5 \leq y \leq 5$

27 Suggestions are: (a) $d = 40t$; (b) $i = 0.06p$; (c) $S = 0.05s + 2.50$;
    (d) $c = 0.30g$; (e) $C = 2\pi r$; (f) $A = s^2$; (g) $p = 6s$
31 For the formulas given in the answer to Exercise 27:

	(a)	(b)	(c)	(d)	(e)	(f)	(g)
Independent variable	t	p	s	g	r	s	s
Dependent variable	d	i	S	c	C	A	p

Sec. 10–4, page 332

1 (a) $f(x) = 3x + 2$; (b) $f(x) = -\frac{1}{2}x + 6$; (c) $f(x) = \frac{3}{2}x$; (d) $y = -5x - 3$;
   (e) $y = x + 3$; (f) $y = -3x + 6$
3 (a) $x = -\frac{2}{3}$; (b) $x = 12$; (c) $x = 0$; (d) $x = -\frac{3}{5}$; (e) $x = -3$; (f) $x = 2$
5 (a) $2x + 3y - 3 = 0$; (b) $4x - y - 5 = 0$; (c) $5x + 4y + 28 = 0$;
   (d) $x - y + 1 = 0$; (e) $x + y - 2 = 0$; (f) $2x + 5y - 10 = 0$;
   (g) $4x - y - 16 = 0$; (h) $y + 3 = 0$; (i) $5x + 3y = 0$
7 (a) $o = 2i - 1$; (b) $o = 2i + 3$
9 $F = \frac{9}{5}C + 32$
11 $C = 2\pi r$
13 $y = 0$; $x = 0$

Sec. 10–5, page 339

1 $x = 1, y = -1$ 3 Inconsistent   5 $x = 6, y = 6$
7 $\{(x,y) \mid y = -0.25x + 1.25$ and x a real number$\}$
9 For $m \neq 0$: $\{(x,y) \mid y = -\dfrac{l}{m}x + \dfrac{h}{m}$ and x a real number$\}$

   For $m = 0$: $\left\{-\dfrac{h}{l}, y\right\}$
11 $x = 10, y = 20$ 13 Inconsistent
15 $x = 19, y = -10$ 17 $x = \dfrac{1}{2}, y = -\dfrac{3}{2}$
19 $x = 1.6, y = 2.5$

Sec. 10–6, page 344

1 $|x| < 2$ 3 $|x - 2| \leq 3$ 5 $|x| \leq 2$ 7 $|x - 11| < 2$
9 $\left|x + \dfrac{3}{2}\right| \leq \dfrac{11}{2}$ 11 $-8 \leq x \leq 8$ 13 $-7 < x < 1$

15 $0 < x < 4$ 17 $x < \dfrac{5}{3}$ 19 $x \leq 2$ 21 $x \leq -1$

Sec. 10–7, page 347

1 48 inches   3 25 pounds   5 136 pounds   7 625 pounds
9 50 feet

Sec. 10–8, page 353

5 (a) January, February, March, April, May, June, and July
   (b) August, September, October, November, and December
   (c) April to May
   (d) October to November
   (e) February and December

Sec. 10–9, page 361

1 $14.40	*3* 42	*5* 41; 42	*7* 499; 501	*9* 89; 14
11 $285	*13* (−6,5)	*15* 72	*17* Triangle, 8 ft; square, 6 ft	

19 Need to know at what angle the streets intersect before problem can be solved

21 $7.10, tax $0.71; $4.20, tax $0.42

23 Dodgers, $12,794; Yankees, $7,874

25 60 miles per hour

INDEX